427.973
K46a

45149

DATE DUE			
Dec 13 '72			
Oct 30 '73			
Dec 3 '73			
Oct 28 '74			
Apr 30 '75			
Apr 30 '77			
Jul 6 '77 M			
Aug 9 '77 P			
Mar 26 79			
Oct 30 '80			
Feb 27 '81			

ASPECTS OF AMERICAN ENGLISH

ASPECTS
OF AMERICAN ENGLISH

ELIZABETH M. KERR
The University of Wisconsin—Milwaukee

RALPH M. ADERMAN
The University of Wisconsin—Milwaukee

Under the General Editorship
of David Levin, Stanford University

Harcourt, Brace & World, Inc.   *New York, Burlingame*

Library of Congress Catalog Card Number: 63-12085

Printed in the United States of America

A NOTE ON THE COVER: Voiceprints, sometimes called visible speech, reveal the patterns of voice energy in the various levels of pitch—patterns that are distinct and identifiable from person to person. The two "contour-map" voiceprints on the cover of this book show the phrase *Aspects of American English* as spoken by two different people. They were produced by Lawrence G. Kersta of Bell Telephone Laboratories and are reprinted with the permission of Bell Telephone Laboratories, Inc.

ACKNOWLEDGMENTS

The editors wish to thank the following for their permission to reproduce material in this book.

Appleton-Century-Crofts, Inc.: The selections from *American English Grammar* by Charles C. Fries. Copyright, 1940, the National Council of Teachers of English and Charles C. Fries. Reprinted by permission of Appleton-Century-Crofts. The selection from *A History of the English Language*, 2d edition, by Albert C. Baugh. Copyright, © 1957, Appleton-Century-Crofts, Inc. Reprinted by permission of Appleton-Century-Crofts.

The College English Association, Inc.: The selection by Albert H. Marckwardt from *The CEA Critic*, Vol. 14 (January, 1952). Reprinted by permission of the author and the College English Association. Copyright © *The CEA Critic*, January, 1952.

Donald P. Costello: The selection by Donald P. Costello from *American Speech*, Vol. 34 (October, 1959). Used by permission of the author.

Bergen Evans: The selection by Bergen Evans from *The Atlantic Monthly*, Vol. 209 (May, 1962). The selection by Bergen Evans from *The Atlantic Monthly*, Vol. 205 (March, 1960). Used by permission of the author.

Robert A. Hall, Jr.: The selections from *Linguistics and Your Language* (Doubleday, 1960) by Robert A. Hall, Jr. Used by permission of the author.

Harcourt, Brace & World, Inc.: The selection from *Introduction to Linguistic Structures* by Archibald A. Hill. © 1958 by Harcourt, Brace & World, Inc., and reprinted with their permission.

Harper & Row, Publishers: The selections from *Understanding English* by Paul Roberts. Copyright © 1958 by Paul Roberts. Reprinted by permission of Harper & Row, Publishers.

The Johns Hopkins Press: The selection by H. L. Mencken from *Philologica: The Malone Anniversary Studies*, edited by Thomas A. Kirby and Henry Bosley Woolf. Used by permission of the publisher.

iv

45-149

July, 1963

Alfred A. Knopf, Inc.: The selections reprinted from *The American Language* by H. L. Mencken, by permission of Alfred A. Knopf, Inc. Copyright 1919, 1921, 1923, 1936 by Alfred A. Knopf, Inc.

Language Learning: The selection by Raven I. McDavid, Jr., from *Language Learning,* Vol. 4 (1952–1953), published by University of Michigan Research Club in Language Learning. Used by permission of the editor of *Language Learning.*

Life: An editorial from *Life* magazine. © 1961 Time Inc. Appearing in *Life* magazine (October 27, 1961), and used with *Life's* permission.

The Macmillan Company: The selections reprinted with permission of the publisher from *Words and Their Ways in English Speech* by James B. Greenough and George Lyman Kittredge. Copyright 1900, 1901 by The Macmillan Company. Copyright 1928, 1929 by Robert Greenough and George Lyman Kittredge.

G. & C. Merriam Company: The selection by J. N. Hook. By permission. From *Word Study,* copyright 1951 by G. & C. Merriam Co., Publishers of the Merriam-Webster Dictionaries. Also used by permission of the author.

The National Council of Teachers of English: The selection by Harold B. Allen from *The English Journal,* Vol. 45 (April, 1956). Reprinted with the permission of the National Council of Teachers of English and Harold B. Allen. The selection by James Sledd from *College English,* Vol. 23 (May, 1962). Reprinted with the permission of the National Council of Teachers of English and James Sledd. The selection by John S. Kenyon from *College English,* Vol. 10 (October, 1948). Reprinted with the permission of the National Council of Teachers of English. The selection by Austin C. Dobbins from *College English,* Vol. 18 (October, 1956). Reprinted with the permission of the National Council of Teachers of English and Austin C. Dobbins.

The New York *Times:* The selection by Raven I. McDavid, Jr., from the *New York Times Magazine* (April 23, 1950). Used by permission of the New York *Times* and the author.

Margaret Nicholson: The selection by Margaret Nicholson from the *Atlantic Monthly,* Vol. 199 (May, 1957). © Margaret Nicholson 1957. Used by permission of the author.

Oxford University Press, Inc.: The selection from *American English* by Albert H. Marckwardt. © 1958 by Oxford University Press, Inc. Reprinted by permission.

Routledge & Kegan Paul, Ltd.: The selections from *The American Language* by H. L. Mencken. Used by permission.

Speech Association of America: The selection by W. Nelson Francis from the *Quarterly Journal of Speech,* Vol. 40 (October, 1954). Used by permission of the Speech Association of America and the author.

Time: The selection from *Time* magazine, Vol. 78 (October 6, 1961). Courtesy *Time;* copyright Time Inc. 1961.

The University of Michigan Press: The selection reprinted from *A Word Geography of the Eastern United States* by Hans Kurath by permission of The University of Michigan Press. Copyright 1949 by The University of Michigan.

The World Publishing Company: The selection from *The Miracle of Language* by Charlton Laird. Copyright 1953 by Charlton Laird. Used by permission of the publisher.

INTRODUCTION

Since language has its own character, developed by the countless generations who have used it, knowing a language well helps one to know the countries and the peoples who have made it and those who are now making it. Americans have adapted the English language to their purposes, and American English has taken on new vigor and distinctive color in the New World. One purpose of this book is to help students understand their linguistic heritage.

We believe that language is a primary concern of the college English course. Some years ago we began working with selected readings on American English as the basis for controlled source papers. One of us has recently used many of the selections included here in a course in expository writing. In this work we anticipated two current trends: the use of sourcebooks for teaching techniques of documentation, and the study of the English language or American English in the composition course. Our personal experience has convinced us of the value of this approach. In such courses students improve their skill in writing, develop a lively curiosity about language, and gain vital and coherent knowledge.

We believe this book has certain distinct virtues. Its concentration on American English will meet the needs of all students, not just those of the English major. Students using it will increasingly come to understand that skill in language underlies distinguished achievement in any branch of learning. They will find that sentence structure, grammar, usage, and vocabulary are not just rules in a handbook or artificial exercises, but the matter about which they will read and write and make their own observations and contributions. Special attention is given to the reasons for the use of standard English, and to the selection of a variety of styles suitable to the purpose and occasion of the communication. The book allows scope, in a two-semester course, for coordination of the material on language with such other readings as modern fiction and drama. The basic principles of the development of the English language are pertinent to historical survey courses in English or American literature. The selections are all suitable for study as examples of modern expository writing. Some can serve as models for techniques of documentation, and all are useful for preparing documented papers of various lengths based on controlled sources, or for research papers involving library work.

The material on dictionaries includes contrasting views of Webster's *Third New International Dictionary* and explications of the functions of a dictionary and the methods of compiling one.

Each selection is followed by study questions, each part by topics for written assignments. At the end are listed topics for long papers, which may be based on the text or extended into research papers. The study questions and topics for papers emphasize the student's observation of language in use and the application of general principles to the particular language of his own environment. The study questions and topics for written papers also stress basic problems in exposition: analysis, comparison, classification, and exemplification are repeatedly called for.

These selections are not technical: the material is modern, much of it recent, and it is addressed to the general reader. Complete chapters or articles are given, with at most minor deletions. The scientific point of view is usually represented, and attention is given also to the contrasting prescriptive view of grammar and usage, and the historical explanation of that view. Although structural linguistics is too specialized a subject for detailed treatment here, the articles by structural linguists will introduce students to the subject, providing a foundation for possible later courses in linguistics or history of the English language. No word lists or glossaries are included; such valuable raw material is available in *American Speech* and *Publications of the American Dialect Society.* Although articles dealing with specific phenomena of language, such as the etymology of single words, or the vocabularies of special subjects or groups, could not be included within the limits of this relatively small volume, a number of our suggestions for theme topics refer to articles which are useful as models to show students how to use their own data.

As the table of contents indicates, the general principles of language are given first. Order within the parts is from general to specific, although the selections can, of course, be used in any order desired. Parts II through V apply the four "approaches to language" identified and explained by Charles C. Fries in the last selection in Part I. Part II, "Historical Aspects," includes material on the history of the English language only as a basis for consideration of American English and of the chief differences between British and American English. (An excellent brief history by Whitehall, listed in the bibliography, is easily available in *Webster's New World Dictionary.*) Part III, "Regional Aspects," provides for stress on whatever regional variety of American English is used by the students. Part IV, "Literary and Colloquial Aspects," includes the indispensable essay by John S. Kenyon which distinguishes between cultural levels and functional varieties of language and recognizes colloquial standard English as a correct variety of style. This part is an excellent basis for the study of varieties of style in literary selections. The material on slang appeals to students but makes clear both its uses and limitations. Part V, "Social or Class Aspects," presents sound linguistic attitudes toward standard and nonstandard English and strengthens the teacher's insistence on standard English by providing realistic motivation: the social and economic advantage to the student of using acceptable English. This point is further stressed in study questions.

As suggested above, this text may be used in various ways: in a two-semester course in composition the first two parts might be used in the first semester, supplemented by other readings exemplifying problems in exposition; in the second semester, the remainder of the book might be supplemented by fiction, drama, and formal and informal essays to illustrate varieties of style and levels of usage. Research papers might be based on the application of material in the text to a work of modern American fiction. In a one-semester course in composition, the material might be streamlined by reducing the reading to the essential selections, which we believe are the following: 1, 2, 3, 4, 5; 6, 8, 10; 12, 13, 14; 17, 18, 21, 22, 23, 24, 27. The book might also be used as a text in an introductory course in language or in a more advanced course if supplemented by some of the many excellent paperback books on linguistics. Whatever the course, teachers can devise their own assignments or adapt suggestions in the text to their own specific needs. Many of the topics can be easily varied, thus allowing for and stimulating student originality, and avoiding repetition of specific subjects. The sources quoted in entries in general dictionaries and the works listed in Wentworth and Flexner, *Dictionary of American Slang,* will suggest modern authors whose works might be suitable for special study of modern written English or dialogue. For papers requiring extensive use of the library, the bibliography will serve as a basis for further research. (This bibliography does not include such standard reference works as Craigie and Hulbert, *Dictionary of American English;* Mathews, *Dictionary of Americanisms;* Murray, *New English Dictionary;* and Wentworth, *American Dialect Dictionary.*) Bibliographies given in the books listed cover both books and articles and thus serve as a guide to the periodicals most valuable for the study of American English.

We wish to acknowledge the valuable expert advice given us by Miss Verna L. Newsome, Professor of English at the University of Wisconsin—Milwaukee. We wish also to thank Dr. Albert H. Marckwardt of the University of Michigan and Dr. Kenneth G. Wilson of the University of Connecticut, who read and criticized earlier versions of the manuscript.

E. M. K.
R. M. A.

Milwaukee, Wisconsin
November, 1962

CONTENTS

IV. LITERARY AND COLLOQUIAL ASPECTS 141

V. SOCIAL OR CLASS ASPECTS 179

ASPECTS OF AMERICAN ENGLISH

I. PRINCIPLES OF LANGUAGE

In recent years students of language have come more and more to recognize that language is a living, changing instrument, that the characteristics of each set of language patterns differ in some details from all others, and that it is impossible to superimpose the grammar of one language upon another. The descriptive or scientific linguist tries to set forth the characteristics of a language without forcing it into a preconceived pattern suitable for a different set of linguistic patterns. The use of Latin grammar to explain the operation of English is a classic misapplication and one which has stubbornly resisted the efforts of scientific linguists to change it. In this section the discussion of different aspects of language by several experts provides a foundation of principles of language upon which the student can build as he examines various aspects of American English. The student should consider these principles when he is working on the topics for short or long papers on specific aspects of American English.

The fact that language is a complex instrument is becoming even more apparent as linguists methodically examine it and apply their discoveries in new theories and hypotheses. The ideas presented in this section are commonly accepted as some of the bases of the new approach to language, an approach marked by cautious impersonality and a vigorous insistence upon describing patterns of linguistic behavior. As the student begins to comprehend some of the principles of the scientific linguist, he can more easily understand some of the aspects of American English.

1. WHAT IS LANGUAGE?

Archibald A. Hill

In the opening chapter of *Introduction to Linguistic Structures* (1958) Professor Hill discusses five of the characteristics of language that distinguish it as a human activity.

1. Some basic assumptions

The subject of linguistics presents an initial difficulty because the word which designates it is unfamiliar. The word can easily be defined as the scientific analysis of language, but it is doubtful if such a definition is meaningful to anyone who lacks familiarity with this kind of analytic activity. It is far better to begin by defining language, since language is closer to the reader's experience. Yet even the definition of language presents unsuspected difficulties and needs preliminary discussion before it is attempted directly.

If a group of educated speakers are asked to define the language they are using, the reply will probably be "All the words and sentences used to express our thoughts." The definition is satisfactory in everyday situations, since long practice has made plain what is meant, and consequently most hearers know how to respond accurately. But for all that, the definition is not sufficiently accurate to be the basis for analysis. Terms like "words and sentences," which seem transparent to a speaker of a Western language, would be more misleading than enlightening if applied to some languages. Moreover, there are phenomena similar to language which this definition does not identify. Most important, the definition identifies language activity by thought. Language activity can be observed, and is therefore subject to verification. Thought can be observed only by subjective introspection, and so is not subject to verification. Language activity is therefore more knowable, thought less knowable. Obviously a definition must define the less knowable by the more knowable if it is to cast light. In what follows, such a definition will be attempted. There must first be a warning, the need for which will be clearer as we advance. A definition is not a description. A definition gives only those characteristics which have diagnostic value for recognition. A description attempts to give all characteristics, preferably in the order of their importance. A definition necessarily leaves out much and may make use of relatively trivial characteristics, but it is not to be condemned for that reason.

Most professional students of language proceed from a few assumptions, one of which is that the fundamental forms of language activity are the sequences of sounds made by human lips, tongues, and vocal cords—the phenomena usually distinguished by the narrower name of "speech."

2

Though this first assumption may seem like a truism, it is important, since many who accept it verbally still act as if they did not believe it. Some few even deny it. There are only two reasons for questioning the assumption. Writing has great permanence and great prestige. Further, the basis of our education is training in the manipulation of written symbols of ever-increasing complexity. Highly literate people, and those who would like to be literate, are therefore apt to think of writing as the real center of language and of speech as peripheral and derived—often badly—from the written forms.

There are a number of facts which should settle this question of priority. First, speech reaches back to the origins of human society; writing has a history of only about seven thousand years.[1] Also, no contemporary community of men is without language, even though it is probably still true that most of the world's several thousand language communities remain in the preliterate stage, without benefit of alphabet or even picture symbol. Individual members of literate communities, furthermore, learn their language some years before they learn to read or write it; and adults, even adults who are professional writers, carry on a good deal more speech activity in daily living than activity involving writing. The final fact is that all writing sys-tems are essentially representations of the forms of speech, rather than representations of ideas or objects in the nonlinguistic world. There are exceptions to this statement, like the Arabic numbers which work independently of the words for numbers in the Western languages. The exceptions. however, are in a minority disproportionate to the majority of symbols which always indicate the forms of language. The point can be driven home by a pair of simple examples. The symbol for *one* in Japanese writing is a single stroke, that for *two* two strokes, and so on. It might be thought that such a symbol has no relation to the Japanese word for *one* (*ichi*) but represents instead the nonlinguistic idea of "oneness." Actually the occurrence of the single stroke is correlated with the occurrence of the word. It occurs not only in the number but also in such forms as *ichiji, primary*. The Japanese symbol, therefore, has a quite different range from the letter sequence *one*

---

[1] The great antiquity of language, as compared with writing, is a reasonable assumption, but it is often presented without evidence. To arrive at the conclusion that language is older than writing, linguists and anthropologists start from the observed fact that in modern communities, all organized cooperative activity rests firmly and necessarily on language as the means of controlling and directing interaction. This being so in all observed communities, it is assumed by archaeological anthropologists that when remains of past communities show material evidence of social organization, these remains are those of communities which possessed language. Communities which show such evidences of social organization also show artifacts or other evidences which are much older than the remains of any communities which show evidences of even primitive systems of writing. It is possible that early human communities possessed some other form of highly organized communication, such as the gesture language which has been occasionally proposed since the days of Locke (cf. Max Müller, *Lectures on the Science of Language*, London, 1862, p. 31). But though possible, such a nonvocal symbol system is unlikely. Language is now a universal activity; it is an extra and unnecessary hypothesis to suppose something else.

of English, which is not used in the dissimilar word *primary*. The one-stroke symbol corresponds with the occurrence of the Japanese word *ichi*, proving that the one-stroke symbol is a representation of the word (though an understandably pictorial one), and not a direct representation of the idea of oneness.

Written symbols can be understood, furthermore, insofar as they fit into a linguistic structure, even when they refer to nothing in the nonlinguistic world. Thus, if an English text should have the sentence "He *sprashes* it," the second word could immediately be recognized as a verb in the third person singular and as a sequence of sounds quite in accord with English structural habits, though it represents nothing in the outside world at all. For the purposes of this book, therefore, the linguist's assumption that language is a set of sounds will be adopted. It is no contradiction of this assumption that the sounds can be secondarily translated into visual marks, grooves on a wax disk, electrical impulses, or finger movements.

Linguists assume that the description and analysis of language must begin with description of the sounds and their patterning and that description of meaning must be put off until the first task is done. Such an attitude is often misunderstood to be a denial of meaning, but this is not true. The linguist's desire to put off analysis of meaning is no more than an application of the principle of working from the more knowable to the less knowable, and though linguistics has not as yet had very striking results in semantic analysis, it can be hoped that the next few decades will see results of real value in semantics.

2. The defining characteristics of language

Working with the assumptions given above, linguists can offer a set of five defining characteristics which serve to set off language from other forms of symbolic behavior and to establish language as a purely human activity. Often animal communication will have one or more of these five characteristics, but never all of them.

First, language, as has been said, is a set of sounds. This is perhaps the least important characteristic, since the communication of mammals and birds is also a set of sounds. On the other hand, the system of communication which is in some ways most strikingly like language, that of bees, is a set of body movements, not sounds. It would be easy, further, to imagine a language based on something else than sound, but no human language is so constructed. Even the manual language of the deaf is derived from the pre-existent spoken language of the community.

Second, the connection between the sounds, or sequences of sounds, and objects of the outside world is arbitrary and unpredictable. That is to say, a visitor from Mars would be unable to predict that in London a given animal is connected with the sound sequence written *dog,* in Paris with the sequence *chien,* in Madrid with *perro.* The arbitrary quality of language symbols is not infrequently denied, for a number of reasons. Sometimes the denial is based on nothing more than the notion that the forms of one's native language are so inevitably right that they must be instinctive for all proper men. Sometimes the denial is more subtle. It is often maintained that all language, even though now largely arbitrary, must once have been a systematic imitation of objects by means of sound. It is true that there are some imitative words in all languages, but they are at best a limited part of the vocabulary. It is easy to imitate the noise of a barking dog, for instance, but difficult if not impossible to imitate a noiseless object, such as a rainbow. Though imitative words show similarity in many languages, absolute identity is rare. A dog goes "bow-wow" in English, but in related languages he often goes "wow-wow" or "bow-bow." The imitative words do not, after all, entirely escape from the general arbitrariness of language. The imitative origin of language appears, therefore, at worst unlikely and at best unprovable. The same injunction holds for theories of language origin which speculate that it is an imitation of facial or other gestures.

If it is assumed that language is arbitrary, what is meant by the statement? Just that the sounds of speech and their connection with entities of experience are passed on to all members of any community by older members of that community. Therefore, a human being cut off from contact with a speech community can never learn to talk as that community does, and cut off from all speech communities never learns to talk at all. In essence, to say that language is arbitrary is merely to say that it is social. This is perhaps the most important statement that can be made about language.

In contrast, much of animal communication is instinctive rather than social. That is to say, all cats mew and purr, and would do so even if they were cut off from all communication with other cats. On the other hand, some animal communication seems to share the social nature of human speech and is therefore learned activity. A striking example is the barking of dogs, which is characteristic only of the domesticated animal, not of dogs in the wild state. Similarly, the honey dances of bees may not be altogether without an arbitrary element. It is also likely that when more is known of the cries and chatterings of the great apes in the wild state, a considerable social element in their communication may be found. Nor should it be thought that all human communication is social. A part of our communication consists of instinctive reactions which accompany language, like the trembling of fear or the suffusion of blood which accompanies anger. Yet even in the nonlinguistic accompaniments of speech, the tones of voice and the gestures, it is now clear that there is more of arbitrary and socially learned behavior than had at one time been supposed.

Third, language is systematic. I cannot hope to make this statement completely clear at this point, since the whole of this book is devoted to an exposition of the system of language. However, some observations may now be made about the system of language. As in any system, language entities are arranged in recurrent designs, so that if a part of the design is seen, predictions can be made about the whole of it, as a triangle can be drawn if one side and two angles are given. Suppose there is an incomplete sentence like "John —s Mary an —." A good deal about what must fill the two blanks is obvious. The first must be a verb, the second a noun. Furthermore, not all verbs will go in the first blank, since it requires a verb whose third person singular is spelled with -s and which can take two objects (that is, not such a verb as *look* or *see*). Nor will all nouns fit in the second place, since an initial vowel is required, and the noun must be one which takes an article. There is no difficulty in deciding that the sentence could be either "John gives Mary an apple" or "John hands Mary an aspirin," but not "John *gaves* Mary an *book*." [2]

Another observation that can be made about language systems is that every occurrence of language is a substitution frame. Any sentence is a series of entities, for each of which a whole group of other entities can be substituted without changing the frame. Thus the sentence "John gives Mary an apple" is such a substitution frame. For *John* there can be replacements like *he, Jack, William, the man, her husband,* or many others. For the verb, entities like *buys, takes, offers,* as well as the alternatives *hands* or *gives,* may be used. This characteristic of extensive substitutability for all parts of any language utterance is of some importance in that it enables us to say that parrots, no matter how startlingly human their utterances may be, are not carrying on language activity. A parakeet may produce the sentence "Birds can't talk!" with human pitch, voice tones, and nearly perfect sounds. But the bird never says "Dogs can't talk!" or "Birds can't write!" His utterance is a unit, not a multiple substitution frame.

Still another characteristic of language systems is that the entities of language are grouped into classes, always simpler, more predictable, and more sharply separated than the infinite variety of objects in the world. For instance, a whole series of objects is grouped under the single word *chair,* and *chair* is put into the large class of nouns. In dealing with objects in the outside world it may be difficult to decide whether something is a chair, a stool, or merely a rock. In language, we think of nouns and verbs as quite separate and are apt to say that the one class represents things, the other events. But in the outside world, as the physicists tell us, it is often hard to decide whether an object is best described as thing or as event.

----

[2] . . . [A]n asterisk placed before a form means that it is believed to be impossible. In historical treatments of language, on the other hand, an asterisk before a form indicates that it has been reconstructed by comparison but is not actually recorded. These two uses of the asterisk should not be confused.

To return once more to the defining characteristics of language, the fourth characteristic is that it is a set of symbols. That is to say, language has meaning. In this form the statement is a platitude and does not distinguish language from other activities which are also symbolic. The nature of language symbols turns out to be rather different from the symbols of other types of communication. The simplest nonlinguistic symbol can be defined as a substitute stimulus. Pavlov's famous dogs, fed at the sound of a bell, eventually began to drool at the sound of the bell even when no food was present. The dogs were responding to a substitute stimulus. Nonlinguistic symbols can also be substitute responses, and these can also be taught to animals. A dog who learns to "speak" at the sight of food has learned such a substitute response. In human speech, however, one of the most striking facts is that we can talk about things which are not present, and we can talk about things which ordinarily produce a strong physical reaction without experiencing that reaction. For instance, I can talk about apples even though there are none in the room, and I can talk about them without always making my mouth water, even when I am hungry. This type of language, which occurs without an immediately present stimulus or response, is called "displaced speech," and it is obviously of great importance. It is what enables man to know something of the past and of the world beyond the limited range of his vision and hearing at a given moment.

The crucial fact in producing this almost miraculous and purely human effect seems to be that a given language entity can be both substitute stimulus and substitute response, and can also be a stimulus for further language responses or a response to other language stimuli. I can talk about apples when they are absent because "something reminds me of them." That is, I can make language responses to what is before me, and these language responses can stimulate the further response *apple* without any direct physical stimulus to my vision, touch, or smell. *Apple* can call forth still further language entities, like *pear* or *banana*, in an endless chain; these entities are also both stimuli and responses. When human speakers do this, they are setting up what philosophers call a "universe of discourse." The ability to make connected discourse within the symbol system is what enables men to talk at length, and profitably, about things they have never seen. By means of language men make elaborate models of distant experience and eventually test their accuracy by acting upon them. All that is known of animal communication leads to the supposition that precisely what is absent from it is the kind of symbolic activity here described, symbolic activity connected not merely with experience but with all parts of the symbol system itself. We believe, in short, that animals are incapable of displaced speech.

The paragraphs above are rather general, so that a concrete example may be helpful. Let us suppose that two speakers of English are together in a room. One of them is cold. A direct response for him would be to close the window.

Instead of this he can use the substitute response, which is also substitute stimulus: "John, please close the window for me." John can either close the window or reply with a further substitute: "Just a minute. Wait until I finish this page." Such a reply may produce acceptance or may lead to a discussion of John's procrastinating character, of the fact that his parents did not discipline him properly in youth and that modern young people are generally rebellious and unmannerly. To all of this John may reply that modern times are marked by progress and the disappearance of old taboos. In the meantime the window may have been quietly closed, or completely forgotten in the warmth of discussion. What is important is that each speaker has begun reacting, not to the immediate situation, but to the other speaker's language and to his own. And in so doing, each has been building a model of general social conditions, of wide scope and ultimately of some value, even in a random and unchecked conversation of the sort described.

We are now ready to turn to the last defining characteristic of language, the fact that it is complete. By this is meant that whenever a human language has been accurately observed, it has been found to be so elaborated that its speakers can make a linguistic response to any experience they may undergo. This complex elaboration is such a regular characteristic of all languages, even those of the simplest societies, that linguists have long ago accepted it as a universal characteristic. Nevertheless, in early books about language, and in the descriptions by linguistically untrained travelers today, there are statements that tribe X has a language with only two or three hundred words in it, forcing the tribe to eke out its vocabulary by gesture.[3] Linguists maintain that all such statements are the product of lack of knowledge, and are false. Skepticism about such statements is borne out by the fact that in all instances where it was possible to check on tribe X, its language proved to be complete as usual, whereupon the statement was

---

[3] A typical recent statement of this sort was reported by Leonard Bloomfield in "Secondary and Tertiary Responses to Language," *Language*, XX, 1944, p. 49 *n*.

"A physician, of good general background and education, who had been hunting in the north woods, told me that the Chippewa language contains only a few hundred words. Upon question, he said that he got this information from his guide, a Chippewa Indian. When I tried to state the diagnostic setting, the physician, our host, briefly and with signs of displeasure repeated his statement and then turned his back to me. A third person, observing this discourtesy, explained that I had some experience of the language in question. This information had no effect."

For a good general account of the completeness of primitive languages and the use of gesture as a substitute among mutually unintelligible language groups, consult Ralph L. Beals and Harry Hoijer, *An Introduction to Anthropology*, Macmillan, New York, 1956, pp. 508–11.

transferred to tribe Y, whose language was as yet unknown. The statement that human language is complete once again serves to distinguish it from animal activity. In the communication of bees, for instance, the subjects of systematic discourse are severely limited. Bees cannot, apparently, make an utterance equivalent to "The beekeeper is coming."

The statement that human language is always complete should not be interpreted to mean that every language has a word for everything. Obviously the ancient Greeks had no words for automobiles or atom bombs, and probably the modern Yahgan of Tierra del Fuego lack them as well. The completeness of language lies rather in the fact that a speaker of ancient Greek would have been perfectly capable of describing an automobile had he seen one, and further that had automobiles become important in ancient Greece, the speakers of Greek would have been perfectly capable of coining a word for them. It is a characteristic of vocabulary that, except in languages which have gone out of use, it is always expansible, in spite of the fact that resistance to new forms may frequently appear. Since language enables the user to make appropriate responses to all things and since vocabulary is thus characteristically "open," differences in vocabulary between two languages are not an accurate measure of the difference in efficiency or excellence of the two tongues. The fact that Eskimo does not have as highly developed a vocabulary of philosophy as does German merely indicates that the Eskimos are less interested in philosophy; on the other hand, Eskimo has a highly developed vocabulary for various kinds of snow, indicating that snow is important in Eskimo society. The completeness of human language and the openness of vocabulary make a groundless chimera of the occasionally expressed fear that a language might so degenerate as to become useless.

We can now attempt a definition of language, though the definition will be cumbersome. Language is the primary and most highly elaborated form of human symbolic activity. Its symbols are made up of sounds produced by the vocal apparatus, and they are arranged in classes and patterns which make up a complex and symmetrical structure. The entities of language are symbols, that is, they have meaning, but the connection between symbol and thing is arbitrary and socially controlled. The symbols of language are simultaneously substitute stimuli and substitute responses and can call forth further stimuli and responses, so that discourse becomes independent of an immediate physical stimulus. The entities and structure of language are always so elaborated as to give the speaker the possibility of making a linguistic response to any experience. Most of the above can be paraphrased by saying that every language is a model of a culture and its adjustment to the world. . . .

Study Questions

1. If possible, discover from people whose native language is not English, what sounds a child learns in imitation of animal sounds, as an American child learns *bowwow* for dog, *meow* for cat, *quack* for duck, *baa* for sheep, and so forth. If various members of a class investigate a number of languages, do the results show identity of sounds, similarity, or dissimilarity? What do the findings imply as to the imitative origin of language? See Noel Perrin, "Old Macberlitz Had a Farm," *The New Yorker* (January 27, 1962), 28–29, and Paul Koht's letter in reply, *The New Yorker* (February 24, 1962), 125.

2. What special "family words" for objects or people do you use in your own home? How did these words originate? In German, *Gift* means "poison"; in French, *lice* means "lists" or "arena." Can you think of other examples to illustrate that language is arbitrary?

3. The four basic sentence patterns in English are:
   a. Birds chirp.
   b. The bird is small.
   c. Birds are travelers.
   d. The child saw the bird. (Verna L. Newsome, *Structural Grammar in the Classroom*, Wisconsin Council of Teachers of English, 1961, p. 13.)
Using these four patterns as "substitution frames" to which modifiers may be added, what do you discover about "extensive substitutability"?

4. From your own earliest memories of nursery rhymes and fairy tales, illustrate how a child talks about things he has never seen. By observing a small child and his speech and responses to words, can you determine what constitutes his "universe of discourse"?

5. To illustrate the expansibility of Greek, look up *stereophonic* in a recent dictionary; note the original meaning of *stereo* and *phonic* and all the words for modern inventions and concepts which have been derived from these roots.

2. LANGUAGE HAS SYSTEM
Robert A. Hall, Jr.

This selection from *Linguistics and Your Language* (1960) examines the approaches toward language systems which the scientific linguist may follow in his investigations.

Up to now, in general, grammarians and teachers and those who have told others how to talk and what to do about their language, have done so on a purely *normative* basis—that is, setting up rules or norms and insisting that people follow them. Sometimes the normative grammarian has justified his dicta by appealing to "logic," sometimes to tradition, and sometimes to just the weight of his own say-so; but his attitude has always been authoritarian, i.e., depending on the force of authority and not on accurate observation and reasoning. The scientific attitude, on the other hand, rejects normative commands, and tries to base its conclusions on the greatest possible accuracy in observing facts, with the greatest possible objectivity, and on as careful reasoning and analysis as we can apply to the facts at our command. A true scientist also wants others to know as much of the truth as he can find out and make known, so that others also can follow his line of argument and, where possible, carry on up to and beyond whatever point he has reached. Now if we were to proceed immediately to the linguistic analyst's recommendations for changing our current ideas and behavior connected with language, we would be skipping an essential step in the process; and the linguist, by presenting his findings and his advice without first giving his reasons for so doing, would be converting himself from a scientist into simply another normative grammarian. In this process, there would be no gain; there is no use of substituting Language Authoritarian No. 2 for Language Authoritarian No. 1. What we need to do is rather to find out how we can escape entirely from the clutches of authoritarianism of any kind in language, and how we can ourselves acquire the essentials of a scientific attitude, and if we need to or want to, go ahead on our own in studying and thinking about language without being dependent on "authority."

When we want to imagine how things would seem to somebody who could look at us in a wholly objective, scientific way, we often put our reasoning in terms of a "man from Mars" coming to observe the earth and its inhabitants, living among men and studying their existence dispassionately and in its entirety. Such a "man from Mars," or some equally impartial observer, would notice, among the first things he saw in any human group, that its members cooperate by means of signals. They lend each other a hand, literally, in many undertakings, and they are able to exchange the use of all their faculties. We can build skyscrapers and bridges, manoeuver airplanes and battleships, warn each other of coming dangers and tell each other of past happenings, by means of signals. Theoretically, of course, any one of the five senses—touch, smell, taste, sight or hearing—could be used to make such signals. But our senses of touch, smell, and taste do not distinguish very clearly or sharply between various feelings, smells or tastes, and our memories for these senses are not as exact as they are for sight or hearing. These last two senses are more nearly on a par with each other, so far as clearness and sharpness of distinction and memory go: we can distinguish a signal that we see, and can remember it, just about as clearly as one that we hear. But hearing has certain advantages over sight, for signalling purposes: we can hear sounds coming from any direction, whereas we can see only things that are more or less in front of us; and we have, built into our bodies from birth, a pretty complex group of organs that we can use for making sounds, and a wide range of sounds that we can make—whereas the range of visible signals we can make unaided is quite limited. Furthermore, we can make sounds with the organs of our respiratory tract (what cigarette advertisements call the "T-zone") without interfering with what we are doing with the rest of our body—working, resting, etc.—but any visible signals we might try to make (say, with arm signals) necessarily involve major disturbance to whatever else we might be trying to do at the same time.

So our "man from Mars" would observe that humans communicate by means of signals, and that these signals are primarily *oral* and *aural*—made with the mouth and other "organs of speech," and heard with the ear. He would observe this in any community he was in, from the Australian Bushmen to the tribes of the Congo, from the Navaho sheep-herders to the aristocracy of Buckingham Palace. In fact, this is the major, basic characteristic that he would find differentiating humans from other living beings: humans talk, and talk extensively. They are not, by any means, the only living beings to communicate by means of auditory signals; but in the various animals that communicate with each other, the range and extent of communication is much less.

Furthermore, our "man from Mars" or our ideal linguistic analyst would see that when humans talk, their talk is not just a continual succession of babble, of sounds no two of which are alike or ever come in a given order. That is the way that monkeys gabble and jabber, or that babies prattle; but in grown people's speech, the world over, the same sounds and the same combinations of sounds keep recurring more or less frequently. In short, there are *partial resemblances* in the utterances that people make; and, because people's utterances have partial resemblances, we can say that all language has *system*—in its sounds and in the way these sounds are put together. If anything has system, we can describe it, by saying briefly and compactly what are the partial resemblances of the elements of the system; our "man from Mars" or our ideal analyst could make a series of statements about these systems of auditory signalling, about these *languages*, he observed among humans, and thus could make a description of their speech. If he were to do this, he would be engaging in the most fundamental type of scientific analysis as applied to language, in *descriptive linguistics*.

Another very important thing that our observer would see is that these signals always occur in connection with other things—in the last analysis, in connection (direct or indirect) with something in the world around us, with reality. (Let's leave aside all philosophical discussion as to the nature of reality, and simply assume reality as something we take as fact, in the way we all do in normal living.) That is to say, when the word *book* occurs in our speech, it normally occurs in connection, direct or indirect, with an object of the general type that might be described as "a series of sheets of paper in some way fastened together, or a composition or part of a composition that might be written on such a series of sheets of paper or other writing materials." The connections in which a word occurs, the situations with respect to which we use it, are the word's *meaning*. If a child has just learned some new word, say *grass*, and uses it to refer to some object that we normally call by some other name, such as a person's hair or the fur on a coat, we simply say that the child "doesn't know what *grass* means"— he hasn't yet learned in what situations it is and is not used. That is one of the basic features of a linguistic signal—it has to have meaning; if it has no meaning, it is not a signal, and does not come under the subject-matter of linguistics.

On the other hand, the meaning of a word is not by any means fixed, not so much as its sound; for instance, the sound of the word *book* is reasonably definite and always predictable throughout the English-speaking world, but it has many different meanings, as in *a big book* (referring to the actual tome), *a long book* (the composition contained in a book, even before it's printed and bound), or *Book I of the poem* (referring to a part of the composition). The word *book* also has many special uses in phrases such as "to throw the book at someone," "to speak by the book," in England "to book a ticket," and so forth. The meanings and uses of even such a simple word as *book* are much less easily definable and predictable, and change much more rapidly, than the sounds and grammatical form of the word. Hence the linguistic scientist considers it better to study language first from the point of view of its *form* (sounds and combinations of sounds), and tries to avoid, as much as possible, basing his analysis on the shifting sands of meaning.

In so doing, the linguistic analyst gets away at the outset from the approach to language that we find in a considerable part of the Latin and English grammar we learn in our schools—the approach based on meaning rather than form. Even our traditional definitions of the "parts of speech" like nouns, adjectives, verbs and so on, are based on meaning more than on anything else. Most of us probably were taught that a noun was supposed to be "the name of a person, place, or thing"; an adjective, "the name of a quality or accidence"; and a verb, "the name of an action or state of being." Unfortunately, however, this approach is inefficient and keeps us from getting an accurate idea of the way the system of signalling, the language itself, as opposed to its meanings, is built. Meanings vary not only from one dialect to another, but from one person to another, or even in one person's usage: how many of us use the words *Communist* or *Fascist* in exactly the same meaning as the next man does, or are absolutely sure of the exact meaning of every word we use? For that matter, some meanings just will not fit into the definitions that grammarians give for linguistic classes such as the "parts of speech." Take the word *reflection*. In English, the word *reflection* is certainly a noun, just as much as *book, typewriter, ribbon, hat* or any of the other thousands of nouns of the language; but is *reflection* the name of a person, place or thing? It is hardly any of these; a reflection always involves motion, whether that of a light-wave or of a sound-wave or of anything else being reflected off something. It is more of an action, a happening, than a thing. Yet the word *reflection,* as any speaker of English who has learned a little grammatical terminology will tell us, is most certainly a noun.

The reason we say that *reflection* is a noun is, not that it refers to a person, place or thing (for *reflection, light, matter* and many other nouns do not), but that it fits into the system of the English language in the same way as do other words which we call nouns. The word *reflection* can take the suffix *-'s* (*reflection's*); it can, if necessary, be used in the plural (*reflections*); it can have the word *the* used before it (*the reflection*). Those things are true of all English nouns; and they are all features, not of the nouns' meaning, but of their form. At this stage of our work, the only use we make of a word's meaning is to determine whether the word is a true linguistic signal or not, and whether it belongs together in our analysis with other signals that have the same meaning (as when we classify *went* as the past of *go*); otherwise, it is much safer to keep to the form, which is constant, and can be identified and described with much less trouble than the meaning.

Our analysis has to be *formal* first of all; this implies that it will also be somewhat on an abstract plane, and that we will be analyzing language itself before we come to examine the situations in which it is used. Language naturally does not exist in a void, nor yet in a lifeless world of logic or abstraction. People talk, and use language in all their activities, from the most everyday, commonplace contacts to the most intellectual type of reasoning; that is, language is above all social in the way it works, and we shall have occasion to take up its social function later on. But we must first find out *what* language is, before we examine *how* it functions in the wider context of human affairs. Similarly the chemist, even though he may ultimately be interested in the function and use of some fertilizer or dyestuff, first analyzes it and studies its formal characteristics in terms of the frame of reference which has been worked out for chemical analysis.

Our study of language, in addition to being formal, needs to be *descriptive* at the outset, before we proceed to further more advanced analyses. What we need, first of all, is to get as clear and complete an idea as we can get of the structure of any language we're working on, as it exists or existed at a particular point of time, without letting our picture of the language be distorted by extraneous considerations. There are two types of undesirable approach which we are especially likely to introduce, and which can easily distract our attention from the work of pure description: the *prescriptive* approach, and the historical. On this first point, the analyst's task is not to prescribe what "should" or "should not" be said; his job is to describe what actually *is* said, with as completely scientific and objective an approach as a human is capable of. He is interested in noting down factors of meaning such as the social connotations of "incorrect" forms, but considerations of "correctness" should never induce him to omit from his study or analysis such forms as *ain't, he done*. From the scientific point of view, the truly sub-standard *it ain't*, the supposedly sub-standard *it's me*, the standard *I'm tired*, and all other types of speech (literary, dialectal, rustic, slang, criminal argot, etc.) are of absolutely equal merit. That is to say, questions of merit or value just do not enter into the picture of linguistic analysis, however important they may be in the study of literature. Matters of "correctness," of standard versus non-standard, are socially determined and are relevant only from the point of view of meaning, not of linguistic form. In the same way, the chemist or the biologist studies all chemical or biological phenomena with an impersonal, scientific attitude. Our culture has come to accept this situation with regard to the physical sciences, before it has extended the same recognition to the social sciences such as anthropology, of which linguistics is a branch. No one would now say to a biologist working on *spirochaeta pallida*: "That organism is the cause of syphilis, and venereal diseases must not even be discussed; therefore you must stop working in your laboratory and reporting your findings on spirochetes."

Likewise, the scientific linguist approaches all linguistic systems with what he hopes is an equally unprejudiced eye, no matter what is the level of culture or civilization of the people who use them. Whether we consider American, West European, Bush Negro African, aboriginal Australian, or American Indian civilization to be the highest and "best," we must use the same approach and the same methods for analyzing their languages. This is true even for such lowly and usually despised media of communication as Pidgin English; and, when we study Pidgin English with a serious intent and go at it without preconceived notions as to its merit or fitness for use, we find that even Pidgin has a structure and a value of its own.

The other distortion we mentioned, that which comes from a premature introduction of the historical viewpoint, is not basically anti-scientific, as is the prescriptive approach; but its bad effects are just as great, and lead to just as faulty a picture of the state of affairs. At present, in English, the Romance languages, and other languages of the Indo-European family, nouns are definitely distinct from adjectives: among other things, nouns in English have their plural in –s, adjectives do not have a plural formation; adjectives can have adverbs in –ly formed on them, nouns cannot. The present state of affairs, however, seems to have developed out of an earlier condition in which, some thousands of years ago, there was no distinction between the two parts of speech. So far, so good; if we state these two situations separately, and then tell the historical relation between the two, no harm is done. But definite harm is done if we do as one scholar did, and make the statement "Grammatically, nouns and adjectives are identical;

their functional differentiation . . . was a later development." Identical
at what point of time?—in Indo-European, yes; in modern English, Romance, etc., or even Latin and Greek, no; and the statement, as it stands,
is inaccurate and confusing. It is as if we were to say "Maine is really a part
of Massachusetts, and Vermont a section of New York; their functional differentiation was a later development," just because that was the situation
in earlier times. Historical considerations should not be allowed to obscure
our first aim, which is to find out the facts as they are or were at whatever
given point of time we are studying; then, if we want to study historical
development, we can do so by comparing two or more sets of descriptive
data.

What the linguistic analyst does, therefore, when he begins to work on
any particular language or on any feature of language in general, is to get
rid of any preconceptions he may have concerning the social standing or
"merit" of language. Then he has to get a clear idea of the language's
structure, of what "makes it tick," at the specific point of time and space
he's interested in—whether it be the present or some time in the past—and
make an accurate description of it, at least for his own use and preferably
published for others' use as well. Such a work is called a *descriptive grammar*. He can then go ahead and study the variations from any particular
dialect which are found either in space (*linguistic geography*) or in time
(*historical grammar*). In any of these kinds of study, the analyst adopts
certain divisions which fit his subject-matter. Just as the chemist, say,
classes certain phenomena under organic chemistry and others under in-
organic chemistry, so the linguistic analyst divides his work into three main
branches: the study of 1) sound, 2) form, and 3) meaning.

Study Questions

1. Explain the difference between the descriptive and the prescriptive linguist's attitude toward such language as "Sure, the window's broke, but it ain't my
fault; Jack done it." Linguistically, are such substandard expressions as valid as
"Father, I cannot tell a lie; I did it with my little hatchet"? What is the social
objection to substandard expressions?

2. Which would provide the prescriptive linguist with more material for a
study of "correct" spoken English, the dialogue in a novel by J. P. Marquand
about upper-class Bostonians or that in J. D. Salinger's *Catcher in the Rye* or
Mark Twain's *Huckleberry Finn*? Of what value to the descriptive linguist would
be the dialogue in realistic fiction dealing with uneducated characters?

3. Without overstressing analogy, compare the botanist's interest in weeds with
the descriptive linguist's interest in substandard speech. To whom and why are
weeds or substandard elements in speech undesirable? What functions do weeds
serve in nature and substandard speech in society?

3. THE CONVENTIONAL CHARACTER OF LANGUAGE

James B. Greenough AND George Lyman Kittredge

Professors Greenough and Kittredge collaborated on *Words and Their Ways in English Speech* (1901), from which this selection is taken. In their pioneering book they anticipated the present-day linguist's insistence upon examining language behavior in its cultural context.

The changes which the meanings of words undergo in the development of a language seem, at first sight, purely fortuitous in some instances. In fact, however, the appearance of chance is due merely to our ignorance of the causes that have operated in each case. Such causes may be simple and easily understood, or so complex as never to be discoverable in their entirety. But so long as thought proceeds in obedience to definite laws, language, which is the expression of thought by means of conventional signs, must also obey rules which, if we could discover them, would account for every variation.

We often speak of the "proper or essential meaning" of a word. The term is convenient, and one could not well dispense with it in etymological study. Yet it may easily become misleading, if certain cautionary limitations are not borne in mind. In the absolute sense of the term a word has no "essential" meaning. Words are conventional signs. They mean what they are intended to mean by the speaker and understood to mean by the hearer. There is no other sense in which language can be properly said to signify anything. Thus when a boy in the street declares that he "hain't seen no dog," it is not true that his "two negatives make one affirmative," for he intends simply an emphatic negation, and we inevitably understand him in that way, however nice we may be about our own *not's*. In other words, two negatives may make an affirmative in logic, but they seldom do in English speech. The rule in Anglo-Saxon and Middle English was like that in Greek: "Use as many negatives as you can." Thus in King Alfred's description of the effects of the harping of Orpheus: "No hart shunned-not no lion, nor no hare no hound, nor no beast knew-not no hatred nor no fear from another, for the pleasure they took in the sound."

Many current social phrases show in a moment how conventional are the meanings of words. Thus, "Beg your pardon!" with a questioning inflection of the voice, has come to mean simply "What?"—an inquiry when one has failed to catch another's remark. The only difference between "Beg pardon" and "What?" is a difference in courtesy,—the former involving an apology for inattention. . . . "So glad to see you!" "Give my love to—," "Sorry to be out when you called!"—are all phrases which mean just as much and just as little as they are understood to mean by the speaker and the person spoken to.

Perhaps the final test of the fact that language is a convention,—that words have no natural and essential meaning which belongs to them more than any other,—is seen in irony. Here we use a word in a sense which is the direct opposite of that which it usually bears,—and we are understood without difficulty. Thus, "He is a very courageous person" may mean, if it is so intended and so taken, "He is an arrant coward!" Nor is it absolutely necessary that the remark should be uttered in any special tone of voice in order to convey this ironical meaning. The intention of the speaker and the understanding of the hearer are all that is required. There is a whole class of expressions (more or less colloquial) which have become idiomatic in an ironical sense: as, "A precious rascal!" "That's a pretty thing to say!" "Fine work, this!" "Here's a pretty how-d'ye do!" . . .

The truth of these considerations may be tested in another way. Many words have so changed their meanings in the course of time that their present sense has no necessary logical connection with that which they formerly bore.

Thus the Latin *rivalis* is an adjective that meant "pertaining to a brook" (L. *rivus;* cf. *river, rivulet*); but a *rival* is a "competitor." There is no necessary connection of thought between the two senses. Philologists know the history of this curious change, and see that it is easy and natural. *Rivales* in Latin came to mean "neighbors who got water from the same stream,"— and it is thus used in the Roman Digest, which discusses the contests that often rose between such persons respecting their riparian rights. But this connection between the senses is a mere matter of history. It does not affect us today. We do not think of brooks when we talk of rivals in politics, or business, or love. . . .

Explodo meant, in Latin, "to drive off an actor by clapping the hands," then "to hoot off" by any noisy sign of disapproval. Thus Cicero speaks of a player as being "exploded not merely by hissing, but by abusive words." The modern intransitive use of *explode* is very modern indeed, but it suggests neither actors nor catcalls. The bridge between the senses is the idea of "driving out" in such phrases as "the ball was exploded from the gun." So powerful, however, are the modern associations of the word that even the bookish phrase "an exploded fallacy," which preserves the old sense, is commonly understood as an error that has been "blown up" or "blown to pieces" by the arguments of an adversary. . . .

These are merely a few examples out of thousands, but they suffice to enforce what has been said of the conventional nature of words.

To be sure, the course by which these same words have strayed so far from their former selves may usually be traced; and the clew which has guided their wanderings may then become evident. But this does not alter the case; for the present signification of each of them *is* its meaning, and something very different *was* its meaning a hundred or a thousand years ago, and between the two is a great gap, which the memory and the linguistic consciousness of the modern speaker does not span, and could not if it would. It is as if the word had been annihilated and created anew. The modern user knows nothing of the former meaning.

Words, then, have no character in themselves. They are merely conventional signs, and consequently they can be good or bad, dignified or vulgar, only in accordance with the ideas which they conventionally denote or suggest in the mind of the speaker and his hearers. Yet under this head of *suggestions* comes in an important consideration, which accounts for a great deal that would otherwise be inexplicable. Most words, from their use, acquire special connotations or associations, which almost seem to give them a character of their own.

Thus the word *fist* means simply "the hand with the fingers doubled up against the palm." In the idiomatic comparison "as big as your fist," it is purely descriptive, and has no particular character, good or bad. The use of the fist in fighting, however, has given a peculiar connotation to the term. We may say "He hit his opponent with his clenched fist," for here again *fist* is purely descriptive and occurs in an appropriate environment. Similarly, we may say "The boy cried dismally, wiping his eyes with his dingy fist," for there there is a certain grotesqueness in the scene which justifies the use of undignified language. But we can no longer say, as was formerly possible, "The lady held a lily in her delicate fist." In other words, the associations of *fist* are either pugnacious, vulgar, or jocose.

These suggestive associations are partly general and partly individual. If certain phrases are habitually associated in our minds with low or disagreeable persons or things, they will inevitably be relegated to the category of unseemly terms; and, on the other hand, phrases that are associated with dignified and reputable persons or circumstances will acquire a kind of respectability independent of the exact meaning which they convey.

The associations in question may be purely personal. Everybody remembers certain words which he dislikes intensely, though they are in common use, convey no bad or disagreeable meaning, and are quite euphonious. We may even remember our reason for such dislikes. Perhaps the word is associated with an unpleasant experience; more likely, however, our antipathy is due to its habitual use by some one whom we do not fancy. Or we may have been bored by hearing the word over-used, so that every new repetition gives us a feeling of satiety.

We have already averted to this doctrine of association in discussing slang. One of the chief objections to the excessive use of this pariah dialect is not that there is anything objectionable about the words themselves, but that their associations are low, or at least undignified, and perhaps disgusting. If they secure a position in the vocabulary, their origin is likely to be forgotten, and they cease to be offensive.

The associations of words are always shifting, even when the meaning remains unchanged. Hence we continually meet with expressions in our older poets which have lost their dignity, and appear to us out of harmony with the context, though they were quite irreproachable when the author used them. . . .

Clearly, then, we are dealing with a very real phenomenon in the operations of language. When a word has been long used in a particular sense, there cluster about it a great variety of traditional associations,—religious, historical, literary, or sentimental, which, though not a part of its meaning, properly so called, are still a considerable factor in its significant power. A rose by any other name would smell as sweet, no doubt; yet no other name would so vividly suggest to us its fragrance. The noun *lily* is no whiter, nor is it more graceful, than, for example, *nilly*. Yet if it were possible to substitute *nilly* for *lily*, it would be long before the new term would call up in our minds either the whiteness or the grace of the lily as the accustomed word presents them,—not by virtue of any inherent quality, but merely because of its traditional and poetic associations.

The power of such connotations becomes very great when the word is an old one, which has been much used, and is in some manner, therefore, bound up with the most intense experiences of great numbers of men. Words like *father, mother, home,* or the name of one's country, may have a tremendous effect in a great crisis. A mob may be roused to fury by the utterance of a single word; yet in all such cases it is of course not the word at all that produces the effect, but its associations. Caesar's mutinous army was reduced to tearful submission by the one word *Quirites!* "fellow-citizens," which reminded them that they were no longer *commilitones,* the "fellow-soldiers" of their beloved leader.

Indeed, language is sometimes translated into conduct. A figure of speech may even suggest a course of action. To "*bridle* one's tongue" is an old and very natural metaphor. Is it too much to believe that it suggested the particular form of gag used in the seventeenth and eighteenth centuries to confine the tongue of a convicted shrew? At all events, the figure of speech is centuries older than the actual "scold's bridle." A mistaken etymology may react in a similar manner. A *forlorn hope* is a body of soldiers who undertake some service of extraordinary peril. The phrase is an adaptation of the Dutch *verloren hoop,* "lost band" (in Fr., *enfants perdus*). *Hoop* is cognate with our *heap,* which formerly signified a multitude of persons as well as of things. Who can doubt that the happy confusion of tongues which illuminated with a ray of *hope* the desperate valor of the old phrase, has had its effect on the fortune of war?

As we have already remarked, we seem to ourselves to speak by nature, for we cannot remember learning to talk. This fact, taken in connection with the powerful influence which words often produce upon our minds through the association of ideas enables us readily to understand how it is often thought that words have some natural power or meaning independently of usage or convention. This idea is widespread, and manifests itself alike in the savage and in the philosopher. . . .

In invoking a god, or other supernatural being, it was customary to use many different names. Often, in later times, the object of this variety was thought to be the winning of the deity's favor by employing that title which he might prefer. Originally, however, the purpose was to make sure of uttering the one true and essential name of the divinity,— that name which would control him instantly and force him to grant your request. It is well known that the real name of the city of Rome was supposed to be kept secret, lest, if it became known to the enemy, they might use it in incantations which would deprive the city of its protecting gods. So, among some savages, it is a deadly insult to call a man by his right name,—an idea which has left its traces in the apologetic Latin formula "quem honoris causa nomino," and in the parliamentary phrase "the gentleman from Ohio."

All these superstitions, primitive as they seem to us, have had considerable effect on men's opinions about language, and, consequently, on language itself. They have even found philosophic expression in the Stoic doctrine of etymology, which has exerted a profound influence on modern thought, and still sways us in our judgment of words.

When, in the fourth or fifth century before Christ, the Greek philosophers began to connect the study of words with that of things, one of the questions which confronted them was, whether words and their meanings came "by nature" . . . , or artificially and "by convention." . . . The Stoics, in accordance with their general theory of the universe, decided in favor of a "natural" origin, and held that if the "true" . . . , or original meaning of a word could only be discovered, we should at once gain an insight into the divinely constituted nature of the thing which the word denotes. The search for this "true meaning" . . . was therefore called *etymology,* or "the science of true meanings."

The doctrine of the Stoics has long been exploded, and the term *etymology* has entirely changed its sense. Yet the old notion dies hard. In the popular mind there still lingers a haunting suspicion that it is true, and accordingly one often hears, from the pulpit or the platform, and even from the professor's chair, serious arguments based on the supposed original or essential meaning of this or that word. The fallacy of such reasoning may be illustrated by an anecdote. The writer recently asked a friend, in jest, whether a particular service came within the functions of an *amanuensis.* "Oh! yes," was the reply, "she does it *with her hands!*" Now, it is true that *amanuensis* comes from *manus,* "the hand"; yet the jocose remark just quoted was none the less an absurdity, as indeed, it was meant to be. The Romans, who were accustomed to dictating their compositions, designated the slaves who wrote for them as *servi a manu*, i.e., "writing-servants," for *manus* was often used for "handwriting" (like our *hand*). Later they made, somewhat irregularly, a noun, *amanuensis* (like *Atheniensis*), and this we have borrowed in the same sense, and in that sense only. Hence the absurdity of drawing from the general meaning of *manus*, "hand," any inferences as to the proper duties of an amanuensis. . . .

The history of every word begins with its root, if the root can be ascertained, as is not always the case. Yet we must not expect the root to contain, as in the germ, all the significance that successive civilizations have attached to the words that have grown out of it. We should never forget that words are conventional symbols, and that any word—whatever its origin—bears, at any moment, that meaning which the speakers of the language have tacitly agreed to assign to it. And this meaning may, or may not, have a direct logical connection with the original sense of the root.

This principle does not do away with the distinctions of right and wrong in speaking a language. The purpose of speech is to express one's thoughts so that they may be understood by others. Hence, the consensus of usage determines the meaning which a word bears, and this consensus is governed at all times by the *Sprachgefühl*, so that a language always remains true to itself, as we have had occasion to remark before. Within the limits of this feeling, however, hardly any influence is too slight to produce a variation in sense.

Study Questions

1. "Words are conventional signs" is another way of saying that the relation between words and meaning is arbitrary. How is this fact established by the different meanings given to common words by special groups, such as common words currently in use by teen-agers?

2. Two negatives, for example, "It is not unlikely that it will rain tomorrow," or "Her visit was not unexpected," or "This fact is not without significance," may be used as a weak affirmative. In dialogue in fiction, drama, or in actual conversation, find examples of this permissible double negative and of the substandard double negative and distinguish between the social and intellectual contexts in which they occur.

3. Some conventional phrases are regional and thus subject to misinterpretation: "May I carry you home?" or "Good evening" used in the afternoon. Can you supply other examples? When you say "goodbye" do you mean "God be with you"? The English expression, contracted to *goodbye*, means the same as the Spanish *Vaya Vd. con Dios*. What other conventional terms do you know in another language? Do they have precise equivalents in English? Are they used with their full meaning? What does *hello* mean?

4. What do *bonfire*, *gossip*, and *amethyst* mean to you? In an unabridged or

a collegiate dictionary, look up these words and note their original meaning as indicated in the etymology given in brackets. What do you conclude?

5. Slang is called "this pariah dialect." What mental image and connotations does *pariah* evoke? Why is analogy based on society and social classes appropriate in dealing with language? What happens to the capable pariah whose origin is unknown or to slang which is accepted or to the weed which proves to have some value?

6. Surprisingly, the root of a word may often contain the germ of all its later significance. Look up *gender, civil, maternal,* and related words. What other examples can you think of?

4. REVOLUTION IN GRAMMAR

W. Nelson Francis

In an article in the *Quarterly Journal of Speech* for October, 1954, Professor Francis sketches some of the ideas and assumptions underlying scientific linguistics.

1

A long overdue revolution is at present taking place in the study of English grammar—a revolution as sweeping in its consequences as the Darwinian revolution in biology. It is the result of the application to English of methods of descriptive analysis originally developed for use with languages of primitive peoples. To anyone at all interested in language, it is challenging; to those concerned with the teaching of English (including parents), it presents the necessity of radically revising both the substance and the methods of their teaching.

A curious paradox exists in regard to grammar. On the one hand it is felt to be the dullest and driest of academic subjects, fit only for those in whose veins the red blood of life has long since turned to ink. On the other, it is a subject upon which people who would scorn to be professional grammarians hold very dogmatic opinions, which they will defend with considerable emotion. Much of this prejudice stems from the usual sources of prejudice—ignorance and confusion. Even highly educated people seldom have a clear idea of what grammarians do, and there is an unfortunate confusion about the meaning of the term "grammar" itself.

Hence it would be well to begin with definitions. What do people mean when they use the word "grammar"? Actually the word is used to refer to three different things, and much of the emotional thinking about matters grammatical arises from confusion among these different meanings.

The first thing we mean by "grammar" is "the set of formal patterns in which the words of a language are arranged in order to convey larger meanings." It is not necessary that we be able to discuss these patterns self-consciously in order to be able to use them. In fact, all speakers of a language above the age of five or six know how to use its complex forms of organization with considerable skill; in this sense of the word—call it "Grammar 1"—they are thoroughly familiar with its grammar.

The second meaning of "grammar"—call it "Grammar 2"—is "the branch of linguistic science which is concerned with the description, analysis, and formulization of formal language patterns." Just as gravity was in full operation before Newton's apple fell, so grammar in the first sense was in full operation before anyone formulated the first rule that began the history of grammar as a study.

The third sense in which people use the word "grammar" is "linguistic etiquette." This we may call "Grammar 3." The word in this sense is often coupled with a derogatory adjective: we say that the expression "he ain't here" is "bad grammar." What we mean is that such an expression is bad linguistic manners in certain circles. From the point of view of "Grammar 1" it is faultless; it conforms just as completely to the structural patterns of English as does "he isn't here." The trouble with it is like the trouble with Prince Hal in Shakespeare's play—it is "bad," not in itself, but in the company it keeps.

As has already been suggested, much confusion arises from mixing these meanings. One hears a good deal of criticism of teachers of English couched in such terms as "they don't teach grammar any more." Criticism of this sort is based on the wholly unproved assumption that teaching Grammar 2 will increase the student's proficiency in Grammar 1 or improve his manners in Grammar 3. Actually, the form of Grammar 2 which is usually taught is a very inaccurate and misleading analysis of the facts of Grammar 1; and it therefore is of highly questionable value in improving a person's ability to handle the structural patterns of his language. It is hardly reasonable to expect that teaching a person some inaccurate grammatical analysis will either improve the effectiveness of his assertions or teach him what expressions are acceptable to use in a given social context.

These, then, are the three meanings of "grammar": Grammar 1, a form of behavior; Grammar 2, a field of study, a science; and Grammar 3, a branch of etiquette.

2

Grammarians have arrived at some basic principles of their science, three of which are fundamental to this discussion. The first is that a language constitutes a set of behavior patterns common to the members of a given community. It is a part of what the anthropologists call the culture of the community. Actually it has complex and intimate relationships with other phases of culture such as myth and ritual. But for purposes of study it may be dealt with as a separate set of phenomena that can be objectively described and analyzed like any other universe of facts. Specifically, its phenomena can be observed, recorded, classified, and compared; and general laws of their behavior can be made by the same inductive process that is used to produce the "laws" of physics, chemistry, and the other sciences.

A second important principle of linguistic science is that each language or dialect has its own unique system of behavior patterns. Parts of this system may show similarities to parts of the systems of other languages, particularly if those languages are genetically related. But different languages solve the problems of expression and communication in different ways, just as the problems of movement through water are solved in different ways by lobsters, fish, seals, and penguins. A couple of corollaries of this principle are important. The first is that there is no such thing as "universal grammar," or at least if there is, it is so general and abstract as to be of little use. The second corollary is that the grammar of each language must be made up on the basis of a study of that particular language—a study that is free from preconceived notions of what a language should contain and how it should operate. The marine biologist does not criticize the octopus for using jet-propulsion to get him through the water instead of the methods of a self-respecting fish. Neither does the linguistic scientist express alarm or distress when he finds a language that seems to get along quite well without any words that correspond to what in English we call verbs.

A third principle on which linguistic science is based is that the analysis and description of a given language must conform to the requirements laid down for any satisfactory scientific theory. These are (1) simplicity, (2) consistency, (3) completeness, and (4) usefulness for predicting the behavior of phenomena not brought under immediate observation when the theory was formed. Linguistic scientists who have recently turned their attention to English have found that, judged by these criteria, the traditional grammar of English is unsatisfactory. It falls down badly on the first two requirements, being unduly complex and glaringly inconsistent within itself. It can be made to work, just as the Ptolemaic earth-centered astronomy can be, but at the cost of great elaboration and complication. The new grammar, like the Copernican sun-centered astronomy, solves the same problems with greater elegance, which is the scientist's word for the simplicity, compactness, and tidiness that characterize a satisfactory theory.

3

A brief look at the history of the traditional grammar of English will make apparent the reasons for its inadequacy. The study of English grammar is actually an outgrowth of the linguistic interest of the Renaissance. It was during the later Middle Ages and early Renaissance that the various vernacular languages of Europe came into their own. They began to be used for many kinds of writing which had previously always been done in Latin. As the vernaculars, in the hands of great writers like Dante and Chaucer, came of age as members of the linguistic family, a concomitant interest in their grammars arose. The earliest important English grammar was written by Shakespeare's contemporary, Ben Jonson.

It is important to observe that not only Ben Jonson himself but also those who followed him in the study of English grammar were men deeply learned in Latin and sometimes in Greek. For all their interest in English, they were conditioned from earliest school days to conceive of the classical languages as superior to the vernaculars. We still sometimes call the elementary school the "grammar school"; historically the term means the school where Latin grammar was taught. By the time the Renaissance or eighteenth-century scholar took his university degree, he was accustomed to use Latin as the normal means of communication with his fellow scholars. Dr. Samuel Johnson, for instance, who had only three years at the university and did not take a degree, wrote poetry in both Latin and Greek. Hence it was natural for these men to take Latin grammar as the norm, and to analyze English in terms of Latin. The grammarians of the seventeenth and eighteenth centuries who formulated the traditional grammar of English looked for the devices and distinctions of Latin grammar in English, and where they did not actually find them they imagined or created them. Of course, since English is a member of the Indo-European family of languages, to which Latin and Greek also belong, it did have many grammatical elements in common with them. But many of these had been obscured or wholly lost as a result of the extensive changes that had taken place in English—changes that the early grammarians inevitably conceived of as degeneration. They felt that it was their function to resist further change, if not to repair the damage already done. So preoccupied were they with the grammar of Latin as the ideal that they overlooked in large part the exceedingly complex and delicate system that English had substituted for the Indo-European grammar it had abandoned. Instead they stretched unhappy English on the Procrustean bed of Latin. It is no wonder that we commonly hear people say, "I didn't really understand grammar until I began to study Latin." This is eloquent testimony to the fact that the grammar "rules" of our present-day textbooks are largely an inheritance from the Latin-based grammar of the eighteenth century.

Meanwhile the extension of linguistic study beyond the Indo-European and Semitic families began to reveal that there are many different ways in which linguistic phenomena are organized—in other words, many different kinds of grammar. The tone-languages of the Orient and of North America, and the complex agglutinative languages of Africa, among others, forced grammarians to abandon the idea of a universal or ideal grammar and to direct their attention more closely to the individual systems employed by the multifarious languages of mankind. With the growth and refinement of the scientific method and its application to the field of anthropology, language came under more rigorous scientific scrutiny. As with anthropology in general, linguistic science at first concerned itself with the primitive. Finally, again following the lead of anthropology, linguistics began to apply its techniques to the old familiar tongues, among them English. Accelerated by the practical need during World War II of teaching languages, including English, to large numbers in a short time, research into the nature of English grammar has moved rapidly in the last fifteen years. The definitive grammar of English is yet to be written, but the results so far achieved are spectacular. It is now as unrealistic to teach "traditional" grammar of English as it is to teach "traditional" (i.e., pre-Darwinian) biology or "traditional" (i.e., four-element) chemistry. Yet nearly all certified teachers of English on all levels are doing so. Here is a cultural lag of major proportions.

4

Before we can proceed to a sketch of what the new grammar of English looks like, we must take account of a few more of the premises of linguistic science. They must be understood and accepted by anyone who wishes to understand the new grammar.

First, the spoken language is primary, at least for the original study of a language. In many of the primitive languages,[1] of course, where writing is unknown, the spoken language is the *only* form. This is in many ways an advantage to the linguist, because the written language may use conventions that obscure its basic structure. The reason for the primary importance of the spoken language is that language originates as speech, and most of the changes and innovations that occur in the history of a given language begin in the spoken tongue.

Secondly, we must take account of the concept of dialect. I suppose most laymen would define a dialect as "a corrupt form of a language spoken in a given region by people who don't know any better." This introduces moral judgments which are repulsive to the linguistic scholar. Let us approach the definition of a dialect from the more objective end, through the notion of a speech community. A speech community is merely a group of people who are in pretty constant intercommunication. There are various types of speech communities: local ones, like "the people who live in Tidewater Virginia"; class ones, like "the white-collar class"; occupational ones, like "doctors, nurses, and other people who work in hospitals"; social

[1] "Primitive languages" here is really an abbreviated statement for "languages used by peoples of relatively primitive culture"; it is not to be taken as implying anything simple or rudimentary about the languages themselves. Many languages included under the term, such as native languages of Africa and Mexico, exhibit grammatical complexities unknown to more "civilized" languages.

ones, like "clubwomen." In a sense, each of these has its own dialect. Each family may be said to have its own dialect; in fact, in so far as each of us has his own vocabulary and particular quirks of speech, each individual has his own dialect. Also, of course, in so far as he is a member of many speech communities, each individual is more or less master of many dialects and shifts easily and almost unconsciously from one to another as he shifts from one social environment to another.

In the light of this concept of dialects, a language can be defined as a group of dialects which have enough of their sound-system, vocabulary, and grammar (Grammar 1, that is) in common to permit their speakers to be mutually intelligible in the ordinary affairs of life. It usually happens that one of the many dialects that make up a language comes to have more prestige than the others; in modern times it has usually been the dialect of the middle-class residents of the capital, like Parisian French and London English, which is so distinguished. This comes to be thought of as the standard dialect; in fact, its speakers become snobbish and succeed in establishing the belief that it is not a dialect at all, but the only proper form of the language. This causes the speakers of other dialects to become self-conscious and ashamed of their speech, or else aggressive and jingoistic about it—either of which is an acknowledgment of their feelings of inferiority. Thus one of the duties of the educational system comes to be that of teaching the standard dialect to all so as to relieve them of feelings of inferiority, and thus relieve society of linguistic neurotics. This is where Grammar 3, linguistic etiquette, comes into the picture.

A third premise arising from the two just discussed is that the difference between the way educated people talk and the way they write is a dialectal difference. The spread between these two dialects may be very narrow, as in present-day America, or very wide, as in Norway, where people often speak local Norwegian dialects but write in the Dano-Norwegian *Riksmaal*. The extreme is the use by writers of an entirely different language, or at least an ancient and no longer spoken form of the language—like Sanskrit in northern India or Latin in western Europe during the later Middle Ages. A corollary of this premise is that anyone setting out to write a grammar must know and make clear whether he is dealing with the spoken or the written dialect. Virtually all current English grammars deal with the written language only; evidence for this is that their rules for the plurals of nouns, for instance, are really spelling rules, which say nothing about pronunciation.

This is not the place to go into any sort of detail about the methods of analysis the linguistic scientist uses. Suffice it to say that he begins by breaking up the flow of speech into minimum sound-units, or phones, which he then groups into families called phonemes, the minimum significant sound-units. Most languages have from twenty to sixty of these. American English has forty-one: nine vowels, twenty-four consonants, four degrees of stress, and four levels of pitch. These phonemes group themselves into minimum meaningful units, called morphemes. These fall into two groups: free morphemes, those that can enter freely into many combinations with other free morphemes to make phrases and sentences; and bound morphemes, which are always found tied in a close and often indissoluble relationship with other bound or free morphemes. An example of a free morpheme is "dog"; an example of a bound morpheme is "un-" or "ex-." The linguist usually avoids talking about "words" because the term is very inexact. Is "instead of," for instance, to be considered one, two, or three words? This is purely a matter of opinion; but it is a matter of fact that it is made up of three morphemes.

In any case, our analysis has now brought the linguist to the point where he has some notion of the word-stock (he would call it the "lexicon") of his language. He must then go into the question of how the morphemes are grouped into meaningful utterances, which is the field of grammar proper. At this point in the analysis of English, as of many other languages, it becomes apparent that there are three bases upon which classification and analysis may be built: form, function, and meaning. For illustration let us take the word "boys" in the utterance "the boys are here." From the point of view of form, "boys" is a noun with the plural ending "s" (pronounced like "z"), preceded by the noun-determiner "the," and tied by concord to the verb "are," which it precedes. From the point of view of function, "boys" is the subject of the verb "are" and of the sentence. From the point of view of meaning, "boys" points out or names more than one of the male young of the human species, about whom an assertion is being made.

Of these three bases of classification, the one most amenable to objective description and analysis of a rigorously scientific sort is form. In fact, many conclusions about form can be drawn by a person unable to understand or speak the language. Next comes function. But except as it is revealed by form, function is dependent on knowing the meaning. In a telegraphic sentence like "ship sails today" [2] no one can say whether "ship" is the subject of "sails" or an imperative verb with "sails" as its object until he knows what the sentence means. Most shaky of all bases for grammatical analysis is meaning. Attempts have been made to reduce the phenomena of meaning to objective description, but so far they have not succeeded very well. Meaning is such a subjective quality that it is usually omitted entirely from scientific description. The botanist can describe the forms of plants and the functions of their various parts, but he refuses to concern himself with their meaning. It is left to the poet to find symbolic meaning in roses, violets, and lilies.

At this point it is interesting to note that the traditional grammar of English bases some of its key concepts and definitions on this very sub-

[2] This example is taken from C. C. Fries, *The Structure of English* (New York, 1952), p. 62. This important book will be discussed below.

jective and shaky foundation of meaning. A recent English grammar defines a sentence as "a group of words which expresses a complete thought through the use of a verb, called its predicate, and a subject, consisting of a noun or pronoun about which the verb has something to say." [3] But what is a complete thought? Actually we do not identify sentences this way at all. If someone says, "I don't know what to do," dropping his voice at the end, and pauses, the hearer will know that it is quite safe for him to make a comment without running the risk of interrupting an unfinished sentence. But if the speaker says the same words and maintains a level pitch at the end, the polite listener will wait for him to finish his sentence. The words are the same, the meaning is the same; the only difference is a slight one in the pitch of the final syllable—a purely formal distinction, which signals that the first utterance is complete, a sentence, while the second is incomplete. In writing we would translate these signals into punctuation: a period or exclamation point at the end of the first, a comma or dash at the end of the second. It is the form of the utterance, not the completeness of the thought, that tells us whether it is a whole sentence or only part of one.

Another favorite definition of the traditional grammar, also based on meaning, is that of "noun" as "the name of a person, place, or thing"; or, as the grammar just quoted has it, "the name of anybody or anything, with or without life, and with or without substance or form." [4] Yet we identify nouns, not by asking if they name something, but by their positions in expressions and by the formal marks they carry. In the sentence, "The slithy toves did gyre and gimble in the wabe," any speaker of English knows that "toves" and "wabe" are nouns, though he cannot tell what they name, if indeed they name anything. How does he know? Actually because they have certain formal marks, like their position in relation to "the" as well as the whole arrangement of the sentence. We know from our practical knowledge of English grammar (Grammar 1), which we have had since before we went to school, that if we were to put meaningful words into this sentence, we would have to put nouns in place of "toves" and "wabe," giving something like "The slithy snakes did gyre and gimble in the wood." The pattern of the sentence simply will not allow us to say "The slithy arounds did gyre and gimble in the wooden."

One trouble with the traditional grammar, then, is that it relies heavily on the most subjective element in language, meaning. Another is that it shifts the ground of its classification and produces the elementary logical error of cross-division. A zoologist who divided animals into invertebrates, mammals, and beasts of burden would not get very far before running into trouble. Yet the traditional grammar is guilty of the same error when it defines three parts of speech on the basis of meaning (noun, verb, and

[3] Ralph B. Allen, *English Grammar* (New York, 1950), p. 187.
[4] *Ibid.*, p. 1.

interjection), four more on the basis of function (adjective, adverb, pronoun, conjunction), and one partly on function and partly on form (preposition). The result is that in such an expression as "a dog's life" there can be endless futile argument about whether "dog's" is a noun or an adjective. It is, of course, a noun from the point of view of form and an adjective from the point of view of function, and hence falls into both classes, just as a horse is both a mammal and a beast of burden. No wonder students are bewildered in their attempts to master the traditional grammar. Their natural clearness of mind tells them that it is a crazy patchwork violating the elementary principles of logical thought.

5

If the traditional grammar is so bad, what does the new grammar offer in its place?

It offers a description, analysis, and set of definitions and formulas—rules, if you will—based firmly and consistently on the easiest, or at least the most objective, aspect of language, form. Experts can quibble over whether "dog's" in "a dog's life" is a noun or an adjective, but anyone can see that it is spelled with " 's" and hear that it ends with a "z" sound; likewise anyone can tell that it comes in the middle between "a" and "life." Furthermore he can tell that something important has happened if the expression is changed to "the dog's alive," "the live dogs," or "the dogs lived," even if he doesn't know what the words mean and has never heard of such functions as modifier, subject, or attributive genitive. He cannot, of course, get very far into his analysis without either a knowledge of the language or access to someone with such knowledge. He will also need a minimum technical vocabulary describing grammatical functions. Just so the anatomist is better off for knowing physiology. But the grammarian, like the anatomist, must beware of allowing his preconceived notions to lead him into the error of interpreting before he describes—an error which often results in his finding only what he is looking for.

When the grammarian looks at English objectively, he finds that it conveys its meanings by two broad devices: the denotations and connotations of words separately considered, which the linguist calls "lexical meaning," and the significance of word-forms, word-groups, and arrangements apart from the lexical meanings of the words, which the linguist calls "structural meaning." The first of these is the domain of the lexicographer and the semanticist, and hence is not our present concern. The second, the structural meaning, is the business of the structural linguist, or grammarian. The importance of this second kind of meaning must be emphasized because it is often overlooked. The man in the street tends to think of the meaning of a sentence as being the aggregate of the dictionary meanings of the words that make it up; hence the widespread fallacy of literal translation—the feeling that if you take a French sentence and a French-English dictionary and write down the English equivalent of each French word you will come out with an intelligible English sentence. How ludicrous the results can be, anyone knows who is familiar with Mark Twain's retranslation from the French of his jumping frog story. One sentence reads, "Eh bien! I no saw not that that frog has nothing of better than each frog." Upon which Mark's comment is, "if that isn't grammar gone to seed, then I count myself no judge." [5]

The second point brought out by a formal analysis of English is that it uses four principal devices of form to signal structural meanings:

1. Word order—the sequence in which words and word-groups are arranged.

2. Function-words—words devoid of lexical meaning which indicate relationships among the meaningful words with which they appear.

3. Inflections—alterations in the forms of words themselves to signal changes in meaning and relationship.

4. Formal contrasts—contrasts in the forms of words signaling greater differences in function and meaning. These could also be considered inflections, but it is more convenient for both the lexicographer and the grammarian to consider them separately.

Usually several of these are present in any utterance, but they can be separately illustrated by means of contrasting expressions involving minimum variation—the kind of controlled experiment used in the scientific laboratory.

To illustrate the structural meaning of word order, let us compare the two sentences "man bites dog" and "dog bites man." The words are identical in lexical meaning and in form; the only difference is in sequence. It is interesting to note that Latin expresses the difference between these two by changes in the form of the words, without necessarily altering the order: "homo canem mordet" or "hominem canis mordet." Latin grammar is worse than useless in understanding this point of English grammar.

Next, compare the sentences "the dog is the friend of man" and "any dog is a friend of that man." Here the words having lexical meaning are "dog," "is," "friend," and "man," which appear in the same form and the same order in both sentences. The formal differences between them are in the substitution of "any" and "a" for "the," and in the insertion of "that." These little words are function-words; they make quite a difference in the meanings of the two sentences, though it is virtually impossible to say what they mean in isolation.

Third, compare the sentences "the dog loves the man" and "the dogs loved the men." Here the words are the same, in the same order, with the

[5] Mark Twain, "The Jumping Frog; the Original Story in English; the Retranslation Clawed Back from the French, into a Civilized Language Once More, by Patient and Unremunerated Toil," *1601 . . . and Sketches Old and New* (n.p., 1933), p. 50.

same function-words in the same positions. But the forms of the three words having lexical meaning have been changed: "dog" to "dogs," "loves" to "loved," and "man" to "men." These changes are inflections. English has very few of them as compared with Greek, Latin, Russian, or even German. But it still uses them; about one word in four in an ordinary English sentence is inflected.

Fourth, consider the difference between "the dog's friend arrived" and "the dog's friendly arrival." Here the difference lies in the change of "friend" to "friendly," a formal alteration signaling a change of function from subject to modifier, and the change of "arrived" to "arrival," signaling a change of function from predicate to head-word in a noun-modifier group. These changes are of the same formal nature as inflections, but because they produce words of different lexical meaning, classifiable as different parts of speech, it is better to call them formal contrasts than inflections. In other words, it is logically quite defensible to consider "love," "loves," "loving," and "loved" as the same word in differing aspects and to consider "friend," "friendly," "friendliness," "friendship," and "befriend" as different words related by formal and semantic similarities. But this is only a matter of convenience of analysis, which permits a more accurate description of English structure. In another language we might find that this kind of distinction is unnecessary but that some other distinction, unnecessary in English, is required. The categories of grammatical description are not sacrosanct; they are as much a part of man's organization of his observations as they are of the nature of things.

If we are considering the spoken variety of English, we must add a fifth device for indicating structural meaning—the various musical and rhythmic patterns which the linguist classifies under juncture, stress, and intonation. Consider the following pair of sentences:

Alfred, the alligator is sick!
Alfred the alligator is sick.

These are identical in the four respects discussed above—word order, function-words, inflections, and word-form. Yet they have markedly different meanings, as would be revealed by the intonation if they were spoken aloud. These differences in intonation are to a certain extent indicated in the written language by punctuation—that is, in fact, the primary function of punctuation.

6

The examples so far given were chosen to illustrate in isolation the various kinds of structural devices in English grammar. Much more commonly the structural meaning of a given sentence is indicated by a combination of two or more of these devices: a sort of margin of safety which permits some of the devices to be missed or done away with without obscuring the structural meaning of the sentence, as indeed anyone knows who has ever written a telegram or a newspaper headine. On the other hand, sentences which do not have enough of these formal devices are inevitably ambiguous. Take the example already given, Fries's "ship sails today." This is ambiguous because there is nothing to indicate which of the first two words is performing a noun function and which a verb function. If we mark the noun by putting the noun-determining function-word "the" in front of it, the ambiguity disappears; we have either "the ship sails today" or "ship the sails today." The ambiguity could just as well be resolved by using other devices: consider "ship sailed today," "ship to sail today," "ship sail today," "shipping sails today," "shipment of sails today," and so on. It is simply a question of having enough formal devices in the sentence to indicate its structural meaning clearly.

How powerful the structural meanings of English are is illustrated by so-called "nonsense." In English, nonsense as a literary form often consists of utterances that have a clear structural meaning but use words that either have no lexical meaning, or whose lexical meanings are inconsistent one with another. This will become apparent if we subject a rather famous bit of English nonsense to formal grammatical analysis:

All mimsy were the borogoves
And the mome raths outgrabe.

This passage consists of ten words, five of them words that should have lexical meaning but don't, one standard verb, and four function-words. In so far as it is possible to indicate its abstract structure, it would be this:

All ....y were the ....s
And the ....s ....

Although this is a relatively simple formal organization, it signals some rather complicated meanings. The first thing we observe is that the first line presents a conflict: word order seems to signal one thing, and inflections and function-words something else. Specifically, "mimsy" is in the position normally occupied by the subject, but we know that it is not the subject and that "borogoves" is. We know this because there is an inflectional tie between the form "were" and the "s" ending of "borogoves," because there is the noun-determiner "the" before it, and because the alternative candidate for subject, "mimsy," lacks both of these. It is true that "mimsy" does have the function-word "all" before it, which may indicate a noun; but when it does, the noun is either plural (in which case "mimsy" would most likely end in "s"), or else the noun is what grammarians call a mass-word (like "sugar," "coal," "snow"), in which case the verb would have to be "was," not "were." All these formal considerations are sufficient to counteract the effect of word order and show that the sentence is of the type that may be represented thus:

All gloomy were the Democrats.

Actually there is one other possibility. If "mimsy" belongs to the small group of nouns which don't use "s" to make the plural, and if "borogoves" has been so implied (but not specifically mentioned) in the context as to justify its appearing with the determiner "the," the sentence would then belong to the following type:

[In the campaign for funds] all alumni were the canvassers.
[In the drought last summer] all cattle were the sufferers.

But the odds are so much against this that most of us would be prepared to fight for our belief that "borogoves" are things that can be named, and that at the time referred to they were in a complete state of "mimsyness."

Moving on to the second line, "And the mome raths outgrabe," the first thing we note is that the "And" signals another parallel assertion to follow. We are thus prepared to recognize from the noun-determiner "the," the plural inflection "s," and the particular positions of "mome" and "outgrabe," as well as the continuing influence of the "were" of the preceding line, that we are dealing with a sentence of this pattern:

And the lone rats agreed.

The influence of the "were" is particularly important here; it guides us in selecting among several interpretations of the sentence. Specifically, it requires us to identify "outgrabe" as a verb in the past tense, and thus a "strong" or "irregular" verb, since it lacks the characteristic past-tense ending "d" or "ed." We do this in spite of the fact that there is another strong candidate for the position of verb: that is, "raths," which bears a regular verb inflection and could be tied with "mome" as its subject in the normal noun-verb relationship. In such a case we should have to recognize "outgrabe" as either an adverb of the kind not marked by the form-contrast ending "ly," an adjective, or the past participle of a strong verb. The sentence would then belong to one of the following types:

And the moon shines above.
And the man stays aloof.
And the fool seems outdone.

But we reject all of these—probably they don't even occur to us—because they all have verbs in the present tense, whereas the "were" of the first line combines with the "And" at the beginning of the second to set the whole in the past.

We might recognize one further possibility for the structural meaning of this second line, particularly in the verse context, since we are used to certain patterns in verse that do not often appear in speech or prose. The "were" of the first line could be understood as doing double duty, its ghost or echo appearing between "raths" and "outgrabe." Then we would have something like this:

All gloomy were the Democrats
And the home folks outraged.

But again the odds are pretty heavy against this. I for one am so sure that "outgrabe" is the past tense of a strong verb that I can give its present. In my dialect, at least, it is "outgribe."

The reader may not realize it, but in the last four paragraphs I have been discussing grammar from a purely formal point of view. I have not once called a word a noun because it names something (that is, I have not once resorted to meaning), nor have I called any word an adjective because it modifies a noun (that is, resorted to function). Instead I have been working in the opposite direction, from form toward function and meaning. I have used only criteria which are objectively observable, and I have assumed only a working knowledge of certain structural patterns and devices known to all speakers of English over the age of six. I did use some technical terms like "noun," "verb," and "tense," but only to save time; I could have got along without them.

If one clears his mind of the inconsistencies of the traditional grammar (not so easy a process as it might be), he can proceed with a similarly rigorous formal analysis of a sufficient number of representative utterances in English and come out with a descriptive grammar. This is just what Professor Fries did in gathering and studying the material for the analysis he presents in the remarkable book to which I have already referred, *The Structure of English*. What he actually did was to put a tape recorder into action and record about fifty hours of telephone conversation among the good citizens of Ann Arbor, Michigan. When this material was transcribed, it constituted about a quarter of a million words of perfectly natural speech by educated middle-class Americans. The details of his conclusions cannot be presented here, but they are sufficiently different from the usual grammar to be revolutionary. For instance, he recognizes only four parts of speech among the words with lexical meaning, roughly corresponding to what the traditional grammar calls substantives, verbs, adjectives, and adverbs, though to avoid preconceived notions from the traditional grammar Fries calls them Class 1, Class 2, Class 3, and Class 4 words. To these he adds a relatively small group of function-words, 154 in his materials, which he divides into fifteen groups. These must be memorized by anyone learning the language; they are not subject to the same kind of general rules that govern the four parts of speech. Undoubtedly his conclusions will be developed and modified by himself and by other linguistic scholars, but for the present his book remains the most complete treatment extant of English grammar from the point of view of linguistic science.

7

Two vital questions are raised by this revolution in grammar. The first is, "What is the value of this new system?" In the minds of many who ask it, the implication of this question is, "We have been getting along all these years with traditional grammar, so it can't be so very bad. Why should we go through the painful process of unlearning and relearning grammar just because linguistic scientists have concocted some new theories?"

The first answer to this question is the bravest and most honest. It is that the superseding of vague and sloppy thinking by clear and precise thinking is an exciting experience in and for itself. To acquire insight into the workings of a language, and to recognize the infinitely delicate system of relationship, balance, and interplay that constitutes its grammar, is to become closely acquainted with one of man's most miraculous creations, not unworthy to be set beside the equally beautiful organization of the physical universe. And to find that its most complex effects are produced by the multi-layered organization of relatively simple materials is to bring our thinking about language into accord with modern thought in other fields, which is more and more coming to emphasize the importance of organization—the fact that an organized whole is truly greater than the sum of all its parts.

There are other answers, more practical if less philosophically valid. It is too early to tell, but it seems probable that a realistic, scientific grammar should vastly facilitate the teaching of English, especially as a foreign language. Already results are showing here; it has been found that if intonation contours and other structural patterns are taught quite early, the student has a confidence that allows him to attempt to speak the language much sooner than he otherwise would.

The new grammar can also be of use in improving the native speaker's proficiency in handling the structural devices of his own language. In other words, Grammar 2, if it is accurate and consistent, *can* be of use in improving skill in Grammar 1. An illustration is that famous bugaboo, the dangling participle. Consider a specific instance of it, which once appeared on a college freshman's theme, to the mingled delight and despair of the instructor:

Having eaten our lunch, the steamboat departed.

What is the trouble with this sentence? Clearly there must be something wrong with it, because it makes people laugh, although it was not the intent of the writer to make them laugh. In other words, it produces a completely wrong response, resulting in total breakdown of communication.

It is, in fact, "bad grammar" in a much more serious way than are mere dialectal divergences like "he ain't here" or "he never seen none," which produce social reactions but communicate effectively. In the light of the new grammar, the trouble with our dangling participle is that the form, instead of leading to the meaning, is in conflict with it. Into the position which, in this pattern, is reserved for the word naming the eater of the lunch, the writer has inserted the word "steamboat." The resulting tug-of-war between form and meaning is only momentary; meaning quickly wins out, simply because our common sense tells us that steamboats don't eat lunches. But if the pull of the lexical meaning is not given a good deal of help from common sense, the form will conquer the meaning, or the two will remain in ambiguous equilibrium—as, for instance, in "Having eaten our lunch, the passengers boarded the steamboat." Writers will find it easier to avoid such troubles if they know about the forms of English and are taught to use the form to convey the meaning, instead of setting up tensions between form and meaning. This, of course, is what English teachers are already trying to do. The new grammar should be a better weapon in their arsenal than the traditional grammar, since it is based on a clear understanding of the realities.

The second and more difficult question is, "How can the change from one grammar to the other be effected?" Here we face obstacles of a formidable nature. When we remember the controversies attending on revolutionary changes in biology and astronomy, we realize what a tenacious hold the race can maintain on anything it has once learned, and the resistance it can offer to new ideas. And remember that neither astronomy nor biology was taught in the elementary schools. They were, in fact, rather specialized subjects in advanced education. How then change grammar, which is taught to everybody, from the fifth grade up through college? The vested interest represented by thousands upon thousands of English and Speech teachers who have learned the traditional grammar and taught it for many years is a conservative force comparable to those which keep us still using the chaotic system of English spelling and the unwieldy measuring system of inches and feet, pounds and ounces, quarts, bushels, and acres. Moreover, this army is constantly receiving new recruits. It is possible in my state to become certified to teach English in high school if one has had eighteen credit hours of college English—let us say two semesters of freshman composition (almost all of which is taught by people unfamiliar with the new grammar), two semesters of a survey course in English literature, one semester of Shakespeare, and one semester of the contemporary novel. And since hard-pressed school administrators feel that anyone who can speak English can in a pinch teach it, the result is that many people are called upon to teach grammar whose knowledge of the subject is totally inadequate.

There is, in other words, a battle ahead of the new grammar. It will have to fight not only the apathy of the general public but the ignorance and inertia of those who count themselves competent in the field of grammar. The battle is already on, in fact. Those who try to get the concepts of the new grammar introduced into the curriculum are tagged as "liberal" grammarians—the implication being, I suppose, that one has a free choice between "liberal" and "conservative" grammar, and that the liberals are a bit dangerous, perhaps even a touch subversive. They are accused of undermining standards, of holding that "any way of saying something is just as good as any other," of not teaching the fundamentals of good English. I trust that the readers of this article will see how unfounded these charges are. But the smear campaign is on. So far as I know, neither religion nor patriotism has yet been brought into it. When they are, Professor Fries will have to say to Socrates, Galileo, Darwin, Freud, and the other members of the honorable fraternity of the misunderstood, "Move over, gentlemen, and make room for me."

Study Questions

1. Test your understanding of "the four principal devices of form" used "to signal structural meanings" by analyzing the first sentence of the selection.
   a. What changes in word order are possible? Upon what principles does the order depend?
   b. What are the function words? Which of these words permit substitutions without destroying all meaning in the sentence?
   c. Which words have inflections? Change *revolution* to *revolutions*. Which other words have to be changed and why?
   d. Change the original sentence to "Studying of English grammar is undergoing a revolution which is long overdue." What changes of function are signaled by formal alterations?
2. What meanings may *revolution* have? What meaning does it have in the first sentence? How does the meaning of *revolution* at the beginning of the sentence change if "the study of English grammar" is changed to "Algeria"? How is the meaning of "taking place in" affected?
3. What use does Francis make of analogy? Are his analogies as pertinent to speech behavior as to other kinds of human behavior?
4. Considering the role played by Latin in the intellectual life of medieval and Renaissance Europe, why might grammarians expect to find Latin influence on English grammar? What does the fact that grammar develops in the spoken language signify about this assumed influence of Latin?
5. Look up the tables of phonemes in *Webster's New World Dictionary* and study them until you understand the references to phonemes in the readings in this text.
6. Look up the definition of *sentence* in six composition texts. Do any define by "the form of the utterance"?
7. If you have studied any foreign language, illustrate the fallacy of literal translation by translating into English some of the common idioms of greeting or

weather—or by translating into another language "How are you?" or "It looks like rain."

8. How do juncture, stress, and intonation, as indicated by punctuation, affect the meaning of this line from a poem by a father to his son:

"Mysonmypigmycounterpart"?

9. How do juncture, stress, and intonation in pronunciation serve to distinguish between such pairs of phrases as these: "clients entered therapy," "client-centered therapy"; "chic hats," "she cats"; "don't you," "don't chew"; "buy cheap," "bite sheep"?

5. APPROACHES TO LANGUAGE
Charles C. Fries

This selection is taken from *American English Grammar* (1940), a study which shows how conclusions about language can be arrived at inductively from a careful analysis of language behavior. In the following passage from Chapter I Professor Fries discusses various aspects of language. In a general way the pattern of these aspects provides a classification of some of the basic approaches to language, and the editors, while recognizing that the categories are not always mutually exclusive, have adopted Professor Fries's four classes as the organizing principle for the remainder of this book.

Underlying many of the controversies concerning words and language forms is a very common attitude which I shall call here the "conventional point of view." Frequently stated explicitly, sometimes only implied, it appears in most handbooks and manuals of correct English, in grammars and rhetorics, in educational tests and measures, and in many editorials of the press. This conventional point of view assumes not only that there is a correctness in English language as absolute as that in elementary mathematics but also that the measures of this correctness are very definite rules. The following quotations are typical:

A college professor rises to defend "ain't" and "it is me" as good English. The reed upon which he leans is majority usage. . . . "Ain't," as a legitimate contraction of "am not," would not require defense or apology if it were not for widespread misuse. Unfortunately the same cannot be said of "it is me." This solecism could not be given the odor of good English by a plurality as great as Warren G. Harding rolled up in 1920. . . . A vast amount of wretched English is heard in this country. The remedy does not lie in the repeal of the rules of grammar; but rather in a stricter and more intelligent enforcement of those rules in our schools. . . . This protest against traditional usage and the rules of grammar is merely another manifestation of the unfortunate trend of the times to lawlessness in every direction. . . . Quite as important as keeping undesirables out of the vocabulary is the maintaining of respect for the rules of grammar, which govern the formation of words into phrases and sentences. . . . Students should be taught that correct speaking is evidence of culture; and that in order to speak correctly they must master the rules that govern the use of the language.[1]

Grammar consists of a series of rules and definitions. . . . Since . . . ninety-five per cent of all children and teachers come from homes or communities where incorrect English is used, nearly everyone has before him the long, hard task of overcoming habits set up early in life before he studied language and grammar in school. . . . Such people are exposed to the ridicule of those who notice the error, and the only way in which they can cure themselves is by eternal vigilance and the study of grammar.[2]

This is a test to see how well you know correct English usage and how well you can select the *rule or principle in accordance with which a usage is correct.* In the left hand column a list of sentences is given. In each sentence there are two forms in parentheses, one correct, and the other incorrect. In the right hand column a list of rules or principles is given, some one of which applies to each sentence. . . .

Sentences	*Principles*
( ) 1. (Whom) (Who) did you meet?	*a.* The indirect object is in the objective case.
( ) 2. He told John and (I) (me) an interesting story.	*b.* The subject of the verb is in the nominative case.
	c. The object of a verb is in the objective case.

Read the first sentence in Section I; then mark out the incorrect form. Read the rules in Section I, until you find one that applies to this first sentence. Place the letter of this rule in the square preceding the first sentence. . . .[3]

One purpose of this report is to describe and illustrate a method of constructing a grammar curriculum upon the basis of the errors of school children. . . . it is apparent that the first step is *to ascertain* the rules which are broken and to determine their relative importance.[4]

The point of view expressed in these quotations, assuming as it does that certain definite rules [5] are the necessary standards by which to measure

[1] From an editorial in *The Detroit Free Press*, December 9, 1928.

[2] W. W. Charters, *Teaching the Common Branches* (New York, The Macmillan Co., rev. ed., 1924), pp. 96, 98, 115.

[3] T. J. Kirby, *Grammar Test*, University of Iowa Standard Tests and Scales.

[4] "Minimal Essentials in Language and Grammar," in *Sixteenth Yearbook* of the National Society for the Study of Education (Bloomington, Ind., Public School Publishing Co., 1917), pp. 86, 87.

[5] For a statement of the development of this point of view see C. C. Fries, *Teaching of the English Language* (New York, Thomas Nelson and Sons, 1927), Ch. I, "The Rules of Grammar as the Measure of Language Errors."

language correctness, also repudiates *general usage* as a valid guide to acceptability, even the usage of the so-called "educated." The following quotation represents dozens of similar statements:

> The truth is, however, that authority of general usage, or even of the usage of great writers, is not absolute in language. There is a misuse of words which can be justified by no authority, however great, and *by no usage however general.*[6]

From this, the "conventional point of view," the problem of the differences in our language practice is a very simple one. Only two kinds of forms or usages exist—correct forms and mistakes. In general, the mistakes are thought to be corrupt forms or illegitimate meanings derived by carelessness from the correct ones. In some cases a grudging acquiescence accepts some forms which are contrary to the rules when these forms are sanctioned by an overwhelming usage, but here the view remains that these forms, although established by usage, are still *incorrect* and must always be incorrect. To this point of view these incorrect forms sanctioned by usage are the "idioms" of the language. In all the matters of differing language practices, therefore, those who hold this point of view regard the obligation of the schools as perfectly clear and comparatively simple—the schools must root out the *mistakes* or *errors* and cultivate the language uses that are *correct according to the rules.*[7]

Opposed to this "conventional point of view" is that held by the outstanding scholars in English language during the last hundred years. I shall call it here "the scientific point of view." Typical expressions of it abound.

> In considering the use of grammar as a corrective of what are called "ungrammatical" expressions, it must be borne in mind that the rules of grammar have no value except as statements of facts: whatever is in general use in a language is for that very reason grammatically correct.[8]

> The grammar of a language is not a list of rules imposed upon its speakers by scholastic authorities, but is a scientific record of the actual phenomena of that language, written and spoken. If any community habitually uses certain forms of speech, these forms are part of the grammar of the speech of that community.[9]

---

[6] R. G. White, *Words and Their Uses* (Boston, Houghton Mifflin Co., rev. ed., 1899), p. 14.

[7] "Some better reason than a custom arising from ignorance . . . is needed for changing the English language. It would seem to be still the part of the schools to teach the language *strictly according to rule*, and to place emphasis on such teaching, rather than to encourage questionable liberties of usage." From an editorial in *The Christian Science Monitor*, Boston, February 23, 1923.

[8] Henry Sweet, *New English Grammar*, Vol. I (Oxford, Clarendon Press, 1891), p. 5.

[9] Grattan and Gurrey, *Our Living Language* (London, Thomas Nelson and Sons, 1925), p. 25

It has been my endeavor in this work to represent English Grammar not as a set of stiff dogmatic precepts, according to which some things are correct and others absolutely wrong, but as something living and developing under continual fluctuations and undulations, something that is founded on the past and prepares the way for the future, something that is not always consistent or perfect, but progressing and perfectible—in one word, human.[10]

A Grammar book does not attempt to teach people how they ought to speak, but on the contrary, unless it is a very bad or a very old work, it merely states how, as a matter of fact, certain people do speak at the time at which it is written.[11]

In these typical expressions of "the scientific point of view" there is, first of all, a definitely stated opposition to the fundamental principle of the "conventional attitude." All of them insist that it is unsound to take the rules of grammar as the necessary norms of correct English and to set out to make all usage conform to those rules. In these expressions of the scientific view there is, also, a clear affirmation of the fundamental principle of the attitude that usage or practice is the basis of all the *correctness* there can be in language.[12] From this, the scientific point of view, the problem presented by the differences in our language is by no means a simple one. Instead of having to deal with a mass of diverse forms which can be easily separated into the two groups of *mistakes* and *correct language* according to perfectly definite measures, the language scholar finds himself confronted by a complex range of differing practices which must be sorted into an indefinite number of groups according to a set of somewhat indistinct criteria called "general usage." [13] Those who hold this scientific point of view insist, therefore, that the first step in fulfilling the obligation of the schools in the matter of dealing with the English language is to record, realistically and as completely as possible, the facts of this usage. . . .

All of us upon occasion note and use for the purpose of identification the many differences in the speech of those about us. By differences in pitch of voice, for instance, we can usually tell whether the person talking to us over the telephone is a man, or a woman, or a child. . . . In similar fashion

---

[10] Otto Jespersen, *A Modern English Grammar* (Heidelberg, 1909), I, Preface.

[11] H. C. Wyld, *Elementary Lessons in English Grammar* (Oxford, Clarendon Press, 1925), p. 12.

[12] This statement must not be taken to imply that *mere correctness* is to be considered the ultimate ideal of language. The scientific point of view does not in any way conflict with the artistic view of *good English*. See the discussion of "The Scientific and the Artistic Points of View in Language," in C. C. Fries, *The Teaching of the English Language*, pp. 102–121.

[13] One should, perhaps, call attention at this point to the fact that the great *Oxford English Dictionary* is the outstanding document in this "scientific view of language." The principle underlying the production of the *Oxford Dictionary*, the very foundation of its method, was the insistence upon use or practice as the sole criterion of the legitimate meaning of words. Compare, for example, the treatment of the word *nice* (especially sense 15) in this dictionary with the usual statements concerning it as given in the conventional handbooks.

we should with little difficulty recognize the speech of a Scot like Harry Lauder as differing from that of a native of Georgia or Alabama. If one could conjure up Shakspere or Spenser or Milton, he would find their English strange to his ears not only in pronunciation but in vocabulary and in grammar as well. The speech of Chaucer and of Wycliffe would sound even less like English. In other words, even if one ignores such details as separate the speech of every single person from that of any other, there are at least four large types of differences to be noted in our discussion here.

First, there are historical differences. Chaucer used, as we do, *they* as the nominative plural of the pronoun of the third person, but he did not use *their* as the genitive and *them* as the dative-accusative form. Instead, he used the forms *her* or *hir*, for the genitive plural, and *hem* for the dative-accusative or objective forms. In Chaucer's language it was still the practice to distinguish carefully between the singular and plural forms of the past tense of many verbs. He would say *I rood* (rode) but we *ride(n)*, *he sang* but they *sunge(n)*. In the late sixteenth century it was no longer the practice to distinguish between the singular and plural in the past tense, and Shakspere therefore used *we rode* as well as *I rode*. For him, however, *learn* was often used with the meaning we give to *teach*, and *thou* was frequently used to address those of inferior rank or intimate friends. Thus the language forms of each age have differed in some respect from those of any other time. Constant change is the outstanding characteristic of a live language used by an intellectually active people. The historical changes do not come suddenly, nor do they affect all the users of a language equally. Thus at any time there will be found those who cling to the older methods and those who use the newer fashion. Many of the differences we note in the language of today find their explanation in this process of historical change. These older forms constitute a fairly large proportion of the materials usually called errors by those who maintain the conventional point of view. The so-called double negative, as in "They didn't take no oil with them," is thus a perpetuation of an old practice exceedingly common in the English language for centuries. It was formerly the normal way of stressing a negative. The form *foot*, in such expressions as "He is six foot tall," "The height of the bar is now six foot and two inches," is again the perpetuation of an old practice in the English language which the modern fashion has abandoned. It is an old genitive plural following the numeral. A few other examples out of dozens of such historical differences are *clomb*, usually spelled *clum*, as the past tense of the verb *climb*, instead of *climbed;* *wrought* [14] as the past tense of the verb *work*, instead of *worked;* *stang* as the past tense of the verb *sting*, instead of *stung*. Such differences belong not only in this group called "historical differences" but often also to some of the other three groups to be explained below. In fact, the four types of

[14] One should note that in the case of *wrought* the old form has not the flavor of "vulgar" English as have the other examples here given but suggests super-refinement.

differences are not by any means mutually exclusive classifications but merely loose divisions with convenient labels.

Second, there are regional differences. In the south of England, in early Modern English, the inflectional ending of the verb in the third person singular present indicative was *-eth*, as in "God *loveth* a cheerful giver." In the north of England this inflectional ending was *-es*, as "God *loves* a cheerful giver." Late Modern English has adopted the form that was used only in the northern region. In the language practice of the United States, *gotten* as a past participle form of *get* is fairly general; in England it seldom appears. *You all* as a plural of *you* is especially characteristic of southern United States. In some colleges one takes a course *under* a professor; in others it is *from* one or *with* one; in still others it is *to* one. Some of the differences we note in the language practices of those about us find their explanation in the fact that the fashions in one community or section of the country do not necessarily develop in others. Regional or geographical differences show themselves more clearly in matters of vocabulary. That part of an automobile that is called a *hood* in the United States is called a *bonnet* in England. That which they call the *hood* in England we call the *top*. *Lumber*, to most of us in the United States means *timber;* in England it still means *rubbish*. In some sections of the United States a *paper bag* is usually called a *sack*, in others a *poke*. Such regional differences become especially noticeable when a person from one section of the country moves into another bringing with him the peculiar fashions of the district from which he comes. In the new community these language differences challenge attention and give rise to questions of correctness and preference.

Third, there are literary and colloquial differences. The language practices of conversation differ in many subtle ways from those used in formal writing. Most apparent is the abundance of contractions in the language of conversation. Thoroughly unnatural would sound the speech of those who in conversation did not constantly use *I'm, you'll, isn't, don't, aren't, they'd better, we've,* instead of the fully expanded *I am, you will, is not, do not, are not, they had better, we have.* And in similar fashion the formal writing that habitually employed such contractions would seem equally unnatural because of the impression of very informal familiarity which they would create. Apparent, too, although less obvious are the differences between conversation and formal writing in the matter of sentence completeness. Conversation abounds in groups of words that do not form conventionally complete and logical sentences. Many verbs are omitted; clauses are uttered which are to be attached to the whole context of the conversation rather than to any particular word in a parsable sentence; single words stand for complete ideas. In formal writing the situation demands much more logical completeness of expression, and most of the sentences appear to satisfy the demands of a conventional grammatical analysis. Less apparent but not less real are the differences which arise out of the fact that many perfectly familiar expressions occur practically only in conversational situations and are found very seldom in literary English unless they appear in attempts to report conversation in writing. Occasions seldom arise in anything except conversational situations to use *Who* (or *whom*) *did you call?* or *It is me* (or *I*).

Many assume that the language practices of formal writing are the best or at least that they are of a higher level than those of colloquial or conversational English. When, therefore, they find an expression marked "colloquial" in a dictionary, as is the phrase "*to get on one's nerves*" in Webster's *New International Dictionary,* they frown upon its use. As a matter of fact, thus to label an expression "colloquial" is simply to say that it occurs in good conversation but not in formal writing.[15] Unless one can assume that formal writing is in itself more desirable than good conversation, the language practices peculiar to conversation cannot be rated in comparison with those of formal writing. Each set of language practices is best in its own special sphere of use; one will necessarily differ from the other.

Fourth, there are social or class differences. Despite the fact that America in its national life has struggled to express its belief in the essential equality of human beings and to free the paths of opportunity from arbitrary and artificial restraints, there still do exist some clear differences between the habits and practices of various social groups. It is, of course, practically impossible to mark the limits of any social class in this country. It is even extremely difficult to describe the special characteristics of any such class because of the comparative ease with which one passes from one social group to another, especially in youth, and the consequent mixture of group habits among those so moving. Our public schools, our churches, our community welfare work, our political life, all furnish rather frequent occasions for social class mixture. All that can be done in respect to such a description is to indicate certain facts which seem generally true for the *core* of any social group, realizing that these same facts may also be true separately of many who have connections with other groups. There are, for example, those who habitually wear formal dress clothes in the evening and those who never wear them. Many of the former frequent the opera and concerts

[15] The word *colloquial* as applied to English words and structures is frequently misunderstood, even by teachers of English. Some confuse it with *localism,* and think of the words and constructions marked "colloquial" as peculiarities of speaking which are characteristic of a particular locality. Others feel that some stigma attaches to the label "colloquial" and would strive to avoid as *incorrect* (or as of a *low level*) all words and phrases so marked. The word *colloquial,* however, as used to label words and phrases in a dictionary like Webster's *New International Dictionary* has no such meaning. It is used to mark those words and constructions whose range of use is primarily that of the polite conversation of cultivated people, of their familiar letters and informal speeches, as distinct from those words and constructions which are common also in formal writing. As a matter of fact, even the language of our better magazines and of public addresses has, during the last generation, moved away from the formal toward the informal.

of the best music; many of the latter find their entertainment solely in the movies. The families of the wealthy, especially those whose wealth has continued for several generations, ordinarily mix but little with the families of unskilled laborers; and the families of college professors even in a small city have usually very little social life in common with the families of policemen and firemen.

Just as the general social habits of such separated social groups naturally show marked differences, so their language practices inevitably vary. Pronunciations such as *"ketch"* for *catch* and *"git"* for *get;* and grammatical forms such as "He *seen* his mistake as soon as he *done* it" or *"You was"* are not the characteristic modes of speech of university professors, or of the clergymen who preach from the pulpits in our large city churches, or of the judges of the supreme court, or of the presidents of our most important banks, or even of those who habitually patronize the opera. Such language practices, therefore, if used in these particular social groups attract as much attention as a pair of overalls might at an evening gathering where custom demands formal dress clothes. In fact, part of the significance of the social differences in language habits can well be illustrated by a comparison with clothes. Fundamentally the clothes one wears fulfill the elementary practical functions of comfort by keeping one warm and of modesty by avoiding indecent exposure of one's person. These two practical purposes could just as well be accomplished by rather shapeless simple garments produced over a standard pattern for every one and worn upon all occasions. Such clothes could be made to fulfill their primary functions very efficiently with a minimum of cost. In such a situation, however, aside from the significance of differing degrees of cleanliness, the clothes would show us very little concerning the individuals who wore them. With our present habits of dress the clothes connote or suggest, in a broad general way, certain information concerning the wearers. Among other things they suggest the *circumstances in which we usually see them worn.* A dress suit suggests an evening party (or in some places a hotel waiter); overalls suggest a piece of dirty work or possibly a summer camp. In like manner language forms and constructions not only fulfill a primary function of communicating meaning; they also suggest the circumstances in which those particular forms and constructions are usually employed. If, then, one uses the pronunciations and grammatical forms given earlier in this paragraph, they may serve to communicate his meaning unmistakably, but they will also suggest that he habitually associates with those social groups for whom these language forms are the customary usage and not with those for whom they are not characteristic. We must, therefore, recognize the fact that there are separate social or class groups even in American communities and that these groups differ from one another in many social practices including their language habits.

As indicated earlier the four kinds of differences in language practice here outlined are by no means mutually exclusive. Many historical differences and some sectional differences have become also social differences. . . .

Study Questions

1. What does Fries mean by the "conventional point of view" toward the English language? Where do you find these views expounded today?

2. According to Fries, what principles constitute the "scientific point of view" toward the English language? In what ways does this point of view differ from the conventional attitude?

3. Explain the similarity and difference between Fries's "differences" and the three "status labels" used in *Webster's Third New International Dictionary* (Preface, 19a).

4. Classify the following usage labels found in *Webster's Collegiate Dictionary* according to Fries's four differences in language practice; give the full term for each abbreviation:

Archaic	Dram.	Obs.	Shak.	Vulgar
Bib.	Hist.	Phil.	Slang	Western U.S.
Brit.	Illit.	Poet.	Southern U.S.	
Colloq.	Local	Rare	U.S.	
Dial.	N. E.	Scot.	U.S. Army	

5. From six columns in different parts of the vocabulary of a collegiate dictionary, collect and classify usage labels which clearly indicate the four differences in language practice. What other usage labels do you find? Do these labels suggest contexts for the designated words which would be related to the four categories? For example, what context is suggested for a term used in carpentry? In aeronautics?

6. Look up *frame*, both verb and noun meanings. How many usage labels do you find? In which sense would *frame* be unsuitable for use in written English in a dignified general context?

7. The Anglo-Saxon forms for *he, she, it* were *he, heo, hit*. Justice William O. Douglas of the United States Supreme Court quotes natives of the Great Smoky Mountains as using *hit* ("The People of Cade's Cove," *The National Geographic* [July, 1962], 60–95). William Faulkner in the short story "Barn Burning" has natives of northern Mississippi use *hit*. The article and the story indicate how these different groups of people dress and live. How would you explain the survival of the old form among widely separated rural groups? Is *hit* bad grammar when used in Cade's Cove, a homogeneous community of a few families? Is *hit* a sign of inferior status when used by Mississippi poor whites in dealing with the upper classes? Is *hit* bad grammar when used by a Mississippi white school teacher who had just been demonstrating to a group of colored teachers how to teach reading? (Hortense Powdermaker, *After Freedom* [New York, 1939], p. 305.)

Part **I.**   *Principles of Language*
        Subjects for Brief Papers or Written Reports

1. In Lewis Carroll's *Alice Through the Looking Glass* look up

> 'Twas brillig, and the slithy toves
>   Did gyre and gimble in the wabe.

In the "frames" of this nonsense poem substitute words that make sense. What do you discover about basic English sentence patterns and structure as distinct from meaning? Write a brief report on how position, word forms—tense, person, number, etc.—and structure words—articles, prepositions, and conjunctions—signal sentence patterns independent of lexical meaning.

2. After studying Chapter 8, "The Poetry in Our Daily Speech," in Harry Warfel, *Language: A Science of Human Behavior,* analyze a poem of your own choice and write a report on how meaning and rhythm are related to structure words.

3. What limits a speaker's "possibility of making a linguistic response to any experience"? What limitations are you most conscious of in your own responses? In what ways can those limitations be reduced and your own possibilities of making linguistic responses be extended? How can knowledge of the basic principles of language and the characteristics of English contribute to your skill in making linguistic responses? Rewrite a paragraph of your own in which you strive for effective use of variety in sentence beginnings and endings; subordination by word, by phrase, by clause; emphasis by inversion; emphasis by climactic series; balanced sentence; periodic sentence; parallel participial phrases; clearing out of dead wood; precise diction.

4. How does Aldous Huxley's *Brave New World* show the arbitrary meaning and the conventional character of language? What familiar English words have different meanings or different connotations? How have these been developed? Write a short theme explaining the language process by which one group of words, such as those dealing with motherhood, acquire connotations opposed to our present ones.

5. Judging by "rules" that college students "know," two of the most common dicta of prescriptive grammarians seem to be that a sentence should not begin with a coordinate conjunction, and that it should not end with a preposition. As a "descriptive linguist," examine the first two pages of "The Conventional Character of Language," written by the oldest and among the most eminent of the linguists represented in this text. What is their practice on these two points? Is the prepositional ending avoided in any sentences? What are your conclusions? Extend your observations by random sampling of other selections and write a report on your observations.

6. Study the word *conventional* and the related words near it in the dictionary. What different meanings of the root, *ven,* can you identify? Classify and illustrate them. How do the meanings of *convention* illustrate both the literal and figurative

meanings? Is the original meaning wholly lost in any words in the group? In a short paper present your findings and your generalizations from them.

7. Examine a recent college English handbook or a freshman composition textbook and determine whether the author follows the scientific or the prescriptive point of view toward language. Write a short paper in which you classify your evidence and draw your conclusions from it.

8. Examine Jacques Barzun's *The House of Intellect*, summarize Barzun's main objections to the scientific linguists, and evaluate his objections on the basis of your readings in Part I.

9. On the basis of your study of Part I and of the Preface of *Webster's Third New International Dictionary*, show how the compilers were following linguistic principles in their work.

10. Write a short paper on William Faulkner's "Barn Burning" as representing Fries's four "Differences in Language Practice," showing how historical differences have become substandard regional, how other regional differences are reflected in words and pronunciation, how literary language and colloquial language are used, and how dialogue reflects difference in social levels.

11. In Evans's *Comfortable Words* look up *albatross* and browse through and collect other examples of words which have no "real" meaning. Write a brief report of your findings and the language processes represented.

II. HISTORICAL ASPECTS

This section deals with some of the historical aspects of language. In dictionaries, the changes in the meaning and pronunciation of words are carefully recorded. Once a student understands the pattern which the dictionary uses in dealing with these changes, he can easily trace the different stages of word history. A study of two different editions of the same dictionary or an examination of the citations in the Oxford English Dictionary *will reveal how the characteristics of words change with the passage of years. (Although linguists look upon this function as the primary one, many other people regard the dictionary as an absolute authority which decides questions of usage, pronunciation, meaning, and appropriateness.) With the aid of the dictionary, then, the student can acquire a sense of historical perspective about words and their role in human communication.*

Many place-names also function historically. Like fossils, they often reflect the prevailing characteristics of a bygone era. The reading, the peculiar interests, the ethnic and religious backgrounds, the prominent personages of a community are a few of the historical implications preserved in place-names long after the nature of the community has otherwise changed completely.

The history of words shows the significance of language as a living, dynamic force. The study of language changes provides information about the flexibility of language—the leveling of inflections, the simplification of sentence patterns, and the tendency toward monosyllabism. Investigation of the history of a language also discloses that new words are added when they become necessary for effective communication and that old words atrophy and drop out of normal usage when they no longer serve a useful function. This process of growth, development, and change, common to all

51

languages, is most easily perceived when words are examined in their historical context.

Since word history is so basic in the study of language, it will reappear in later sections, often masquerading as an element of the regional quality of words or as a determining factor in the literary or social implications of words. This overlapping and fusion serves to stress the basic historical quality inherent in words. In fact, it is the historical element which makes words so flexible and, at times, so perplexing.

6. THE LEXICOGRAPHER'S UNEASY CHAIR

James Sledd

In a review of *Webster's Third New International Dictionary* in *College English*, May, 1962, Professor Sledd appraises the book as a scientific linguist and responds to criticisms made by unscientific and linguistically conservative reviewers of the book.

> This latest dictionary to bear the Merriam-Webster label is an intellectual achievement of the very highest order.
> —Sumner Ives in *Word Study*

> The anxiously awaited work that was to have crowned cisatlantic linguistic scholarship with a particular glory turns out to be a scandal and a disaster.
> —Wilson Follett in the *Atlantic*

> Somebody had goofed.
> —Ethel Merman in *Webster's Third New International Dictionary*

But who? Is the goof trademarked, a Merriam-Webster, or is scholarship in Springfield trans-*Atlantic?* The experts will have to answer that question, and thoughtful laymen after using the new dictionary for a long time. This review has more modest aims. Mainly it examines a few issues which less inhibited critics have already raised, suggests some possible limitations of their criticisms, and urges that the serious work of serious scholars must be seriously judged.

Everyone knows that the *Third International* is an entirely new dictionary for use today. In this eighth member of a series which began in 1828, the Merriam Company has invested over $3,500,000, almost three times the cost of the 1934 *New International*, so that the statements in *Webster's Third* are backed by over a century of experience, by the evidence of more than 10,000,000 citations, and by the knowledge and skill of a large permanent staff and more than 200 special consultants. To a reviewer, those facts should be rather sobering.

Some editors, however, and some reviewers have not been restrained from prompt attacks. They have criticized the *Third International* for its failure to include expected encyclopedic matter, for its technique of definition, and especially for its treatment of what is called usage; and they have charged Dr. Gove and his associates with unwise innovations motivated by the desire to destroy all standards of better and worse in the use of English. While insisting upon the responsibility of lexicographers, some of the attackers have not been equally alert to the responsibility of critics.

The question of motives can be dismissed at once. The lexicographers at the Merriam Company, it may safely be assumed, have just one motive: to make the best possible dictionaries. They may have failed, in one respect or another; but such innovations as they actually have made have not been made without the most serious and responsible consideration.

The charge of unwise innovation has two parts: first, that an innovation has been made; and second, that it is unwise. Some of the critics have assumed that the editors of the *Third International* have departed from established lexicographical custom by assuming the role of historians, not lawgivers. One reviewer, indeed, to prove his accusation that the lexicographers had abandoned authority for permissiveness, quoted a part of their statement that "the standard of English pronunciation . . . is the usage that now prevails among the educated and cultured people to whom the language is vernacular." He had not bothered to read precisely the same statement in the 1934 *New International*.

More generally, too, many of the unfavorable critics have ignored the whole history of English lexicography since Samuel Johnson: they have hurried to denounce an innovation as unwise before establishing the fact of innovation. Already in the eighteenth century, the ideal of the standard and standardizing dictionary had been sharply questioned. The encyclopedist Ephraim Chambers declared his view that "the Dictionary-Writer is not supposed to have any hand in the things he relates; he is no more concerned to make the improvements, or establish the significations, than the historian" to fight the battles he describes. Even Johnson said of himself that he did not "form, but register the language," that he did not "teach men how they should think, but relate how they have hitherto expressed their thoughts"; and when Englishmen a century later set out to make the great *Oxford Dictionary*, they assumed from the beginning that the lexicographer is "an historian" of the language, "not a critic." It may be that professional lexicographers have been on the wrong track for two centuries and that in two hours an amateur can set them straight; but in that event the amateur and not the lexicographer would be the innovator. He would do well, before attempting to put his lawgiving theory into practice, to face Johnson's doubts in that magnificent "Preface" and to ask himself the unanswerable question how rational choice among the resources of a language is possible for the man who does not know what those resources are.

The relation between a dictionary and an encyclopedia is another problem whose history should have been better known to some reviewers. Few lexicographers are likely to solve it either to their own full satisfaction or to the satisfaction of all their readers. From the *Third International*, the objectors miss the gazetteer and the biographical dictionary of the 1934 volume, and they dislike the new decision to restrict the word-list "to generic words . . . as distinguished from proper names that are not generic." Other readers might just as well make opposite complaints. The hairy-nosed wombat and the hickory shuckworm do not greatly interest the average American, who has equally little need to know the incubation period of the ostrich or the gestation period of the elephant, to contemplate the drawing of a milestone marked "Boston 20 miles," or to examine a colorplate of fishes which is a slander to the catfish and the brook trout; and the occasional philologist might hope for a dictionary which explains words and leaves to the encyclopedia, as Murray said, the description of things. But who can say that he knows infallibly how such decisions should be made? Murray did not claim infallibility but admitted inconsistency in his omission of *African* and inclusion of *American*. Since man and the universe cannot be put between two covers, some things must be omitted; "selection is guided by usefulness"; and usefulness can be guessed at but not measured. Readers who can get the use of a Webster's unabridged will have access to an encyclopedia. They should consult it when they need to know about people and places. Meanwhile they may be grateful that the *Third International* has made space for as many quotations as it now includes. A dictionary without quotations is like a table of contents without a book.

There remain, of the critics' favorite subjects, the technique of definition and the matter of usage. The technique of definition is briefly explained in the editor's preface:

> The primary objective of precise, sharp defining has been met through development of a new dictionary style based upon completely analytical one-phrase definitions throughout the book. Since the headword in the definition is intended to be modified only by structural elements restrictive in some degree and essential to each other, the use of commas either to separate or to group has been severely limited, chiefly to units in apposition or in series. The new defining pattern does not provide for a predication which conveys further expository comment. . . . Defining by synonym is carefully avoided by putting all unqualified or undifferentiated terms in small capital letters. Such a term in small capitals should not be considered a definition but a cross-reference to a definition of equivalent meaning that can be substituted for the small capitals.
>
> A large number of verbal illustrations mostly from the mid-twentieth century has been woven into the defining pattern with a view to contributing considerably to the user's interest and understanding by showing a word used in context.

If it is not naively optimistic to expect most critics of a dictionary to agree on anything, general approval may be expected for careful synonymies and for the distinction between a synonym and a definition; and the value of illustrative quotations has been demonstrated by centuries of English lexicography. The objection that not many mid-century authors deserve quotation has already been answered, for it is only another form of the notion that the lexicographer should be a lawgiver and not a historian. It would, moreover, be rash to suggest either that many of the quotations are not particularly informative or that identification by the mere names of the authors makes it impossible to check the quotations or to examine them in their contexts: with 10,000,000 quotations to choose from, the editors must know the possibilities of choice more fully than any critic, and precise references would take up much valuable space.

The definitions themselves are another matter. Without advancing any claim to special competence, an ordinary reader may fairly report that he finds some of the definitions extraordinarily clumsy and hard to follow and that as an English teacher he would not encourage his students to follow the new Merriam-Webster model. The one-phrase definitions of nouns in particular may become confusing because in English it is hard to keep track of the relations among a long series of prepositional phrases, participial phrases, and relative clauses; the reader may simply forget what goes with what, if indeed he ever can find out. A less serious criticism is that the new typeface and the long entries unbroken by indentation are bad for middle-aged eyes. Real mistakes, of course, are extremely rare, but a fisherman may be pardoned an objection to the fourth numbered definition of the noun *keeper* as "a fish large enough to be legally caught." The crime is not catching but keeping an undersized or oversized fish.

Perhaps such a quibble is itself no keeper, and some criticism of the dictionary's treatment of usage has been equally frivolous. An excellent bad example appeared in *Life*, whose editors compressed a remarkable amount of confusion into a single sentence when they attacked "Editor Gove" for "saying that if a word is misused often enough, it becomes acceptable." Though one can argue how much use and by what speakers is enough, consistency would force *Life's* editors into silence. Their sacred kye are scrawnier than Pharaoh's seven kine, and it is shocking that the influence of such a magazine should force learning to debate with ignorance.

Yet so loud a stridulation of critics cannot simply be ignored. There is a real question whether the *Third International*, though justly called "the most comprehensive guide to usage currently available," has recorded usage as precisely as it might have done. Were the editors right to abandon "the status label *colloquial*"? Have they adequately reported not only what people say and write but also those opinions concerning speech and writing which properly enter into their own definitions of *standard* and of *Standard English*? Those are legitimate questions to ask of a dictionary "prepared with a constant regard for the needs of the high school and college student" and of the general reader. However diffidently and respectfully, a reviewer must give the best answers that he can.

Several reasons have been offered, by various authorities, for the abandonment of the label *colloquial*. Those reasons are not all alike. It is one thing to say that we cannot know "whether a word out of context is colloquial or not" (Gove), that lexicographers cannot distinguish the "many different degrees of standard usage" by status labels but can only suggest them by quotations (Gove), or that "the bases for discrimination are often

too subtle for exact and understandable verbal statement" (Ives); it is quite
another thing to argue against marking words *colloquial* because many
readers have wrongly concluded that a word so marked is somehow bad
(Ives). In a matter to which the editors must have given their best thought,
the variety itself of these justifications and the failure to order them in any
coherent and inclusive statement is somewhat puzzling; and the impertinent
might be tempted to inquire how 200,000 quotations will enable the inex-
pert reader to do what 10,000,000 quotations did not make possible for the
expert lexicographer or how a dictionary can be made at all if nothing can
go into it which the ignorant might misinterpret. One reason for the widespread misinterpretation of the policy adopted is surely that the underlying
theory has not been clearly explained.

And that is not all. The very defenses of the new policy appear sometimes to refute the contention that finer discriminations are not possible
than those in *Webster's Third*. When the newspapers attack the dictionary
for listing words like *double-dome* and *finalize* as standard, defenders reply
by citing other slangy or colloquial or much reprobated terms from the
columns of those same newspapers. What is the force of the attack or the
defense unless the intelligent layman can draw precisely that distinction
between "the formal and informal speech and writing of the educated"
which the *Third International* refuses to draw for him? If he lacked that
ability, both attackers and defenders would be wasting their citations.

Much can be said, of course, about the confusion of styles in modern
writing. Perhaps distinctions among styles are now indeed less clear and
stable than they were in a less troubled age; perhaps the clumsier writers
do ignore the existing distinctions while the sophisticated use them to play
sophisticated tunes; perhaps the scrupulously objective lexicographer cannot establish those distinctions from his quotation slips alone. For all that,
distinctions do exist. They exist in good writing, and they exist in the linguistic consciousness of the educated. Dr. Gove's definers prove they exist
when they give *egghead* as a synonym for *double-dome* but then define
egghead in impeccably formal terms as "one with intellectual interests or
pretensions" or as "a highly educated person." Such opposition between
theory and practice strikes even a timid and generally admiring reviewer
as rather odd, as though some notion of scientific objectivity should require
the scientist to deny that he knows what he knows because he may not
know how he knows it.

In the absence, then, of convincing argument to the contrary, a simple
reader is left with the uneasy feeling that the abandonment of *"Colloq."*
was a mistake which the introduction of more quotations does not quite
rectify and that as a teacher he must now provide foreigners and inexperi-
enced students both with some general principles of linguistic choice and
with specific instruction in instances where the new dictionary does not
discriminate finely enough among stylistic variants. The dictionary leaves

unlabeled many expressions which this teacher would not allow a beginning writer to use in serious exposition or argument except for clearly intended and rather special effects: (*to be caught*) *with one's pants down, dollarwise, stylewise* (*s.v. –wise*), (*to give one*) *the bird, dog* "something inferior of its kind," *to enthuse, to level* "deal frankly," *schmaltz, chintzy, the catbird seat, to roll* "rob," *to send* "delight," *shindig, shook-up, square* "an unsophisticated person," *squirrelly, to goof,* and the like. Enforcing such modest niceties will now be more difficult; for classroom lawyers and irate parents will be able to cite the dictionary which the teacher has taught Johnny how to read but which has collapsed the distinction between formal and informal Standard English. Similar difficulties could occur with various mild obscenities, such as *pissed off* and *pisspoor*, which should be marked not only as slang but with some one of the warning labels that the dictionary attaches to the almost quite adequately recorded four-letter words; and the label *slang* itself might well be more freely used with the various synonyms for *drunk—stewed, stinko, stoned, tight, tanked, sozzled, potted, pie-eyed, feeling no pain, blind, looped, squiffed, boiled, fried, high,* etc. Odzooks!

The convenience of a classroom teacher, however, is a rather petty criterion by which to judge a great dictionary, and the tiny handful of evidence here alleged must not be taken as justifying the shrill lament that *Webster's Third* is "a scandal and a disaster." The wake has been distinctly premature. Both the dictionary and the language it records are likely to survive the keening critics, whose exaggerations are something of a stumbling block themselves. The mere extent of the information in a dictionary unabridged should fix in a reviewer's mind the salutary knowledge that as no one man can make such a book, so no one man can judge it; but the popular reviews of the *Third International* have merely skimmed its surface and have said little of its technical features or substantial accomplishments. The present discussion will conclude with a few slight remarks on some such matters and with the renewed insistence that longer use and more expert study will be necessary before the dictionary can be definitively judged.

Teachers of elementary composition may be especially interested in the dictionary's three well-filled pages on English punctuation. As several recent grammarians have done, the editors attempt to establish definite relations between pointing and intonation, and they pursue that end with some care and vigor: the theory that punctuation may in part be taught by relating it to pitch-contours and to pauses here receives a better-than-average statement.

Yet the composition teacher may still be sceptical. For one thing, no account of English intonation has deserved or won universal acceptance. The editors themselves thus seem to postulate more than the three "pauses" allowed in the Trager-Smith phonology, which their description directly or indirectly follows. What is worse is the failure of the proposed relationships between speech and pointing as one moves from dialect to dialect: rules that may hold in one region do not hold in another. For much Southern American speech and for much Southern British, it is simply not the case that "the rising pause . . . is usually indicated in writing by a comma"; for many speakers and writers in many areas, an exclamation point may correspond to a *low*-pitched "terminal stress" as well as to a high one; and a colon may be used in writing not just for "a fading or sustained pause in speech" but for a "rising pause" or for no pause at all. The editors have weakened their case by stating it too simply and too strongly.

For the linguistically inclined, Mr. Edwin Artin's extensive "Guide to Pronunciation" will have a particular attraction. The "Guide" is just that— a guide; "not a treatise on phonetics" or a structural dialectologist's systematic account of American pronunciation, but an explanation of the way the editors have used their new alphabet in their transcriptions. Though the forgetful will regret that the key is no longer before them at each opening, and though a stern phonemicist might call the whole system sloppy, the new alphabet is an arguable solution to an extremely complex theoretical and practical problem and a definite improvement over the more complicated yet less accurate and more misleading diacritical key in the *Webster's* of 1934. The objective in devising the alphabet "was a set of symbols which would represent each speech sound which distinguishes one word from another and each difference in sound which is associated with some large region of the country" (Ives), so that the editors might record both the formal and the informal pronunciations actually heard in cultivated conversation from speakers of the standard dialects in the various regions. The *Third International* can thus do fuller justice than its predecessor did to regional variation and to modes of speech less artificial than the "formal platform speech" of the earlier work.

Like every competent writer on American pronunciation, Mr. Artin will be criticized as well as praised. He writes, indeed, at a particularly difficult time, when phonological theory is so unsettled that rival groups among the linguists can scarcely communicate with one another. Since pleasing one group of theorists means displeasing its opponents, since it is easily possible to please neither or none, and since Mr. Artin does not include in his "Guide" the sort of general and historical information which could be found in the corresponding section of the 1934 dictionary, perhaps he will not have so large an audience as Kenyon reached. His readers will be the kind who will argue the results of equating the medial consonants of *tidal* and *title* because in some dialects they are phonetically identical or of distinguishing them because the preceding diphthongs may be of different lengths and because the consonants of *tide* and *titular* clearly differ. Other readers, if they find the "Guide" hard going, will not risk too much confusion by limiting their study to the table of symbols and to the short section on pronunciation in the "Explanatory Notes."

Within the dictionary proper, the word-list first invites examination. Like the addenda to the later editions of the *Second,* the vexing miscellaneous entries at the bottoms of the pages are now gone from *Webster's Third,* either dropped or worked into the main alphabet; numerous obsolete words have disappeared, since the cut-off date has been advanced from 1500 to 1755; and further space for additions has been found by rejecting many no longer useful terms from the rapidly changing and never generally current technical vocabulary with which both the *Second* and the *Third International* are stuffed. This plethora of scientific and technical terms, carefully gathered in an elaborate reading program, is of course no plethora at all but only a comfortable supply for the scientist and technologist, who seem pleased with the dictionary's coverage of their fields; and a general dictionary must make room as well for some regionalisms, for a certain amount of recent slang, and for the new words in general use which so eloquently damn our culture. When all this has been done, it would be unfair to complain that perhaps not enough attention has been paid to the distinctive vocabularies of English-speaking nations other than Britain and the United States.

Beyond the word-list, neither space nor the reviewer's competence will allow him to go. He has few complaints about spelling, the only loud one being against *alright;* as far as a layman's knowledge goes, the etymologies are accurate, and beyond that point they remain clear and comprehensible; the discrimination and the arrangement of senses impose silence on the reader who has not studied them with the same care that went into their making; and the synonymies have already proved their practical value. A sweeping conclusion will not be expected of a review whose thesis is that the prematurity of sweeping conclusions has already been sufficiently exemplified, but a moderately serious examination has made a few things perfectly plain about the *Third International.* As a completely new, independent, responsibly edited, unabridged dictionary, no other work can rival it on precisely its own ground. Its merits are infinitely greater than those of the reviews which have lightly questioned them. Time and the experts will ultimately decide its just rank in the world of English lexicography, whether above, below, or alongside its predecessor; but meanwhile it can usefully fill a place in the libraries of a generation.

Study Questions

1. Look up one of the articles cited by Sledd attacking *Webster's Third New International Dictionary.* Does Sledd give a fair account of the tone and the basis of the adverse criticism? (See pp. 98–100.)

2. What is the literal meaning of *innovation?* What innovation, so far as the history of English lexicography is concerned, did critics seek in *Webster's Third New International Dictionary?* Do the critics regard themselves as innovators or as traditionalists? With which type of grammarian, prescriptive (normative) or descriptive (scientific), would the adverse critics be likely to be in accord? With which type would Sledd agree?

3. What does *colloquial* mean? Explain the reasons for the omission of *colloq.* as a usage label in the *Third International* and Sledd's objection to the omission. If you were writing a theme, impersonal in tone and literary in subject, would you try to avoid colloquial expressions? Would such expressions be suitable in a first-person account of a humorous experience? Look up in the *Third International* a term in your own vocabulary, labeled *colloq.* in your collegiate dictionary. Would the *Third International* entry make clear to you that the term would be unsuitable in a formal context?

4. What technical features in the *Third International* are absent from or are different from your collegiate dictionary? What features in your collegiate dictionary are absent from the *Third International?* Where does Sledd assume most users of the *Third International* will be when they consult it? Where do you most often use your collegiate dictionary? Does Sledd have a valid point in his answer to this criticism?

5. Why does Sledd refrain from judging *Webster's Third New International Dictionary?* Did the critics he cited withhold judgment?

7. BUT WHAT'S A DICTIONARY FOR?

Bergen Evans

Professor Bergen Evans, long a student of American usage and grammar, answers adverse critics of the *Webster's Third New International Dictionary* in an article in the *Atlantic Monthly* for May, 1962.

The storm of abuse in the popular press that greeted the appearance of *Webster's Third New International Dictionary* is a curious phenomenon. Never has a scholarly work of this stature been attacked with such un-bridled fury and contempt. An article in the *Atlantic* viewed it as a "disappointment," a "shock," a "calamity," "a scandal and a disaster." The New York *Times,* in a special editorial, felt that the work would "accelerate the deterioration" of the language and sternly accused the editors of betraying a public trust. The *Journal* of the American Bar Association saw the publication as "deplorable," "a flagrant example of lexicographic irresponsibility," "a serious blow to the cause of good English." *Life* called it "a non-word deluge," "monstrous," "abominable," and "a cause for dismay." They doubted that "Lincoln could have modeled his Gettysburg Address" on it—a concept of how things get written that throws very little light on Lincoln but a great deal on *Life*.

What underlies all this sound and fury? Is the claim of the G. & C. Merriam Company, probably the world's greatest dictionary maker, that the preparation of the work cost $3.5 million, that it required the efforts of three hundred scholars over a period of twenty-seven years, working on the largest collection of citations ever assembled in any language—is all this a fraud, a hoax?

So monstrous a discrepancy in evaluation requires us to examine basic principles. Just what's a dictionary for? What does it propose to do? What does the common reader go to a dictionary to find? What has the purchaser of a dictionary a right to expect for his money?

Before we look at basic principles, it is necessary to interpose two brief statements. The first of these is that a dictionary is concerned with words. Some dictionaries give various kinds of other useful information. Some have tables of weights and measures on the flyleaves. Some list historical events, and some, home remedies. And there's nothing wrong with their so doing. But the great increase in our vocabulary in the past three decades compels all dictionaries to make more efficient use of their space. And if something must be eliminated, it is sensible to throw out these extraneous things and stick to words.

Yet wild wails arose. The *Saturday Review* lamented that one can no longer find the goddess Astarte under a separate heading—though they point out that a genus of mollusks named after the goddess is included! They seemed to feel that out of sheer perversity the editors of the dictionary stooped to mollusks while ignoring goddesses and that, in some way, this typifies modern lexicography. Mr. Wilson Follett, folletizing (his mental processes demand some special designation) in the *Atlantic*, cried out in horror that one is not even able to learn from the Third International "that the Virgin was Mary the mother of Jesus"!

The second brief statement is that there has been even more progress in the making of dictionaries in the past thirty years than there has been in the making of automobiles. The difference, for example, between the much-touted Second International (1934) and the much-clouted Third International (1961) is not like the difference between yearly models but like the difference between the horse and buggy and the automobile. Between the appearance of these two editions a whole new science related to the making of dictionaries, the science of descriptive linguistics, has come into being.

Modern linguistics gets its charter from Leonard Bloomfield's *Language* (1933). Bloomfield, for thirteen years professor of Germanic philology at the University of Chicago and for nine years professor of linguistics at Yale, was one of those inseminating scholars who can't be relegated to any

department and don't dream of accepting established categories and procedures just because they're established. He was as much an anthropologist
as a linguist, and his concepts of language were shaped not by Strunk's
Elements of Style but by his knowledge of Cree Indian dialects.

The broad general findings of the new science are:

1. All languages are systems of human conventions, not systems of natural laws. The first—and essential—step in the study of any language is
observing and setting down precisely what happens when native speakers
speak it.

2. Each language is unique in its pronunciation, grammar, and vocabulary. It cannot be described in terms of logic or of some theoretical, ideal
language. It cannot be described in terms of any other language, or even
in terms of its own past.

3. All languages are dynamic rather than static, and hence a "rule" in
any language can only be a statement of contemporary practice. Change is
constant—and normal.

4. "Correctness" can rest only upon usage, for the simple reason that
there is nothing else for it to rest on. And all usage is relative.

From these propositions it follows that a dictionary is good only insofar
as it is a comprehensive and accurate description of current usage. And to
be comprehensive it must include some indication of social and regional
associations.

New dictionaries are needed because English has changed more in the
past two generations than at any other time in its history. It has had to
adapt to extraordinary cultural and technological changes, two world wars,
unparalleled changes in transportation and communication, and unprecedented movements of populations.

More subtly, but pervasively, it has changed under the influence of mass
education and the growth of democracy. As written English is used by increasing millions and for more reasons than ever before, the language has
become more utilitarian and more informal. Every publication in America
today includes pages that would appear, to the purist of forty years ago,
unbuttoned gibberish. Not that they are; they simply show that you can't
hold the language of one generation up as a model for the next.

It's not that you musn't. You *can't*. For example, in the issue in which
Life stated editorially that it would follow the Second International, there
were over forty words, constructions, and meanings which are in the Third
International but not in the Second. The issue of the New York *Times*
which hailed the Second International as the authority to which it would
adhere and the Third International as a scandal and a betrayal which it
would reject used one hundred and fifty-three separate words, phrases,
and constructions which are listed in the Third International but not in the
Second and nineteen others which are condemned in the Second. Many
of them are used many times, more than three hundred such uses in all.

The Washington *Post,* in an editorial captioned "Keep Your Old Webster's," says, in the first sentence, "don't throw it away," and in the second, "hang on to it." But the old Webster's labels *don't* "colloquial" and doesn't include "hang on to," in this sense, at all.

In short, all of these publications are written in the language that the Third International describes, even the very editorials which scorn it. And this is no coincidence, because the Third International isn't setting up any new standards at all; it is simply describing what *Life,* the Washington *Post,* and the New York *Times* are doing. Much of the dictionary's material comes from these very publications, the *Times,* in particular, furnishing more of its illustrative quotations than any other newspaper.

And the papers have no choice. No journal or periodical could sell a single issue today if it restricted itself to the American language of twenty-eight years ago. It couldn't discuss half the things we are interested in, and its style would seem stiff and cumbrous. If the editorials were serious, the public—and the stockholders—have reason to be grateful that the writers on these publications are more literate than the editors.

And so back to our questions: what's a dictionary for, and how, in 1962, can it best do what it ought to do? The demands are simple. The common reader turns to a dictionary for information about the spelling, pronunciation, meaning, and proper use of words. He wants to know what is current and respectable. But he wants—and has a right to—the truth, the full truth. And the full truth about any language, and especially about American English today, is that there are many areas in which certainty is impossible and simplification is misleading.

Even in so settled a matter as spelling, a dictionary cannot always be absolute. *Theater* is correct, but so is *theatre.* And so are *traveled* and *travelled, plow* and *plough, catalog* and *catalogue,* and scores of other variants. The reader may want a single certainty. He may have taken an unyielding position in an argument, he may have wagered in support of his conviction and may demand that the dictionary "settle" the matter. But neither his vanity nor his purse is any concern of the dictionary's; it must record the facts. And the fact here is that there are many words in our language which may be spelled, with equal correctness, in either of two ways.

So with pronunciation. A citizen listening to his radio might notice that James B. Conant, Bernard Baruch, and Dwight D. Eisenhower pronounce *economics* as ECKuhnomiks, while A. Whitney Griswold, Adlai Stevenson, and Herbert Hoover pronounce it EEKuhnomiks. He turns to the dictionary to see which of the two pronunciations is "right" and finds that they are both acceptable.

Has he been betrayed? Has the dictionary abdicated its responsibility? Should it say that one *must* speak like the president of Harvard or like the president of Yale, like the thirty-first President of the United States or like the thirty-fourth? Surely it's none of its business to make a choice. Not because of the distinction of these particular speakers; lexicography, like God, is no respecter of persons. But because so widespread and conspicuous a use of two pronunciations among people of this elevation shows that there *are* two pronunciations. Their speaking establishes the fact which the dictionary must record.

Among the "enormities" with which *Life* taxes the Third International is its listing of "the common mispronunciation" *heighth*. That it is labeled a "dialectal variant" seems, somehow, to compound the felony. But one hears the word so pronounced, and if one professes to give a full account of American English in the 1960s, one has to take some cognizance of it. All people do not possess *Life's* intuitive perception that the word is so "monstrous" that even to list it as a dialect variation is to merit scorn. Among these, by the way, was John Milton, who, in one of the greatest passages in all literature, besought the Holy Spirit to raise him to the "highth" of his great argument. And even the *Oxford English Dictionary* is so benighted as to list it, in full boldface, right alongside of *Height* as a variant that has been in the language since at least 1290.

Now there are still, apparently, millions of Americans who retain, in this as in much else, some of the speech of Milton. This particular pronunciation seems to be receding, but the *American Dialect Dictionary* still records instances of it from almost every state on the Eastern seaboard and notes that it is heard from older people and "occasionally in educated speech," "common with good speakers," "general," "widespread."

Under these circumstances, what is a dictionary to do? Since millions speak the word this way, the pronunciation can't be ignored. Since it has been in use as long as we have any record of English and since it has been used by the greatest writers, it can't be described as substandard or slang. But it is heard now only in certain localities. That makes it a dialectal pronunciation, and an honest dictionary will list it as such. What else can it do? Should it do?

The average purchaser of a dictionary uses it most often, probably, to find out what a word "means." As a reader, he wants to know what an author intended to convey. As a speaker or writer, he wants to know what a word will convey to his auditors. And this, too, is complex, subtle, and forever changing.

An illustration is furnished by an editorial in the Washington *Post* (January 17, 1962). After a ringing appeal to those who "love truth and accuracy" and the usual bombinations about "abdication of authority" and "barbarism," the editorial charges the Third International with "pretentious and obscure verbosity" and specifically instances its definition of "so simple an object as a door."

The definition reads:

a movable piece of firm material or a structure supported usu. along one side and swinging on pivots or hinges, sliding along a groove, rolling up and down, revolving as one of four leaves, or folding like an accordion by means of which an opening may be closed or kept open for passage into or out of a building, room, or other covered enclosure or a car, airplane, elevator, or other vehicle.

Then follows a series of special meanings, each particularly defined and, where necessary, illustrated by a quotation.

Since, aside from roaring and admonishing the "gentlemen from Springfield" that "accuracy and brevity are virtues," the *Post's* editorial fails to explain what is wrong with the definition, we can only infer from "so simple" a thing that the writer takes the plain, downright, man-in-the-street attitude that a door is a door and any damn fool knows that.

But if so, he has walked into one of lexicography's biggest booby traps: the belief that the obvious is easy to define. Whereas the opposite is true. Anyone can give a fair description of the strange, the new, or the unique. It's the commonplace, the habitual, that challenges definition, for its very commonness compels us to define it in uncommon terms. Dr. Johnson was ridiculed on just this score when his dictionary appeared in 1755. For two hundred years his definition of a network as "any thing reticulated or decussated, at equal distances, with interstices between the intersections" has been good for a laugh. But in the merriment one thing is always overlooked: no one has yet come up with a better definition! Subsequent dictionaries defined it as a mesh and then defined a mesh as a network. That's simple, all right.

Anyone who attempts sincerely to state what the word *door* means in the United States of America today can't take refuge in a log cabin. There has been an enormous proliferation of closing and demarking devices and structures in the past twenty years, and anyone who tries to thread his way through the many meanings now included under *door* may have to sacrifice brevity to accuracy and even have to employ words that a limited vocabulary may find obscure.

Is the entrance to a tent a door, for instance? And what of the thing that seals the exit of an airplane? Is this a door? Or what of those sheets and jets of air that are now being used, in place of old-fashioned oak and hinges, to screen entrances and exits. Are they doors? And what of those accordion-like things that set off various sections of many modern apartments? The fine print in the lease takes it for granted that they are doors and that spaces demarked by them are rooms—and the rent is computed on the number of rooms.

Was I gypped by the landlord when he called the folding contraption that shuts off my kitchen a door? I go to the Second International, which the editor of the *Post* urges me to use in preference to the Third International. Here I find that a door is

> The movable frame or barrier of boards, or other material, usually turning on hinges or pivots or sliding, by which an entranceway into a house or apartment is closed and opened; also, a similar part of a piece of furniture, as in a cabinet or bookcase.

This is only forty-six words, but though it includes the cellar door, it excludes the barn door and the accordion-like thing.

So I go on to the Third International. I see at once that the new definition is longer. But I'm looking for accuracy, and if I must sacrifice brevity to get it, then I must. And, sure enough, in the definition which raised the *Post's* blood pressure, I find the words "folding like an accordion." The thing *is* a door, and my landlord is using the word in one of its currently accepted meanings.

We don't turn to a work of reference merely for confirmation. We all have words in our vocabularies which we have misunderstood, and to come on the true meaning of one of these words is quite a shock. All our complacency and self-esteem rise to oppose the discovery. But eventually we must accept the humiliation and laugh it off as best we can.

Some, often those who have set themselves up as authorities, stick to their error and charge the dictionary with being in a conspiracy against them. They are sure that their meaning is the only "right" one. And when the dictionary doesn't bear them out they complain about "permissive" attitudes instead of correcting their mistake.

The New York *Times* and the *Saturday Review* both regarded as contemptibly "permissive" the fact that one meaning of one word was illustrated by a quotation from Polly Adler. But a rudimentary knowledge of the development of any language would have told them that the underworld has been a far more active force in shaping and enriching speech than all the synods that have ever convened. Their attitude is like that of the patriot who canceled his subscription to the *Dictionary of American Biography* when he discovered that the very first volume included Benedict Arnold!

The ultimate of "permissiveness," singled out by almost every critic for special scorn, was the inclusion in the Third International of *finalize*. It was this, more than any other one thing, that was given as the reason for sticking to the good old Second International—that "peerless authority on American English," as the *Times* called it. But if it was such an authority, why didn't they look into it? They would have found *finalize* if they had.

And why shouldn't it be there? It exists. It's been recorded for two generations. Millions employ it every day. Two Presidents of the United States—men of widely differing cultural backgrounds—have used it in formal statements. And so has the Secretary-General of the United Nations, a man of unusual linguistic attainments. It isn't permitting the word but omitting it that would break faith with the reader. Because it is exactly the sort of word we want information about.

To list it as substandard would be to imply that it is used solely by the ignorant and the illiterate. But this would be a misrepresentation: President Kennedy and U Thant are highly educated men, and both are articulate and literate. It isn't even a freak form. On the contrary, it is a classic example of a regular process of development in English, a process which has given us such thoroughly accepted words as *generalize, minimize, formalize,* and *verbalize.* Nor can it be dismissed on logical grounds or on the ground that it is a mere duplication of *complete.* It says something that *complete* doesn't say and says it in a way that is significant in the modern bureaucratic world: one usually *completes* something which he has initiated but *finalizes* the work of others.

One is free to dislike the word. I don't like it. But the editor of a dictionary has to examine the evidence for a word's existence and seek it in context to get, as clearly and closely as he can, the exact meaning that it conveys to those who use it. And if it is widely used by well-educated, literate, reputable people, he must list it as a standard word. He is not compiling a volume of his own prejudices.

An individual's use of his native tongue is the surest index to his position within his community. And those who turn to a dictionary expect from it some statement of the current status of a word or a grammatical construction. And it is with the failure to assume this function that modern lexicography has been most fiercely charged. The charge is based on a naïve assumption that simple labels can be attached in all instances. But they can't. Some words are standard in some constructions and not in others. There may be as many shades of status as of meaning, and modern lexicography instead of abdicating this function has fulfilled it to a degree utterly unknown to earlier dictionaries.

Consider the word *fetch,* meaning to "go get and bring to." Until recently a standard word of full dignity ("Fetch me, I pray thee, a little water in a vessel"—I Kings 17:10), it has become slightly tainted. Perhaps the command latent in it is resented as undemocratic. Or maybe its use in training dogs to retrieve has made some people feel that it is an undignified word to apply to human beings. But, whatever the reason, there is a growing uncertainty about its status, and hence it is the sort of word that conscientious people look up in a dictionary.

Will they find it labeled "good" or "bad"? Neither, of course, because either applied indiscriminately would be untrue. The Third International lists nineteen different meanings of the verb *to fetch.* Of these some are labeled "dialectal," some "chiefly dialectal," some "obsolete," one "chiefly Scottish," and two "not in formal use." The primary meaning—"to go after and bring back"—is not labeled and hence can be accepted as standard, accepted with the more assurance because the many shades of labeling show us that the word's status has been carefully considered.

On grammatical questions the Third International tries to be equally exact and thorough. Sometimes a construction is listed without comment, meaning that in the opinion of the editors it is unquestionably respectable. Sometimes a construction carries the comment "used by speakers and writers on all educational levels though disapproved by some grammarians." Or the comment may be "used in substandard speech and formerly also by reputable writers." Or "less often in standard than in substandard speech." Or simply "dial."

And this very accurate reporting is based on evidence which is presented for our examination. One may feel that the evidence is inadequate or that the evaluation of it is erroneous. But surely, in the face of classification so much more elaborate and careful than any known heretofore, one cannot fly into a rage and insist that the dictionary is "out to destroy . . . every vestige of linguistic punctilio . . . every criterion for distinguishing between better usages and worse."

Words, as we have said, are continually shifting their meanings and connotations and hence their status. A word which has dignity, say, in the vocabulary of an older person may go down in other people's estimation. Like *fetch*. The older speaker is not likely to be aware of this and will probably be inclined to ascribe the snickers of the young at his speech to that degeneration of manners which every generation has deplored in its juniors. But a word which is coming up in the scale—like *jazz*, say, or, more recently, *crap*—will strike his ear at once. We are much more aware of offenses given us than of those we give. And if he turns to a dictionary and finds the offending word listed as standard—or even listed, apparently—his response is likely to be an outburst of indignation.

But the dictionary can neither snicker nor fulminate. It records. It will offend many, no doubt, to find the expression *wise up*, meaning to inform or to become informed, listed in the Third International with no restricting label. To my aging ears it still sounds like slang. But the evidence—quotations from the *Kiplinger Washington Letter* and the *Wall Street Journal* —convinces me that it is I who am out of step, lagging behind. If such publications have taken to using *wise up* in serious contexts, with no punctuational indication of irregularity, then it is obviously respectable. And finding it so listed and supported, I can only say that it's nice to be informed and sigh to realize that I am becoming an old fogy. But, of course, I don't have to use it (and I'll be damned if I will! "Let them smile, as I do now, At the old forsaken bough Where I cling").

In part, the trouble is due to the fact that there is no standard for standard. Ideas of what is proper to use in serious, dignified speech and writing are changing—and with breathtaking rapidity. This is one of the major facts of contemporary American English. But it is no more the dictionary's business to oppose this process than to speed it up.

Even in our standard speech some words are more dignified and some more informal than others, and dictionaries have tried to guide us through these uncertainties by marking certain words and constructions as "colloquial," meaning "inappropriate in a formal situation." But this distinction, in the opinion of most scholars, has done more harm than good. It has created the notion that these particular words are inferior, when actually they might be the best possible words in an informal statement. And so—to the rage of many reviewers—the Third International has dropped this label. Not all labels, as angrily charged, but only this one out of a score. And the doing so may have been an error, but it certainly didn't constitute "betrayal" or "abandoning of all distinctions." It was intended to end a certain confusion.

In all the finer shades of meaning, of which the status of a word is only one, the user is on his own, whether he likes it or not. Despite *Life's* artless assumption about the Gettysburg Address, nothing worth writing is written *from* a dictionary. The dictionary, rather, comes along afterwards and describes what *has been* written.

Words in themselves are not dignified, or silly, or wise, or malicious. But they can be used in dignified, silly, wise, or malicious ways by dignified, silly, wise, or malicious people. *Egghead*, for example, is a perfectly legitimate word, as legitimate as *highbrow* or *long-haired*. But there is something very wrong and very undignified, by civilized standards, in a belligerent dislike for intelligence and education. *Yak* is an amusing word for persistent chatter. Anyone could say, "We were just yakking over a cup of coffee," with no harm to his dignity. But to call a Supreme Court decision *yakking* is to be vulgarly insulting and so, undignified. Again, there's nothing wrong with *confab* when it's appropriate. But when the work of a great research project, employing hundreds of distinguished scholars over several decades and involving the honor of one of the greatest publishing houses in the world, is described as *confabbing* (as the New York *Times* editorially described the preparation of the Third International), the use of this particular word asserts that the lexicographers had merely sat around and talked idly. And the statement becomes undignified—if not, indeed, slanderous.

The lack of dignity in such statements is not in the words, nor in the dictionaries that list them, but in the hostility that deliberately seeks this tone of expression. And in expressing itself the hostility frequently shows that those who are expressing it don't know how to use a dictionary. Most of the reviewers seem unable to read the Third International and unwilling to read the Second.

The *American Bar Association Journal*, for instance, in a typical outburst ("a deplorable abdication of responsibility"), picked out for special scorn the inclusion in the Third International of the word *irregardless*. "As far as the new Webster's is concerned," said the *Journal*, "this meaningless verbal bastard is just as legitimate as any other word in the dictionary." Thirty seconds spent in examining the book they were so roundly condemning would have shown them that in it *irregardless* is labeled "nonstand"—which means "nonstandard," which means "not conforming to the usage generally characteristic of educated native speakers of the language." Is that "just as legitimate as any other word in the dictionary"?

The most disturbing fact of all is that the editors of a dozen of the most influential publications in America today are under the impression that *authoritative* must mean *authoritarian*. Even the "permissive" Third International doesn't recognize this identification—editors' attitudes being not yet, fortunately, those of the American people. But the Fourth International may have to.

The new dictionary may have many faults. Nothing that tries to meet an ever-changing situation over a terrain as vast as contemporary English can hope to be free of them. And much in it is open to honest, and informed, disagreement. There can be linguistic objection to the eradication of proper names. The removal of guides to pronunciation from the foot of every page may not have been worth the valuable space it saved. The new method of defining words of many meanings has disadvantages as well as advantages. And of the half million or more definitions, hundreds, possibly thousands, may seem inadequate or imprecise. To some (of whom I am one) the omission of the label "colloquial" will seem meritorious; to others it will seem a loss.

But one thing is certain: anyone who solemnly announces in the year 1962 that he will be guided in matters of English usage by a dictionary published in 1934 is talking ignorant and pretentious nonsense.

Study Questions

1. What basic principles or general findings of linguistic science does Evans summarize? How do these ideas compare with the linguistic principles set forth in Part I?

2. What reasons for needing new dictionaries does Evans give? Can you furnish concrete examples to back up his statement?

3. According to Evans, what are the functions of a dictionary? Does he find *Webster's Third International* fulfilling these functions? Explain.

4. Why does Evans feel that dictionaries should not attempt to set up absolute standards regarding words?

5. Read Wilson Follett's "Sabotage in Springfield," *Atlantic Monthly* (January, 1962), 73–77, and sum up his position on usage and grammar. Where does Bergen Evans take issue with him? Why?

6. Read other reviews of *Webster's Third New International Dictionary* and evaluate the linguistic positions of the reviewers. (See pp. 98–100.)

7. Compare Evans's article with Sledd's: their basic attitudes, their coverage of distinctive features of *Webster's Third New International Dictionary*, their attitudes toward changes from the *Second International.*

8. What personal aversions do Sledd and Evans express to terms accepted as standard in *Webster's Third International?* Do they question the validity of the acceptance?

9. Look up *fetch* in your own dictionary and classify the meanings under the "four differences in language practice." Are any of the meanings literary?

8. THE HALLMARKS OF AMERICAN

H. L. Mencken

H. L. Mencken describes the distinctive characteristics of the English language used in the United States. The following selection is taken from *The American Language* (1937), an extensive examination of the American variant of English with many examples gleaned from Mencken's reading and the reports of his informants.

The characters chiefly noted in American English by all who have discussed it are, first, its general uniformity throughout the country; second, its impatient disregard for grammatical, syntactical and phonological rule and precedent; and third, its large capacity (distinctly greater than that of the English of present-day England) for taking in new words and phrases from outside sources, and for manufacturing them of its own materials.

The first of these characters has struck every observer, native and foreign. In place of the discordant local dialects of all the other major countries, including England, we have a general *Volkssprache* for the whole nation, and if it is conditioned at all it is only by minor differences in pronunciation and vocabulary, and by the linguistic struggles of various groups of newcomers. No other country can show such linguistic solidarity, nor any approach to it—not even Canada, for there a large minority of the population resists speaking English altogether. . . . Even in the United Kingdom there are wide divergences.[1] "When we remember," says the New International Encyclopedia [sic], "that the dialects of the counties in England have marked differences—so marked, indeed, that it may be doubted whether a Lancashire miner and a Lincolnshire farmer could understand each other—we may well be proud that our vast country has,

---

[1] W. W. Skeat distinguishes 9 principal dialects in Scotland, 3 in Ireland and 30 in England and Wales. See his *English Dialects From the Eighth Century to the Present Day*, Cambridge, 1911, pp. 107 ff.

strictly speaking, only one language." There are some regional pecularities in pronunciation and intonation, . . . but when it comes to the words they habitually use and the way they use them all Americans, even the less tutored, follow pretty much the same line. A Boston taxi-driver could go to work in Chicago or San Francisco without running any risk of misunderstanding his new fares. Once he had flattened his *a*'s a bit and picked up a few dozen localisms, he would be, to all linguistic intents and purposes, fully naturalized.

Of the intrinsic differences that separate American from English the chief have their roots in the obvious disparity between the environment and traditions of the American people since the Seventeenth Century and those of the English. The latter have lived under a relatively stable social order, and it has impressed upon their souls their characteristic respect for what is customary and of good report. Until the World War brought chaos to most of their institutions, their whole lives were regulated, perhaps more than those of any other people save the Spaniards, by a regard for precedent. The Americans, though partly of the same blood, have felt no such restraint, and acquired no such habit of conformity. On the contrary, they have plunged to the other extreme, for the conditions of life in their country have put a high value upon the precisely opposite qualities of curiosity and daring, and so they have acquired that character of restlessness, that impatience of forms, that disdain of the dead hand, which now broadly marks them. From the first, says a literary historian, they have been "less phlegmatic, less conservative than the English. There were climatic influences, it may be; there was surely a spirit of intensity everywhere that made for short effort." [2] Thus, in the arts, and thus in business, in politics, in daily intercourse, in habits of mind and speech. The American is not, of course, lacking in a capacity for discipline; he has it highly developed; he submits to leadership readily, and even to tyranny. But, by a curious twist, it is not the leadership that is old and decorous that commonly fetches him, but the leadership that is new and extravagant. He will resist dictation out of the past, but he will follow a new messiah with almost Russian willingness, and into the wildest vagaries of economics, religion, morals and speech. A new fallacy in politics spreads faster in the United States than anywhere else on earth, and so does a new fashion in hats, or a new revelation of God, or a new means of killing time, or a new shibboleth, or metaphor, or piece of slang. Thus the American, on his linguistic side, likes to make his language as he goes along, and not all the hard work of the schoolmarm can hold the business back. A novelty loses nothing by the fact that it is a novelty; it rather gains something, and particularly if it meets the national fancy for the terse, the vivid, and, above all, the bold and imaginative. The characteristic American habit of re-

[2] F. L. Pattee, *A History of American Literature Since 1870*, New York, 1916. See also *The American Novel*, Carl Van Doren, New York, 1921.

ducing complex concepts to the starkest abbreviations was already notice-able in colonial times, and such highly typical Americanisms as *O.K.*, *N.G.*, and *P.D.Q.*, have been traced back to the early days of the Republic. Nor are the influences that shaped these tendencies invisible today, for in-stitution-making is yet going on, and so is language-making. In so modest an operation as that which has evolved *bunco* from *buncombe* and *bunk* from *bunco* there is evidence of a phenomenon which the philologian recognizes as belonging to the most lusty stages of speech.

But of more importance than the sheer inventions, if only because much more numerous, are the extensions of the vocabulary, both absolutely and in ready workableness, by the devices of rhetoric. The American, from the beginning, has been the most ardent of recorded rhetoricians. His politics bristles with pungent epithets; his whole history has been bedizened with tall talk; his fundamental institutions rest far more upon brilliant phrases than upon logical ideas. And in small things as in large he exercises con-tinually an incomparable capacity for projecting hidden and often fan-tastic relationships into arresting parts of speech. Such a term as *rubber-neck* is almost a complete treatise on American psychology; it reveals the national habit of mind more clearly than any labored inquiry could ever reveal it. It has in it precisely the boldness and contempt for ordered forms that are so characteristically American, and it has too the grotesque humor of the country, and the delight in devastating opprobriums, and the acute feeling for the succinct and savory. . . . Verbs are fashioned out of substantives by the simple process of prefixing the preposition: *to engineer, to stump, to hog, to style, to author.* Others grow out of an in-termediate adjective, as *to boom.* Others are made by torturing nouns with harsh affixes, as *to burglarize* and *to itemize*, or by groping for the root, as *to resurrect* and *to jell.* Yet others are changed from intransitive to transi-tive; a sleeping-car *sleeps* thirty passengers. So with the adjectives. They are made of substantives unchanged: *codfish, jitney.* Or by bold combina-tions: *down-and-out, up-state, flat-footed.* Or by shading down suffixes to a barbaric simplicity: *scary, classy, tasty.* Or by working over adverbs until they tremble on the brink between adverb and adjective: *right, sure* and *near* are examples.

All these processes, of course, are also to be observed in the history of the English of England; at the time of its sturdiest growth they were in the most active possible being. They are, indeed, common to all tongues; "the essence of language," says Dr. Jespersen, "is activity." But if you will put the English of today beside the American of today you will see at once how much more forcibly they are in operation in the latter than in the former. The standard Southern dialect of English has been arrested in its growth by its purists and grammarians, and burdened with irrational affectations by fashionable pretension. It shows no living change since the reign of Samuel Johnson. Its tendency is to combat all that expansive gusto which made for its pliancy and resilience in the days of Shakespeare.[3] In place of the old loose-footedness there is set up a preciosity which, in one direction, takes the form of clumsy artificialities in the spoken language, and in another shows itself in the even clumsier Johnsonese of so much current English writing—the jargon denounced by Sir Arthur Quiller-Couch in his Cambridge lectures. This "infirmity of speech" Quiller-Couch finds "in parliamentary debates and in the newspapers; . . . it has become the medium through which Boards of Government, County Councils, Syndicates, Committees, Commercial Firms, express the processes as well as the conclusions of their thought, and so voice the reason of their being." Distinct from journalese, the two yet overlap, "and have a knack of assimilating each other's vices." [4]

American, despite the gallant efforts of the pedagogues, has so far escaped any such suffocating formalization. We, too, of course, have our occasional practitioners of the authentic English Jargon, but in the main our faults lie in precisely the opposite direction. That is to say, we incline toward a directness of statement which, at its greatest, lacks restraint and urbanity altogether, and toward a hospitality which often admits novelties for the mere sake of their novelty, and is quite uncritical of the difference between a genuine improvement in succinctness and clarity, and mere extravagant raciness. "The tendency," says one English observer, "is . . . to consider the speech of any man, as any man himself, as good as any other." [5] The Americans, adds a Scots professor, "are determined to hack their way through the language, as their ancestors through forests, regardless of the valuable growths that may be sacrificed in blazing the trail." [6] But this Scot dismisses the English neologisms of the day when

---

[3] Rather curiously, the two authorities who were most influential, during the Nineteenth Century, in keeping it to a rigid pattern were both Americans. They were Lindley Murray (1745–1826) and Joseph E. Worcester (1784–1865). Murray, a Pennsylvanian, went to England after the Revolution, and in 1795 published his Grammar of the English Language. It had an extraordinary sale in England, and was accepted as the court of last resort in usage down to quite recent times. Worcester's Universal and Critical Dictionary of the English Language, 1846, divided the honors of authority in England with B. H. Smart's Dictionary, published during the same year. It was extensively pirated. Thus, says Thomas R. Lounsbury (The Standard of Pronunciation in English, New York, 1904, p. 220), "the Londoner frequently got his pure London pronunciation from a citizen of this country who was never outside of New England for more than a few months of his life." Worcester was also accepted at Harvard and at the University of Virginia, but elsewhere in the United States Webster prevailed.

[4] See the chapter "Interlude on Jargon," in Quiller-Couch's On the Art of Writing, New York, 1916. Appropriately enough, large parts of the learned critic's book are written in the very Jargon he attacks. See also Ch. VI of Growth and Structure of the English Language, by O. Jespersen, 3rd ed., rev., Leipzig, 1919, especially pp. 143 ff. See also "Official English," in English, March, 1919, p. 7; April, p. 45; and August, p. 135; and "The Decay of Syntax," in the London Times Literary Supplement, May 8, 1919, p. 1.

[5] Alexander Francis, Americans: An Impression, New York, 1900.

[6] Breaking Priscian's Head, by J. Y. T. Greig, London, 1929.

ranged beside the American stock, as "dwiny, feeble stuff"; "it is to America," he admits, "that we must chiefly look in future for the replenishment and freshening of our language." I quote one more Briton, this time an Englishman steeped in the public school tradition:

> The English of the United States is not merely different from ours; it has a restless inventiveness which may well be founded in a sense of racial discomfort, a lack of full accord between the temperament of the people and the constitution of their speech. The English are uncommunicative; the Americans are not. In its coolness and quiet withdrawal, in its prevailing sobriety, our language reflects the cautious economies and leisurely assurance of the average speaker. We say so little that we do not need to enliven our vocabulary and underline our sentences, or cry "Wolf!" when we wish to be heard. The more stimulating climate of the United States has produced a more eager, a more expansive, a more decisive people. The Americans apprehend their world in sharper outlines and aspire after a more salient rendering of it.[7]

This revolt against conventional bonds and restraints is most noticeable, of course, on the lower levels of American speech; in the regions above there still linger some vestiges of Eighteenth Century tightness. But even in those upper regions there are rebels a-plenty, and some of them are of such authority that it is impossible to dismiss them. . . . In recent years certain English magnificoes have shown signs of going the same route, but whenever they yield the corrective bastinado is laid on, and nine times out of ten they are accused, and rightly, of succumbing to American influence.

Let American confront a novel problem alongside English, and immediately its superior imaginativeness and resourcefulness become obvious. *Movie* is better than *cinema;* and the English begin to admit the fact by adopting the word; it is not only better American, it is better English. *Billboard* is better than *hoarding*. *Office-holder* is more honest, more picturesque, more thoroughly Anglo-Saxon than *public-servant*. . . . American is full of what Bret Harte called the "saber-cuts of Saxon"; it meets Montaigne's ideal of "a succulent and nervous speech, short and compact, not as much delicated and combed out as vehement and brusque, rather arbitrary than monotonous, not pedantic but soldierly, as Suetonius called Caesar's Latin." One pictures the common materials of English dumped into a pot, exotic flavorings added, and the bubblings assiduously and expectantly skimmed. What is old and respected is already in decay the moment it comes into contact with what is new and vivid. "When we Americans are through with the English language," says Mr. Dooley, "it will look as if it had been run over by a musical comedy."

All this boldness of conceit, of course, makes for vulgarity. Unrestrained by any critical sense—and the critical sense of the pedagogues counts for

[7] *Pomona, or The Future of English*, by Basil de Selincourt, London, 1929.

little, for they cry wolf too often—it flowers in such barbaric inventions as *tasty, alright, go-getter, he-man, go-aheadativeness, tony, goof, semi-occasional,* and *to doxologize.* But vulgarity, after all, means no more than a yielding to natural impulses in the face of conventional inhibitions, and that yielding to natural impulses is at the heart of all healthy language-making. The history of English, like the history of American and of every other living tongue, is a history of vulgarisms that, by their accurate meeting of real needs, have forced their way into sound usage, and even into the lifeless catalogues of the grammarians. The purist performs a useful office in enforcing a certain logical regularity upon the process, and in our own case the omnipresent example of the greater conservatism of the English restrains, to some extent, our native tendency to go too fast, but the process itself is as inexorable in its workings as the precession of the equinoxes, and if we yield to it more eagerly than the English, it is only a proof, perhaps, that the future of what was once the Anglo-Saxon tongue lies on this side of the water. Standard English now has the brakes on, but American continues to leap in the dark, and the prodigality of its movement is all the indication that is needed of its intrinsic health, its capacity to meet the ever-changing needs of a restless and emotional people, inordinately mongrel, and disdainful of tradition. Language, says A. H. Sayce,

is no artificial product, contained in books and dictionaries and governed by the strict rules of impersonal grammarians. It is the living expression of the mind and spirit of a people, ever changing and shifting, whose sole standard of correctness is custom and the common usage of the community. . . . The first lesson to be learned is that there is no intrinsic right or wrong in the use of language, no fixed rules such as are the delight of the teacher of Latin prose. What is right now will be wrong hereafter; what language rejected yesterday she accepts today.[8]

Study Questions

1. Why and how has the American language resisted the formalism often found in British English?
2. Summarize the characteristics of American English which Mencken discusses and evaluate his attitude toward each of them.
3. Check Mencken's examples of the extension of American vocabulary in the *Dictionary of Americanisms, Dictionary of American English,* and *Webster's Third New International Dictionary* to determine when the changes took place and how long it took for them to be accepted as standard usage.
4. Examine Mencken's *The American Language* and its *Supplements* for pertinent illustrations of the unconventionality of the grammar and vocabulary of American English. On the basis of your findings discuss the various aspects of linguistic unconventionality.

[8] *Introduction to the Science of Language,* 4th ed., London, 1900, Vol. II, pp. 33–34.

5. What is Mencken's attitude toward the prescriptive grammarians? Although Mencken is more concerned with vocabulary than with grammar, which words or groups of words that he discusses involve questions of grammar?

6. Does Mencken's style illustrate the "hallmarks of American"? Are American words and idioms prominent in this selection? Check the etymology of his most notable words.

7. Except in the terms cited as examples, would a British reader have any difficulty in understanding Mencken? Considering the context of Mencken's article and the contexts in which most of the italicized words would be used, what generalization can you make about British and American literary language and British and American colloquial language?

9. AMERICAN PLACE-NAMES

H. L. Mencken

In another section of *The American Language* H. L. Mencken classifies the sources of American place-names and illustrates his points with unusual examples from all sections of the United States.

A study of American place-names reveals eight general classes, as follows: (a) those embodying personal names, chiefly the surnames of pioneers or of national heroes; (b) those transferred from other and older places, either in the Eastern States or in Europe; (c) Indian names; (d) Dutch, Spanish, French, German and Scandinavian names; (e) Biblical and mythological names; (f) names descriptive of localities; (g) names suggested by local flora, fauna or geology; (h) purely fanciful names. The names of the first class are perhaps the most numerous. Some consist of surnames standing alone, as *Washington, Cleveland, Bismarck, Lafayette, Taylor* and *Randolph;* others consist of surnames in combination with various old and new *Grundwörter,* as *Pittsburgh, Knoxville, Bailey's Switch, Hagerstown, Franklinton, Dodge City, Fort Riley, Wayne Junction* and *McKeesport;* and yet others are contrived of given-names, either alone or in combination, as *Louisville, St. Paul, Elizabeth, Johnstown, Charlotte, Williamsburg* and *Marysville.* All our great cities are surrounded by grotesque *Bensonhursts, Bryn Joneses, Smithvales* and *Krauswoods.* The number of towns in the United States bearing women's given-names is enormous. I find, for example, eleven postoffices called *Charlotte,* ten called *Ada* and no less than nineteen called *Alma.* Most of these places are small, but there is an *Elizabeth* with nearly 125,000 population, an *Elmira* with 50,000, and an *Augusta* with more than 60,000.

The names of the second class . . . are betrayed in many cases by the prefix *New;* more than 600 such postoffices are recorded, ranging from *New Albany* to *New Windsor.* Others bear such prefixes as *West, North* and *South,* or various distinguishing affixes, *e.g., Bostonia, Pittsburgh Landing, Yorktown* and *Hartford City.* One often finds Eastern county names applied to Western towns and Eastern town names applied to Western rivers and mountains. Thus, *Cambria,* which is the name of a county but not of a postoffice in Pennsylvania, is a town in seven Western States; *Baltimore* is the name of a glacier in Alaska, and *Princeton* is the name of a peak in Colorado. In the same way the names of the more easterly States often reappear in the West, *e.g.,* in *Mount Ohio,* Colo., *Delaware,* Okla., and *Virginia City,* Nev. The tendency to name small American towns after the great capitals of antiquity has excited the derision of the English since the earliest days; there is scarcely an English book upon the States without some fling at it. Of late it has fallen into abeyance, though sixteen *Athenses* still remain, and there are yet many *Carthages, Uticas, Spartas, Syracuses, Romes, Alexandrias, Ninevehs* and *Troys.*[1] The third city of the nation, *Philadelphia,* got its name from the ancient stronghold of Philadelphus of Pergamon. To make up for the falling off of this old and flamboyant custom, the more recent immigrants brought with them the names of the capitals and other great cities of their fatherlands. Thus the American map now bristles with *Berlins, Bremens, Hamburgs, Warsaws* and *Leipzigs,* and also shows *Stockholms, Venices, Belgrades* and *Christianias.*[2]

The influence of Indian names upon American nomenclature is obvious. No fewer than twenty-six of the States have names borrowed from the aborigines,[3] and the same thing is true of large numbers of towns and coun-

[1] See Classical Place-Names in America, by Evan T. Sage, *American Speech,* April, 1929. Mr. Sage says that Pennsylvania shows more classical place-names than any other State, with Ohio ranking second, New York third, Texas fourth, and Connecticut last. He calls attention to the pseudo-classical names: *Demopolis* (Ala.), *Cosmopolis* (Wash.), *Gallipolis* (O.), *Indianapolis* (Ind.), *Thermopolis* (Wyo.), *Coraopolis* (Pa.), and *Opolis* (Kans.). See also Origin of the Classical Place-Names of Central New York, by Charles Maar, *Quarterly Journal of the New York State Historical Association,* July, 1926.

[2] See Amerikanska Ortnamn af Svenskt Ursprung, by V. Berger, New York, 1915. The Swedish names listed by Mr. Berger are chiefly to be found in Minnesota, Iowa, Kansas, Nebraska and the Dakotas. See also Scandinavian Place-Names in the American Danelaw, by Roy W. Swanson, *Swedish-American Historical Bulletin* (St. Peter, Minn.), Aug., 1929.

[3] In most of the States local antiquaries have investigated the State names. See, for example, The Origin and Meaning of the Name *California,* by George Davidson, San Francisco, 1910; *California,* the Name, by Ruth Putnam, Berkeley, 1917; *Arizona,* Its Derivation and Origin, by Merrill P. Freeman, Tucson, 1913; *Ohio,* 1803–1903, by Maria Ewing Martin, New Straitsville, 1903; The Naming of *Indiana,* by Cyrus W. Hodgin, Richmond (Ind.), 1903; *Idaho,* Its Meaning, Origin and Application, by John E. Rees, Portland (Ore.), 1917. See also The Origin of American State Names, by F. W. Lawrence, *National Geographic Magazine,* Aug., 1920. The literature on the

ties. The second city of the country bears one, and so do the largest American river, and the greatest American water-fall, and four of the five Great Lakes, and the scene of the most important military decision ever reached on American soil. "In a list of 1,885 lakes and ponds of the United States," says Louis N. Feipel,[4] "285 are still found to have Indian names; and more than a thousand rivers and streams have names derived from Indian words." Walt Whitman was so earnestly in favor of these Indian names that he proposed substituting them for all other place-names, even the oldest and most hallowed. "California," he said in "An American Primer,"[5] "is sown thick with the names of all the little and big saints. Chase them away and substitute aboriginal names. . . . Among names to be revolutionized: that of the city of *Baltimore.* . . . The name of *Niagara* should be substituted for the *St. Lawrence.* Among places that stand in need of fresh, appropriate names are the great cities of *St. Louis, New Orleans, St. Paul.*" But eloquent argument has also been offered on the other side, chiefly on the ground that Indian names are often hard to pronounce and ever harder to spell. In 1863 R. H. Newell (Orpheus C. Kerr), a popular humorist of the time, satirized the more difficult of them in a poem called "The American Traveler," beginning:

> To Lake *Aghmoogenegamook,*
> All in the State of Maine,
> A man from *Wittequergaugaum* came
> One evening in the rain.[6]

I can find neither of these names in the latest report of the Geographic Board, but there are still towns in Maine called *Anasagunticook, Mattawamkeag, Oquossoc* and *Wytopitlock,* and lakes called *Unsuntabunt* and *Mattagomonsis.* But many Indian names began to disappear in colonial days. Thus the early Virginians changed the name of the *Powhatan* to the *James,* and the first settlers in New York changed the name of *Horicon* to *Lake George.* In the same way the present name of the *White* Mountains displaced *Agiochook;* and *New Amsterdam* (1626), and later *New York* (1664), displaced *Manhattan,* which survived, however, as the name of the island, and was revived in 1898 as the name of a borough. In our own time *Mt. Rainier* has displaced *Tacoma* (or *Tahoma*).[7] By various linguistic

---

names of cities is rather meager. A model contribution to the subject is *Baltimore—What Does the Name Mean?*, by Hermann Collitz, *Johns Hopkins Alumni Magazine,* Jan., 1934. Baltimore, of course, gets its name from the title of the Barons Baltimore, Lords Proprietor of Maryland. Dr. Collitz shows that the name comes from the Irish *ball-ti-more,* signifying "the place of the great lord."

[4] American Place-Names, *American Speech,* Nov., 1925, p. 79.

[5] *Atlantic Monthly,* April, 1904, pp. 468–69.

[6] It is reprinted in Local Discolor, by Mamie Meredith, *American Speech,* April, 1931.

[7] This substitution, I am informed, was due to the jealousy of Seattle, the citizens of which objected to having the greatest American peak south of Alaska bear the name of the rival city of Tacoma. But it is still called *Tacoma* in Tacoma.

devices changes have been made in other Indian names. Thus, *Mauwau-waming* became *Wyoming*, *Maucwachoong* became *Mauch Chunk*, *Oue-messourit* became *Missouri*, *Nibthaska* became *Nebraska*, *Rarenawok* became *Roanoke*, *Asingsing* became *Sing-Sing*, and *Machihiganing* became *Michigan*.

The Dutch place-names of the United States are chiefly confined to the vicinity of New York, and a good many of them have become greatly corrupted. *Brooklyn*, *Wallabout* and *Gramercy* offer examples. The first-named was originally *Breuckelen*, the second was *Waale Bobht*, and the third was *De Kromme Zee*. *Hell-Gate* is a crude translation of the Dutch *Helle-Gat*. During the early part of the last century the more delicate New Yorkers transformed the term into *Hurlgate*, but the change was vigorously opposed by Washington Irving, and *Hell-Gate* was revived. The Dutch *hoek* was early translated into the English *hook*, and as such is found in various place-names, *e.g.*, *Kinderhook*, Sandy *Hook*, Corlaers's *Hook* and *Hook* Mountain. The Dutch *kill*, meaning channel, is in *Kill* van Kull, *Peekskill*, *Catskill* and *Schuylkill*. *Dorp* (village) is in New *Dorp*.[8] *Kloof* (valley, ravine) survives, in the Catskills, in Kaatersill *Clove*, North *Clove* and *Clove* Valley. *Bosch* (corrupted to *bush*), *wijk* (corrupted to *wick*) and *vlei* (usually written *vly* or *fly*) are also occasionally encountered. The first means a wood, the second a district, and the third either a valley or a plain. Very familiar Dutch place-names are *Harlem*, *Staten*, *Flushing* (from *Vlissingen*), *Cortlandt*, *Nassau*, *Coenties*, *Spuyten Duyvel*, *Yonkers*, *Barnegat* and *Bowery* (from *bouwerij*, a farmstead). *Block* Island was originally *Blok*, and Cape *May*, according to Schele de Vere, was *Mey*. The French place-names have suffered even more severely than the Dutch. Few persons would recognize *Smackover*, the name of a small town in Arkansas, as French, and yet in its original form it was *Chemin Couvert*. Schele de Vere, in 1871, recorded the degeneration of the name to *Smack Cover*; the Postoffice, always eager to shorten and simplify names, has since made one word of it and got rid of the redundant *c*. In the same way *Bob Ruly*, a Michigan name, descends from *Bois Brulé*; *Glazypool*, the name of an Arkansas mountain, from *Glaise à Paul*; *Low Freight*, the name of an Arkansas river, from *L'Eau Frais*; *Loose* creek, in Missouri, from *L'Ours*; *Swashing* creek from *San Joachim*; *Baraboo*, in Wisconsin, from *Baribault*; *Picketwire*, in Arkansas, from *Purgatoire*; and *Funny Louis*, in Louisiana, from *Funneleur*. A large number of French place-names, *e.g.*, *Lac Supérieur*, were translated into English at an early day, and nearly all the original *Bellevues* are now *Belleviews* or *Bellviews*. *Belair*, La.,

---

[8] The name of Jamaica, L.I., was originally *Rustdorp* and that of Westchester was *Ostdorp*. To this day Schenectady is commonly called the *Dorp* locally, and its people pass as *Dorpians*. See Dialectical Evidence in the Place-Names of Eastern New York, by Edward E. Hale, *American Speech*, Dec., 1929. Mr. Hale's errors in Dutch are corrected by A. E. H. Swaen, in Dutch Place-Names in Eastern New York, *American Speech*, June, 1930.

represents the end-product of a process of decay which began with *Belle Aire*, and then proceeded to *Bellaire* and *Bellair*. All these forms are still to be found, together with *Bel Air* and *Belle Ayr*. The Geographic Board's antipathy to names of more than one word has converted *La Cygne* in Kansas, to *Lacygne*. *Lamoine*, *Labelle*, *Lagrange* and *Lamonte* are among its other improvements, but *Lafayette* for *La Fayette*, long antedated the beginning of its labors.[9] Sheer ignorance has often been responsible for the debasement of French place-names. Consider, for example, the case of *Grande Ronde*. It is the name of a valley and a river in Eastern Oregon, and it used to be the name of a town in Yamhill county. But then a big lumber company came along, enlarged the town-site, put a mortgage on it, and issued bonds against it. On these bonds, as in the incorporation papers of the company, the name was spelled *Grand Ronde*. The Oregon Geographic Board protested, but when it was discovered that rectifying the blunder would cost many hundreds of dollars, the lumber company refused to move, and so the place is now *Grand Ronde*—in French, a sort of linguistic hermaphrodite.[10]

According to Harold W. Bentley [11] no less than 2,000 American cities and towns have Spanish names, and thousands more are borne by rivers, mountains, valleys and other geographical entities. He says that there are more than 400 cities and towns of Spanish name in California alone. They are numerous all over the rest of the trans-Mississippi region, and, curiously enough, are even rather common in the East. The Mexican War was responsible for many of the Eastern examples, but others, *e.g.*, *Alhambra*, *Altamont* and *Eldorado*, seem to reveal nothing more than a fondness for mellifluous names. The map of California is studded with lovely specimens: *Santa Margarita*, *San Anselmo*, *Alamagordo*, *Terra Amarilla*, *Sabinoso*, *Las Palomas*, *Ensenada*, *San Patricio*, *Bernalillo*, and so on. Unfortunately, they are intermingled with horrifying Anglo-Saxon inventions, *e.g.*, *Oakhurst*, *Ben Hur*, *Drytown*, *Skidoo*, *Susanville*, *Uno* and *Ono*, in-

[9] The Geographic Board of Canada is naturally more tender with French names, but some of them are so long that it is forced to shorten them. *Le Petit Journal* of Montreal reported on Nov. 22, 1931 that there was a *Coeur-Très-Pur-de-la-Bienheureuse-Vierge-Marie-de-Plaisance* (commonly reduced to *Plaisance*) in Quebec, and a *Ste. Marie-Madeleine-du-Cap-de-la-Madeleine* to keep it company. The board also makes war on the numerous *k*'s in Canadian Indian names on the ground that *k* is not a French letter. Examples: *Kapikikikakik*, *Kakekekwaki*. In general, the board opposes the abandonment of French names. Thus it has decided for *Matissard* (lake) as against *Horsetail*, and for *Laberge* (creek) as against *Lizard*. Some of the Canadian names show strange combinations. When the French-speaking rustics found a village they commonly give it a saint's name and then tack on the name of the district. The result is such marvels as *St. Evariste de Forsyth*, *St. Hippolyte de Kilkenny* and *St. Louis du Ha Ha*.
[10] I am indebted here to Mr. Lewis A. McArthur, secretary to the Oregon Geographic Board. He tells me also of the fate of *Psyche*, a town in Clallam county. The local residents, baffled by the name, called it *Pysht*, and in the end the Postoffice succumbed, and *Pysht* it is today.
[11] *A Dictionary of Spanish Terms in English*, New York, 1932, p. 17.

cluding harsh bastard forms, e.g., *Sierraville, Hermosa Beach, Point Loma* and *Casitas Springs.* Many names originally Spanish have been translated, e.g., *Rio de los Santos Reyes* into *Kings* river, and *Rio de las Plumas* into *Feather* river, or mauled by crude attempts to turn them into something more "American," e.g., *Elsinore* in place of *El Señor,* and *Monte Vista* in place of *Vista del Monte.* Probably a fifth of the Spanish place-names in California are the names of saints. The names of the Jewish patriarchs and those of the holy places of Palestine are seldom, if ever, encountered: the Christianity of the early Spaniards seems to have concerned itself with the New Testament far more than with the Old, and with Catholic doctrine even more than with the New Testament. There are no *Canaans* or rivers *Jordan* in the Southwest, but *Concepcions, Sacramentos* and *Trinidads* are not hard to find.

The Americans who ousted the Spaniards were intimately familiar with both books of the Bible, and one finds copious proofs of it on the map of the United States. There are no less than eleven *Beulahs,* nine *Canaans,* eleven *Jordans* and twenty-one *Sharons. Adam* is sponsor for a town in West Virginia and an island in the Chesapeake, and *Eve* for a village in Kentucky. There are five postoffices named *Aaron,* two named *Abraham,* two named *Job,* and a town and a lake named *Moses.* Most of the *St. Pauls* and *St. Josephs* of the country were inherited from the French, but the two *St. Patricks* show a later influence. Eight *Wesleys* and *Wesleyvilles,* eight *Asburys* and twelve names embodying *Luther* indicate the general theological trend of the plain people. There is a village in Maryland, too small to have a postoffice, named *Gott,* and I find *Gotts Island* in Maine (in the French days, *Petite Plaisance*) and *Gottville* in California, but no doubt these were named after German settlers of that awful name, and not after the Lord God directly. There are four *Trinities,* to say nothing of the inherited *Trinidads.* And in Arkansas and New York there are *Sodoms.*

Names wholly or partly descriptive of localities are very numerous throughout the country, and among the *Grundwörter* embodied in them are terms highly characteristic of American and almost unknown to the English vocabulary. *Bald Knob* would puzzle an Englishman, but the name is so common in the United States that the Geographic Board has had to take measures against it. Others of that sort are *Council Bluffs, Patapsco Neck, Delaware Water Gap,*[12] *Walden Pond, Sandy Hook, Key West, Bull Run, Portage, French Lick, Jones Gulch, Watkins Gully, Cedar Bayou, Keams Canyon, Poker Flat, Parker Notch, Sucker Branch, Frazier's Bottom* and *Eagle Pass. Butte Creek,* in Montana, a small inland stream, bears a name made up of two Americanisms. There are thirty-five postoffices whose names embody the word *prairie,* several of them, e.g., *Prairie du*

---

[12] *Gap* occurs in England, but it is very rare. There is a Goring *Gap* between the Chiltern Hills and the Berkshire Downs, on the railway from London to Oxford.

Chien, Wis., inherited from the French. There are seven *Divides,* eight *Buttes,* eight town-names embodying the word *burnt,* innumerable names embodying *grove, barren, plain, fork, cove* and *ferry,* and a great swarm of *Cold Springs, Coldwaters, Summits, Middletowns* and *Highlands.* The flora and fauna of the land are enormously represented. There are twenty-two *Buffalos* beside the city in New York, and scores of *Buffalo Creeks, Ridges, Springs* and *Wallows.* The *Elks,* in various forms, are still more numerous, and there are dozens of towns, mountains, lakes, creeks and country districts named after the *beaver, martin, coyote, moose* and *otter,* and as many more named after such characteristic flora as the *paw-paw,* the *sycamore,* the *cottonwood,* the *locust* and the *sunflower.* There is an *Alligator* in Mississippi, a *Crawfish* in Kentucky and a *Rat Lake* on the Canadian border of Minnesota. The endless search for mineral wealth has besprinkled the map with such names as *Bromide, Oil City, Anthracite, Chrome, Chloride, Coal Run, Goldfield, Telluride, Leadville* and *Cement.*

There was a time, particularly during the gold rush to California, when the rough humor of the country showed itself in the invention of extravagant and often highly felicitous place-names, but with the growth of population and the rise of civic spirit they have tended to be replaced by more seemly coinages. *Catfish* creek, in Wisconsin, is now the *Yakara* river; the *Bulldog* mountains, in Arizona, have become the *Harosomas.* As with natural features of the landscape, so with towns. Nearly all the old *Boozevilles, Jackass Flats, Three Fingers, Hell-For-Sartains, Undershirt Hills, Razzle-Dazzles, Cow-Tails, Yellow Dogs, Jim-Jamses, Jump-Offs, Poker Citys* and *Skunktowns* have yielded to the growth of delicacy, but *Tombstone* still stands in Arizona, *Goose Bill* remains a postoffice in Montana, and the Geographic Board gives its imprimatur to the *Horsethief* trail in Colorado, to *Burning Bear* in the same State, and to *Pig Eye* lake in Minnesota. Various other survivors of a more lively and innocent day linger on the map: *Blue Ball,* Pa., *Hot Coffee,* Miss., *Cowhide,* W. Va., *Dollarville,* Mich., *Oven Fork,* Ky., *Social Circle,* Ga., *Sleepy Eye,* Minn., *Bubble,* Ark., *Shy Beaver,* Pa., *Shin Pond,* Me., *Gizzard,* Tenn., *Rough-and-Ready,* Calif., *Non Intervention,* Va., *T.B.,* Md., *Noodle,* Tex., *Vinegar Bend,* Ala., *Matrimony,* N.C., *Wham,* La., *Number Four,* N.Y., *Oblong,* Ill., *Stock Yards,* Neb., *Stout,* Iowa, and so on.[13] West Virginia, the wildest of the Eastern States, is full of such place-names. Among them I find *Affinity,*

---

[13] See Picturesque Town-Names in America, by Mamie Meredith, *American Speech,* Aug., 1931; American Towns Bear Odd Names, New York *Times,* Feb. 7, 1932; and Strangers in Mississippi Find *Hot Coffee* is Place, Baltimore *Evening Sun,* Oct. 21, 1932. During the Winter of 1934–35 the *Evening Sun* printed a series of lists of odd place-names on its editorial page. Some grotesque English names, almost fit to match the specimens above, are listed in Queer Names, *American Church Monthly,* Sept., 1931, p. 173, *e.g., Upper Swell, Little Snoring, Nether Peover, Appledram, Swaffham, Eye Over, Fetcham, Snailwell, High Easter, Wooton, Wawen, Mutford.*

Annamoriah (*Anna Maria?*), *Bee, Bias, Big Chimney, Bille, Blue Jay, Bulltown, Caress, Cinderella, Cyclone, Czar, Cornstalk, Duck, Halcyon, Jingo, Left Hand, Raven's Eye, Six, Skull Run, Three Churches, Uneeda, Wide Mouth, War Eagle* and *Stumptown.* The Postal Guide shows two *Ben Hurs,* five *St. Elmos* and ten *Ivanhoes,* but only one *Middlemarch.* There are seventeen *Roosevelts,* six *Codys* and six *Barnums,* but no *Shakespeare. Washington,* of course, is the most popular of American place-names. But among names of postoffices it is hard pushed by *Clinton, Centerville, Liberty, Canton, Marion* and *Madison,* and even by *Springfield, Warren* and *Bismarck.* A number of charming double names dot the American map, *e.g., Perth Amboy, Newport News, Front Royal, Wilkes-Barre, Princess Anne, Port Tobacco, The Dalles, Baton Rouge, Walla Walla, Winston-Salem.* In the older States they are supported by some even more charming names for regions and neighborhoods, *e.g., Dame's Quarter, My Lady's Manor* and *Soldiers' Delight* in Maryland. . . .

Study Questions

1. Mencken's classification is illogical in separating names that in type of meaning belong together: i.e., *Vermont* would go under (*d*) and the *Green Mountains* under (*f*), although *vert mont* in French means green mountain. Names from other languages may in meaning include classes (*a*), (*b*), (*e*), (*f*), and (*g*). *Stillwater* and *Eau Claire,* the French form, logically belong together in (*f*). A large number of Indian names belong in (*f*) and (*g*), where translations of Indian names, a common type, would be classified. Work out a classification that does not overlap and that is based on purpose as suggested by the kind of name: to honor a person, to retain familiar place-names from other regions, to describe a locality, and so forth.

2. For each of your classes, give examples from your own state or locality, including as much variety in language as can be noted: English, French, Indian, and so forth.

3. What can you infer from place-names about your own state and the stages in its development? What people discovered and explored it? Where did the first settlers come from? Who were some of the leading settlers? Did later European immigration leave its mark? What are the dominant physical features?

4. From consideration of place-names, what do you conclude about the relationship of historical and regional aspects of language? Can regional aspects be understood without consideration of historical aspects?

5. Within a community, further aspects of place-names can be observed. List and give examples of as many categories of names in towns and cities as you can, from street names to names of apartment buildings or business buildings. How many of your previous classes are represented? Do you find any new ones? What is the effect of the need for many names, in a large city?

6. What seem to you to be the most American kinds of place-names, according to "The Hallmarks of American"? Give examples.

10. LANGUAGE DOESN'T STAY THE SAME

Robert A. Hall, Jr.

In this chapter from *Linguistics and Your Language* Professor Hall considers the constantly changing character of language. Like the people who use it, language is flexible and adaptable, meeting each new situation as it arises. Often regularity and consistency are cast aside for more effective modes of expression which are a source of distress and alarm to linguistic conservatives.

[In the preceding section, Hall examined instances of linguistic borrowing.] . . . This [linguistic borrowing] is one way in which a language can change—by importation of features from some source outside itself, from some external source; and we can therefore call this kind of change in language *external* change. All external change is, by its nature, borrowing, whether the source is a dialect closely or distantly related to the dialect which does the borrowing, or an unrelated language. It was to this kind of change—primarily to obsolescence and revival of archaic forms (i.e., borrowing from an earlier stage of the language)—that Horace was referring to when he wrote in his *Art of Poetry:*

> Multa renascentur quae iam cecidere, cadentque
> Quae nunc sunt in honore vocabula, si volet usus

"Many words which have already gone out of use come back to life again, and words which are now in honor fall into disuse, if usage so wills it."

This observation is quite well-founded and justified. Languages change, over the centuries, so much as to render them completely different in the space of only a thousand years or so. If Horace, for instance, were to come to life today and converse with a speaker of Modern French, the two would be completely unable to understand each other. Imagine a speaker of Old French (of, say, around the year 1000) added to the conversation, and the situation would not be much better. The speaker of Old French would not be able to act as interpreter, but instead would have great difficulty in understanding either his linguistic ancestor (Horace) or his linguistic descendant (the present-day speaker of French). They would have in common a great many words that were related historically, but which would be too different from each other to be understood—such as the word for "August," which Horace would pronounce *augustum,* the speaker of Old French *aúst,* and the modern Frenchman with just one phoneme, a vowel similar to our "oo" sound. The entire linguistic systems of Latin, Old

French, and Modern French differ so greatly that speakers of the three languages would each have to learn two other languages in order to grasp what the others were saying. The same would hold true for a speaker of the English of King Alfred's time, one of Chaucer's time, and one of our own time, if they could try to converse together.

However, when Horace discusses borrowing of archaic forms, he is seeing and presenting only a part of linguistic change; and so would we, if we took into account only the results of external borrowing, such as we study in linguistic geography. Theoretically, it might be possible to keep an otherwise-normal speech-community hermetically sealed off from all outside sources of borrowing (including knowledge of past stages of their language), and maybe even—by extremely detailed supervision like that of a super-police-state—to prevent inter-dialectal borrowing within the speech-community. But even in such a completely isolated, regulated community, the language would still change, no matter how much effort was made to keep it stable. For, in addition to borrowing or external change, there is another force at work to keep language constantly changing, which would work no matter how little external influence were exerted on the language: *internal* change. Internal change is, in its turn, of two subvarieties: *internal borrowing*, and *evolution* or *organic change*. The inner evolution of a language, particularly in its phonemes, goes on gradually, and speakers of the language are often not even aware that it is going on, or else they see only such a small part of the total pattern of change that they don't realize its import. After some hundreds or thousands of years have passed, however, a language comes to be very different from what it was at an earlier stage; and the changes have taken place so gradually and so inevitably that no one could possibly have halted them.

Internal borrowing, or *analogy*, is the kind of change that takes place when a child says *foots* instead of *feet*, *oxes* instead of *oxen*, *sticked* instead of *stuck*, or *breaked* instead of *broke*. We usually call such forms as *foots, oxes, sticked, breaked* "mistakes" and all of us—even the most illiterate users of sub-standard English—train our children to say *feet*, not *foots*, and so on. Yet what lies at the root of these "mistakes" is an extremely widespread process, which we call *analogical replacement*. What has happened when the child has said *foots* or *sticked?* Simply this: he has heard and learned a whole host of "regular" formations—plural formations such as *root—roots, hat—hats, book—books, map—maps, box—boxes,* and past formations like *kick—kicked, lick—licked, trick—tricked, rake—raked,* in the hundreds and thousands. He has simply made his new formation of a plural for *foot* or *ox* by abstracting (unconsciously, for the most part) the "regular" ending –s –es and adding it to *foot* or *ox*. Likewise, he has taken the "regular" past ending –ed or *breaked* "on the analogy" of other pasts like *kicked, raked,* and so on. He is making what we often call an *analogical new-formation,* by borrowing an element of linguistic form or construction (here the noun-plural suffix *-s -es* or the verb past suffix *-ed*) from one part of our linguistic structure (here the "regular" formations) and adding it to another (here the "irregular" forms). This is a kind of borrowing, just like external borrowing; but the source of borrowing is not somewhere outside but within the language itself, and so we call it internal borrowing.

Analogical changes of this kind are often presented in the shape of proportional formulas, with x standing for the new-formation, thus

$$hat : hats = foot : x \quad (\text{"}hat \text{ is to } hats \text{ as } foot \text{ is to } x\text{"})$$
$$box : boxes = ox : x$$
$$kick : kicked = stick : x$$
$$rake : raked = break : x$$

Sometimes, objections are made to our statement of analogical replacements in a proportional formula, such as those we have just given; critics say that naive speakers would not be capable of exact enough reasoning to make up a formula of this sort and carry it out. There are two answers to this objection: 1) that what we are giving here is a description of what takes place, not a statement of reasoning that we might necessarily expect from a naive speaker, who speaks normally without abstract analysis and who habitually does perfectly many things he could not possibly describe; and 2) that even naive speakers from time to time are perfectly conscious of the basis for their analogical formations. The great Danish linguist Otto Jespersen tells the story of a Danish child who should, according to normal Danish usage, have said *nikkede* "nodded" as the past of *nikker* "nod," but said *nak* instead on the analogy of *stak* "stuck," whose present is *stikker*. When the child was corrected, he immediately retorted "*Stikker–stak, nikker–nak*," showing that he knew perfectly well on what analogy he had made the new past tense form, and stating it in the form of a proportion.

From the point of view of the present language, analogical new-formations like *oxes* or *taked* are "mistakes," forms that would be uttered only by children or others learning the language, or by adults when tired or flustered (that is, as "slips of the tongue"), and that would not be accepted by any native speaker at present. But there are always some forms with regard to which our usage is not fully settled, even that of normal adult native speakers of the language, and for which we may use first one and then another alternative. We have, for instance, the "irregular" plural formation *hoof–hooves*, and the "strong" past tenses *wake–woke, dive–dove*; yet we often hear and make regularized forms for these words: *hoofs, waked, dived*. That is to say, in some respects our usage is *fluctuating*; and in the course of time, we will gradually come to favor one competing form over the other (say, *dived* over *dove*), until at last one is triumphant and drives out the other completely in normal everyday usage.

What we often fail to realize, however, is that some forms which seem fully fixed in our present language were, in earlier times, analogical new-formations, and went through a period of newness, and then of fluctuation, before displacing older forms entirely. Our plurals *days* and *cows* are both analogical replacements of earlier forms which would have sounded quite different if they had developed normally into Modern English. Old English had the singular *dag* "day," plural *dagas*, and *cū* "cow," plural *cȳ* (in which the letter *y* stands for a vowel like that spelled *u* in French or *ü* in German); the Old English plurals, had they developed normally, would have given *dawes* and *kye* (rhyming with *high*) in present-day English. But we do not say *day–dawes* or *cow–kye*; we use the regularized plurals *days* and *cows* instead. This is because around the year 1200, our linguistic ancestors made an analogical new-formation, borrowing the stem *day* from the singular to replace the stem *dawe–* in the plural before the ending *–s*. In the plural of *cow*, there were two successive analogical formations. Around the year 1300, people started to use the plural *kyn*, with the analogical plural ending *–n* (which was then very frequent, but survives now only in *oxen*, *children*, *brethren*). The form *kyn* survives at present as an archaism, *kine*; in its turn, it was replaced around 1600 by the plural *cows*, in which the plural ending *–s* was borrowed from the majority of nouns and added to the singular *cow*. There must have been a time when *days* seemed as much of a "mistake" as *foots* does now, and—slightly later—a period when *days* and *dawes* were in competition just as *hoofs* and *hooves* are now. If we extend our time-perspective far enough back, we can see that we use relatively few plural formations which are direct continuations of those in use four or five thousand years ago.

These considerations are of importance when it comes to judging forms like *hisn*, *hern*, and so forth, or *he done*. . . . When an "ignorant" person borrows the ending *–n* from the possessive pronoun *mine* and adds it to the adjectives *his, her, our, your* and *their*, to make the distinctive possessive pronouns *hisn, hern, ourn, yourn, theirn*, this procedure on his part is not due to ignorance or stupidity. It is due to exactly the same process of analogizing, of regularizing the forms of the language, that we saw in the instances of *cows* or *days*, and that has gone on in producing a great many other forms we now use. The analogy in this instance is, of course:

$$my \; : \; mine = his \; : \; x$$

and so forth. Likewise, such a past tense as *he done* is traceable to some such analogy as this:

$$he \; has \; kicked \; : \; he \; kicked = he \; has \; done \; : \; x$$

That such forms as *hisn* or *he done* are not accepted as part of the standard language is not due to any defect in the forms themselves—they are perfectly respectable analogical forms, with as much right to existence as *cows* and *days;* the thing that makes them unacceptable is simply the connotation of social disfavor which has been attached to them.

Very often, internal borrowing (analogy) comes into play when linguistic forms become irregular and grammatical relationships are obscured as a result of changes in phonemes. This is what happened in the case of English *day—dawes;* it has happened in recent centuries in such instances as those of the old plurals *eye—eyen, shoe—shoon, brother—brethren,* which have now been replaced by the more transparent and easily understandable formations *eyes, shoes, brothers* respectively; or in such past tenses of verbs as *help—holp, work—wrought,* now regularized by analogy in the new-formations *helped, worked.* In English noun plurals and verb pasts and past participles, the trend of development is slowly but surely towards analogical leveling of irregularities; even though forms like *gooses, mouses* or *drinked, writed* are simply "errors" or "blunders" now, they may perhaps be perfectly normal by two or three hundred years from now. Today's analogical "mistakes" are often tomorrow's competing forms, and day-after-tomorrow's "correct" forms.

In other instances, analogy works rather to restore distinctions that have been lost through phonemic change. The Italian imperfect singular is an excellent example of this. The three forms of the imperfect singular in Latin—first, second, and third persons—ended in *–bam, –bās, –bat* respectively, as in

> 1.sg. *cantābam* "I used to sing"
> 2.sg. *cantābās* "you (sg.) used to sing"
> 3.sg. *cantābat* "he, she, or it used to sing"

During the development of Latin into Italian, final *–m, –s,* and *–t* ceased to be pronounced, and all three of these forms would have developed normally into Italian *cantava.* In other tenses of the verb, however, changes in sound did not obscure the distinction between first, second, and third singular; and hence there was a strong pressure from the pattern of the rest of the language, to re-establish such a distinction where it had been lost through the disappearance of final *–m, –s, –t.* Even before the earliest documents were written in Italian, the second person singular of the imperfect was distinguished from the other two persons by the substitution of the ending *–i,* taken ultimately from the second singular of the present in verbs like *audīs* "you (sg.) hear," whose ending *–is* developed regularly to *–i.* The second person singular of the imperfect was thus remade analogically into *cantavi;* in Old Italian, the first and third singular both were *cantava,* the normal development of both *cantābam* and *cantābat.* In later times, the ending *–o* was borrowed from the first singular of the present (as in *canto* "I sing") and used instead of *–a* as a distinctive first singular ending in the imperfect also. The following table shows the historical development of the imperfect singular from Latin to Italian, with daggers placed before the forms which are analogical replacements:

	LATIN	LATE LATIN	OLD ITALIAN	MODERN ITALIAN
1.sg.	cantābam	cantaba	cantava	†cantavo
2.sg.	cantābās	cantaba	†cantavi	†cantavi
3.sg.	cantābat	cantaba	cantava	cantava

Analogical change is always at work in language—not only in inflectional forms like *foots* and *taked*, but also on the level of word-formation, syntax and meaning. We are always deriving new words from already existing ones, by extending the use of some prefix, suffix, or other formative element. On the analogy of *Jacobite* "follower of King James," *Adamite* "descendant of Adam," *Hamite* "descendant of Ham," and similar formations in *–ite*, we can coin such terms as *Hicksite* or *Buchmanite*. We take the prefix *de-* from formations like *decode, deface, derail*, and add it to other nouns to make new words such as *delouse, degut*. Sometimes we separate the elements of a word differently from the way earlier speakers did, and thus remodel the word: so, for example, in the Middle English phrases *a naddere* "a certain kind of snake" and *a napron* "a small cloth," the *n* was taken as being part of the indefinite article *an*, and the phrases were redivided as *an addere* (Modern English *an adder*) and *an apron*, respectively. The analogy in these instances was something of this kind:

an other : other = a naddere : x

Syntactical constructions are often extended by analogy; as Leonard Bloomfield points out (*Language*, p. 407):

> From the sixteenth century on, we find English subordinate clauses introduced by the word *like*. We can picture the innovation in this way:
> *to do better than Judith : to do better than Judith did = to do like Judith : x*
> where the outcome is the construction *to do like Judith did.* . . .

Study Questions

1. How was the process of external change accelerated in American English, in comparison with British English? From what American sources did Americans borrow and what language needs prompted this borrowing? What are some of the words that are characteristic of American English—names of plants, animals, food, clothing, utensils, and so forth? What borrowings, from what sources, appear in the following sentence? The khaki-clad campers, wearing moccasins, carried their canoe as they trekked along the portage.

2. Conscious humorous analogy illustrates the slow and largely unconscious process of organic change. Add a few examples of your own to these analogous parallels: *mouse, mice, spouse, spice, house, hice; cat, kitten, rat, ritten, mat,*

mitten; stink, stank, stunk, think, thank, thunk; goose, gosling, geese, moose, mosling, meese; tooth, teeth, booth, beeth. In which pairs is the analogy sound and in which is it based merely on similarity of words in different categories, as with *cat* and *mat?*

3. Some common spelling errors are due to spelling by analogy: the word *similar*, unconsciously associated with the word *familiar* despite the obvious difference in pronunciation, is often spelled *similiar*. Without—or even by means of— dictionaries, such analogous spellings may become established. Sledd objects to *alright*, given in *Webster's Third International*. Bergen Evans, in *Comfortable Words*, cites as analogies *already* and *all ready*, and *always* and *all ways*. From a list of commonly misspelled words select those you have trouble with, identify those which involve faulty analogy, and study carefully the differences between the words you have unconsciously or illogically associated. Can you cite other examples of spelling errors due to analogy? Can you cite examples of such "errors" becoming accepted spelling?

4. In words cited by Sledd or Evans as accepted by *Webster's Third International*, can you find any examples of analogy that have completed the transition from error to competing form to correct form?

5. Look up in *Webster's Second* and *Webster's Third New International Dictionaries* the following terms: *to contact, to implement, to enthuse, to finalize.* Which ones have become standard English? Which ones changed their status between the two editions?

11. THE BIRTH OF NEW VERBS
H. L. Mencken

In this essay contributed to *Philologica: The Malone Anniversary Studies* (1949), H. L. Mencken describes some of the methods used to coin new verbs. If he were revising and expanding the essay today, he would be able to include additional examples resulting from the increased spread of bureaucratic jargon, among them some of the verbs included in the *Webster's Third New International Dictionary*.

The hostility with which neologisms are sometimes received is a commonplace to all persons who look into the history of language. The bitter wars once waged upon *mob* and *reliable* were typical. The former, though it had been used by Dryden, was attacked by Swift in No. 230 of the *Tatler* (1710), and he was later joined furiously by Johnson, perhaps the most ignorant man, before 1919, who ever dabbled in lexicography. The latter, when it was revived in America in the last years of the eighteenth century (it has been traced in England to 1569), was denounced by the British reviewers of the time as a shining example of Yankee barbarism, and to this day there are hunkers in England and Scotland who object to it, as they object to *lengthy, influential* and *talented.* Swift, in the *Tatler* paper I have just mentioned, also censured *sham, bully, bubble* and *banter,* and said of the last that it "was first borrowed from the bullies in White Friars, then fell among footmen, and at last retired to the pedants." Johnson, in his Dictionary of 1755, described *to bamboozle* as "low" and *to wabble* as "low and barbarous," and at other times and in other places sought idiotically to put down *to coax, to budge, to fib, to swap* and *to derange.* Most of these were actually old in English, but purists are seldom bothered by such considerations. When they dislike a word they give no heed to its history, its linguistic plausibility or even the respectability of its associations, but have at it in a violent and all-out manner, as if using it were a sin against the Holy Ghost.

Taking one day with another, new verbs seem to outrage them more than new nouns, perhaps because the nouns commonly come in hitched to new objects that cannot be escaped, *e.g.,* the telephone, the submarine, the movies and the radio. There was no apparent resistance when *television* appeared, and I have heard no serious criticism of it since. But when *to contact* dawned in the early '20's a howl went up from the American Holoferneses, and presently it was echoed *fortissimo* in England, and to this day it reverberates from crag to crag of the precipices of Athene. I must confess at once that I share this priggish loathing, and never use the word myself, just as I never use *alright,* but the plain fact remains that there is plenty of excuse for it in the genius of the English language, and that many other verbs in daily use are no more legitimate. I offer as examples *to feast, to stock, to stream, to stitch* and *to master,* and if you crave more you will find many in Dr. Donald W. Lee's excellent historical study, "Functional Change in Early English." [1] *To contact* flowed quite naturally out of the noun *contact* in the sense of an acquaintance, a connection which Eric Partridge lists as arising in the commercial jargon of this great Republic some time before 1925. The etymologists have so far failed to establish the precise date, but in my own collectanea I find a pamphlet entitled "Observations on the Duties of *Contact Men,*" written in 1924 by John H. Bartlett, then the First Assistant Postmaster General, in which *contact work* also appeared. Apparently, *contact* and *contact man* were both then understood, at all events in the Postoffice, for the pamphlet offered no explanation of them. *To contact* must have followed soon afterward, for the Oxford Supplement offers an example dated 1929.

But at the start it encountered a great deal of what its users called sales resistance. So late as July 7, 1931, a syndicated editorial in a string of Class B newspapers was describing it as still below the salt, and so late as June 1, 1938, the *New Republic* was denouncing it as "dreadful." This denunciation, however, was promptly challenged by the distinguished linguist,

---

[1] Menasha, Wis., 1948.

Westbrook Pegler, who pointed out that the *New Republic* itself constantly used *to implement* in its lamentations on the current European situation, and that *to implement*, etymologically speaking, was exactly on all fours with *to contact*. To this the *New Republic* made the childish answer that *to implement* had been "perfectly good English since the days of Walter Scott," thus inviting the riposte that if there had been a *New Republic* then the verb would have been challenged and perhaps barred from the language. *To contact*, in fact, had got into the Oxford Supplement in 1933 and into Webster's New International in 1934 (albeit marked "slang" in the latter) and after that its progress was but little impeded. In 1940 it entered gloriously into the gobbledegook beginning to flourish at Washington, and by 1941 it was in wide use in the Army and Navy. In the latter year it was formally adopted by the British Army in Greece, and soon thereafter it began to appear in all the less straitlaced English newspapers. It is now at least half a dozen years since I last encountered a really full-dress excoriation of it.

To process has done even better. It had existed in English for centuries as a law term, but it was not until the early '80's that it began to branch out. Then it came into use to signify the manipulations used in photo-engraving, and after that it began to be applied gradually to other such mechanical or chemical operations, *e.g.*, the sharpening of pins and the canning of fruits and vegetables. But it was not until the Washington jobholders began rolling up their fearful and wonderful argot that it took on the multitudinous meanings it now enjoys. So far as I have been able to determine, the first human beings *processed* were the conscripts collared by the Selective Service Act of September 16, 1940, but very soon thereafter the bureaucrats began to *process* all sorts of other persons, and by 1942 the verb had taken on the range of a counter-word, signifying almost anything involving change. Unlike *to contact*, which is still frowned upon by intellectual popinjays, it has had its chief success on the higher levels, and in my archives are examples of its use by dignitaries as varied as Secretary of War Henry L. Stimson, the chief of the Manuscript Division of the New York Public Library, the editors of the *Journal of the American Medical Association*, and Dr. Harlow Shapley, the Harvard astronomer. It seems to be especially esteemed by librarians, and the Library of Congress has a *Processing* Committee to coördinate the doings of its numerous divisions. Webster (1934) heard of this new and swollen verb only as "slang, U.S.," but by 1947 it was listed without comment by the New College Standard. The dispatches of the Associated Press are now *processed* before being sent out to its client newspapers; the records of paupers are *processed* by social workers; felons are *processed* on being received in prison; Germans suspected of Nazi activity are *processed* by the Nürnberg catchpolls; college freshmen are *processed* by the goons of their deans; orators hired to whoop up Community Fund drives are *processed* before being turned loose; and the Army *proc-*

esses not only enlisted men, but also line and staff officers, doctors, dentists, nurses, and war correspondents. The word has taken on all the shades of meaning of *examined, inspected, instructed, investigated, organized, registered, manipulated, studied, sorted, tested, screened, judged* and *edited.*

New verbs of the same general sort have appeared in great number since Elizabethan times, and though most of them have had short lives a sufficiency have always survived to give the language constant reinforcement and refreshment. Shakespeare failed with *to spaniel* but not with *to dwindle.* Thomas Jefferson was denounced by the English pedants for *to belittle,* but by 1862 it was being used without thought of sin by Trollope. *To rubberneck,* when it was launched by George Ade in 1896, made a very painful impression upon the delicate, but by 1929 Professor J. Y. T. Greig, the Scottish philologian, was hailing it as "one of the best words ever coined."

The embryologist of speech discerns several processes in the making of such novelties. Some are simply nouns unchanged, *e.g., to contact, to author, to style, to decision, to taxi, to pressure* and *to signature;* others are back-formations from nouns, *e.g., to locate, to enthuse, to reune, to resurrect, to intermiss, to aggravate, to liase, to vamp, to commute, to reminisce, to typewrite* and *to jell;* yet others are made by adding ancient suffixes to nouns common or proper, *e.g., to glamorize, to slenderize, to hospitalize, to simonize, to hooverize, to publicize, to finalize* and *to funeralize* (I have encountered *to obituarize* more than once in the Literary Supplement to the London *Times*); or by prefixing a particle, *e.g., to entruck.* Again, there are new verbs made of old verbs, mainly with negative prefixes, *e.g., to debamboozle, to dewater* and *to disadmire.* Sometimes, yet again, the original word is neither a noun nor a verb, but an adjective, as in *to thin, to peeve, to slim* and *to safen,* or a preposition, as in *to up, to plus* and *to over,* or even a conjunction, as in *to if.* So far I have heard of no verb made of what appears to be a pronoun save *to self* (used by plant breeders to indicate pollination by hand), but it certainly would not surprise me to hear that *to it* and *to me* and even *to him* and *to her* had been born.

The motives behind these coinages are various. In the majority of cases, perhaps, there is nothing save a desire to get rid of circumlocution and the waste of words, as in *to contact* for *to make contact with* and *to process* for *to subject to the process of.* To this class belong many familiar examples, *e.g., to referee* (apparently invented by the literati of the Intercollegiate Football Association in 1884), *to thumb* (a ride), *to radio, to press-agent, to glad-hand, to onion* (a hamburger), *to host* (or *hostess*), *to high-pressure, to professor, to front-page, to prima donna, to lone-wolf, to wastebasket, to feud, to pancake, to third-degree, to program, to racketeer, to gavel, to propaganda, to steam-roller, to belly-ache, to accession* and *to bible* (used by the Gideons for *to supply a hotel with Bibles*). There is, of course, nothing new here: *to park* is in Piers Plowman, *to demagogue* was used by James Harrington in *The Commonwealth of Oceana* in 1656, and *to orator* goes back to Thomas Heywood. What is peculiar to American speech today is simply the increasing copiousness of such inventions and their accelerating boldness. But that is only saying what everyone knows, including even a minority of linguists, to wit, that American speech is now in a stage of unprecedented growth, not infrequently approaching the carcinomatous. If some of the novelties devised by *Variety, Time* and Walter Winchell and his imitators would have been unimaginable in a more decorous era, then these great journals and publicists would have been equally unimaginable.

But behind some of the new verbs made of nouns unchanged there is something more than a desire for directness and succinctness. There is also the fact that they are felt to be more precise than the words or phrases they displace. This, I believe, may account for the rise of such forms as *to author, to package, to proposition, to audition* and *to service. To audition* does not mean simply to hear; it means to hear for the express purpose of estimating the performer's worth in the market. The audience that gathers at a concert *hears* the performers, but the agent or manager who *auditions* them hears them as a guide to his booking them. So with *to author.* It arose on the movie lots to designate the preparation of a script. To say that a given author *writes* a given script may be inaccurate, for a great deal goes into it beside the mere writing of its text, and sometimes the text is the least part of it. So *to author* was born—and now, as new verbs have a way of doing, it has begun to displace *to write* in situations where *to write* would be quite as accurate and a great deal less slobbergomptious. In the same way, *to service* is by no means identical with *to serve,* though it includes *to serve,* and *to package* means much more than to thrust into a box or bag, and *to proposition,* at least in the field of amour, is not only distinct from *to propose,* but in sense antithetical to *propose.* When a gentleman who *propositions* a lady later finds himself marching with her to the altar of God he is commonly very greatly surprised and vexed.

Many of the new verbs are engendered by new technical devices and processes, and fill genuine needs. They often seem unpleasant when they first appear, but if they are really useful they soon become commonplace. The Oxford Supplement's earliest example of *to motor* is from an American whodunit of 1928, and so late as February 13, 1937, a correspondent of the New York *Times* was noting that it had but recently appeared in that great family newspaper; but no one would see anything uncouth in it today, for it has become as sound English, or at all events as sound American, as *to boat* or *to toboggan. To entruck,* an Army term first used in World War II, is quite as "good," etymologically speaking, as *to entrain* (1568), *to entomb* (1578), *to enslave* (1656) and *to entangle* (1555), and soon or late may be as familiar. I confess that when I read an advertisement of a firm offering *to permanize* baby's first shoe in bronze I had a sinking feeling, but how else, without a mouthful of words, could the process have been described? Again, what is the matter with *to dewater*, "used by construction engineers in the sense of to remove water from a tunnel"? Or *to debulk* in the sense of to reduce in bulk? Or *to overprocess* in the sense of to spoil the broth? Or *to clipper* in the sense of to travel by a *Clipper* airship? Or *to tirade, to bodyguard, to trailer, to brain-trust, to tax-exempt, to dissave* (used by the CIO's department of education, 1948, to indicate "spending more than you earn"), *to obsolete, to bristle* (brush advertisement in the *DuPont Magazine*, June, 1945), *to subway, to cold-wave, to Ku Klux, to combust* (used by heating engineers as more precise than *to burn*), *to chiropract, to secretary, to deadhead, to highlight, to model* (for *to serve as a clothes model*), *to alert, to gate-crash, to chairman, to baton, to architect* (*Architectural Forum*, May, 1937, p. 8), *to angel* (one of *Variety's* coinages), *to impresario* (another), *to mastermind* (a third), *to showcase* (a fourth), *to background* (a fifth), *to baritone* (a sixth), *to questionnaire, to guest* (as an orchestra conductor), *to bankroll* (another *Variety* invention, often abbreviated *to b.r.*), *to ash-can, to headquarter, to commentator, to wax* (to make a phonograph record), *to landslide, to town-plan, to toastmaster, to true-bill* (to indict), *to ladder* (to produce ladders in stockings), *to streamline* and *to referend?*

Many of these verbs, of course, come from what may be called the sub-cellars of language, but surely not all. In the jargon of every profession, however learned, there are many more. The plastics engineers have contributed *to depolish* as the refrigeration engineers have contributed *to defrost* and the dirt engineers *to dewater*. The medical men, though their writing is commonly very prosy, have invented many new verbs, some of them dreadful, *e.g., to blood-count, to hemorrhage, to intern, to cystoscope, to wassermann* and *to obstetricate*. They use *to operate* without the usual terminal *on*, and those in the Army and Navy use *to survey* as a short substitute for *to retire from the service after a medical survey*. They are constantly devising such novelties as *to degerm* (*Journal of Infectious Diseases*, Nov.-Dec., 1938, p. 301) and *to anoxiate* (to reduce the oxygen in the blood and tissues), and they seem to have a great liking for such current counter-words as *to process, to author, to burp* and *outstanding*. Back in 1886, when the electric chair was a popular novelty, one of them invented the verb *to electrize* to designate the processing of its patients. When this was challenged, by whom I do not know, they substituted the mellifluous *to electrocute*, which still survives. But one thing lying within their line of duty they have persistently failed to do, and that is to run down the etymology of the great American verb *to goose*. Every schoolboy knows what it means, but no one seems to know its origin. I have been in correspondence on the subject with eminent American physicians and surgeons for years, but they seem to be still as far from agreement about it as they are about the cause of stomach ulcers.

Study Questions

1. For each of Mencken's processes in verb formation, add some examples of your own.

2. In the space-age vocabulary, can you find examples of new verbs?

3. Verbs formed of proper names plus *ize* are often of only temporary usefulness. *Fletcherize* and *Hooverize* may well be followed by such words as *simonize* if that particular product ceases to be manufactured. *Bowdlerize,* however, and *mesmerize* and *mercerize* are likely to continue in use. Look up these words in the dictionary to determine their origin and the factors causing their use or disuse. Can you think of any other such *ize* verbs? Can you formulate a principle governing such verbs by which their life expectancy can be predicted?

Part II.   *Historical Aspects*
Subjects for Brief Papers or Written Reports

1. Compare Sledd's article with one of those he refers to, or compare the articles by Bergen Evans and Wilson Follett. Deal with basic assumptions about the functions of a dictionary and specific criticisms of *Webster's Third New International Dictionary,* and arrive at your own conclusions as to the tone and reasoning used in each argument.

2. In the editorial comment from *Life,* quoted below, check every major word in the sentence "concocted from words found in Webster's." Which words would *not* be so used by a person seriously concerned with correctness in written English? Look up the same words in *Webster's Second International.* Which do you find? Classify your findings—words designated as nonstandard, words not found in the form used, and so forth—and report your conclusions as to the soundness of the basic criticism that *Webster's Third International* does not "distinguish between good and bad usage." Comment on the validity of the implication that the sentence "concocted" represents only expressions which *Webster's Third International* presents as unquestionably used by the most eminent modern writers in the precise sense in which *Life* uses them.

A Non-Word Deluge

"Bet you a dollar you'll never find it in Webster's!" This familiar challenge, whether from a player of Scrabble or merely someone proud of his wordsmanship, will be a risky one to make from now on. For the chances are, whatever "it" is, you *will* find it in Webster's Third New International Dictionary, just out.

It appears 27 years after its predecessor, contains 100,000 brand-new terms, but has only 2,662 pages (*vs.* 3,194 for the Second Edition) by virtue of dropping the gazetteer, biographical dictionary and such "nonlexical" terms as the characters in Dickens. But that's not the biggest change. Webster's, joining the say-as-you-go school of permissive English, has now all but abandoned any effort to distinguish between good and bad usage—between the King's English, say, and the fishwife's. Its rule of thumb seems to be: anything people say goes into the book.

Thus, that most monstrous of all non-words—"irregardless"—is included. So is Madison Avenue's abomination of adding "-wise" to those nouns ("Yes, but how is he wisdomwise?") which it hasn't already corrupted by adding "-ize" ("As soon as we can concretize the program, we will finalize it"). The hayseed's "hain't" (as well as "ain't") is listed, and all such enormities are compounded by approving "enormity" as a synonym of "enormousness," "like" for "as," and the common mispronunciation "heighth" as a "dialect variant."

We don't want to be stuffy about it. We're glad to see Webster's recognizing such new terms as beatnik, litterbug, two-way stretch, potty-chair and jungle juice. We don't object to "ain't"—since it's a justifiable contraction, and "aren't I" is ungrammatical. But we will continue to doubt that Lincoln could have modeled his Gettysburg Address, or Churchill his immortal speeches, on a word book so lax that even the following sentence could be concocted from words found in Webster's:

"Irregardless of the enormity of the upsurge, none of us are able, governmentwise, in a time of normalcy, to act like we can ignore it; we don't mean to infer otherwise in saying so." Or, to coin a slogan for that beer everybody in their homes is going to enthuse about: "*We brew good, like we used to could.*"

We're not opposed to progress, but we'll just keep Webster's Second Edition around awhile for little matters of style, good English, winning at Scrabble and suchwise.

Life (October 27, 1961), 4.

3. Compare the *Life* editorial with the following review from *Time*, considering the writer's concept of what a dictionary should be, his purpose, and his method, and giving your own evaluation of each.

Vox Populi, Vox Webster

When he set out in 1746 to write the first great English dictionary, Samuel Johnson intended his definitions to be laws that would firmly establish meanings. But usage thumbs its nose at laws; the dictionary nowadays is more a *Social Register* of words than a Supreme Court of language. In the 27 years since the G. & C. Merriam Co. published the Second Edition of its unabridged *Webster's New International Dictionary*, thousands of new words have clamored to be listed. Last week, after investing $3,500,000 and 757 "editor-years," Merriam responded with a brand-new edition ($47.50 and up). It is the most radical version yet of the nation's most famous dictionary.

G. & C. Merriam Co. is the only direct descendant, corporately speaking, of Noah Webster,* who in 1828 produced the first truly American dictionary, which in its 70,000 listings stressed the New World's lusty new words, from *applesauce* to *skunk*. The descendants have never matched Noah's style, clarity and wit. He was a practical man given to phonetic spelling (*ake, crum, skreen*). He was a feeling man given to personalizing his definitions: "All sin is *hateful* in the sight of God and of good men." Or: "In short, we *love* whatever gives us pleasure and delight, whether animal or intellectual; and if our hearts are right, we *love* God above all things. . . ." The newest Webster's sacrifices all such eloquence for dry and technical accuracy.

Nonetheless, from *A* to *zyzzogeton* (a genus of South American leaf hoppers), Merriam-Webster's Third Edition is lighter and brighter than its immediate predecessor. It weighs 13½ v. 16½ lbs., has 2,662 v. 3,194 pages, contains 450,000 v. 600,000 entries. Gone are the gazetteer, the biographical dictionary, and 100,000 obsolete or non-lexical terms, such as the names of characters in Dickens. In are 100,000 brand-new terms, from *astronaut, beatnik, boo-boo, countdown, den mother* and *drip-dry*, to *footsie, hard sell, mccarthyism, no-show, schlemiel, sit-in, wage dividend* and *zip gun.*

THAT OLD *Sprachgefühl.* The result may pain purists, who will even find four-letter words ("usu. considered vulgar") in the new lexicon. They appear now because the most cultured (*urbane, polished*) Americans are used to earthier speech in fiction and drama. According to Merriam-Webster, even *ain't* is "used orally in most parts of the U.S. by many cultivated speakers." Nor could the editors fail to *dig cool cats* who make *stacked chicks flip*. Without *drips* and *pads* and *junkies*, who *bug* victims for *bread* to buy *horse* for a *fix*, the dictionary of 1961 would not be *finalized*.

Yet *wordwise*, science by far outdoes slang in supplying neologisms. Chemistry alone accounts for 17,000 words, culled from 250,000 new derivatives since 1934. Medicine yields the longest word, topping *antidisestablishmentarianism* (28 letters) with *pneumonoultramicroscopicsilicovolcanoconiosis* (45), a lung disease afflicting miners. Conversely, one of the shortest words, *set*, requires the longest definition—more than a full page, which took one editor 6½ weeks to write.

Headed by scholarly Philip B. Gove, 59, a onetime English teacher at New York University, Merriam-Webster's Ph.D.-proud editors toil in a Georgian edifice in Springfield, Mass., that looks more like a college library than a company HQ. They began collecting a new batch of commonly used words before their last edition came out (complete with a misspelling—*Brünnehilde* for *Brünnhilde*—that competitors ignorantly cribbed). They used a worldwide network of "word watchers"—avid amateurs with *Sprachgefühl* (feeling for speech), who constantly peruse novels, menus, labels, ticket stubs, and even small-town newspaper accounts of obscure murders. The head of Merriam's own shipping department, for example, is the part-time scholar who netted *piggyback*, as used in railroad freight hauling.

* His heirs sold the rights to Printers George and Charles Merriam of Springfield, Mass., but the Merriams failed to get sole right to Webster's name, which is now in the public domain—hence the modern multiplicity of "Webster's" dictionaries.

INDESTRUCTIBLE BONES. Whenever word watchers spotted a new usage, editors filled out a "citation slip"—6,200,000 in all—to record its frequency and nuances. Words that got enough "cits" (pronounced sites) were discussed with Merriam's 200 outside consultants, who cover every field, from Knots and Logic, Mosses and Liverworts, to Cocktails and Girl Guiding. Their expert opinion clarified each new definition.

The most conspicuous change in the *Third New International Dictionary* is that every definition is really new. Instead of thumbnail essays, they run to single phrases. To illustrate new shades of meaning, they include 200,000 quotations that draw on sources as diverse as *Variety, Lingerie Merchandising,* and TIME (probably the most frequently quoted magazine), along with "pungent, lively remarks" by 14,000 modern notables from Winston Churchill to Mickey Spillane. The old edition brushed off *goof* as "a ridiculous, stupid person." Now, in amplification, Dwight Eisenhower is quoted as complaining that someone "made a *goof.*" Elizabeth Taylor broadens *sick* by speaking of "a room smelling rather of *sick.*" Ethel Merman says, "Two shows a day *drain* a girl," and Willie Mays warns, "Hit too many homers and people start *puffing* you up."

Says Editor Gove: "The English language is not a system of logic. What we start with is an inchoate heterogeneous agglomerate that retains the indestructible bones of innumerable tries at orderly communication." In short, writing dictionaries ain't easy.

Time (October 6, 1961), 49.

4. Compare the selection from *Life* with the remarks made about it by Sledd and Evans. Are the comments of Sledd and Evans justified? Evaluate the tone and reasoning of the three selections.

5. For either of the reviews given above, examine the issue of the magazine from which it was taken and report on the use of "words, constructions, and meanings," such as Evans mentions, which are not given in *Webster's Second International.* Is Evans's comment on the relation between the language of these publications and the *Third International* sound?

6. Compare the Prefaces of the *Second* and the *Third International Dictionary.* What differences are apparent? Are there any innovations in basic principles? In techniques?

7. Compare Sledd's and Evans's articles, using Selection 7, Study Question 7.

8. Bergen Evans is not only an authority on American English but also a versatile user of it. Study his Introduction and a number of the short essays in *Comfortable Words* and analyze the "hallmarks of American" exhibited in his style.

9. Analyze the "hallmarks of American" which you recognize in one of Mencken's critical articles in any of the six series of *Prejudices,* in the Vintage selection from *Prejudices* (1959), or in *The American Mercury* during the 1920's.

10. Study Mencken's "American" version of the "Declaration of Independence," in *Parodies* (Random House, 1960), and discuss how it differs from the English of the original, distinguishing between standard and non-standard American. What "hallmarks" do you find? Is Mencken's version an example of "current standard American"?

11. Read Robertson and Cassidy on Mencken, in *The Development of Modern*

English. What criticism do they make of Mencken's comparison between British and American English? On the basis of "The Hallmarks of American," decide whether their criticism is justified and in a short paper state their views, your opinion, and your reasons.

12. In an essay on Ring Lardner, Mencken comments on how "magnificently" Lardner handles the American vulgate. Read Lardner's "Haircut" or one of his "You know me, Al" baseball stories and write a paper on the unconventionality of grammar and vocabulary.

13. Mencken alludes to the great conservative influence of Lindley Murray and Joseph E. Worcester. Investigate the linguistic activities of either one and write a brief report of your findings.

14. Analyze the differences between British and American English in the dialogue in Harry Leon Wilson's *Ruggles of Red Gap.*

15. In a brief paper present your own scheme of classification of place-names in your home county. Illustrate with examples, and arrive at a conclusion as to dominant trends exhibited.

16. Classify the names of buildings and physical features on your campus, and report on the categories represented and the origin of the chief names. (P. Burwell Rogers' "Tidewater Virginians Name Their Homes," *American Speech* [December, 1959], 251–57, may be helpful as a model.)

17. Examine a selection from colonial American literature dealing with American life and report on the "borrowed" terms that represent external change. Or compare an early work such as William Byrd's *History of the Dividing Line* (1728) with William Bartram's *Travels* (1791).

18. Using the vocabulary of the space age or another rapidly developing area of science or technology, make a list of new verbs, classify them, and prepare a paper on the processes of verb formation in the area selected.

III. REGIONAL ASPECTS

In his classification of language differences Fries included the regional peculiarities of pronunciation, grammar, and usage. A traveler going from Chicago to Boston or New Orleans quickly recognizes marked differences in the way people in various sections of the United States use language. In order to have a record of the distinctive sectional characteristics, investigators have been making field surveys of the language patterns before their distinctive elements are changed as a result of the homogenizing process caused by today's radio, television, and rapid transportation. These investigators are interested merely in recording scientifically the facts of language which they discover; they are not interested in judging the social acceptability of the pronunciation, vocabulary, grammar, or syntax of a particular area. This latter task they leave to the arbiters of manners and behavior.

In this section we shall consider some of the objective aspects of language in a region: the gathering of evidence, the study of dialects and usage, and the generalizations about them. The social or class implications of these regional aspects of language will be treated more fully in Part V.

12. THE AMERICAN DIALECTS
Albert C. Baugh

"The American Dialects" is a section of Professor Baugh's *A History of the English Language* (1957). The bibliography included in this selection indicates the wide range of American dialect studies and lists some of the leading scholars in that field.

Certain features of pronunciation characteristic of a part of New England and others associated with many parts of the South are so easily recognized and so well known that for a long time it was customary to distinguish three main dialects in American English—the New England dialect, the Southern dialect, and General American, meaning the dialect of all the rest of the country. Such a division, in a broad way, is not unjustified since each of the dialect types is marked by features which distinguish it clearly from the others. But it is not sufficiently exact. Not all of New England shares in the features—such as the so-called "broad *a*" and the loss of [r] finally and before consonants—which are thought of as most characteristic. Parts of the South were settled from Pennsylvania and are not typically southern in speech. And finally, General American itself shows regional differences which, while not so obvious to the layman, can be recognized by the linguist and charted.

Our ability to distinguish more accurately the various speech areas which exist in this country is due to the fact that we now have a large mass of accurate data gathered by field workers for the *Linguistic Atlas of the United States and Canada* and a growing number of detailed studies of regional pronunciation and other features. These are too numerous to be detailed here, but they have contributed greatly to a clearer understanding of some of the speech areas of the country.[1]

---

[1] The following studies may be mentioned by way of illustration: the seven articles by C. K. Thomas, "Pronunciation in Upstate New York," published in *American Speech* (otherwise cited as *AS*), Vols. X–XII; the same author's "Pronunciation in Downstate New York," *AS*, XVII (1942), 30–41, 149–57 (the results of these and other studies are embodied in his *An Introduction to the Phonetics of American English*, New York, 1947); Allan F. Hubbell, *The Pronunciation of English in New York City* (New York, 1950); Edwin F. Shewmake, *English Pronunciation in Virginia* (Davidson, N.C., 1928), and "Distinctive Virginia Pronunciation," *AS*, XVIII (1943), 33–38; Argus Tresidder, "Notes on Virginia Speech," *AS*, XVI (1941), 112–20, and "The Sounds of Virginia Speech," *AS*, XVIII (1943), 261–72; the same author's "The Speech of the Shenandoah Valley," *AS*, XII (1937), 284–88; Lester V. Berrey, "Southern Mountain Dialect," *AS*, XV (1940), 45–54; Joseph S. Hall, *The Phonetics of Great Smoky Mountain Speech* (New York, 1942); Oma Stanley, *The Speech of East Texas* (New York, 1937). The distribution of various dialect features is studied in Hans Kurath, "Mourning and Morning," *Studies for William A. Read* (University, La., 1940), pp. 166–73; C. K. Thomas,

104

In 1949 Professor Hans Kurath published a study of the first importance, *A Word Geography of the Eastern United States*. On the basis of lexical evidence, mainly in the Atlantic Coast states as far south as South Carolina, he distinguished eighteen speech areas, which he grouped into three main groups: Northern, Midland, and Southern. The line separating Northern from Midland, confirmed by a number of isoglosses, runs through northern Pennsylvania, turns southeast about halfway across the state, and continues this general course across New Jersey. The division between Midland and Southern, proceeding in the opposite direction, begins at the Atlantic Ocean at a midpoint on the Delmarva peninsula, describes a northward arc through Maryland, and turns southwest, skirting the eastern edge of the Blue Ridge Mountains in Virginia and North Carolina and turning west just north of Atlanta, Georgia. To the east lie the Piedmont and the coastal plain. Such a threefold division has the virtue of simplicity, and when the evidence is all in it may prove a valid classification for the country as far west as the Mississippi.[2] As for the region farther west it would be rash to hazard an opinion, since this area contains a greater mixture of people from different parts of the country than does the eastern third of the United States. The classification has the weakness of suggesting a greater homogeneity for the Northern type than it has, containing as it does the dialect of eastern New England, which must be recognized as a distinct variety

"Notes on the Pronunciation of *hurry*," *AS*, XXI (1946), 112–15, and "Notes on the Pronunciation of *on*," *AS*, XXII (1947), 104–07; Albert H. Marckwardt, "Middle English ŏ in the American English of the Great Lakes Area," *Papers of the Michigan Acad.*, XXVI (1941), 561–71, and "Middle English *wa–* in the Speech of the Great Lakes Region," *AS*, XVII (1942), 226–34; Raven I. McDavid, Jr., "Low-back Vowels in the South Carolina Piedmont," *AS*, XV (1940), 144–48, "Derivatives of Middle English [o:] in the South Atlantic Area," *Quar. Jour. of Speech*, XXXV (1949), 496–504, and (with Virginia G. McDavid) "*h* before Semivowels in the Eastern United States," *Language*, XXVIII (1952), 41–62; E. Bagby Atwood, "*Grease* and *greasy*–a Study of Geographical Variation," *Texas Stud. in English*, XXIX (1950), 249–60, to which may be added the same author's *Survey of Verb Forms in the Eastern United States* (Ann Arbor, 1953), and Albert H. Marckwardt, "Folk Speech in Indiana and Adjacent States," *Indiana History Bull.*, XVII (1940), 120–40, which is particularly interesting for its evidence of the extent of southern penetration into the state of Indiana. Mention may also be made of R. I. McDavid's "Postvocalic /–r/ in South Carolina: A Social Analysis," *AS*, XXIII (1948), 194–203, suggesting that the loss of *r* in the tidewater area is an aristocratic feature, and the same author's "The Position of the Charleston Dialect," *Pubns. of the Amer. Dialect Soc.*, XXIII (1955), 35–49. Untechnical but scholarly accounts of the more important dialect areas will be found in chapters contributed by Hans Kurath to *The Cultural Approach to History*, ed. C. R. Ware (New York, 1940), and *Regionalism in America*, ed. Merrill Jensen (Madison, 1951). The *Pronunciation of English in the Eastern States*, by Kurath and McDavid, is eagerly awaited.

2 Studies such as Frederic G. Cassidy, "Some New England Words in Wisconsin," *Language*, XVII (1941), 324–39, and Alva L. Davis and Raven I. McDavid, Jr., "Northwestern Ohio, a Transition Area," *ibid.*, XXVI (1950), 264–73, suggest, however, that the pattern may prove to be one of mixture and a scattered distribution of features, determined by the predominance of northern or midland (or southern) settlers in different communities. This is also the pattern suggested for Wyoming in Wilson O. Clough, "Some Wyoming Speech Patterns," *AS*, XXIX (1954), 28–35.

of American English, and that, let us say, or most of the state of New York, which on the basis of pronunciation is a part of General American. But such inconsistencies between lexical and phonological criteria are probably inevitable, since words are more easily transferred than regional types of pronunciation.

In the present state of our knowledge it seems best to recognize seven regional dialects in the United States:

1. *Eastern New England.* This includes the whole or parts of states that lie to the east of the Connecticut River in Massachusetts and Connecticut and east of the Green Mountains in Vermont. While all features of the dialect are not uniform in their distribution we may recognize as characteristic the retention of a rounded vowel in words like *hot* and *top*, which the rest of the country has unrounded to a shortened form of the *a* in *father*, the use of the broad *a* in *fast, path, grass,* etc., and, as we have seen, the loss of the *r* in *car, hard,* etc., except before vowels (*carry, Tory*). Boston is its focal area.[3]

2. *New York City.* Although often considered a part of the Eastern New England dialect, the speech of New York City and adjacent counties is on the whole quite different.[4] While it has generally lost the *r*, *cot* and *caught* are phonemically contrasted [kɑt, kɔt] since the *o* in words like *cot* and *top*, before voiceless stops, is almost always unrounded. The pronunciation of *curl* like *coil, third* as *thoid* is the characteristic most distinctive of New York City in the popular mind, although it should be added that among cultivated New Yorkers *curl* and *coil* are phonemically distinct [kɜɪl, kɔɪl].

3. *Middle Atlantic.* This includes the eastern third of Pennsylvania below the Northern-Midland line, the southern half of New Jersey, the northern half of Delaware, and the adjacent parts of Maryland. It preserves the *r* in all positions, has the unrounded vowel in *forest* as well as in *hot*, always pronounces [æ] in *fast, ask, grass,* etc. In all these features except the unrounded vowel in words like *forest* and *closet* it agrees with General American. Philadelphia is its focal area.

4. *Western Pennsylvania.* We may ultimately find it better to speak of this area as Western Midland when we know how far westward it extends beyond the Pennsylvania line. It spreads into Western Maryland and the adjacent parts of West Virginia on the south. In its over-all pattern it belongs to General American, with the *r* always pronounced, and with [æ] in *ask, path,* etc. *Cot* and *caught* are generally homonyms [kɒt].

5. *Southern Mountain.* It is not possible as yet to mark with confidence the limits of this area, especially on its southern and western boundaries.

---

[3] A focal area is one which because of its political, commercial, cultural or other importance (e.g., social) has influenced the speech of surrounding areas. *Tonic* (soft drink), for instance, has spread apparently only to communities served by distributors whose headquarters are in Boston.

[4] See Hubbell, *op. cit.,* p. 3: Except for a small minority of New Yorkers "divergences from the New England pattern are far more numerous than similarities."

It includes, however, all of West Virginia except the counties bordering on Pennsylvania and Maryland, the mountain regions of Virginia and North Carolina, most of Kentucky and Tennessee, with a small portion of the contiguous states to the south. Settled first from Pennsylvania and later from the South, the region shows in its speech the mixed character which is to be expected under the circumstances. Thus the r is sounded as in Midland, but [ar] is generally pronounced [aɛ], or in the southern part of the area [aə, a] as in many parts of the South. It is impossible at present to say whether it should be considered a variety of Midland or of Southern, and while it appears to be a Midland type modified by Southern, it seems best for the present to designate it by a name that is mainly topographical in character.

6. *Southern.* The Southern dialect covers a large area, the old plantation country, and it would be unreasonable to expect uniformity in it. Important focal areas are the Virginia Piedmont and the low country near the coast of South Carolina. In many districts it agrees with eastern New England in the loss of r finally and before consonants, as in *car* and *hard,* but tends to go even further and omit the r before a word beginning with a vowel, as in *far away* [fɑː ə'we]. But it does not have the rounded vowel in words like *top* and *hot,* or the broad a in *grass, dance.* In the latter words it shows a preference for [æə, æ [5]]. A distinctive feature of the Southern dialect is the treatment of the diphthong in *out.* Instead of the usual [aʊ] the Southern speaker begins this diphthong with [æ] before voiced consonants and finally, while in Virginia and South Carolina this diphthong takes the form [əʊ, ʌʊ] before voiceless consonants. Equally characteristic is the so-called Southern drawl. This is not only a matter of slower enunciation, but involves a diphthongization or double diphthongization of stressed vowels. In its most pronounced form this results in *yes* becoming [jɛɪs] or [jejəs], *class* becoming [klæɪs] or [klæjəs], etc. Final consonant groups are likely to suffer from a weakened articulation: *las', kep', fin',* etc. for *last, kept, find,* especially in substandard use. There are considerable local differences in the speech of the South, enabling a southerner at times to tell from a short conversation the particular state which another southerner comes from. But a northerner can seldom do this.

7. *General American.* General American is characterized by the flat a (in *fast, path,* etc.), the unrounded vowel in *hot, top,* etc., the retention of a strong r in all positions, and less tendency than British English to introduce a glide after the vowels [e] and [o], *late, note.* The dipthong heard in the Southern British pronunciation of words like *note, go* [əʊ] is absent from most parts of General American. All the regions enumerated above except eastern New England, metropolitan New York, and Southern are often spoken of as constituting General American. Local preference for cer-

[5] In the southern and eastern part of West Virginia the influence of Virginia speech is strong.

tain words or expressions does not preclude familiarity with other expressions for the same thing. A Philadelphian who usually says *baby coach* also knows *baby carriage* and may occasionally use it. The general pattern is felt in the major features mentioned, especially the flat *a* and the retention of the /r/ phoneme. In this wider sense General American covers about two thirds of the area of the United States and contains two thirds of the total population. It has been called "the most distinctly American manner of speaking." [6]

The most plausible attempt to account for the different dialects of this country is that which seeks the explanation in a study of the districts in England from which the earliest settlers came.[7] If this explanation is valid, we must believe that the English spoken by the first colonists—mainly those who came during the seventeenth century—determined the speech of the communities in which they settled, and that later accretions to the population of districts already occupied were made sufficiently gradually to be assimilated to the speech that had become established there. There is nothing in the facts to contradict this assumption. Now, the nucleus of the New England colonies was in the district around Massachusetts Bay, and the earliest settlements in the South were in the tidewater district of Virginia. It is fortunately for just these sections that we have the fullest information concerning the English homes of the earliest settlers. In the *Atlas of the Historical Geography of the United States* [8] the evidence has been collected. Of the settlers in New England before 1700, 1281 have been traced to their source in England, and for Virginia during the same period the English homes have been found for 637. These numbers, to be sure, are not large, but it is believed that the group of colonists identified in each case is representative of the two settlements. The result shows that the predominant element in New England was from the southeastern and southern counties of England.[9] Sixty-one per cent of those traced are accounted

[6] Hans Kurath, *American Pronunciation* (Oxford, 1928; *S.P.E. Tract No. XXX*), p. 286. This brief essay contains a convenient enumeration of the principal phonological features of the main dialects, as do G. P. Krapp, *The English Language in America* (2v., New York, 1925), I, 37–42, and C. K. Thomas, *An Introduction to the Phonetics of American English* (New York, 1947), pp. 155–60.

[7] For an excellent statement of this view see Hans Kurath, "The Origin of the Dialectal Differences in Spoken American English," *Modern Philology*, XXV (1928), 385–95.

[8] Prepared by Charles O. Paullin and John K. Wright (Washington and New York, 1932), pp. 46–7. To this may now be added Marcus L. Hansen, *The Atlantic Migration, 1607–1860* (Cambridge, Mass., 1940) and the same author's account of the settlement of New England contributed to the *Handbook of the Linguistic Geography of New England* mentioned on p. 458.

[9] "The number of settlers from London for New England was 193, or 15 per cent; for Virginia 179, or 28 per cent. The counties (with numbers) sending the most settlers to New England are as follows: Norfolk 125, Suffolk 116, Kent 106, Essex 100, Devon 76, Wiltshire 69; to Virginia, Gloucester 44, Kent 42, Yorkshire 30, and Lancaster 22. Of the emigrants from Gloucester both to New England and Virginia more than half came from Bristol. Of the Norfolk emigrants to New England half came from Hingham and Norwich." (Paullin and Wright, *op. cit.*, p. 46.)

for by the larger counties mentioned in the footnote, and since the figures for the smaller counties are not given, we may conservatively say that two thirds of the New England colonists before 1700 came from the south of England, especially the southeast. For Virginia the percentage is not quite so large, but is still decisive. Forty-two per cent were derived from London, Gloucester, and Kent, all in the south. Again figures for the smaller counties are omitted. From the map which these statistics accompany, however, it appears that the south Midlands and the west were more fully represented among the settlers of Virginia than in the New England colonies. In any case, it is certain that more than 50 per cent of the Virginia settlers traced came from the southern half of England. The inference is that the English brought to New England and Virginia was that spoken in the southern parts of England, and that the similarity of the New England and Southern dialects in this country to present-day Standard English is due to the preponderance of settlers from the south of England in these colonies. The importance of Virginia in the later settlements of the South has already been pointed out, and doubtless accounts for the spread of the early Virginia form of speech in the southern states.

We unfortunately do not have the same sort of information about the early settlers in the middle colonies. But we are not without a basis for inference. We know that the Quakers played the principal part in the settlements along the Delaware, and that this sect had its largest following in the north of England and the north Midlands. We should expect a good many of the settlers in eastern Pennsylvania and the adjacent parts of New Jersey and Delaware to have come from the northern half of England. We know also that large numbers of Scotch-Irish settled in Pennsylvania and were later prominent in the settlement of parts of the South and the West. They were mostly Scots who had been settled for a few generations in northeastern Ireland. They, of course, spoke Northern English. The Germans, who formed a large element in the population of the middle colonies, acquired their English from the English-speaking colonists among whom they settled. It would seem likely that the population of the Middle States was much more northern than that of New England and Virginia, and that the preservation of the *r* and other characteristics of Northern English found in the dialect of these states is to be accounted for in this way. It may not be too much to assert that the prominence of the Scotch-Irish in the constant advance of the western frontier was an influential factor in carrying the form of English spoken in the middle colonies into the newer territories of the West and in making this speech the basis of General American.

In describing the principal dialect areas that can be distinguished in the language of this country we have spoken only of distinctive features of the pronunciation. This does not mean that there are no other local differences. There are also peculiarities of vocabulary or idiom that may repre-

sent a survival of some older form of expression or some special development whose origin cannot be traced. They are especially characteristic of
the popular speech. When a man calls a certain kind of cheese *smearcase*,
we suspect contact at some time with the Pennsylvania Dutch settlements.
In the neighborhood of Boston one may call for a *tonic* when he wants only
a *soft drink*. In different parts of the country he may get sugar in a *bag*,
a *sack*, or a *poke*, and he may either *carry* it or, in the South, *tote* it. The
Philadelphian uses the word *square* not only for a small city park but also
for what Baedeker describes as "a rectangular mass of buildings bounded
by four streets," and what is elsewhere known as a *block*. In most parts of
the country one *parks* a car, but until very recently he might *rank* it in
Trenton and, for all I know to the contrary, may still *file* it in a certain
little town in southern Delaware. Within a small area a number of interesting variants for the same thing can often be found in the half-hidden
recesses of popular speech. Thus in different New England communities
the *earthworm* exists under the name *angleworm, angledog, easworm* (with
variants *eastworm* and *easterworm*), *fishworm, mudworm,* and *rainworm*.[10]
There are also odd deviations of idiom from the standard speech. Such are
the Middle Western *phone up* and *I want in,* or the expression reported
from South Dakota, "I got up at six o'clock this morning although I don't
belong to get up until seven." It would be easy to multiply local peculiarities of word or phrase in all parts of America, as in other countries. In
this country they are not always genuine examples of dialect, since they
are not peculiar to a particular dialectal region, but may occur in numerous parts of the country, often at a considerable distance from one
another. In any case they should not by themselves be made the basis for
distinguishing major dialect areas.

In connection with this discussion of American dialects it is necessary to
recall what was said above about the general uniformity of the English language in this country. The differences between the English of one section
and that of another are not great. The universal spread of education in modern times and the absence of any sharp differentiation of social classes in
this country are not favorable to the development or maintenance of dialect.
While a southerner or a man from "down East" can usually be recognized
by his speech, there are large sections of the country in which it would be
impossible to tell within a thousand miles the district from which an individual came. That such differences as exist are more noticeable in the
East and are greater from north to south than from east to west is
but a natural consequence of the geographical configuration of colonial
America. . . .

[10] Cf. Rachel S. Harris, "New England Words for the Earthworm," *American Speech,*
VIII, No. 4 (1933), 12–17, and maps 139 and 140 in Kurath, *Word Geography,* mentioned above.

Study Questions

1. Consult the Preface to *Webster's Third New International Dictionary* to find out what regional restrictions it designates. How do these areas compare with those in Kurath's *Word Geography of the Eastern United States?*

2. What principle of name formation is illustrated by *Delmarva,* in "Delmarva peninsula"?

3. Which colonies did the original settlers of your community come from or, if you live in the Eastern United States, which division of the colonies does your community belong to? What evidence are you aware of, in place-names, for example, of the districts in England or in the Eastern United States from which settlers came to your community? Are you familiar with other characteristics of pronunciation, vocabulary, or idiom which identify your area? Record and classify them as Baugh does.

4. If any of the articles listed in the first footnote deal with the area in which you live or one with which you are familiar, read one such article and note to what extent the author's findings agree with your own observation. Can you add evidence to support him? Do you find contradictory evidence? Can you suggest an explanation for any differences between the author's observations and your own?

5. Do you know any local expressions which you realize are characteristic of your area, such as names of food? If so, can you explain how such terms became established? Consult *Webster's Third New International Dictionary,* the word geographies cited in this book, and the historical facts about the community.

6. Do any of your college friends or teachers from different areas use different names for things or different pronunciations from those used in your own town? Do the general facts given by Baugh serve to explain the variations?

7. John Steinbeck in *The Grapes of Wrath* has a migratory worker comment that "ever'body says words different," Arkansas folks and "Oklahomy folks says 'em different," and a Massachusetts "lady . . . said 'em differentest of all." How do the facts given by Baugh explain the regional differences between Oklahoma or Arkansas and Boston speech?

13. THE WAY WE TALK
Raven I. McDavid, Jr.

In the following article, which originally appeared in the New York *Times Magazine* in 1950, Professor McDavid describes some of the procedures followed by interviewers for the *Linguistic Atlas of the United States*. His discussion enables the reader to see where the substantiating evidence for many of Professor Baugh's generalizations comes from.

"Just one more question, Ma'am," the Government agent said, pencil poised over his notebook. "Do you folks have a sugar bush?"

The woman stirring up the fire in her Indiana farm kitchen drew herself up in surprise. "Young man, don't you know that sugar don't come from no bush?"

The agent was no less surprised. In his Michigan home town, sugar did come from a "bush"—a grove of sap-running trees. But between Michigan and this southern Indiana farm region some barrier to understanding had occurred in what he had always assumed to be a common language.

Scholars who have been making a systematic study of American dialects would explain it this way: The Government agent had gone beyond an isogloss.

The term "isogloss" has been developed by linguistic geographers—students of the local variations in a language spoken over a wide area—as a means of interpreting their data. When they plot on maps the names for simple, everyday objects they notice that some words (or grammatical constructions, or pronunciations) are confined to a certain area. An isogloss is the line surrounding the area in which the word is used. Isoglosses might be compared to the meteorologist's "isotherms" or "isobars"—lines of equal temperature or barometric pressure.

For the last two decades trained investigators have been recording the living language of English-speaking North America and plotting its isoglosses. Inaugurated in 1930 under the sponsorship of the American Council of Learned Societies and directed by Professor Hans Kurath of the University of Michigan, The Linguistic Atlas of the United States and Canada now has material from about 800 communities in twenty-four states and five Canadian provinces along the entire Atlantic seaboard.

Adapting techniques that have been used successfully in Europe, the atlas relies on personal interviews with selected natives of representative communities. Interviews are conducted by the investigators in as near an approximation to ordinary conversation as they can achieve, and the data for each item are recorded in a phonetic alphabet designed to show minute differences in speech sounds.

In each community the people interviewed are chosen to represent the natural local usage of various age and educational levels. Usually there are two interviews in each community, one with a member of the oldest living native generation who has a minimum of education and travel, the other with someone younger, or better educated, or both. In large centers, or those with definite social prestige, there are interviews with college-trained or otherwise well-read natives. Although interviews are limited to those whose native language is English, an effort is made to check the local influence of foreign-language settlements by including people of Dutch descent in the Hudson Valley, German in central Pennsylvania, Scandinavian and Finnish in Minnesota.

Investigators for the atlas generally have worked outside the areas where they grew up. Although this has been largely accidental, there are real advantages. A South Carolinian like myself, for example, may take for granted both words and pronunciations he has been accustomed to, and in his own region may overlook much significant data; in an environment where the speech patterns and the entire community life are strange, he will be more alert. Natives concede to the outsider the right to ask about the simple things of everyday life which they might expect someone from their region to know.

Ideally, an interviewer should gather all his material without telling what he is after until he is through. In practice, curiosity seldom will wait; so the interviewer usually says he is after information about old times, especially the old names people used to call things but don't use any more. Following this procedure, he concentrates on the vocabulary items, leaving pronunciation and grammar items to be picked up at the end of the interview if he has not caught them in free conversation.

The items in the atlas questionnaire deal with topics of everyday conversation—the time of day, the weather, household and furniture, the farm, tools and implements, clothing, topography, farm animals and ways of calling them, crops, cooking, fruits and vegetables, wild animals and insects, trees and shrubs, kinship and social relations, body parts, health and disease, religion and superstition, business and sports.

The Michigan man's term "sugar bush" is familiar enough to people of New York State, where the largest group of early Michigan settlers came from. In fact the term with its less widely used synonym "sap bush," seems to have originated in the Hudson Valley—"bush" being an English adaptation of the Dutch *busch* or *bosch* meaning "grove."

"Sugar bush" is rarely heard in New Jersey, but in Pennsylvania it is the normal term throughout the Yankee settlements that make up the northern tier of counties. In the Middle West (in places where the tree occurs) it is heard in those areas settled by Yankee and York Staters—Michigan,

Wisconsin, the northern counties of Indiana and Illinois, and the Western Reserve in Ohio. But in southern Indiana, where the Michigan man was making his Government survey, the local term was probably "sugar camp," which is common in the Ohio Valley from Pittsburgh west, and occurs fairly far north in Ohio.

Study of such regional variations in speech has led to the conclusion that the Atlantic seaboard from Maine to Florida can be divided into eighteen dialect areas, set off by isoglosses that approximately coincide. (No two isoglosses coincide exactly; it is axiomatic in linguistic geography that every word has its own history.)

In crossing a dialect boundary a common object may take on an almost inconceivable variety of names. Window shades, for example, are popularly known as "curtains" in the North and South but as "blinds" in the Midland. The New England "stone wall" becomes a "stone fence" in Pennsylvania and western New York, a "rock" fence from West Virginia south, a "stone row" in northern New Jersey. The Northern "milk pail" is a "bucket" in the Midland and South; if used for farm garbage it is respectively a "swill pail" and a "slop bucket." The water faucet is normally a "spicket" in the Midland and South; in New York State, "spigot" (as it is usually pronounced here) refers to a wooden spout on a barrel. . . .

To me a "brat" is a noisy, poorly behaved child; when I once applied the name to some faculty children at a Midwestern university, a colleague almost started a fight with me. I later learned that in the part of Indiana he came from one never uses "brat" if a child is legitimate.

Words of course spread with the people who use them, following routes of migration. Since the English have not investigated their dialects as systematically as we have ours, it is difficult to trace our dialect words to particular British dialects. But the northern Connecticut "angle-dog" and the Rhode Island "eace-worm" are Devon and Kent names, respectively, for the earthworm.

Despite these various examples, and the misunderstandings they sometimes create, one must not exaggerate them. The fact is that any native speaker of American English usually will be pretty well understood in any American community. Differences in pronunciation are rarely so great as to cause ambiguity, and all Americans have in common the overwhelming bulk of their grammar and their vocabulary. English-speaking North America is probably the largest and most populous area in the world in which all local dialects are mutually intelligible. In fact, by comparison with most European and Asiatic languages, we may hardly be said to possess any dialects at all.

The reasons for the overwhelming similarities, as well as the sharp differences, in American speech are found in the settlement history and social structure of the country. From the beginning, every American community was characterized by dialect mixture, having settlers from many parts of the British Isles. Most of the early settlers, too, were middle class—true peasants were about as scarce as true aristocrats—who almost certainly spoke regional rather than strictly local varieties of British English. It is probable that the colonies in 1776 had a higher percentage of literacy than the mother country, and literacy always blunts the edge of dialects.

The frontier was another leveler of dialect differences, as it was of other social differences. The development of mass education and of means of transportation and communication—the rivers, the railroads, the automobile, the airplane, the radio, and now television—have familiarized people in one section with the way Americans in other sections talk. Nor must we forget national magazines, national advertising, and the nationally-distributed mail-order catalogue. When farmers in all sections buy "window shades" by mail they soon forget that their parents called them "curtains" or "blinds."

Nor is movement merely geographical. There is nothing approximating the sharp class lines that distinguish social groups in Europe. It is significant that the most sharply divergent native American dialect is that of the Gullah Negroes, spoken in isolated communities in the oldest settled part of the United States, among a minority group shut off from the patterns of the dominant group by a caste system founded on chattel slavery and maintained by legal segregation and for a long time by peonage.

All the influences affecting the development of dialects—national origins, migration and metropolitan prestige—can be found in operation in New York State. The Linguistic Atlas materials show that the state includes parts of three of the eighteen dialect areas of the Atlantic seaboard: Greater New York; the Dutch, English and Palatinate German sphere of the Hudson Valley (including east Jersey); and the up-state Yankee extension of northwestern New England.

The speech of New York City, like that of most metropolitan areas, is more easily identified by its pronunciation than by its vocabulary. Whatever the language, it seems that nearly every large city lacks most or all of the folk vocabulary of the surrounding countryside. Only one expression recorded by the atlas seems peculiar to Greater New York: "school gets out" at three o'clock alongside the more widespread "school lets out" or "school closes." (Long Island has one peculiar term—"pightle," rhyming with "title"—for a barnyard.)

But the chief influence of New York City on vocabulary has been the spreading of Hudson Valley terms through commercial channels. The Manhattan term "round clam" has spread along the Sound to the Connecticut River; the Hudson Valley Dutch term "pot cheese" for cottage cheese —a commercial term in New York City—has spread as far as the Finger Lakes, replacing the Western New England "Dutch cheese."

The up-state area has few words which it does not share with either the Hudson Valley or New England. To the older people a frying pan is generally a "spider," a pantry a "buttry," a funnel a "tunnel"; and an un-raised doughnut is usually a "fried cake."

The usual question asked of students of American English is: "Do you think we will all talk alike some day?" We can only guess at the answer. It is true that all the forces of our civilization are tending to iron out local and social differences: increasing urbanization, easy travel, a higher average educational level, the radio, the moving pictures, national advertising and the mail-order catalogue.

On the other hand, several regional types of standard (or socially preferred) speech are fairly well established. With typical American democracy we generally consider each regional standard as good as the others—an attitude practically unknown in other countries: Southern British, Parisian French, Castilian Spanish are the norms encouraged by courts and academies; some American-Russian manuals prepared during the last war were condemned because they used grammatical forms and pronunciations not sanctioned by the Moscow authorities; Chiang Kai-shek's government would not stand having American soldiers taught any variety of Chinese except Peiping Mandarin.

But the standards of Boston, New York, Philadelphia, Richmond, Charleston, Atlanta, Chicago, St. Louis, San Francisco and Seattle are equally acceptable; and a person growing up in the area around such a community will develop a type of speech modeled on that of his own metropolitan area, not that of any other. We will see vocabulary differences go first, and education and communication will erase purely local pronunciations.

But a single type of pronunciation to which all Americans will conform? Probably never. The country is too big, the population too large, regional traditions too strong—and few people are willing to let an outsider dictate the way they should talk. No one in his right mind can imagine a Commissar of Pronunciation in Washington.

Study Questions

1. Look up *isogloss*. What is its etymology? What other words are derived from the two root words? Which root is directly related to speech and what other basic language terms are derived from it?

2. Why do investigators work outside their native area? Does your own observation and experience, outside your own area or in relation to strangers in your area, confirm the "real advantages" of the practice followed by investigators?

3. See how many of the topics covered by items in the atlas questionnaire you can illustrate by at least one variant to the term used in your region.

4. Of the common objects listed by McDavid, which of the terms given would you use? Which have you heard but would not use? Would you use a different term from any given?

5. If you have traveled in the United States, especially by automobile, what

unfamiliar terms have you noted for geographical features—*run*, as in *Bull Run*, *notch* as in *Franconia Notch*, and so forth; for road signs and instructions—"Look out—squeeze ahead"; for food—"toasted snails" (a kind of roll)? Has difference in terminology or in pronunciation ever caused any real confusion or difficulty? Do you agree that "any native speaker of American English usually will be pretty well understood in any American community"?

6. Do you find any influence of non-English-speaking groups upon the speech patterns of your community? If so, in what ways have these groups affected the topics of everyday conversation?

7. Is the preferred speech of your locality determined by the metropolitan area of which you are a part?

8. Have you observed enough retention of individual speech patterns by a person who has long resided in a region where those patterns are not current, to verify McDavid's concluding paragraph?

14. THE LINGUISTIC ATLASES: OUR NEW RESOURCE
Harold B. Allen

Professor Allen's observations about linguistic fieldwork result from many years of close association with the *Linguistic Atlas* project. This discussion of some of the applications of *Linguistic Atlas* data originally appeared in the *English Journal* for April, 1956.

A few years ago a teacher in South Carolina was pushing her less than enthusiastic pupils through a grammar drill book, painfully but relentlessly. The class struggled on to an exercise intended to teach the correct use of the negative of *ought*. Here the students found sentences with the approved construction *ought not*. But they found also some sentences with a construction they were supposed to cross out, *hadn't ought*. This the pupils had never seen or heard before, and they were delighted with it. True, the book said it was wrong, and teacher, as always, agreed with the book. But there it was—in the book—as plain as anything could be; and somehow it seemed marvelously sensible. *He hadn't intended to do it: He hadn't ought to do it. I hadn't wanted to go: I hadn't ought to go.* Why not? So within a week or two the puzzled teacher began to find more and more of her pupils using *hadn't ought*, pupils who up until then had used *ought not* with unconscious ease.

Such an incident can not happen in the future if teachers and textbook writers know and use the new data now becoming accessible to them. This is the body of facts about American English coming from the great research projects collectively designated the Linguistic Atlas of the United States and Canada.

Of course, this is not the first mass of information about American usage available to teachers of English. During the past forty years an increasing number of studies have effectively demonstrated the unreliability of much that had been accepted as truth. The NCTE itself has led in the publication of the significant and familiar studies by Sterling Andrus Leonard, Albert H. Marckwardt and Fred Walcott, and Charles C. Fries. Dozens of articles on specific items of usage have appeared in our own Council publications as well as in *Language, American Speech,* and a few other periodicals. Also there have been published the increasingly reliable commercial dictionaries and our first pronouncing lexicon, Kenyon and Knott's *Pronouncing Dictionary of American English.*

Now all this weight of evidence has had its clearly perceptible effects upon the handbooks and the school grammars. A comparison of those published in 1920 and those appearing since 1950 reveals a much higher proportion of sweet reasonableness, of honest recognition of the facts of linguistic life. But influential as this evidence has been, it generally has had one important limitation. On the whole, these studies and investigations of usage have assumed the validity of the criterion of national use, a criterion enunciated by the Scottish rhetorician Alexander Campbell in the late eighteenth century. Campbell insisted that national use must be one of the determinants of what is good usage. Following him, these studies assume that what is true in the determination of usage in a smaller country like England or France, with one cultural capital, is equally true for the vast United States with its cultural diversification and many cultural centers.

A second limitation of these studies is that generally they ignore the lexical and grammatical usage of the normal everyday, informal speech of cultivated people (though Leonard did record opinions classifying forms as "colloquial"). Part of this limitation, of course, is also the fact that these studies generally have not treated matters of pronunciation in informal speech. An exception, again, is Kenyon and Knott's dictionary, which did record conversational pronunciations reported by independent mail surveys.

These limitations are reflected naturally enough in the contents of the textbooks. The laudable improvement in the general treatment of usage is accompanied by conspicuous inadequacy in the treatment of any language matters having variations which correlate with geographical distribution. This improvement, furthermore, is offset also by the persistence of considerable misapprehension concerning various matters of pronunciation whether regional or not.

But any textbook or reference book with these inadequacies will soon be obsolete. Already valuable evidence about regional usage in words and grammar and pronunciation is beginning to emerge from the tremendous research activity within the framework of the Linguistic Atlas of the United States. Already enough evidence from this source is available so that textbook makers will shirk responsibility if they do not take these new facts into account.

Data on pronunciation

What is the Linguistic Atlas of the United States? It is not a single project; it is a number of regional research projects using similar procedures and collecting the same kinds of evidence, hence producing results that can be added together and compared.

Essentially this evidence is gathered like this. Using a tested selective sampling technique, linguistically trained fieldworkers interview native residents representing three groups, older and uneducated speakers, middle-aged secondary school graduates, and younger college graduates. From each of these persons information is sought about more than 800 language items (in the first project there were 1200). Each response is recorded in a finely graded phonetic transcription, so that all responses have value as pronunciation evidence. Some items are included for that reason only; others are included for their lexical or grammatical or syntactic significance. The basic list of items in the questionnaire is usually modified slightly in each area through the dropping of some which are irrelevant there and the adding of others significant there. (It is pointless to ask a North Dakota farmer what he calls the Atlantic round clam, a /kwáhɑg/, /kwɔhɔg/, or /kwəhɔg/. He never heard of it by any name!) But this basic list is essentially the same countrywide, so that national comparative studies will be possible when the fieldwork is finished.

At present, organizations to gather this evidence have been effected in eight different areas: New England, Middle Atlantic States, South Atlantic States, North Central States, Upper Midwest, Rocky Mountain States, Pacific Coast, and Louisiana. The New England Atlas has been completed and published. From it and the unpublished materials of the other eastern surveys has come the evidence presented by Hans Kurath in 1949 in his *Word Geography of the Eastern United States* and by E. B. Atwood in 1953 in his *Verb Forms of the Eastern United States*. Derivative articles by Raven I. McDavid, Jr., Atwood, Alva Davis, Walter Avis, Thomas Pearce, David Reed, Marjorie Kimmerle, and others have made public additional usage evidence in *American Speech, College English* and *The English Journal, Orbis, Language,* and *Language Learning*. The volume by Kurath and McDavid on the pronunciation of the Eastern United States is shortly to appear, and Mrs. McDavid is about to complete her dissertation on the verb forms of the North Central and Upper Midwest regions. These publications, together with the Atlas files, constitute a vast accumulation of data for the use of teachers and textbook writers.

When we look at the information now available about regional usage we find that probably the most important single fact is the reconstruction of the picture of American language areas. It has been assumed for years that we have Eastern, Southern, and Northern (sometimes called General American) dialect divisions in this country. But evidence from the Atlantic field records presented by Kurath has led to the recognition of a quite different structure consisting of Eastern New England, Northern, Midland, and Southern, with various subdivisions in each region and, of course, with some overlapping of regions. Midland is the speech of the Pennsylvania-Delaware settlement area and of its derivative areas in central Ohio, northern Indiana, central Illinois, southern Iowa, and so on. It exists also in the variety called South Midland, which extends south along the Appalachians as "Mountain English" and into southern Illinois, Missouri, Arkansas, eastern Oklahoma, and eastern Texas.

For significant matters of pronunciation I would suggest reference to McDavid's excellent article, "Some Social Differences in Pronunciation," in *Language Learning* in 1953.[1] McDavid's thesis here is that, although certain pronunciations may lack recognition or distribution nationally, they can enjoy high prestige in a given region through the influence of such a focal center as Boston, New York, Philadelphia, Richmond, or Charleston. Differences in pronunciation, in other words, are not merely a matter of social and educational background; they may also be related to geographical differences.

For example, despite the tendency of the schools toward spelling-pronunciation, the unaspirated forms /wɪp/ "whip," /wɪlbæro/ "wheelbarrow," and /wɔrf/ "wharf" are in common cultured use in the Midland area and, as a matter of fact, occur sporadically elsewhere among cultured speakers. A few years ago a teacher in Utica, N.Y., yielding to the probably normal impulse to consider one's own speech or that of a textbook as the proper one, wrote to *College English* that she had never observed a person of true culture who lacked the /hw/ cluster in such words. Yet, as McDavid has observed, this teacher would have had to go only a few miles south to central Pennsylvania to observe thousands of cultivated speakers who say /wɪp/ and /wɪlbæro/; indeed, even in her own community the Atlas' cultivated informant is recorded as having /w/ and not /hw/ in these words. In the function words, of course, the customary lack of stress has resulted in the loss of aspiration everywhere, not just in certain areas; yet in my own state of Minnesota the new guide for instruction in the language arts enjoins the teacher to insist upon distinguishing /wɪč/ "witch" and /hwĭč/ "which" and /weðər/ "weather" and /hweðər/ "whether."

Similarly, the /hy/ consonant cluster in *humor* reveals primary geographical distribution. This cluster commonly occurs in Northern speech,

[1] IV, 102–16.

but elsewhere in the nation the usual form among all speakers is simply /yumər/.

In Northern American English and in South Carolina, probably in some other sections, a restressing of the second vowel in *because* has led to the form /bɪkɔ́z/ as usual among cultivated speakers. Yet many teachers, likely influenced by spelling and lacking the information forthcoming from the Atlas studies, insist punctiliously upon /bɪkɔz/.

The sounds represented by the letter *o* in *orange*, *horrid*, and *forest* also vary according to region. In much of New York state and in eastern Pennsylvania, for example, an unround /ɑ/ appears instead of the more common /ɔ/. Not long ago a teacher came to Minnesota from New York state and promptly began insisting that her pupils say only /ɑrɪnj̆/ and /fɑrɪst/; and recently a textbook came out with the same injunction, that the only correct form is /ɑrɪnj̆/.

The diphthong /ɪu/, mistakenly called "long *u*," offers another case in point. In the South, as in British English, a strongly consonantal /y/ beginning is heard in this diphthong in post-alveolar contexts, as in *newspaper*, *tube*, and *due* or *dew*. But in the North this beginning is quite weak, often almost imperceptible, and it is gone completely in northeastern New England and in Midland. Yet many teachers in the Middle West diligently drill their pupils in the pronunciation /nyuz/ instead of their normal /nuz/. More than half my own students each year report that this was their high school experience, although on only a few of them did the attempted inoculation "take." (To prevent misunderstanding, it should be clear that there can of course be no objection to the form /nyuz/ where it is the normal prestige form. What is objectionable is well-meaning but unenlightened tampering with acceptable speech.)

The same kind of thing, but with a much more complicated geographical picture, occurs with the pronunciation of a group of words spelled with *oo*. I should be surprised if many of the readers of this article, or of the original audience hearing it read, would have for all of these words the same pronunciation which I, a native of southern Michigan, have: /rʊf, rʊt, hʊf, hʊp, hʊpɪŋ kɔf, kup, rum, brum, fud, spuk/ (with /ʊ/ as in *put* and /u/ as in *moon*). But I should also be surprised if you have not sometime been in a situation—on either the giving or the receiving end—where someone was being instructed to pronounce *root* and *roof*, perhaps even *soot*, with /u/ rather than /ʊ/. The Atlas files reveal a complicated distribution of these forms, each word having its own distinctive regional pattern; and nothing in this information supports the familiar injunctions.

Another vowel dilemma with historical roots in Middle English is that offered by *creek*. Many Northern teachers, probably swayed by the double *ee* spelling, for years have insisted upon their pupils learning the Southern standard pronunciation /krik/ despite the fact, which should be obvious to an objective listener in a Northern community and which is fully attested by the Atlas records, that the basic Northern form is /krɪk/. Even in Battle Creek, Michigan, I am informed, there is this attempt to lift at least the school population to the cultural heaven, Southern division, where /krik/ is the shibboleth.

There are numerous other moot matters of pronunciation upon which Atlas research now can provide information making possible an enlightened approach. I think, for instance, of such *loci critici* as /hɑg/ and /hɔg/, /rɑzbɛriz/ and /ræzbɛriz/, /grisi/ and /grizi/, /iðər/ and /ɑiðər/, /kɑfi/ and /kɔfi/, /kɑnt/ and /kænt/ and /kent/ "can't," /ves/ and /vɑz/, /kɛč/ and /kæč/, /wɑter/ and /wɔtər/, /tord/ and /təwɔrd/, /sɝˑəp/ and /sɪrəp/, /təmetoz/ and /təmɑtoz/, /rædɪš/ and /rədɪš/, and /dɪfθɪryə/ and /dɪpθɪryə/—for information about which the Atlas sources are invaluable.

Data on grammar and idiom

Then the category of grammar and idiom is another in which Atlas materials contribute to our knowledge about usage. As with pronunciation we quite humanly yield to the notion that what is standard or customary for us either is, or ought to be, standard for others. A recent rhetoric textbook for the college freshman course was written by two authors of southern background. They say, "*Bucket* is more likely to be the ordinary word [;] *pail* . . . a little more old-fashioned and endowed with more 'poetic' suggestions." Any freshman speaking Northern English who finds this statement on page 372 must find it rather puzzling, for to him *bucket* refers to some unfamiliar wooden vessel in a well and is a word invariably preceded by *old oaken*. The Atlas files provide evidence for a much more objective statement about the relationship between *bucket* and *pail*.

Again, more than one textbook writer has condemned *sick to one's stomach* in favor of *sick at one's stomach*, but the Atlas findings reveal *sick to* as the usual Northern locution and *sick at* as a Midland variant, along with *sick from* and *sick with* and *sick in*.

Even those who have confidently relied upon the data in the 1932 Leonard report will now need to revise their statements in the light of what Atlas evidence tells them about *depot* (~railroad station), *in back of* (~behind), *mad* (~angry), *off of* (~from), and *like* (~as if)—all of them rated as disputable usages by Leonard—as well as about the expressions *the dog wants in* and *all the further*, both of which actually are rated there as illiterate.

Now such matters of pronunciation and of vocabulary may readily be accepted by the teacher as likely to be clarified by research in regional language. We are accustomed to thinking of dialect as consisting of differences in sounds and words. Actually, regional linguistic studies may also considerably illumine certain other matters of high importance to the teacher, those in the field of grammar,

At least seven of the grammatical items that Leonard's monograph listed as disputable were included in the Atlas worksheets. These are *dived~ dove, I'll~I shall, eat~et, aren't I?~ain't I?~am I not?, it (he) don't ~doesn't, these kind~those kind,* and *sang~sung.* At least eight more Atlas items appeared in the group classified by Leonard as illiterate: *have drank~have drunk, began~begun, lay down~lie down, a orange~an orange, hadn't you ought~ought not you, run~ran, set down~sit down,* and *you was~you were.*

The Atlas records offer data, some of it surprising, about these items. For instance, the frequently found textbook admonition about the preterit *dove* implies that this is non-standard in contrast with the historical form *dived.* But the records show plainly that *dove* is the usual form among speakers of Northern English and *dived* is Midland and Southern. In other words, the present-day distinction is regional and not social.

But besides these items the Atlas files include comprehensive information about the social and regional distribution of many others that have been in controversy, such as the preterit forms *give* and *gave, did* and *done, dreamed* and *dremt, swam* and *swum, fitted* and *fit, shrank* and *shrunk, saw* and *seen, kneeled* and *knelt, taught* and *learned;* the participial forms *worn out* and *wore out, have taken* and *have took, I been thinking* and *I've been thinking, spoiled* and *spoilt, was bitten* and *was bit, have drove* and *have driven;* together with *you* and *you-all* and *it wasn't me* and *it wasn't I.*

Application of the data

For teachers of English, clearly the immediate application of this new source of information about our language is in the revision of previous statements about usage. In the simple interest of accuracy this revision is demanded. Those of us who have anything to do with the training of future teachers have the responsibility of using such revision in attention paid to usage items in our language and methods classes. The classroom teacher has the special responsibility of using the new information in class drills, in class discussion, and in the evaluation of student oral and written language. As the experience of the South Carolina teacher with *hadn't ought* indicates, the teaching of standard forms must be done in full awareness of frequency and distribution of the contrasting non-standard forms.

But the teacher's application ordinarily must result from revision of usage statements in books of reference and in textbooks. Those who prepare texts, workbooks, drill exercises, and the like cannot in all conscience ignore the findings of the Atlases. Such revision is normal, of course, in the editing procedure of the main dictionaries, which constantly note the new evidence in published research. Full use of Atlas evidence is being made in the Council's own projected dictionary, the *Dictionary of Cur-*

rent American Usage, under the direction of Professor James B. McMillan. Here is an example. Preliminary treatments of various items are sent by McMillan to members of the advisory committee. In a recent batch of treatments appeared this tentative statement about the phrase *all the farther:* "In the sense of 'as far as,' this phrase is often heard, especially in the popular speech of the West. Cultivated speakers and writers, however, still avoid it. The preferred locution, therefore, is *as far as.*"

After checking the Atlas record for the Upper Midwest, I was able to write McMillan that the imputation of western popularity to this expression, if not incorrect, needs clarification, for actually the incidence of its occurrence drops from about forty per cent in Iowa and twenty per cent in Minnesota to about four per cent in the area settled by the next wave of migration in the Dakotas and Nebraska. I could write him also that at least in the eastern half of the Upper Midwest area fifty per cent of the cultivated speakers use *all the farther.* When he receives additional data from the other regional atlases, he will be able to revise the treatment of this locution so as to represent much more accurately just where and by whom it is used.

But we may look forward to a second kind of application of Atlas materials in the classroom. It is high time to recognize the validity of some regional speech in the scope of standard American English. There *are* standard forms which are regional and not national. The label *dial.* in a dictionary does not necessarily consign a linguistic form to either the linguistic slums or the linguistic backwoods. If you want to refer to the strip of grass between the sidewalk and the street, you are driven to awkward circumlocution unless you use a dialect word; there simply is no national word for it. But the cultivated speakers who in various parts of the country call this strip of grass the *boulevard, berm, treelawn, curb, parking, terrace, curb strip, sidewalk plot,* or any of several other names would be surprised, if not disgruntled, to be told that they were not speaking standard English.

Recognizing the validity of our own regional speech as standard means also that we recognize the validity of the standard of speech of other regions. The time is surely long past when we need to take seriously such an unenlightened statement as this which appeared in a speech textbook several years ago: "There is perhaps no deviation from standard English that sounds as provincial and uncultivated as [the retroflex or inverted r-sound]. . . . Inverted sounds are not used in standard English pronunciation. They will do more to make one's speech sound uncultivated than any other one thing."

Students can be helped toward recognition of this regional validity through various kinds of inductive exercises, especially in the vocabulary. Through such an exercise students for the first time approach objectively the language of their family, their neighbors, the community leaders, and speakers of other areas whom they hear. This particular investigative activity, it may be observed, fits naturally also into a language arts program that seeks to draw upon community resources.

Then, finally, a further utilization of the Atlas data, possible in both college and secondary school, would be for the aim of developing awareness that language is a complex, changing, and always relative structure, not a set of absolutes. The use of regional language information can help our students attain a desirable degree of objectivity in their observation of language matters, can help them see that language is essentially a system of habits related at every point to non-language habits of behavior. And this kind of awareness, this kind of objectivity, is at the heart of a disciplined and informed ability to use language effectively for the communication of meaning.

Study Questions

1. Does Allen's story of students adopting "hadn't ought" recall any experience in your own schooling in which you were cautioned against "errors" which were not current in your community? What method would you suggest by which a teacher could determine which deviations from standard English are serious and frequent enough to require special attention?

2. Have you ever been drilled on any of the pronunciation "problems" cited? Did the person or persons "correcting" your pronunciation come from another region in which the "correct" pronunciation was used? If not, were you aware of personal attitudes, such as a desire to be "elegant," which resulted in overzealous purism? A Middle Western school teacher held up as an ideal a professor from the East. The teacher said to her students: "*You* would probably say *p'raps*, and *I* should probably say *per-haps*, but Miss Lowell says *pair-hops*." What would Allen say about that teacher's attitude?

3. Look up in *Webster's Third International* half a dozen of the expressions you have been taught to avoid but which you consider standard in your region to see whether they are listed as standard, regional standard, or regional substandard.

4. From common expressions or pronunciations which are sometimes questioned, choose one which you have verified as standard, one which is standard regional, and one which is substandard. Ask a dozen college students to classify them under the three categories. Do you find any consistent relation between a person's social, educational, and geographical background and his sense of what is regarded as acceptable by authoritative lexicographers, according to recorded usage?

5. Check the entry for *all the farther* in Bryant's *Current American Usage* in light of Allen's discussion. What conclusions can you draw about the use of data from the *Linguistic Atlas*?

6. How do Allen's article and the other articles in this section demonstrate the fact that "language is a complex, changing, and always relative structure, not a set of absolutes"?

15. REGIONAL AND LOCAL WORDS

Hans Kurath

The words discussed below are taken from A Word Geography of the Eastern
United States (1949), edited by Professor Kurath. The factual details are based
on the field reports of investigators for the Linguistic Atlas.

In the present chapter the regional and local vocabulary is arranged from
the point of view of meaning. All synonyms for one and the same thing or
situation are here treated together under one heading, so that the geographic variations in vocabulary can be seen at a glance. . . .

Whenever it seemed desirable to give a more precise indication of the
area in which a word is current, the names of bays, rivers, watersheds,
mountain ranges, and other topographical features have been employed to
orient the reader. . . .

The social distribution of words is also carefully noted. Some are used
only by the simple folk—especially the strictly local expressions; some are
restricted to the cultured. Others are current among the simple folk and
the large middle class, or among the cultured and the middle class. Others
again can be heard from all the people in a given area. Whenever no comment is offered on social distribution it is to be assumed that the word has
general currency within the stated geographic limits.

Care has been exercised to point out whether a given expression is in
general use, common, infrequent, or rare; also, whether it is spreading or
receding, an innovation or a relic. In some cases the apparent focus of
dissemination has been identified—at least tentatively.

Striking trends from local to regional usage and from regional to national
currency are duly noted. The general trend in the American vocabulary is
unmistakably in these directions.

It will be observed that some words occur in two or more geographically
separate areas, partly as the result of independent importation from the
British Isles, partly as survivals in conservative areas.

Although pains have been taken to describe the geographic and the social
spread of each word treated here as accurately as possible, many details—
especially scattered occurrences—have not always been mentioned. The
need for brevity and a desire to emphasize the more striking features of
distribution have prompted this simplification. . . .

The wealth of detail recorded for the Linguistic Atlas is exhibited in the
figures that are included in this chapter. The reader should bear in mind

that more than 1,200 informants were interviewed in the Eastern States and that all statements made below concerning the currency of words rest upon this extensive record of usage.

quarter of eleven

Of, *to*, and *till* are all used over large areas in this phrase.

In the Northern area, on Delaware Bay, and on Chesapeake Bay *of* and *to* stand side by side in this expression. *Quarter of* predominates in the Boston area and in the Hudson Valley, elsewhere *of* and *to* seem to be in balance.

The greater part of the Southern area (Eastern Virginia, northeastern North Carolina, and the Low Country of South Carolina) has exclusively *quarter to*, the South Midland *quarter till*. The Midland *till* has been carried seaward along the Cape Fear and the Peedee rivers and even competes with the Southern *to* on the Neuse.

Pennsylvania presents a picture of great confusion. In the central part of the state the characteristic Midland *till* is still common, but it is yielding ground in the east to *of*, which now predominates in Philadelphia and the southeastern part of the state; and in the Pittsburgh area *of* and *to* are gradually superseding *till*.

(the wind is) rising

Along the Atlantic coast, from New Brunswick to Cape Fear in North Carolina, the wind is said to *breeze up*, *breeze on* (less commonly simply to *breeze*) when it gets stronger. This is one of a number of seafaring terms that are current the full length of the Atlantic coast but are known only to those who live within easy reach of the sea.

living room

In all the Eastern states *living room* and *sitting room* (*settin' room* among the common folk) are the usual names for the room in which the family gathers evenings, and receives and entertains friends. *Sitting room* is now rather a rural expression. *Living room* is fully established in the cities and among the younger generation in the country.

Only the larger houses have (or had) a "best" room for formal occasions such as weddings, funerals, and the reception of honored guests, which is known as the *parlor* from Maine to the Carolinas. The old-time *parlor* is now largely a thing of the past. Some now call it the *front room*.

All these terms are current nearly everywhere in the Eastern States, but with varying frequency.

In the simple homes of the piedmont and the mountains of North Carolina (also on the Peedee in South Carolina, rarely in West Virginia) the living room is called the *big-house* or the *great-house,* on the Eastern Shore of Virginia the *big-room.* . . .

andirons

The andirons in the fireplace are generally known as *fire dogs, dogs,* or *dog irons* in the greater part of the South, the South Midland, and in southwestern Pennsylvania. *Dog irons* predominates from the lower James River (the Norfolk area) to the lower Neuse in North Carolina and in the South Midland, *fire dogs* in South Carolina and the greater part of North Carolina.

Scattered instances of *fire dogs* occur also in Eastern Pennsylvania, and the term is not unknown in New England; but the usual expression in Pennsylvania and the North is *andirons,* which has also become well established on Chesapeake Bay and on the Potomac. As a literary term *andirons* is current also in Southern cities.

In the *andirons* area the common folk not infrequently say *hand irons,* especially (1) in an area extending from Delaware Bay to the Rappahannock in Virginia and (2) in the northern counties of Pennsylvania.

mantel shelf

The shelf over the opening of the fireplace is known as the *mantel* or *mantel piece* in most parts of the Eastern States. (These terms also denote the entire decorative frame of the opening, the uprights together with the shelf.) In eastern Virginia and adjoining parts of North Carolina, except for the central part of the Virginia Piedmont, *shelf* is widely used instead of, or by the side of, *mantel (piece).*

The South Midland, including the drainage basin of the Kanawha, has the distinctive expression *fire board,* which has spread down to the Atlantic between the Cape Fear and the Peedee rivers.

In the vicinity of Raleigh, North Carolina, the strictly local term *frontis* is in use.

roller shades

Roller shades are a recent invention. The term *(roller) shades* has general currency in the Hudson Valley, the Virginia Piedmont, and the greater part of the Carolinas, and it is widely used in urban areas elsewhere. But in large parts of the Eastern States people still pull down the *curtains* or the *blinds.*

Curtain is widely used in this sense (1) in New England and the New England settlement area, (2) in the Philadelphia area, and (3) on Chesapeake Bay and in the coastal part of northeastern North Carolina. Scattered instances of it have also been noted in the Midland.

The Midland term is *blinds.* In the Philadelphia area and on Delamarvia *blinds* competes with *curtains;* in the remainder of Pennsylvania and in all of the South Midland *blinds* has complete sway. There this term is never used as a synonym of shutters; only the *curtains* area has *blinds* in this sense.

clothes closet

Throughout the New England settlement area and the North Midland, including the Shenandoah Valley and northern West Virginia, *clothes press* is still a common term for the clothes closet in rural areas. On Narragansett Bay, where *closet* is the usual designation for the pantry, and in Western Pennsylvania and the adjoining counties of Ohio and West Virginia, *clothes press* is current among all social classes in the country as well as in the cities. On the other hand, the urbanized areas around Boston, in the lower Connecticut Valley, in the lower Hudson Valley, and around Philadelphia now use (*clothes*) *closet* almost entirely. Since the Southern area has no trace of *clothes press,* the common occurrence of this expression on the Eastern Shore must be due to earlier Philadelphia influence, even though this term is now rare there.

store room

Many houses have a room in the attic or the cellar for storing old furniture and utensils. In the South Atlantic States we find a variety of terms to denote it: *lumber room, plunder room, trumpery room, junk room, catch-all.*

Lumber room is the Virginia Piedmont and Tidewater term, which is now current also on the Eastern Shore of Virginia (but not of Maryland) and in the Valley of Virginia. The greater part of North Carolina and adjoining parts of South Carolina have *plunder room,* and this term is not uncommon, by the side of *lumber room,* in Virginia south of the James. From Albemarle Sound to the lower Neuse *trumpery room* is current, on Delaware Bay, *catch-all.*

The expressions for this storeroom were not systematically recorded in the Middle Atlantic States and in New England, except for the eastern half of Pennsylvania. *Store room* appears to be the usual term in the Philadelphia area, *junk room* from the Susquehanna westward. *Junk room* is in use also in the Pennsylvania settlements of the piedmont of North Carolina and on the Cape Fear River by the side of *plunder room.*

porch

The screened porch and the sleeping porch are recent additions to man's comfort; they are known everywhere as *porches.* The unscreened porches of earlier days are also widely called *porches,* but other names are current, too: *piazza, stoop, veranda, gallery,* sometimes with different shades of meanings.

Piazza is found (1) in all of New England and, though less commonly, in the Hudson Valley and on Long Island; (2) in the Carolinas and south of the lower James in Virginia; (3) in southern Maryland west of Chesapeake Bay. The occurrence of *piazza* in southern Maryland permits the inference that this expression was once current all the way from Chesapeake Bay to the Georgia coast and that in the section of the Virginia Tidewater lying between the Potomac and the James, which is under Piedmont influence, the term has been given up.

The old-time *piazza* is usually long and narrow and sheltered by a roof supported by pillars.

Stoop is in general use in the Dutch settlement area—the Hudson Valley, northern New Jersey, and Long Island; it is common to Western New England and the New England settlements of New York State and northern Pennsylvania and has spread into Eastern New England to the very door of Boston. From Narragansett Bay to Cape Cod and on the coast of Maine *stoop* is known, but little used.

Stoop is one of the few Dutch words that have become established beyond the limits of the Dutch settlement area. The reason for the adoption of *stoop* in New England is that the Dutch type of entry to the house, the raised platform, became fashionable in New England. To this day *piazza* and *stoop* mean different things in the New England area.

gutters (on the roof)

Gutters is in regular use on all social levels (1) in the Southern area, (2) in the Hudson Valley, Long Island, and nearly all of New Jersey, and (3) in Eastern New England. In southwestern Connecticut and in Philadelphia and vicinity *gutters* is now very common, but older regional expressions are still used by many. Elsewhere *gutters* is strictly a trade name.

Most parts of the North and the Midland still possess vigorous regional terms.

Eaves troughs (sometimes *eaves troths*) is current in all of New England, except the coastal section from Cape Cod to Maine, and in the New England settlement area. Scattered instances of *eaves troughs, water troughs,* and simply *troughs* occur on Delaware Bay, Chesapeake Bay, the Carolina coast, and in western Virginia and North Carolina, mostly in the speech of older people who have not yet adopted *gutters.* Moreover, *eaves troughs* is rather common in west-central West Virginia, especially in the Ohio Valley section of it, where the *eaves troughs* of the New England settlements of Marietta and vicinity across the river supported this older Southern term.

The North Midland and all of West Virginia have the expressions *the spouting* and *the spouts,* the latter being most frequent in West Virginia.

A related *eaves spouts* is common in the Upper Connecticut Valley and to the east thereof, except for the coastal area; and relics of it are found in Rhode Island, on Cape Cod, and on Nantucket, all parts of Eastern New England.

Whether the *eaves spouts* of the northern counties of Pennsylvania and the Western Reserve of Ohio is a direct descendant of this New England expression or, at least in part, a blend of the New England *eaves troughs* and the Pennsylvania *spouting, spouts* is an open question. It is a very striking fact that the New England settlements in New York State have only *eaves troughs*, whose original home is in southwestern New England. . . .

corn crib

Indian corn is often stored in sheds with flaring sides and a projecting roof. In the Midland and the entire New England settlement area this structure is called a *corn crib*, usually shortened to *crib* in Rhode Island. The simplex *crib* is characteristic of all of North Carolina and adjoining parts of Tidewater Virginia (south of the James), and of westernmost Virginia and South Carolina.

The Virginia Piedmont, the Tidewater area north of the James, and the Western Shore of Maryland have the distinctive term *corn house* to the exclusion of *corn crib*.

In New England the two expressions stand side by side, but only scattered relics of *corn house* are found in the New England settlement area.

Two local expressions are worth noting, the *crib house* of southern New Jersey and the *corn stack* of southern Delamarvia (southern Delaware to Cape Charles).

hay cock

For the temporary small heaps of hay in the meadow two regional terms are widely current, *cock* in the New England area and the North Midland, *shock* in the Southern area and in the South Midland. The Midland *cock*, however, is still common in the Valley of Virginia, not uncommon in Western North Carolina, and relics of it have survived in central West Virginia. Moreover, this Midland term has spread all the way down to the mouth of Chesapeake Bay on Delamarvia and to the James River on the western shore of the Bay.

The Southern *shock*, on the other hand, has become established in the greater part of the South Midland and bids fair to replace *cock* altogether in that section. On the Eastern Shore *shock* is no longer common, and it is clearly losing ground in Maryland west of the Bay.

Other terms for the haycock, more local in character, are: *heap* (1) in parts of New England and (2) in the Pennsylvania German area (cf. Pennsylvania German *Haufe*); *tumble*, scattered in northern New England; *doodle*, (1) in Western Pennsylvania and (2) on the lower Kanawha in West Virginia; *hand stack*, scattered in Pennsylvania; *pile*, (1) on the Atlantic coast from Delaware to Georgia and (2) in Eastern Pennsylvania.

picket fence

Fences with pointed or blunt upright slats which commonly surround the dwelling and the garden are known as *picket fences* in the New England settlement area, and as *paling fences, paled fences*, or simply as *palings* in the Midland and the Southern area. The variant *paled fence* is characteristic of the Philadelphia area.

Picket fence appears as a modern term in large parts of the Midland and the South, especially in the Ohio Valley, on Chesapeake Bay, in northeastern North Carolina, and in the Charleston area in South Carolina.

rail fence

The old-fashioned rail fence built of overlapping rails laid zigzag fashion is simply called a *rail fence* in the Southern area, in New York State, and in the northern counties of Pennsylvania. This term is also widely current in West Virginia and is in regular use in the mountains farther south. In New England this type of fence is commonly known as a *Virginia rail fence* to distinguish it from the *post-and-rail fence* of New England.

The Midland term for the zigzag fence is *worm fence,* an expression that predominates in Pennsylvania, West Virginia, New Jersey, and Delamarvia and has made its way into northern Virginia.

Sporadic terms for this kind of fence are *zigzag fence* and *snake fence.*

Other types of fences are built of rails: the *post-and-rail* fence of New England, also known as the *Connecticut rail fence,* in which the rails are inserted in sturdy posts; the *herring-bone fence = stake-and-rider fence = buck fence* (Eastern Pennsylvania) *= rip-gut fence,* in which the rails are supported by crossed stakes. . . .

pail

The well-known metal container is called a *pail* in the entire New England settlement area and in the Hudson Valley, a *bucket* in all of the Midland and the South. However, on the New England coast north of Boston *bucket* is still used beside *pail* in this sense (sporadically also elsewhere in New England). On the other hand, *pail* has spread southward to central New Jersey and is now also current in Philadelphia beside *bucket.*

In parts of the Southern area *pail* has survived as the name of a wooden milk or water container which has one long stave serving as a handle.

Bucket, in turn, survives in New England in such compounds as *well bucket* and *fire bucket* (but cf. *cedar pail*).

Note also Northern *swill pail,* and Midland and Southern *slop bucket.*

frying pan (of cast iron)

The flat-bottomed cast-iron frying pan is now often called simply a *frying pan,* especially in urban areas. However, two older expressions, *skillet* and *spider,* are still extensively used for the cast-iron pan to distinguish it from the modern sheet-metal frying pan.

Skillet is current in all of the Midland from New Jersey to western South Carolina and westward. It is also the old term in the Virginia Piedmont, but it has here been largely supplanted by *frying pan.*

Spider occurs in two large separate areas: (1) in the New England settlement area (all the way to the Western Reserve of Ohio), and (2) in the tidewater area from the Potomac southward to the Peedee in South Carolina. It appears also on the Jersey coast from Sandy Hook to Cape May.

faucet

The water *faucet* is known by that name only in the Northern area. The entire Midland and the South have *spicket* (occasionally *spigot*). *Faucet*, to be sure, is not entirely unknown in this sense in the Midland and the South. . . .

paper bag

Paper bag and *paper sack* are both widely used in the Eastern States.

Poke is current, often by the side of *bag* or *sack*, in a large area extending from central Pennsylvania westward, and southward to the Carolinas. In Virginia the Blue Ridge forms the eastern boundary of the *poke* area, in North Carolina the Yadkin.

To the east of the *poke* area, in the bilingual Great Valley of Pennsylvania (from Reading to Frederick in Maryland), the Pennsylvania German term *toot*, riming with *foot*, is in common use in the English spoken there.

burlap bag

Burlap sack or *bag* is the most common term in the Eastern States for the rough loose-woven sack in which potatoes and other farm produce are shipped. It is regularly current throughout the North and the North Midland, and not uncommon in Tidewater Virginia and on the Kanawha. However, most of the Southern area and parts of the Midland have vigorous regional and local terms.

Sea-grass sack, grass sack is current on the coast from Delaware Bay to Albemarle Sound and also on the Western Shore of Chesapeake Bay north of the James River.

Croker sack, crocus sack is in common use (1) in the southern part of the Virginia Piedmont, (2) in South Carolina and Georgia (also in Wilmington at the mouth of the Cape Fear), and (3) on Martha's Vineyard off Cape Cod.

Tow sack is the North Carolina term. It is common throughout the state and rare outside of it, except around Norfolk, Virginia.

Guano sack is common in Maryland, both east and west of the Bay, and in the Shenandoah Valley—presumably as a Baltimore trade name. (Much guano was imported by way of Baltimore and distributed to the farm lands from there.)

Gunny sack is the regular term for the burlap bag in the Ohio Valley from Wheeling downstream. Scattered instances of it have been noted in Eastern Pennsylvania, in Metropolitan New York, and in New England.

Study Questions

1. Make your own list of terms by selecting the term in each group which you would normally use or which sounds most familiar. After each term indicate where, to the best of your knowledge, you learned it: at home, school, through playmates, older friends, advertising, or fiction. Compare your lists with your classmates'.

2. Make a class list showing which terms in each group are used and by how many individuals.

3. Where there are decided individual variations—that is, only a few people use one term and the majority use another—investigate to discover where each of the nonconformists learned the term. Do facts in the person's previous environment or in the family history explain the deviations? Do several persons who use the same term have similar backgrounds?

4. List the terms you recognize from reading but would never use, perhaps terms like *bucket*, in "old oaken bucket." For example, Southern stories use *croker sack, tote,* and *poke;* English stories use *lumber room* and *drawing room.*

5. List the terms you have heard but would not use.

6. List the terms that are completely new to you.

7. Do your findings confirm or contradict the generalization that regional differences are slight and do not cause misunderstanding?

8. From what sources do people learn most of the words with which *Linguistic Atlas* investigators are concerned?

9. In your findings, are any variations related to social distribution?

10. Do your findings show the trend from local to regional to national? One example of the trend would be the national currency of *blinds* due to the popularity of Venetian blinds.

16. LINGUISTIC GEOGRAPHY AND FRESHMAN ENGLISH

Albert H. Marckwardt

In this discussion, which was published in the *CEA Critic* for January, 1952, Dr. Marckwardt suggests that *Linguistic Atlas* data can be used to show how regional variations in pronunciation and usage are perfectly natural and acceptable in their cultural context.

Every autumn approximately half a million students enter the colleges and universities of the country. Virtually all of them are required to take a course in freshman English. Over a ten-year period their number mounts to a total of five or six million. Year in and year out several thousand instructors in English devote most of their time to teaching these students.

In one sense this is a thumbnail sketch of the most amazing linguistic enterprise in the history of the civilized world. Varied as are the aims and outlines of freshman English the country over, the hundreds of courses which fall into this category have one element in common: they seek to give the individual student a mastery of standard American English as a medium of communication. Never before has any educational system committed itself to the teaching of a national standard, that is to say a prestige dialect, on so vast a scale.

This common aim poses certain problems. First, it is still true that many high school and college students come from homes where standard English is not habitually spoken or written. For these, this phase of the English program of school and college means that the individual student must be trained to forego his habitual use of certain language features characteristic of the regional and social dialects of English and to substitute for these features of that prestige dialect which we call Standard English.

At the same time we must recognize that this so-called Standard English is not absolutely identical the country over, although most college handbooks and rhetorics are blandly written upon the assumption that it is. To select just a single instance, the use of *for* in "I would like for you to write me a letter," is characteristic of cultivated speech and writing over large parts of the South and totally absent from most other sections of the country, yet college textbooks often quite unreasonably legislate against this particular construction. I recall very vividly my own bewilderment when, as an undergraduate, I read in the textbook we used in those days that the use of *taken* as an active past-tense form—*I taken it*—was one of the worst errors that anyone could make. As I learned much later, this statement undoubtedly made a great deal of sense to students in some parts of the country, but to my classmates and me, with our particular regional linguistic background, it was wholly meaningless. We simply couldn't imagine anyone's doing it.

The situation is similar, if not even more aggravated, in the speech field with respect to matters of pronunciation. I say more aggravated because a good many manuals of speech are written from a more rigid, authoritarian point of view than are the best hand-books of composition. For example, when even a usually careful and competent phonetician applies the label "substandard" to the voiced *t* in *better,* the diphthongal pronunciation of the vowel in *bird,* the *w* of *somewhat,* and the voiceless initial fricative of *thither,* one feels the need of a body of objective fact to put these impressionistic judgments to the test. We have only to remember that even today, all candidates for teaching positions in New York City must demonstrate by examination that they have mastered the south-eastern British-so-called Received Standard—pronunciations recorded in Daniel Jones's *Pronouncing Dictionary of the English Language,* for which the editor claims no validity whatsoever outside of the particular area from which they were gathered.

The problem then becomes one of securing authoritative data about standard American English, as it exists in various parts of the country. One source of such data is to be found in the materials which have been collected for the Linguistic Atlas of the United States and Canada. At present this consists of the published *Linguistic Atlas of New England,* the completely collected field records of the Linguistic Atlas of the South-Atlantic States and of the Linguistic Atlas of the Middle Atlantic States, together with the fragmentary materials of at least four other linguistic atlas projects in various stages of completion throughout the country.

There is no question that these materials, even in their present incomplete state, present a more complete body of carefully gathered information concerning pronunciation than the most authoritative dictionaries are based on today. The second edition of *Webster's New International Dictionary* employed 104 consultants on pronunciation, and subsequent analysis showed these to be very unevenly distributed throughout the country. The cultured informants represented in the three coastal atlases alone comprise more than half again that number. When the country is completely covered, there will undoubtedly be from two to three times as many. Moreover, the atlas will contain affirmative evidence of substandard speech in quantity. That is to say, the evidence will be there and will not have to be guessed at negatively in terms of whatever does not happen to be known to, or habitually used by, the author or lexicographer. Finally, the wide variety of pronunciation characteristic of the cultured informants should serve to check some of the excessive dogmatism found in speech classes.

With respect to problems of vocabulary, morphology, and syntax the situation is much the same. Any examination of a dozen or more college textbooks in composition will demonstrate that in large measure the authors of these books have copied one another as assiduously as have the lexicographers. Or even if they have gone to the current factual sources of the language on many moot points, what help can they expect to get? A dictionary label of "colloquial" or a classification of "popular English" in a standard work on syntax is, after all, just another man's subjective judgment, often based upon somewhat meager evidence. It is reasonable to maintain that the selective sampling technique employed by the atlases and the sheer mass of evidence they have collected impart a greater validity to their findings than most collections of fact relative to current use of the language.

Early in 1951 a minor furore was created in one of the pedagogical journals when someone insisted that the apparent relaxation of standards in English grammars and handbooks over the past quarter-century could be accounted for by the fact that the linguistic habits of the freshmen were influencing, and indeed overcoming, those of the instructors. This somewhat startling conclusion was purportedly based upon a comparison covering twenty points of form and syntax between the 1949 Norman Lewis survey of the language of college professors, editors, lexicographers, authors, etc., and a presumably similar survey of the usage of a group of freshmen.

What the author of the article overlooked, and what so far few of his critics have pointed out, was that the instructions given to the two groups differed so radically that the results of the surveys simply did not admit of a valid comparison. To make his point, the author might much more profitably have consulted the atlas materials for the normal usage of the cultured informants. Had he done so, however, his point might well have vanished, for a spot check of one or two items considered in the study shows the cultured informants closer to the reported usage of the freshmen than to the so-called authorities consulted by Mr. Lewis.

There is still another way in which atlas findings can be of considerable service. In our attempt to assure our students, on the secondary as well as the college level, of a habitual command of standard English equal to the demands of any situation in which their abilities may place them, we must operate with a high degree of efficiency. Language habits are formed only by dint of constant repetition. Even in the twelve or sixteen years of schooling through the high school and college levels, the number of new habits which can be formed and of the old ones which may be eradicated is not too great. This calls for a highly judicious selection of the particular language features to be attacked and replaced by new habits. It demands careful curriculum planning.

We know now that it can no longer be assumed that all substandard forms and syntactical patterns are alike the country over. Professor E. Bagby Atwood, of the University of Texas, in analyzing the field records of the three coastal atlases, has found sharp lines of demarcation in the inflectional forms of folk speech. The same is also true with such syntactical matters as the choice of preposition in "sick (to) (at) or (in) one's stomach." If it is decided that there is enough prejudice against, or social stigma connected with *sick to his stomach* to make the substitution of *at* a justifiable item somewhere in the language curriculum, in those areas where *sick at his stomach* is the characteristic folk form, this item may be safely omitted. It does not constitute a problem. The same conclusion will apply to *all the farther, dog-bit* as a past participle, or *taken* as a past-tense form. Atlas results merit the attention of those who are charged with framing courses of English instruction at virtually all levels of schooling.

There are, of course, many broader implications of the splendid work that has been done and that which is now under way in determining the regional features of American English. My only purpose here is to suggest that since so many of us are concerned with the teaching of the English language on a practical level, the work of the linguistic geographer is by no means merely a remote endeavor, presenting a few research scholars with an opportunity to demonstrate their virtuosity, but rather an activity that can touch intimately and affect profoundly our everyday classroom practices.

Study Questions

1. Which of the problems involved in teaching or learning standard English has been of most concern to you personally? Which problems do you recognize as being common in the elementary schools you attended? In high school? In college or university?

2. Why, do you suppose, is *Webster's Third New International Dictionary* based on much more accurate pronunciation data than the previous edition? Check your own "educated guess" with the Preface.

3. At what age and grade level should children begin to learn to avoid forms to which social stigma is attached?

4. What are the social implications of the American democratic ideal of providing most high school graduates with some college education?

5. This selection is addressed to teachers. What are the responsibilities of college students in speech and writing? Is "social stigma" of vital consequence to migratory workers? To unskilled laborers? To factory workers? To parents who are ambitious for their children? To artists, teachers, doctors, lawyers? To you?

6. To which of these expressions do you think "social stigma" would be attached—that is, which ones might damage one's chances to get or keep a good position, to marry a cultured person of good social position, to be accepted socially by people of prestige in the community?

"Grammar never done me no good."
"Between you and I, she don't know nothing."
"If I would of been invited sooner, I could of went."
"It is not for nothing that men seek public positions with low pay; there is always payola."
"Is that you, John?" "No, Mary, it's me, Bill."
"Who have you written to since last Sunday?"
"The building was not open to tourists, but Tom's father, who knew some official, got us in."
"I've had more annoying distractions than any person should be expected to put up with."
"You speak as you dress, conforming to the standards and customs of the group you belong to."

Check your decisions by looking up the key expression or construction in one of the books on usage in the bibliography.

Part III. Regional Aspects
Subjects for Brief Papers or Written Reports

1. Summarize briefly the English-speaking background of your community as revealed by such aspects of language as place-names, pronunciation, vocabulary, and idiom which you have recorded and classified and verified in historical sources.

2. Read one of the articles referred to by Baugh in "The American Dialects" that deals with an area you know and write a comparison or comparison-contrast of the author's findings and your own.

3. Collect data on vocabulary and pronunciation variants among college students and in a brief report present your observations and your explanatory comments.

4. Write a short paper on unfamiliar terms you have collected in traveling outside your native area.

5. Select a foreign-language group in your town or city with whose speech you are familiar and write a brief account of their contributions to local vocabulary and idiom.

6. Report on the status, in *Webster's Third International,* of a short list of expressions you have been taught are incorrect. Where possible, compare *Webster's* classification with that in Bryant, *Current American Usage* or Evans and Evans, *Dictionary of Contemporary American Usage.*

7. Report on your findings for the fourth question on Allen's article, "The Linguistic Atlases," and give the relevant information about the individuals questioned, their answers, and your conclusions.

8. In paragraph three Allen refers to the studies of American usage by Leonard, Marckwardt and Walcott, and Fries. Examine one of these books, or Margaret M. Bryant's *Current American Usage,* and summarize the attitudes toward usage.

9. From Kurath's list of terms, in "Regional and Local Words," make your own list of the term in each group which you would use. Classify the terms according to your source—family, friends, reading—and write a paper upon the influences apparent in your familiar vocabulary.

10. Have each member of the class make a list of terms used, from Kurath's list. Collect these lists and report on the results, comparing your data with Kurath's.

11. Study terms for common objects used in national advertising and report on the relation of your own vocabulary to the nationally adopted terms, with special attention to terms you adopted from such sources and terms you retain despite your awareness of the national norms.

12. Analyze briefly your chief problems in learning and using standard English: the nature of your problems, the chief causes of them, the ways in which the scientific approach to language and usage may aid you in solving them.

13. In the sixth question on Marckwardt's "Linguistic Geography and Freshman English," classify the sentences as substandard and standard, give your authority for your classifications, and explain the principle involved.

IV. LITERARY AND COLLOQUIAL ASPECTS

In this section the articles deal with some of the distinctions between the spoken and written uses of language. Many students, intimidated by over-zealous parents or teachers, have misinterpreted the label colloq. *in the dictionary and have come to regard colloquial language as improper language. Nothing could be further from the truth.* Colloquial *in its literal sense means "pertaining to speaking together," and difficulty arises in trying to group all types of spoken expressions under one heading. Slang, jargon, trade talk, clichés, cultivated conversation, and a formal oration are all colloquial in the sense that they are spoken; but as Professor Kenyon points out, they differ widely in their cultural levels and functions. Too often* colloquial *is used as a term of disapproval, largely because many spoken words and phrases are culturally substandard and inappropriate for a higher social level. The student should observe the spoken and written expressions around him and adjust his vocabulary and mode of expression to fit the occasion. Other details of this problem will be treated in the section on the social and cultural aspects of language.*

The question of appropriateness confronts every user of language. Some individuals, apparently more sensitive than others, can adapt themselves unerringly to each situation; but more frequently, through lack of skill or sensitivity, people are unable to adjust their speech or writing to the circumstances. The result can be confusion, embarrassment, or both. It is important for the linguistic fledgling to observe, analyze, and classify patterns and functions so that he can use his words effectively and appropriately.

In written communication appropriateness is also important. A note to a friend differs in tone and vocabulary from a closely reasoned formal argu-

141

ment. *The more formal statements ordinarily use a larger proportion of learned words either because these are more appropriate to the circumstances or because there are no colloquial words to express the idea. For most writing in college a combination of learned and popular words used flexibly and informally is the best solution. Again, however, it is necessary for the student to determine what style and tone are most suitable for his purposes. Since absolute standards of appropriateness do not exist, the student must choose his pattern of expression on the basis of careful, sensitive evaluation of his purpose and the occasion.*

17. LEARNED WORDS AND POPULAR WORDS

James B. Greenough AND George Lyman Kittredge

This chapter from *Words and Their Ways in English Speech* (1901) deals with two aspects of vocabulary—words derived from a literary source and those coming from the spoken language.

In every cultivated language there are two great classes of words which, taken together, comprise the whole vocabulary. First, there are those words with which we become acquainted in ordinary conversation,—which we learn, that is to say, from the members of our own family and from our familiar associates, and which we should know and use even if we could not read or write. They concern the common things of life, and are the stock in trade of all who speak the language. Such words may be called "popular," since they belong to the people at large and are not the exclusive possession of a limited class.

On the other hand, our language includes a multitude of words which are comparatively seldom used in ordinary conversation. Their meanings are known to every educated person, but there is little occasion to employ them at home or in the market-place. Our first acquaintance with them comes not from our mother's lips or from the talk of our schoolmates, but from books that we read, lectures that we hear, or the more formal conversation of highly educated speakers, who are discussing some particular topic in a style appropriately elevated above the habitual level of everyday life. Such words are called "learned," and the distinction between them and "popular" words is of great importance to a right understanding of linguistic process.

The difference between popular and learned words may be easily seen in a few examples. We may describe a girl as "lively" or as "vivacious." In the first case, we are using a native English formation from the familiar noun *life*. In the latter, we are using a Latin derivative which has precisely the same meaning. Yet the atmosphere of the two words is quite different. No one ever got the adjective *lively* out of a book. It is a part of everybody's vocabulary. We cannot remember a time when we did not know it, and we feel sure that we learned it long before we were able to read. On the other hand, we must have passed several years of our lives before learning the word *vivacious*. We may even remember the first time that we saw it in print or heard it from some grown-up friend who was talking over our childish heads. Both *lively* and *vivacious* are good English words, but *lively* is "popular" and *vivacious* is "learned."

143

From the same point of view we may contrast the following pairs of synonyms: [1] *the same, identical; speech, oration; fire, conflagration; choose, select; brave, valorous; swallowing, deglutition; striking, percussion; building, edifice; shady, umbrageous; puckery, astringent; learned, erudite; secret, cryptic; destroy, annihilate; stiff, rigid; flabby, flaccid; queer, eccentric; behead, decapitate; round, circular; thin, emaciated; fat, corpulent; truthful, veracious; try, endeavor; bit, modicum; piece, fragment; sharp, acute; crazy, maniacal; king, sovereign; book, volume; lying, mendacious; beggar, mendicant; teacher, instructor; play, drama; air, atmosphere; paint, pigment.*

The terms "popular" and "learned," as applied to words, are not absolute definitions. No two persons have the same stock of words, and the same word may be "popular" in one man's vocabulary and "learned" in another's.[2] There are also different grades of "popularity"; indeed there is in reality a continuous gradation from infantile words like *mamma* and *papa* to such erudite derivatives as *concatenation* and *cataclysm*. Still, the division into "learned" and "popular" is convenient and sound. Disputes may arise as to the classification of any particular word, but there can be no difference of opinion about the general principle. We must be careful, however, to avoid misconception. When we call a word "popular," we do not mean that it is a favorite word, but simply that it belongs to the people as a whole,—that is, it is everybody's word, not the possession of a limited number. When we call a word "learned," we do not mean that it is used by scholars alone, but simply that its presence in the English vocabulary is due to books and the cultivation of literature rather than to the actual needs of ordinary conversation.

Here is one of the main differences between a cultivated and an uncultivated language. Both possess a large stock of "popular" words; but the cultivated language is also rich in "learned" words, with which the ruder tongue has not provided itself, simply because it has never felt the need of them.

In English it will usually be found that the so-called learned words are of foreign origin. Most of them are derived from French or Latin, and a considerable number from Greek. The reason is obvious. The development of English literature has not been isolated, but has taken place in close connection with the earnest study of foreign literatures. Thus, in the fourteenth century, when our language was assuming substantially the shape which it now bears, the literary exponent of English life and thought,

---

[1] Not all the words are exact synonyms, but that is of no importance in the present discussion.

[2] It is instructive to study one's own vocabulary from this point of view,—making a list of (1) those words which we feel sure we learned in childhood, (2) those which we have learned in later life, but not from books, (3) those which have entered our vocabulary from books. We shall also find it useful to consider the difference between our reading vocabulary and our speaking vocabulary.

Geoffrey Chaucer, the first of our great poets, was profoundly influenced by Latin literature as well as by that of France and Italy. In the sixteenth and seventeenth centuries, the Greek and Latin classics were vigorously studied by almost every English writer of any consequence, and the great authors of antiquity were regarded as models, not merely of general literary form, but of expression in all its details. These foreign influences have varied much in character and intensity. But it is safe to say that there has been no time since 1350 when English writers of the highest class have not looked to Latin, French, and Italian authors for guidance and inspiration. From 1600 to the present day the direct influence of Greek literature and philosophy has also been enormous,—affecting as it has the finest spirits in a peculiarly pervasive way,—and its indirect influence is quite beyond calculation. Greek civilization, we should remember, has acted upon us, not merely through Greek literature and art, but also through the medium of Latin, since the Romans borrowed their higher culture from Greece.

Now certain facts in the history of our language have made it peculiarly inclined to borrow from French and Latin. The Norman Conquest in the eleventh century made French the language of polite society in England; and, long after the contact between Norman-French and English had ceased to be of direct significance in our linguistic development, the reading and speaking of French and the study of French literature formed an important part of the education of English-speaking men and women. When literary English was in process of formation in the fourteenth and fifteenth centuries, the authors whose works determined the cultivated vocabulary were almost as familiar with French as with their mother tongue, and it was therefore natural that they should borrow a good many French words. But these same authors were also familiar with Latin, which, though called a dead language, has always been the professional dialect of ecclesiastics and a *lingua franca* for educated men. Thus the borrowing from French and from Latin went on side by side, and it is often impossible to say from which of the two languages a particular English word is taken. The practice of naturalizing French and Latin words was, then, firmly established in the fourteenth century, and when, in the sixteenth century, there was a great revival of Greek studies in England, the close literary relations between Greece and Rome facilitated the adoption of a considerable number of words from the Greek. Linguistic processes are cumulative: one does not stop when another begins. Hence we find all of these influences active in increasing the modern vocabulary. In particular, the language of science has looked to Greece for its terms, as the language of abstract thought has drawn its nomenclature from Latin.

It would, however, be a great mistake to suppose that all our "popular" terms are of native origin, and that all foreign derivatives are "learned." The younger and less cultivated members of a community are naturally inclined to imitate the speech of the older and more cultivated. Hence, as time has passed, a great number of French and Latin words, and even some that are derived from the Greek, have made themselves quite at home in ordinary conversation. Such words, whatever their origin, are as truly popular as if they had been a part of our language from the earliest period.

Examples of such popular [3] words of foreign derivation are the following:—

From French: *army, arrest, bay, card, catch, city, chase, chimney, conveyance, deceive, entry, engine, forge, hour, letter, mantle, mason, merchant, manner, mountain, map, move, navy, prince, pen, pencil, parlor, river, rage, soldier, second, table, veil, village.*

From Latin: *accommodate, act, add, adopt, animal, anxious, applause, arbitrate, auction, agent, calculate, cancer, circus, collapse, collision, column, congress, connect, consequence, contract, contradict, correct, creation, cucumber, curve, centennial, decorate, delicate, dentist, describe, diary, diffident, different, digest, direct, discuss, divide, educate, elect, emigrant, equal, erect, expect, extra, fact, genius, genuine, graduate, gratis, horrid, imitate, item, joke, junction, junior, major, magnificent, medicine, medium, miser, obstinate, omit, pagan, pastor, pauper, pedal, pendulum, permit, picture, plague, postpone, premium, prevent, prospect, protect, quiet, recess, recipe, reduce, regular, salute, secure, series, single, species, specimen, splendid, strict, student, subscribe, subtract, suburb, suffocate, suggest, tedious, timid, urge, vaccinate, various, ventilation, vest, veto, victor, vim, vote.*

From Greek: *anthracite, apathy, arsenic, aster, athlete, atlas, attic, barometer, biography, calomel, catarrh, catholic, catastrophe, catechism, caustic, chemist, crisis, dialogue, diphtheria, elastic, encyclopedia, hector, homeopathy, iodine, lexicon, microscope, monotonous, myth, neuralgia, panic, panorama, photograph, skeleton, strychnine, tactics, telegraph, tonic, zoölogy.*

No language can borrow extensively from foreign sources without losing a good many words of its own. Hence, if we compare the oldest form of English (Anglo-Saxon) with our modern speech, we shall discover that many words that were common in Anglo-Saxon have gone quite out of use, being replaced by their foreign equivalents. The "learned" word has driven out the "popular" word, and has thereupon, in many cases, become "popular" itself. Thus instead of A.S. *herë* we use the French word *army;* instead of *thegn* or *thëow*, the French word *servant;* instead of *sipherë* (a compound of the Anglo-Saxon word for *ship* and that for *army*), we use *navy;* instead of *micel*, we say *large;* instead of *sigë, victory;* instead of *swithë, very;* instead of *lāf*, we say *remainder* or *remnant,*—and so on.

Curiously enough, it sometimes happens that when both the native and the foreign word still have a place in our language, the latter has become

[3] The exact grade of "popularity" differs in these examples.

the more popular,—the former being relegated to the higher or poetical style. Thus it is more natural for us to say *divide* (from L. *divido*) than *cleave* (from A.S. *clīfan*); *travel* than *fare*;[4] *river* than *stream*; *castle* than *burg*; *residence* than *dwelling*; *remain* than *abide*; *expect* than *ween*; *pupil* or *scholar* than *learner*; *destruction* than *bale*; *protect* or *defend* than *shield*; *immediately* than *straightway*; *encourage* than *hearten*; *present* than *bestow*; *firm* than *steadfast*; *direct* than *forthright*; *impetuous* than *heady*; *modest* than *shamefaced*; *prince* than *atheling*; *noise* or *tumult* or *disturbance* than *din*; *people* than *folk*;[5] *prophet* than *soothsayer*; *fate* than *weird*; *lancer* than *spearman*; I *intend* than I *am minded*; *excavate* than *delve*; *resist* than *withstand*; *beautiful* than *goodly*; *gracious* than *kindly*. The very fact that the native words belong to the older stock has made them poetical; for the language of poetry is always more archaic than that of prose.

Frequently we have kept both the native and the foreign word, but in different senses, thus increasing our vocabulary to good purpose. The foreign word may be more emphatic than the native: as in *brilliant, bright*; *scintillate, sparkle*; *astonishment, wonder*; a *conflagration*, a *fire*; *devour, eat up*; *labor, work*. Or the native word may be more emphatic than the foreign: as in *stench, odor*; *straightforward, direct*; *dead, deceased*; *murder, homicide*. Often, however, there is a wide distinction in meaning. Thus *driver* differs from *propellor*; *child* from *infant*; *history* from *tale*; *book* from *volume*; *forehead* from *front*; *length* from *longitude*; *moony* from *lunar*; *sunny* from *solar*; *nightly* from *nocturnal*; *churl* from *villain*; *wretch* from *miser*; *poor man* from *pauper*; *run across* from *occur*; *run into* from *incur*; *fight* from *debate*.

From time to time attempts have been made to oust foreign words from our vocabulary and to replace them by native words that have become either obsolete or less usual (that is to say, less popular). Whimsical theorists have even set up the principle that no word of foreign origin should be employed when a native word of the same meaning exists. In English, however, all such efforts are predestined to failure. They result, not in a simpler and more natural style, but in something unfamiliar, fantastic, and affected. Foreign words that have long been in common use are just as much English as if they had been a part of our language from the beginning. There is no rational theory on which they should be shunned. It would be just as reasonable for an Englishman whose ancestors had lived in the island ever since the time of King Alfred, to disown as his countrymen the descendants of a Frenchman or a German who settled there three hundred years ago. The test of the learned or the popular character of a word is not its etymology, but the facts relating to its habitual employment by plain speakers. Nor is there any principle on which, of two expressions, that which is popular should be preferred to that which is

---

[4] *Fare* is still common as a noun and in figurative senses.
[5] But the irregular plural *folks* is a common colloquialism.

learned or less familiar. The sole criterion of choice consists in the appropriateness of one's language to the subject or the occasion. It would be ridiculous to address a crowd of soldiers in the same language that one would employ in a council of war. It would be no less ridiculous to harangue an assembly of generals as if they were a regiment on the eve of battle. The reaction against the excessive Latinization of English is a wholesome tendency, but it becomes a mere "fad" when it is carried out in a *doctrinaire* manner. As Chaucer declares:—

> Ek Plato seith, whoso that can him rede,
> "The wordes mot be cosin to the dede."

Every educated person has at least two ways of speaking his mother tongue. The first is that which he employs in his family, among his familiar friends, and on ordinary occasions. The second is that which he uses in discoursing on more complicated subjects, and in addressing persons with whom he is less intimately acquainted. It is, in short, the language which he employs when he is "on his dignity," as he puts on evening dress when he is going to dine. The difference between these two forms of language consists, in great measure, in a difference of vocabulary. The basis of familiar words must be the same in both, but the vocabulary appropriate to the more formal occasion will include many terms which would be stilted or affected in ordinary talk. There is also considerable difference between familiar and dignified language in the manner of utterance. Contrast the rapid utterance of our everyday dialect, full of contractions and clipped forms, with the more distinct enunciation of the pulpit or the platform. Thus, in conversation, we habitually employ such contractions as *I'll, don't, won't, it's, we'd, he'd,* and the like, which we should never use in public speaking, unless of set purpose, to give a markedly colloquial tinge to what we have to say.

Study Questions

1. A well-known example of "translation" from popular into learned words is Dr. Samuel Johnson's two comments on the Duke of Buckingham's farce, "The Rehearsal": Johnson's first comment, "It has not wit enough to keep it sweet," he rephrased as, "It has not vitality enough to preserve it from putrefaction." Proverbs offer excellent material for similar substitution of learned for popular words as a demonstration of the vocabulary resources of the language and of the difference of effect due to connotation and to the scarcity of exact synonyms. Try substitution of learned words in such proverbs as the following:

> A rolling stone gathers no moss.
> It's a long lane that has no turning.
> Out of sight, out of mind. ("Invisible, insane"
>   does *not* express the same idea!)

In union there is strength.
Give a man enough rope and he will hang himself.
Birds of a feather flock together.
The early bird gets the worm.

2. Look up the etymology of the words in the above proverbs and of the words you used as substitutes. What are the most common languages of origin in each group? What generalization can you make about the kind of words, popular or learned, used in folk sayings, and the languages from which popular and learned words are derived?

3. If you know any foreign language, try the same exercise of rephrasing its proverbs in more learned terms. Do you find differences in etymology between the two versions as you did in the two versions of English proverbs? Does the English language prove to have distinctive characteristics in vocabulary? If so, what is the historical explanation?

4. Give the *closest* learned equivalent of these popular words: *burial, deadly, good will, happiness, hearty, liveliness, motherhood, sight, thoughtful, wedding.*

5. Give a "borrowed" equivalent of these words of native origin: *chapman, forspent, godhood, maker* (archaic meaning), *ruth, uncouth, wold.* What generalization made by Greenough and Kittredge is illustrated?

6. Follow the footnote suggestion on page 144 and make a list of ten typical words in your vocabulary from each of the three sources. For words from books, try to list words you have seldom or never *heard.*

7. Give some examples of words of foreign origin which are more emphatic than equivalent native words. Give some examples of native words which are more emphatic than equivalent words of foreign origin.

8. Give the *literal* meaning of each of these words: *Bible, chivalrous, evangel, vigilant, sinister* and *dextrous.* Can you give other pairs of "borrowed" and native words with the same literal meaning but with widely different connotations and uses?

18. CULTURAL LEVELS AND FUNCTIONAL VARIETIES OF ENGLISH

John S. Kenyon

In this article published in *College English* for October, 1948, Professor Kenyon has provided a simple workable pattern of classification of language into levels with social or cultural connotations and into functional varieties of words used in a formal or informal context.

The word *level,* when used to indicate different styles of language, is a metaphor, suggesting higher or lower position and, like the terms *higher* and *lower,* figuratively implies "better" or "worse," "more desirable" or "less desirable," and similar comparative degrees of excellence or inferiority in language.

The application of the term *level* to those different styles of language that are not properly distinguished as better or worse, desirable or undesirable, creates a false impression. I confess myself guilty of this error along with some other writers. What are frequently grouped together in one class as different levels of language are often in reality false combinations of two distinct and incommensurable categories, namely, *cultural levels* and *functional varieties.*

Among *cultural levels* may be included, on the lower levels, illiterate speech, narrowly local dialect, ungrammatical speech and writing, excessive and unskilful slang, slovenly and careless vocabulary and construction, exceptional pronunciation, and, on the higher level, language used generally by the cultivated, clear, grammatical writing, and pronunciations used by the cultivated over wide areas. The different cultural levels may be summarized in the two general classes *substandard* and *standard.*

Among *functional varieties* not depending on cultural levels may be mentioned colloquial language, itself existing in different degrees of familiarity or formality, as, for example, familiar conversation, private correspondence, formal conversation, familiar public address; formal platform or pulpit speech, public reading, public worship; legal, scientific, and other expository writing; prose and poetic belles-lettres. The different functional varieties may roughly be grouped together in the two classes *familiar* and *formal* writing or speaking.

The term *level,* then, does not properly belong at all to functional varieties of speech—colloquial, familiar, formal, scientific, literary language. They are equally "good" for their respective functions, and as classifications do not depend on the cultural status of the users.

The two groupings *cultural levels* and *functional varieties* are not mutually exclusive categories. They are based on entirely separate principles of classification: *culture* and *function.* Although we are here principally concerned with the functional varieties of standard English (the highest cultural level), yet substandard English likewise has its functional varieties for its different occasions and purposes. Thus the functional variety colloquial English may occur on a substandard cultural level, but the term *colloquial* does not itself designate a cultural level. So the functional variety formal writing or speaking may occur on a lower or on a higher cultural level according to the social status of writer or speaker, and sometimes of reader or audience. It follows, for instance, that the colloquial language of cultivated people is on a higher cultural level than the formal speech of the semiliterate or than some inept literary writing.

Semiliterate formal speech is sometimes heard from radio speakers. I recently heard one such speaker solemnly announce, "Sun day will be Mother's Day." Because the speaker, in his ignorance of good English, thought

JOHN S. KENYON 151

he was making himself plainer by using the distorted pronunciation *sun day* instead of the standard pronunciation *sundy,* he was actually misunderstood by some listeners to be saying, "Some day will be Mother's Day." About forty years ago the great English phonetician Henry Sweet used this very example to show that "we cannot make words more distinct by disguising them." [1] He was referring to the use, as in this instance, of the full sound of vowels in unaccented syllables where standard English has obscure vowels. On the same page Sweet gives another example of the same blunder: "Thus in the sentence *I shall be at home from one to three* the substitution of tuw for tə [ə = the last sound in *sofa*] at once suggests a confusion between the preposition and the numeral." This was also verified on the radio. Not long ago I heard a radio speaker announce carefully, "This program will be heard again tomorrow from one two three." I have also recorded (among many others) the following such substandard forms from the radio: *presidEnt* for the standard form *presidənt,* the days of the week ending in the full word *day* instead of the standard English syllable *-dy, ay man* for the correct ə *man, cahnsider* for *cənsider, tooday* for *təday, too go* for *tə go, Coalumbia* for *Cəlumbia,* etc. This is merely one sort among many of substandard features in the formal speech of the semiliterate. [2]

To begin my strictures at home, in *American Pronunciation* (9th ed., 4th printing, p. 17), I use the page heading "Levels of Speech." This should be "Functional Varieties of Standard Speech," for the reference is solely to the different uses of speech on the one cultivated level. Similarly, in the Kenyon-Knott *Pronouncing Dictionary of American English* (p. xvi, § 2), I carelessly speak of "levels of the colloquial" where I mean "styles of the colloquial," as three lines above. For though there are different cultural levels of colloquial English, the reference here is only to standard colloquial.

S. A. Leonard and H. Y. Moffett, in their study, "Current Definition of Levels in English Usage," [3] say (p. 348): "The levels of English usage have been most clearly described in Dr. Murray's Preface ["General Explanations," p. xvii] to the *New English Dictionary.* I have varied his diagram a little in order to illustrate better the overlapping between the categories." It appears to me that Leonard and Moffett have so varied the diagram as to obscure Murray's intention. For he is not here primarily exhibiting levels of speech but is showing the "Anglicity," or limits of the English vocabulary for the purposes of his dictionary. [4] The only topical divisions of his diagram that imply a cultural level are "slang" and "dialectal," and the only statement in his explanation of the diagram that could imply it is, "Slang words

---

[1] Henry Sweet, *The Sounds of English* (Oxford, 1910), p. 78.
[2] See further *American Speech,* VI, No. 5 (June, 1931), 368–72.
[3] *English Journal,* XVI, No. 5 (May, 1927), 345–59.
[4] The word *Anglicity* is a coinage of the *Oxford Dictionary.* They define it as "English quality, as of speech or style; English idiom."

ascend through colloquial use." This may imply that slang is on a lower cultural level than "colloquial, literary, technical, scientific, foreign." We may also safely infer that Murray would place "Dialectal" on a lower level than colloquial and literary if he were here concerned with cultural levels. Murray's diagram rests consistently on the same basis of classification throughout ("Anglicity"), and he emphasizes that "there is absolutely no defining line in any direction [from the central nucleus of colloquial and literary]." Moreover, Murray's exposition here concerns only vocabulary, with no consideration of the other features that enter so largely into "levels" of language—grammatical form and structure, pronunciation, spelling, and meaning—of styles, in short, only so far as they are affected by vocabulary. These he treats of elsewhere but without reference to levels.

It is not quite clear just how far Leonard and Moffett intend their grouping "literary English," "standard, cultivated, colloquial English," and "naïf, popular, or uncultivated English" to be identical with what they call Murray's "levels," his description of which they commend. But it is clear that they call their own grouping "three levels of usage" (p. 357) and classify them together as a single descending scale (cf. "the low end of the scale," p. 358). The inevitable impression that the average reader receives from such an arrangement of the scale is: Highest level, literary English; next lower level, colloquial English; lowest level, illiterate English; whereas, in fact, the first two "levels" are functional varieties of the one cultural level standard English, while the third ("illiterate or uncultivated," p. 358) is a cultural level.

Krapp has a chapter on "The Levels of English Speech," [5] in which he reveals some awareness of the confusion of cultural levels with functional varieties. He says:

Among those who pay any heed at all to convention in social relationships, a difference of degree is implicit in all use of English. This difference of degree is usually thought of in terms of higher and lower, of upper levels of speech appropriate to certain occasions of more formal character, of lower levels existing, if not necessarily appropriate, among less elevated circumstances. These popular distinctions of level may be accepted without weighting them too heavily with significance in respect of good, better, and best in speech. A disputatious person might very well raise the question whether literary English, ordinarily regarded as being on a high level, is really any better than the spoken word, is really as good as the spoken word, warm with the breath of the living moment.

At the risk of having to own the hard impeachment of being disputatious, I must express the fear that the logical fallacy in treating of levels, which Krapp rather lightly waves aside, is having a serious effect on general ideas of speech levels, and especially of the significance of colloquial English in

[5] George Philip Krapp, *The Knowledge of English* (New York, 1927), pp. 55–76.

good usage. Krapp's grouping, frankly on a scale of "levels" throughout, constitutes a descending scale from the highest, "Literary English," through "Formal Colloquial," "General Colloquial," "Popular English," to the lowest, "Vulgar English." Here the fallacy is obvious: Literary English, Formal Colloquial, and General Colloquial are not cultural levels but only functional varieties of English all on the one cultural level of standard English. The last two, Popular English and Vulgar English, belong in a different order of classification, cultural levels, without regard to function.

So in his succeeding discussion *level* sometimes means the one, sometimes the other; now a functional variety of standard English, and now a cultural level of substandard or of standard English. It is functional on page 58 ("a choice between two levels") and on page 60 ("level of general colloquial"), cultural on page 62 ("popular level" and "cultivated level") and on pages 63–64 ("popular level," "level of popular speech"), functional on page 64 ("general colloquial level"), cultural again on the same page ("popular level," "still lower level"), cultural on page 67 ("vulgar . . . level of speech," "applying the term 'vulgar' to it at certain levels"), cultural on page 68 ("its own [popular] level"), cultural and functional in the same phrase on page 68 ("speakers from the popular and the general colloquial level meet and mix"), and so on most confusingly to page 75.

The same kind of mixture of cultural levels and functional varieties is thrown into one apparently continuous scale by Kennedy: "There is the formal and dignified language of the scholarly or scientific address or paper. . . . The precision and stateliness of this uppermost level . . . is a necessary accompaniment of thinking on a high plane." [6] Next in order he mentions colloquial speech, which he refers to as "the second level, . . . generally acceptable to people of education and refinement." Clearly this is not a cultural level but a functional variety of standard English, like the "uppermost level." The third level is, however, a cultural one: "the latest slang," workmen's "technical slang and colloquialisms which other persons cannot comprehend," "grammatical solecisms." "The speech of this third level can fairly be ranked as lower in the social scale." His fourth level is also cultural: "At the bottom of the scale is the lingo, or cant, of criminals, hobos, and others of the lowest social levels."

Finally, Kennedy fixes the false mental image of a continuous and logically consistent descent from "the cold and lonely heights of formal and highly specialized scientific and scholarly language" to "the stupid and slovenly level of grammatical abuses and inane slang." In reality there is no cultural descent until we reach his third "level," since "formal and dignified language" and "colloquial speech" are only functional varieties of English on the one cultural level of standard English.

In Perrin's excellent and useful *Index*,[7] under the heading "Levels of

[6] Arthur G. Kennedy, *Current English* (Boston, 1935), pp. 15–17: "Speech Levels."
[7] Porter G. Perrin, *An Index to English* (Chicago, 1939), pp. 364–65.

Usage," he names "three principal levels": "Formal English" (likened to formal dress), "Informal English" (described as "the typical language of an educated person going about his everyday affairs"), and "Vulgate English." From his descriptions it appears clearly that Formal and Informal English are functional varieties of standard English, while Vulgate is a substandard cultural level. A similar classification appears in his table on page 365.

On page 19 Perrin uses *level* apparently in the sense of functional variety, not of cultural level: "Fundamentally, good English is speaking or writing in the level of English that is appropriate to the particular situation that faces the speaker or writer. It means making a right choice among the levels of usage." His advice, however, involves two choices: (1) choice of a standard cultural level and (2) choice of the appropriate functional variety of that level.

A clear instance of the inconsistent use of the term *level* is found in Robert C. Pooley's *Teaching English Usage* (New York, 1946), chapter iii, "Levels in English Usage." He names five levels: (1) the illiterate level; (2) the homely level; (3) standard English, informal level; (4) standard English, formal level; and (5) the literary level. In (1) and (2) *level* has an altogether different meaning from that in (3), (4), and (5). In the first two *level* plainly means "cultural level"; in the last three it just as plainly means "functional variety of standard English," all three varieties being therefore on the one cultural level of standard English. So *level* in the two groups belongs to different orders of classification. All misunderstanding and wrong implication would be removed from this otherwise excellent treatment of levels if the last three groups were labeled "Standard English Level, Informal Variety"; "Standard English Level, Formal Variety"; and "Standard English Level, Literary Variety." Pooley's groups contain three cultural levels (illiterate, homely, standard) and three functional varieties of the standard cultural level (informal, formal, literary).

The misapplication to colloquial English of the term *level*, metaphorically appropriate only to cultural gradations, is especially misleading. We often read of English that is "on the colloquial level." For example, Krapp writes: "*Who do you mean?* . . . has passed into current spoken use and may be accepted on the colloquial level."[8] This implies that colloquial English is on a different cultural level from formal English (literary, scientific, etc.), and a too frequent assumption, owing to this and other misuses of the term *colloquial*, is that its cultural level is below that of formal English. This supposition, tacit or explicit, that colloquial style is inferior to formal or literary style, leads inescapably to the absurd conclusion that. whenever scientists or literary artists turn from their formal writing to familiar conversation with their friends, they thereby degrade themselves to a lower social status.

[8] *A Comprehensive Guide to Good English* (New York, 1927), p. 641.

This misuse of *level* encourages the fallacy frequently met with of contrasting colloquial with standard English, logically as fallacious as contrasting white men with tall men. For instance, Mencken writes: " 'I have no doubt *but* that' . . . seems to be very firmly lodged in colloquial American, and even to have respectable standing in the standard speech." [9] This contrast, not always specifically stated, is often implied. For example, Kennedy writes: "Colloquial English is, properly defined, the language of conversation, and especially of familiar conversation. As such it may approximate the standard speech of the better class of English speakers, or it may drop to the level of the illiterate and careless speaker." [10] *May approximate* should be replaced by *may be on the level of*.

Similarly, on page 440: "Some measure words [are] still used colloquially without any ending in the plural . . . ; but most of these are given the *s* ending in standard English usage." Here *standard* is confused with *formal*.

Kennedy (pp. 534, 616) several times contrasts colloquial English with "standard literary English." This implies that colloquial English is not standard, while literary English is. If he means to contrast standard colloquial with standard literary, well and good; but I fear that most readers would understand the contrast to be of colloquial with standard.[11]

The term *colloquial* cannot properly designate a substandard cultural level of English. It designates a functional variety—that used chiefly in conversation—and in itself says nothing as to its cultural level, though this discussion, and the dictionary definitions, are chiefly concerned with cultivated colloquial, a functional variety of standard English. When writers of such standing as those I have mentioned slip into expressions that imply lower cultural status of colloquial English, it is not surprising that some teachers fall into the error. One teacher expressed the conviction that colloquialisms should not be represented as standard American speech. But the context of the statement indicated that its author was using *colloquialism* in the sense of "localism." I could hardly believe how frequent this gross error is, until I heard it from a well-known American broadcaster.[12]

The best dictionaries, at least in their definitions, give no warrant for the various misuses of *colloquial, colloquially, colloquialism, colloquiality*. I urge the reader to study carefully the definitions in the *Oxford English Dictionary*, with its many apt examples from standard writers, and in

[9] H. L. Mencken, *The American Language* (4th ed.; New York, 1936), p. 203.
[10] *Op. cit.*, p. 26.
[11] Greenough and Kittredge in *Words and Their Ways in English Speech* (New York, 1909), chap. vii, only apparently treat literary English as the sole standard form: "What is the origin of standard or literary English?" (p. 80). They use *standard* in a special sense for their particular purpose, calling it "the common property of all but the absolutely illiterate," "the language which all educated users of English speak and write" (therefore including colloquial). For the usual current meaning, see the definitions of *standard* quoted in *American Pronunciation* (6th and subsequent eds.), pp. 14–15.
[12] Leonard and Moffett also mention the frequency of this blunder (*op. cit.*, p. 351, n. 5).

Webster's New International Dictionary, Second Edition, with its quotations from George Lyman Kittredge. Kittredge's views on the standing of colloquial English are well known. It is said that somebody once asked him about the meaning of the label "Colloq." in dictionaries. He is reported to have replied, "I myself speak 'colloke' and often write it." I cannot verify the story, but it sounds authentic.

It seems to me inevitable that the frequent groupings of so-called "levels" such as "Literary, Colloquial, Illiterate," and the like, will lead the reader to suppose that just as Illiterate is culturally below Colloquial, so Colloquial is culturally below Literary. While I can scarcely hope that my humble remonstrance will reform all future writing on "levels of English," I believe that writers who confuse the meaning of the term *level* must accept some part of the responsibility for the popular misunderstanding of the true status of colloquial English; for I cannot avoid the belief that the popular idea of colloquial English as something to be looked down upon with disfavor is due in part to the failure of writers on the subject to distinguish between *cultural levels of English* and *functional varieties of standard English.*

Study Questions

1. Note the definition of *level,* as a noun, which Kenyon has in mind in the first sentence. Quote the definitions of *standard* and *substandard* which apply to the English language. How do these definitions confirm the evaluative implication of *levels* as used in reference to language?

2. Of the functional varieties listed in the fourth paragraph, which ones might be used on the substandard level by (1) an uneducated laborer, (2) a preacher in a poor church in a backward area, (3) a politician with a "plain-folks" approach to uneducated constituents? Which varieties would be used on the standard level by (1) a college-educated business man, (2) an eminent clergyman, (3) a noted scientist, (4) a statesman, (5) a celebrated novelist?

3. In Robert Penn Warren's *All the King's Men,* study the public speeches of Willie Stark in Chapters One and Six and his private conversations in Chapters Three and Six. What varieties of style can you identify? Select sentences or passages to illustrate each. In each selection, identify deviations from standard English, their purpose and effect. When Willie uses standard English, do "borrowed" words of foreign derivation or native words from Anglo-Saxon predominate?

4. In G. B. Shaw's *Pygmalion,* Acts I and V, study the speeches of Alf Doolittle for varieties of style on the substandard level. Does he ever rise to and *maintain* standard English? What are the chief deviations from standard English in his more formal speech?

5. From radio, television, or other listening situations, collect examples of "substandard" features in "the formal speech of the semi-literate."

6. *Webster's Third New International Dictionary* omits *colloq.* as a "Status Label." Consult the Preface to find out why. On the basis of Kenyon's article, do the reasons seem valid—that is, would the label *colloq.* be incorrectly interpreted by most dictionary users?

7. Drama and fiction have been the chief *recorded* sources of examples of colloquial language. Have modern recording devices greatly extended records of truly conversational English? In the quotations in *Webster's Third International,* what kinds of sources are likely to represent the colloquial variety of style?

8. Look up in *Webster's Second International* or *Webster's Collegiate Dictionary* one of the following verbs and list the idiomatic phrases marked *colloq.:* come, do, go, make, take. In *Webster's Third International,* look up these idiomatic phrases. Are the examples sufficient, in suggesting context, to serve as a guide to appropriate use? Refer to Sledd's and Evans's remarks on the omission of *colloq.* in *Webster's Third International.* Do you agree or do you think that the omission is no disadvantage to the student?

9. In a passage of dialogue from a modern American play or work of fiction, select the words and idiomatic phrases which you consider more suited to conversation than to formal situations. Compare the contexts with the examples in *Webster's Third International* illustrating those words or phrases. Do the examples suggest appropriate use in a context comparable to that in the literary source you used?

10. The analogy between language and dress is one of the most valid and helpful ways of showing that language is social and that it should suit the occasion. A snapshot of a person alone, with no background, gives no information about the suitability of his clothes, but a background and other persons will suggest the situation. A girl in a bathing suit on a dance floor would look as absurd as a girl in a formal gown on a beach. Do the "snapshots" of words in quotations in the dictionary give enough background? Collect ten or more examples of quotations and decide what variety of style each suggests. Do any fail to suggest variety?

19. SLANG AND ITS RELATIVES
Paul Roberts

Professor Roberts discusses the role and relevance of slang in human communication in *Understanding English* (1958), from which this selection is taken.

Slang is one of those things that everybody can recognize and nobody can define. Not only is it hard to wrap slang in a definition; it is also hard to distinguish it from such similar things as colloquialisms, provincialisms, jargon, trade talk. As we shall see, these areas blend into one another, and it is often a waste of time to look for the boundary.

One characteristic of a slang term is that it exists side by side with another, more general term for the same thing. Take for example the word *chick,* which has been used by some speakers in the meaning *girl* or *young woman.* The difference between *chick* and *girl* can be stated only in reference to the people who use the words: some say, "This chick is my sister"; others "This girl is my sister." *Chick* is slang and *girl* is not, because *chick* is used by a limited part of the population, mostly young people, whereas *girl* is used by everybody, including those who use *chick*.

It is often said that a slang term ceases to be slang when it is "accepted by the dictionary." This is not really the test. You will find many slang terms duly registered in dictionaries and still slang terms. The term ceases to be slang when it drives out of use its respectable synonym, or when it acquires a meaning that cannot be expressed otherwise. If, for instance, people ceased to use the word *girl* and all used *chick* instead, then *chick* could no longer be called a slang term.

Such things have happened. The term *hot dog* was once a slang term, but it couldn't be considered so now. No one in America would go up to a counter and order a "sausage sandwich." Similarly *varsity*, originally a slang contraction of *university*, has acquired special meanings which only it expresses and is no longer slang. *Jazz*, when it means a particular kind of music, is scarcely a slang term, since there is no more respectable word meaning that kind of music.

Certainly respectability must enter into any discussion of slang. Slang is essentially not respectable. There is always a more elegant way of saying the thing but one chooses the slang term for reasons. The reason may be a desire to be thought witty or clever or up to date. More often it is a desire to show, by a particular use of language, that one is a member in good standing of a particular group of people.

Criminals have always been prolific producers of slang because they are so obviously marked off from respectable society. They deliberately widen the gulf by multiplying language differences, and they often use the differences for practical purposes: to recognize one another, to shield their conversation from hostile ears. Criminal groups of the seventeenth and eighteenth centuries in England developed large vocabularies of slang— or *cant*, as it was then called—which rendered their talk almost meaningless to an outsider.

Much of the slang in common use today comes ultimately from characters on the other side of the law. This will be recognizable, for example, in words relating to American money. For "money" in general we have such terms as *dough, lettuce,* the *green* or the *big green, folding stuff,* and various others. The different denominations all have their slang terms: *singles* or *fish* for one dollar bills; *fin* for a five; *sawbuck* for a ten and *double sawbuck* for a twenty; *C-note* or *century* for a hundred; *grand* for a thousand. All of these are old, well-weathered terms and are familiar to many people who wouldn't dream of holding up a drugstore. But it is clear that they have their highest frequency in those districts where policemen would prefer to go in pairs.

In games slang is common everywhere, but it is most prolific in those games which are more or less disreputable. Bridge and golf have their slang terms, but gambling games have more, and roulette, for which the participants may wear evening clothes, has fewer than craps or poker, for which they usually do not. Poker has a wide variety of slang terms—or at least had when the writer had the game explained to him by an obliging friend. Thus in addition to the general names for the cards—*ace, deuce, king*—another set of slang terms are, or were, in use: *bull* or *bullet* for "ace," *cowboy* for "king," a *pair of ducks* for "a pair of deuces." Two aces and two eights are a *dead man's hand*, three tens are *thirty miles* or *thirty miles of railroad*, a flush of any sort is *all blue*.

Dice, even more disreputable than poker, has a correspondingly higher incidence of slang terms.

The connection between slang and the criminal element is seen again in the dope racket, the terms of which have been made more or less generally familiar by the movies and television. (The word *dope* itself is originally slang, but it is now in more general use than *narcotics*. Within the racket, terms abound. The words *marijuana* and *heroin* seem scarcely to occur among users or peddlers of the drugs, as is suggested by the fact that addicts speaking of heroin on a television program pronounced it to rhyme with *groin*. Usually, apparently, they say *H* or *big H* or *horse* or *caballito* (a Spanish word meaning "little horse" or "horsey"). Marijuana is referred to by several slang terms, of which *hay* seems to be most enduring. An injection of a narcotic is a *fix*. To inject it in the vein is to *mainline*. A salesman or peddler is a *pusher*. An addict is a *junkie*. To rid onself of an addiction is to *kick the habit*. It will be seen that a narcotics addict can discuss his troubles at some length without being understood by anyone outside the circle.

Musicians are another fertile source of slang terms. Again the element of more or less respectability enters: symphony orchestras are less prolific of slang terms than are purveyors of more popular music—jazz, swing, bebop, rock 'n' roll bands. Many of the slang terms in this area, as in others, have only the briefest existence, but others linger. Even the youngest readers will be acquainted with *dig* (understand or appreciate), *cool* (excellent or moving), *crazy* (inspired), *cat* (talented musician or knowledgeable music lover), *real* (exceptionally moving).

High school and college slang probably derives as much from music language as from any other source. More than one college professsor in the 1950's had to learn that the expression "dig that crazy course," coming from one of his earnest young disciples, was not a criticism but a high tribute. But colleges fill out their slang with terms that apply particularly to college activities. Many of these terms are simple abbreviations: *math, prof, exam, poly sci, econ, phys ed*. Others are names, varying from year to year and from campus to campus, for hard or easy courses, hard or easy teachers, passing and failing, studying, cheating, flattering the teacher (*apple-polishing* is an old term that persists). There are slang terms for those who raise class averages and for those who don't, for campus politicians, for campus reporters, for deans and college presidents, for football players, for serious students, for frivolous students, for fraternity and sorority men and women, for nonfraternity and nonsorority men and women, for pretty girls, for other girls, and for girls in general. Everyone and everything connected with college life can be referred to by a slang term as well as by a more general one.

Slang words are mostly nouns and verbs, but the adjective class has its slang too. Any college group at any given time uses one adjective to express general approval. This can be anything at all, even a newly coined noise. It is just something that slips into the pattern "That's very _____," and means that the speaker likes whatever is referred to. When the writer was in college the word was *gruesome*. If, in those days, you said "She's a real gruesome girl," you meant that she attracted you strongly and compelled your admiration.

Since then scores of words have successively taken the place of *gruesome*. The life expectancy of slang in this particular slot is not great. Middle-aged readers will perhaps remember *zorch* and *George*, both illustrations of the truth that all a word has to do to become an adjective is to occur in an adjective pattern. *George*, which until 1952 or so had been an unassuming proper noun, became an adjective as soon as people started saying "That's very George," or, more likely, "That's real George." This started the practice, short-lived, to be sure, of pushing other proper nouns into this position: "That's real Robert" (good), "That's real Tom" (bad), "That's strictly Alexander" (genuine).

Slang connects with grammatical structure at more points than one. For example, it could be stated almost as a law of language that an irregular word which picks up a slang meaning will be regularized. Thus the irregular verb *slay* at one time acquired, in addition to its older meaning of "kill," the slang meaning "interest, amuse": "You really slay me, kid." In this meaning it never occurs with the old past form *slew*. One would say not "He slew me" but always "He slayed me." Similarly *louse* has the plural *lice* when it refers to insects but *louses* when it refers to people.

It is sometimes said that the trouble with slang is that it is constantly changing, that a term becomes old-fashioned almost at birth. It is certainly true that some terms, particularly those that get quick and heavy use, wither faster than the rose. One has only to consider how obsolete terms like *zorch, George, hot* (hot music), *skirt* (girl), *flame* (girl or boy friend), *squire* (escort) sound today.

However, a short but merry life is by no means the rule for slang terms. Some linger on decade after decade, century after century indeed, never becoming quite respectable and never dying out either. The word *dough* for money is just as hardy as it ever was, though no more reputable. Others which seem likely to outlive the century are *cop* (policeman), *nuts* (insane), *plastered* (drunk), *wino* (drunkard), *limey* (Englishman), *jalopy* (automobile), *cram* (study hard). There are thousands of such—well below the salt but also well established at the table.

Teachers of English are often libeled to the effect that they are dedicated to a relentless pursuit of slang and are never so happy as when they are stamping out a slang term. This is part of the larger charge that teachers of English aren't people. Everybody uses slang as a natural result of speaking a language, though it is presumably true that the young and effervescent like to play with language more than their elders do. It is also true that what sounds gay and cute and clever to the young may sound merely banal to older ears.

The effect of slang is closely bound with the personality of the user. It is not simply a question of whether the slang is new or not or clever or not or incisive or not. It is a question of the total effect of the speaker. The writer can remember a friend who used a rather small selection of slang, none of it particularly witty, and used it rather constantly with no infusion of new terms; yet his conversation always seemed to have a pleasant sparkle to it, presumably because he himself sparkled pleasantly. On the other hand, there was another character who always—*always*—greeted one with the salutation, "Dig that crazy cat." He usually prefaced this with the expression "Hey, hey!" This grew tiresome.

Slang spreads fast sometimes, but it doesn't transfer very easily. A person who moves into a new group and brings with him an old group's slang *may* find his language admired and imitated. More likely people will consider him boring or affected or unpleasantly foreign. If he persists with his old talk and doesn't adopt that of the new group, he will find that people begin saying, "Here comes that type; let's get out of here."

The language that we call slang merges imperceptibly with other varieties. Every trade or profession, vocation or avocation has a set of terms more or less peculiar to it and often differing little or not at all from what we think of as slang. Trade talk often serves much the same purpose that slang does—to give coherence to the group and to exclude outsiders. If you think of peddling dope as a profession, then such terms as *fix, mainline, horse, junkie* are not slang but technical terms of the business.

A familiar example of terms of a trade are those employed on ships. Since sailors have for centuries led a life apart, a whole vocabulary has grown up, not only for those activities peculiar to the sea but also for many that go on under other names ashore. Thus a sailor speaks of a *ladder,* not a *staircase;* a *deck,* not a *floor;* a *bulkhead,* not a *wall;* a *head,* not a *toilet;* a *companionway,* not a *corridor;* a *galley,* not a *kitchen; fore* and *aft* and *port* and *starboard,* not *front* and *back* and *left* and *right.*

These terms, as in many other trades, are often jealously guarded. The landlubber inspecting the ship, the apprentice making his first trip are likely to evoke the seaman's cheerful scorn as they use land words for sea things. On the other hand, the landsman isn't any better off if he comes aboard with the proper vocabulary. During the Second World War, when young men were trained ashore in their duties before being assigned to ships, they would often come onto the ships with the right words and lisp assuredly of going below and going aloft, of galley and messroom and fo'c'sle. This also would irritate the oldtimers, who sometimes revenged themselves by talking of going downstairs instead of below and out on the front porch instead of to the bow.

Ship talk is but an obvious example of the kind of special language that any trade or profession or occupation, indeed any coherent human activity cultivates. In printing, in wrestling, in dentistry, in the automobile trade, the participants tend to develop terms which they use and the outside world does not. One difference between this trade talk and slang is that the trade term has a respectability that the slang term lacks. Thus one can say that *dope addict* is more dignified than *junkie, policeman* more dignified than *cop*. But one could hardly say that ship's *wall* is more dignified than ship's *bulkhead*.

Slang and much trade talk too merge imperceptibly with that broad area of language that we call *colloquialism*. "Colloquial" is a rather vague word with different meanings for different people, but it would seem most generally to mean words and constructions that occur more commonly in speech than in writing. As such it would include slang but would not be limited to slang. It would include all the forms that people—educated as well as uneducated—use in conversation but tend to avoid in writing. A further distinction is that *slang* usually denotes words rather than phrases, whereas *colloquialism* can mean a word, a phrase, a sentence—indeed can apply to the whole tone of the utterance.

Compare the sentences "He better take it easy" and "He should proceed carefully." Both might be uttered by people of impeccable breeding and both might occur in writing as well as in speech. The difference is simply one of frequency and likelihood. "He better take it easy" is what you are likely to say if you are chatting casually with someone about the activity of a mutual friend. "He should proceed carefully" is what you are likely to write in a letter to the newspaper.

Colloquialisms are not hard to find, since they make up the bulk of our daily conversation. At random we can compare such colloquial and literary expressions as "do your darndest" (strive), "put something over on someone" (fool), "lend a hand" (assist), "kept his mouth shut" (refused to divulge something), "hit the books pretty hard" (studied diligently), "an awfully cute kid" (a strikingly handsome young man), "who you trying to fool" (whom are you seeking to mislead).

At some periods of history people have had the idea that writing is better the farther it is from speech and that colloquialisms should therefore regularly be avoided. But this is scarcely the mood of the present day. Naturally, if you want to sound dignified—and one *does* want to sound dignified some-times—you choose dignified language and eschew terms that smack of shirt-sleeves and ginger ale. If you're seeking a position with a corporation, you might damage your chances by writing, "I sure hope you'll let me take a crack at the job. I got a notion I'd do real well at it. Sure would try anyhow." It would normally be better sense to say, "I am hoping that you will find it possible to try me in the position. I feel that I would be able to do the work successfully. Certainly I would try very hard."

However, it is undeniable that the trend of much modern writing is toward a more colloquial tone. Not only in advertising, which is ever pally, but also in more or less serious books, magazine articles, newspaper accounts, the tendency is to reflect more and more the words and rhythms of ordinary speech. One finds, for example, a greater use than formerly of contracted forms: *don't, shouldn't, he'll,* in place of *do not, should not, he will.* Plain or folksy or even slang words are often preferred to elegant ones, and writers pay less attention than their predecessors did to the niceties of schoolbook grammar.

The explanation of this trend is no doubt to be sought in sociological developments. The educated class, formerly a pretty exclusive group, is now the great mass of the population. Reading and writing, even a hundred years ago, was the accomplishment of relatively few; now everybody does it. Today's writer is talking not to the country club set but to everybody in town, and he tries to talk everybody's language.

But he shouldn't try too hard. Writing should above all be consistent and natural and honest, and the writer who labors the "jus' us plain folks" approach is spotted as a phoney by the plain folks as well as the fancy ones. Here, from a cereal box, is an example of nobody's language:

> Often, when I'm out ridin' the range, I find myself thinkin' about all the dare-devil deeds the Indian Chiefs did in days gone by, and of the unforgettable adventures of the gallant scouts and frontiersmen who met them in battle. I reckon all you young pardners of mine would like to hear all about them, too!

Even the youngest pardners may have an inkling that this cowboy rides the range on his portable typewriter.

One of the troubles of colorful language, slang or other, is that its color rubs off. The first time you hear and understand an expression like "Dig that crazy cat" you may find it exceptionally expressive, piquant, and moving. The second time you hear it, it isn't quite so exciting. The tenth time it has no effect at all. The fiftieth time it grates a little. The five hundredth time it may make you want to brain the speaker with a trombone.

If language isn't colorful to begin with, it doesn't pale. You can hear the sentence "Listen to that musician" five hundred times with no more pain the last time than the first. Clichés, or trite expressions, are simply dried up metaphors, figures of speech. They are racy ways of saying things but they have slowed down.

The first person who said "It was like walking on eggs" thought up a pretty clever comparison. When you read this for the first time, you get not only the information that the situation was delicate but a picture that reinforces and impresses the message. But this happens the first time only. After that you get only the information that the situation was delicate plus the fact that the writer is not very inventive. So also with "He fought like a tiger," "He behaved like a lamb," "He ran like a deer," "He ate like a pig," "He took a powder," "He pulled the wool over my eyes," "He's all wool and a yard wide," "She's pretty as a picture," "He spelled out the government's policy," "We'd better shake a leg," "An ocean of faces looked up at him," "A forest of masts filled the harbor," "She led him a merry chase," "It slid off him like water off a duck's back," "You can't fly on one wing," "He was as drunk as a lord, but his brother was as sober as a judge." All of these were more or less effective once.

Some groups of people seem to run more to clichés than others. Politicians are notorious, and some of their clichés, like "point with pride" and "view with alarm," have been laughed out of use. Sports writers and announcers also have difficulty avoiding trite phrases. One thinks of such expressions as "the fourth and final quarter" (one knows that the fourth quarter of a football game is the final one, but announcers seldom fail to point it out), "the bags are bulging," "circus catch," "smart little field general." All quarterbacks are smart little field generals, though some of them are also magicians. Line drives, proceeding toward the outfield, always scream, unless they go past something, like first, in which case they whistle. Pitchers are mostly big right-handers or little southpaws. Successful players come through in the clutch.

In fairness we should realize that sports writers and sports announcers deserve sympathy as much as criticism. They have to report, day after day and year after year, activities in which the same features are endlessly repeated. Moreover, they must always report these activities feverishly. The announcer is scarcely at liberty to say that today's football game is a pretty routine affair and the performers of no more than average competence. He must, every Saturday, bubble about how this is the most exciting grid spectacle that he and his colleagues have been privileged to see in a long time and how he wishes all us fans could be out there in the stadium with him to see these two great teams fighting their hearts out.

The cliché is every writer's enemy. Good writers fight clichés all the time, but few, even among the very best, win all the time. The triter the phrase, the more readily it comes to the mind, the more likely it is to slip into the sentence. You want to describe a mob, and you don't want to just say it was a big mob. You want to impress the reader with its size. "Sea of faces," you think, and you write it down. The trouble is that so many other writers have also written it down that it's lost all its blood. It no longer means anything more than "big mob," so you might as well have written "big mob" and been done with it.

The cliché is a difficulty for the young writer particularly, because he may not recognize the cliché when he sees it. "Sea of faces" may strike him as a bright new figure, not only expressive but original. One solution to this problem is experience. As we mature as readers, we become better equipped to recognize the stock phrases of the language as stock phrases. But the principal solution is to learn to distrust the pleasing phrase that comes too readily. It is only reasonable to suppose that the metaphor that jumps at you will have jumped at thousands of others before you.

It is very easy to write, to speak, to think in clichés. That's what most people do. They don't think for themselves but let the popular mind think for them. Their language is not personal but general, composed of public sentences with a few names changed to fit private conditions. There is nothing sinful about talking in clichés, and nobody can avoid it altogether. But those who don't avoid it at all betray laziness and mediocrity.

Study Questions

1. If you read crime stories or watch crime programs on television, list as many slang variants as you can think of or collect for such terms as *dope, gun, money, policeman, robbery*. Which of these slang terms would you avoid using among strangers as likely to suggest your association with criminals?

2. List as many slang terms current among college students as you can. What classifications are represented, such as abbreviations or initials for standard terms, terms for activities characteristic of college, local or temporary allusions, and so forth? Which slang terms would be familiar to most college-age young people? Which would be familiar to college students in general? Which would be familiar only to students on your own campus?

3. What are the current slang adjectives and nouns signifying approval? Signifying disapproval? Do you find the slang meanings in a general dictionary? In a slang dictionary?

4. Collect slang terms used by children and those used by your parents' generation. Do you use the same terms? Which terms can you find labeled as slang in a general dictionary? In a slang dictionary?

5. Conformity to current fads in dress is usually most noticeable among teen-agers. What fads in dress and slang are now current? Are they intended to identify the individual with the group and to dissociate him from other groups? What comparison can you make between teen-agers and trade groups? Is adult disapproval of certain styles of dress and haircuts analogous to disapproval of some speech habits as suggesting undesirable associations and fostering undesirable attitudes?

6. In view of Roberts's remarks about the present trend toward colloquialism,

is the omission of *colloq.* in *Webster's Third International* in harmony with current trends in language?

7. Compare styles in dress of the 1860's, the gay '90's, pre-World War I, the roaring '20's, and present styles: how may the trends in fashions be related to the trends in language? For what occasions in your life do you "dress up"? What people do you call by titles rather than by first names? Are you more likely to risk being too informal in speech and dress or being too formal? How can you apply your attitudes in matters of dress to your use of language? Some modern ministers are disturbed by members of their congregation coming to church in sports clothes. Ask your parents and grandparents if this is a new problem or, like many complaints about modern times, one characteristic of every older generation deploring the ways of youth.

8. Look up the literal meaning of *cliché* and *stereotype*. How does the origin of the terms emphasize the lack of individuality they stand for in language?

9. Frank Sullivan has written a number of "cliché expert" interviews. Look up one of them, in a subject you are fairly familiar with, and analyze the characteristics of the clichés used.

10. Supply the missing term in these pairs or triplets of clichés: "nip and —————," "hale and —————," "bright and —————," "kith and —————," "sink or —————," "live or —————," "survive or —————," "hammer and —————," "free, white, and —————," "wine, woman, and —————," "without regard to race, creed or —————."

11. Turn to the appendix of Wentworth and Flexner's *Dictionary of American Slang* and study the slang expressions relating to *boy, eater, fiend, head, jockey, man,* and *pusher.* Analyze the slang patterns into which these words fall in combined forms.

12. In a collegiate dictionary, select an alphabetical section, such as "dod-dol," either two consecutive columns or two separate ones, and compare with the same alphabetical area in Wentworth and Flexner's *Dictionary of American Slang.* Which words appear in both dictionaries? Which *definitions* of those words in Wentworth and Flexner do not appear in the collegiate dictionary? Which *words* in Wentworth and Flexner do not appear in the collegiate dictionary? What seems to be the relation between slang and nonslang vocabulary?

13. Browse through a collegiate dictionary and collect a dozen entries marked *Slang.* Look up the same terms in an older unabridged dictionary and in *Webster's Third International.* Have you found examples of slang which became acceptable, of slang that died out, of slang that survives as slang? What conclusions can you draw from your small list of terms as to what kind of slang survives and why?

14. In the Preface to Wentworth and Flexner, *Dictionary of American Slang,* pp. ix–x, read the two linguistic "case histories." Using them as models, do a case history of yourself or a close friend, showing contacts with subgroups and a few examples of slang acquired from each. How does this case history illustrate Flexner's "three cultural conditions" (p. x)?

15. List as many slang terms as you can which are used among your own subgroup to describe people and actions. Do these terms show subgroup criteria? Do they illustrate Flexner's statement, in the Preface to the *Dictionary of Ameri-*

can Slang (p. xi), that slang "tends toward degradation rather than elevation"?
16. If you belong to an occupational subgroup, list a dozen or so terms found
in the cant or jargon of that group. Are any of these terms offensive or vulgar?
Would any of these terms be unintelligible outside the group?
17. Test the awareness of slang as an entity by collecting from students who
are not in your English class definitions and examples of slang. How do their definitions of slang compare with those in the discussion by Roberts and in Flexner's
Preface to the *Dictionary of American Slang?* Are the students' examples classed
as slang in the dictionary? Would the general public be more aware or less aware
of slang as an entity than college students are?

20. THE LANGUAGE OF THE CATCHER IN THE RYE

Donald P. Costello

Professor Costello analyzes the dialogue used in J. D. Salinger's *The Catcher in
the Rye,* one of the most popular novels among college and high school students
in recent years. This study first appeared in *American Speech* for October, 1959.

A study of the language of J. D. Salinger's *The Catcher in the Rye* can
be justified not only on the basis of literary interest, but also on the basis
of linguistic significance. Today we study *The Adventures of Huckleberry
Finn* (with which many critics have compared *The Catcher in the Rye*)
not only as a great work of literary art, but as a valuable study in 1884
dialect. In coming decades, *The Catcher in the Rye* will be studied, I feel,
not only as a literary work, but also as an example of teenage vernacular
in the 1950s. As such, the book will be a significant historical linguistic
record of a type of speech rarely made available in permanent form. Its
linguistic importance will increase as the American speech it records becomes less current.

Most critics who looked at *The Catcher in the Rye* at the time of its
publication thought that its language was a true and authentic rendering
of teenage colloquial speech. Reviewers in the Chicago *Sunday Tribune,*
the London *Times Literary Supplement,* the *New Republic,* the New York
Herald Tribune Book Review, the New York *Times,* the *New Yorker,* and the
Saturday Review of Literature all specifically mentioned the authenticity
of the book's language. Various aspects of its language were also discussed
in the reviews published in *America,* the *Atlantic,* the *Catholic World,* the
Christian Science Monitor, the *Library Journal,* the Manchester *Guardian,*
the *Nation,* the *New Statesman and Nation,* the New York *Times Book Re-*

view, Newsweek, the *Spectator,* and *Time.*[1] Of these many reviews, only the writers for the *Catholic World* and the *Christian Science Monitor* denied the authenticity of the book's language, but both of these are religious journals which refused to believe that the "obscenity" was realistic. An examination of the reviews of *The Catcher in the Rye* proves that the language of Holden Caulfield, the book's sixteen-year-old narrator, struck the ear of the contemporary reader as an accurate rendering of the informal speech of an intelligent, educated, Northeastern American adolescent.[2]

In addition to commenting on its authenticity, critics have often remarked —uneasily—the "daring," "obscene," "blasphemous" features of Holden's language. Another commonly noted feature of the book's language has been its comic effect. And yet there has never been an extensive investigation of the language itself. That is what this paper proposes to do.

Even though Holden's language is authentic teenage speech, recording it was certainly not the major intention of Salinger. He was faced with the artistic task of creating an individual character, not with the linguistic task of reproducing the exact speech of teenagers in general. Yet Holden had to speak a recognizable teenage language, and at the same time had to be identifiable as an individual. This difficult task Salinger achieved by giving Holden an extremely trite and typical teenage speech, overlaid with strong personal idiosyncrasies. There are two major speech habits which are Holden's own, which are endlessly repeated throughout the book, and which are, nevertheless, typical enough of teenage speech so that Holden

---

[1] See reviews in *America,* LXXV (August 11, 1951), 463, 464; *Atlantic,* CLXXXVIII (1951), 82; *Catholic World,* CLXXIV (1951), 154; Chicago *Sunday Tribune,* July 15, 1951, Part 4, p. 3; *Christian Science Monitor,* July 19, 1951, p. 9; *Library Journal,* LXXVI (1951), 1125; *Times* [London] *Literary Supplement,* September 7, 1951, p. 561; *Manchester Guardian,* August 10, 1951, p. 4; *Nation,* CLXXIII (September 1, 1951), 176; *New Republic,* CXXV (July 16, 1951), 20, 21; *New Statesman and Nation,* XLII (August 18, 1951), 185; New York *Herald Tribune Book Review,* July 15, 1951, p. 3; New York *Times Book Review,* July 15, 1951, p. 5; New York *Times,* July 16, 1951, p. 19; *New Yorker,* XXVII (August 11, 1951), 71–76; *Newsweek,* XXXVIII (July 16, 1951), 89, 90; *Saturday Review of Literature,* XXXIV (July 14, 1951), 12, 13; *Spectator,* CLXXXVII (August 17, 1951), 224; *Time,* LVIII (July 16, 1951), 96, 97.

[2] If additional evidence of the authenticity of the book's language is required, one need only look at the phenomenal regard with which *The Catcher in the Rye* is held by today's college students, who were about Holden's age at the time the book was written. In its March 9, 1957, issue, the *Nation* published a symposium which attempted to discover the major influences upon the college students of today. Many teachers pointed out the impact of Salinger. Carlos Baker, of Princeton, stated: "There is still, as there has been for years, a cult of Thomas Wolfe. They have all read J. D. Salinger, Wolfe's closest competitor." Stanley Kunitz, of Queens College, wrote: "The only novelist I have heard praised vociferously is J. D. Salinger." Harvey Curtis Webster, of the University of Louisville, listed Salinger as one of the "stimulators." R. J. Kaufman, of the University of Rochester, called *The Catcher in the Rye* "a book which has complexly aroused nearly all of them." See "The Careful Young Men," *Nation,* CLXXXIV (March 9, 1957), 199–214. I have never heard any Salinger partisan among college students doubt the authenticity of the language of their compatriot, Holden.

can be both typical and individual in his use of them. It is certainly common for teenagers to end thoughts with a loosely dangling "and all," just as it is common for them to add an insistent "I really did," "It really was." But Holden uses these phrases to such an overpowering degree that they become a clear part of the flavor of the book; they become, more, a part of Holden himself, and actually help to characterize him.

Holden's "and all" and its twins, "or something," "or anything," serve no real, consistent linguistic function. They simply give a sense of looseness of expression and looseness of thought. Often they signify that Holden knows there is more that could be said about the issue at hand, but he is not going to bother going into it:

. . . how my parents were occupied and all before they had me (5.) [3]
. . . they're *nice* and all (5.)
I'm not going to tell you my whole goddam autobiography or anything (5.)
. . . splendid and clear-thinking and all (6.)

But just as often the use of such expressions is purely arbitrary, with no discernible meaning:

. . . he's my *brother* and all (5.)
. . . was in the Revolutionary War and all (6.)
It was December and all (7.)
. . . no gloves or anything (7.)
. . . right in the pocket and all (7.)

Donald Barr, writing in the *Commonweal,* finds this habit indicative of Holden's tendency to generalize, to find the all in the one:

> Salinger has an ear not only for idiosyncrasies of diction and syntax, but for mental processes. Holden Caulfield's phrase is "and all"—"She looked so damn *nice,* the way she kept going around and around in her blue coat and all"— as if each experience wore a halo. His fallacy is *ab uno disce omnes;* he abstracts and generalizes wildly.[4]

Heiserman and Miller, in the *Western Humanities Review,* comment specifically upon Holden's second most obvious idiosyncrasy: "In a phony world Holden feels compelled to reenforce his sincerity and truthfulness constantly with, 'It really is' or 'It really did.'"[5] S. N. Behrman, in the *New Yorker,* finds a double function of these "perpetual insistences of Holden's." Behrman thinks they "reveal his age, even when he is thinking much older," and, more important, "he is so aware of the danger of slipping into phoni-

---

[3] Whenever *The Catcher in the Rye* is substantially quoted in this paper, a page number will be included in the text immediately after the quotation. The edition to which the page numbers refer is the Signet paperback reprint.

[4] Donald Barr, "Saints, Pilgrims, and Artists," *Commonweal,* LXVII (October 25, 1957), 90.

[5] Arthur Heiserman and James E. Miller, Jr., "J. D. Salinger: Some Crazy Cliff," *Western Humanities Review,* X (1956), 136.

ness himself that he has to repeat over and over 'I really mean it,' 'It really does.'" [6] Holden uses this idiosyncrasy of insistence almost every time that he makes an affirmation.

Allied to Holden's habit of insistence is his "if you want to know the truth." Heiserman and Miller are able to find characterization in this habit too:

> The skepticism inherent in that casual phrase, "if you want to know the truth," suggesting that as a matter of fact in the world of Holden Caulfield very few people do, characterizes this sixteen-year-old "crazy mixed up kid" more sharply and vividly than pages of character "analysis" possibly could.[7]

Holden uses this phrase only after affirmations, just as he uses "It really does," but usually after the personal ones, where he is consciously being frank:

> I have no wind, if you want to know the truth. (8.)
> I don't even think that bastard had a handkerchief, if you want to know the truth. (34.)
> I'm a pacifist, if you want to know the truth. (44.)
> She had quite a lot of sex appeal, too, if you really want to know. (53.)
> I was damn near bawling, I felt so damn happy, if you want to know the truth. (191.)

These personal idiosyncrasies of Holden's speech are in keeping with general teenage language. Yet they are so much a part of Holden and of the flavor of the book that they are much of what makes Holden to be Holden. They are the most memorable feature of the book's language. Although always in character, the rest of Holden's speech is more typical than individual. The special quality of this language comes from its trite-ness, its lack of distinctive qualities.

Holden's informal, schoolboy vernacular is particularly typical in its "vulgarity" and "obscenity." No one familiar with prep-school speech could seriously contend that Salinger overplayed his hand in this respect. On the contrary, Holden's restraints help to characterize him as a sensitive youth who avoids the most strongly forbidden terms, and who never uses vulgarity in a self-conscious or phony way to help him be "one of the boys." *Fuck*, for example, is never used as a part of Holden's speech. The word appears in the novel four times, but only when Holden disapprovingly discusses its wide appearance on walls. The Divine name is used habitually by Holden only in the comparatively weak *for God's sake, God,* and *goddam.* The stronger and usually more offensive *for Chrissake* or *Jesus* or *Jesus Christ* are used habitually by Ackley and Stradlater; but Holden uses them only when he feels the need for a strong expression. He almost never uses

---

[6] S. N. Behrman, "The Vision of the Innocent," *New Yorker,* XXVII (August 11, 1951), 72.

[7] Heiserman and Miller, *op. cit.,* p. 135.

for Chrissake in a unemotional situation. *Goddam* is Holden's favorite adjective. This word is used with no relationship to its original meaning, or to Holden's attitude toward the word to which it is attached. It simply expresses an emotional feeling toward the object: either favorable, as in "goddam hunting cap"; or unfavorable, as in "ya goddam moron"; or indifferent, as in "coming in the goddam windows." *Damn* is used interchangeably with *goddam;* no differentiation in its meaning is detectable.

Other crude words are also often used in Holden's vocabulary. *Ass* keeps a fairly restricted meaning as a part of the human anatomy, but it is used in a variety of ways. It can refer simply to that specific part of the body ("I moved my ass a little"), or be a part of a trite expression ("freezing my ass off"; "in a half-assed way"), or be an expletive ("Game, my ass."). *Hell* is perhaps the most versatile word in Holden's entire vocabulary; it serves most of the meanings and constructions which Mencken lists in his *American Speech* article on "American Profanity." [8] So far is Holden's use of *hell* from its original meaning that he can use the sentence "We had a helluva time" to mean that he and Phoebe had a decidedly pleasant time downtown shopping for shoes. The most common function of *hell* is as the second part of a simile, in which a thing can be either "hot as hell" or, strangely, "cold as hell"; "sad as hell" or "playful as hell"; "old as hell" or "pretty as hell." Like all of these words, *hell* has no close relationship to its original meaning.

Both *bastard* and *sonuvabitch* have also drastically changed in meaning. They no longer, of course, in Holden's vocabulary, have any connection with the accidents of birth. Unless used in a trite simile, *bastard* is a strong word, reserved for things and people Holden particularly dislikes, especially "phonies." *Sonuvabitch* has an even stronger meaning to Holden; he uses it only in the deepest anger. When, for example, Holden is furious with Stradlater over his treatment of Jane Gallagher, Holden repeats again and again that he "kept calling him a moron sonuvabitch" (43).

The use of crude language in *The Catcher in the Rye* increases, as we should expect, when Holden is reporting schoolboy dialogue. When he is directly addressing the reader, Holden's use of such language drops off almost entirely. There is also an increase in this language when any of the characters are excited or angry. Thus, when Holden is apprehensive over Stradlater's treatment of Jane, his *goddams* increase suddenly to seven on a single page (p. 39).

Holden's speech is also typical in his use of slang. I have catalogued over a hundred slang terms used by Holden, and every one of these is in widespread use. Although Holden's slang is rich and colorful, it, of course, being slang, often fails at precise communication. Thus, Holden's *crap* is used in seven different ways. It can mean foolishness, as "all that David Copper-

[8] See H. L. Mencken, "American Profanity," *American Speech,* XIX (1944), 242.

field kind of crap," or messy matter, as "I spilled some crap all over my gray flannel," or merely miscellaneous matter, as "I was putting on my galoshes and crap." It can also carry its basic meaning, animal excreta, as "there didn't look like there was anything in the park except dog crap," and it can be used as an adjective meaning anything generally unfavorable, as "The show was on the crappy side." Holden uses the phrases *to be a lot of crap* and *to shoot the crap* and *to chuck the crap* all to mean "to be untrue," but he can also use *to shoot the crap* to mean simply "to chat," with no connotation of untruth, as in "I certainly wouldn't have minded shooting the crap with old Phoebe for a while."

Similarly Holden's slang use of *crazy* is both trite and imprecise. "That drives me crazy" means that he violently dislikes something; yet "to be crazy about" something means just the opposite. In the same way, to be "killed" by something can mean that he was emotionally affected either favorably ("That story just about killed me.") or unfavorably ("Then she turned her back on me again. It nearly killed me."). This use of *killed* is one of Holden's favorite slang expressions. Heiserman and Miller are, incidentally, certainly incorrect when they conclude: "Holden always lets us know when he has insight into the absurdity of the endlessly absurd situations which make up the life of a sixteen-year-old by exclaiming, 'It killed me.'" [9] Holden often uses this expression with no connection to the absurd; he even uses it for his beloved Phoebe. The expression simply indicates a high degree of emotion—any kind. It is hazardous to conclude that any of Holden's slang has a precise and consistent meaning or function. These same critics fall into the same error when they conclude that Holden's use of the adjective *old* serves as "a term of endearment." [10] Holden appends this word to almost every character, real or fictional, mentioned in the novel, from the hated "old Maurice" to "old Peter Lorre," to "old Phoebe," and even "old Jesus." The only pattern that can be discovered in Holden's use of this term is that he usually uses it only after he has previously mentioned the character; he then feels free to append the familiar *old*. All we can conclude from Holden's slang is that it is typical teenage slang: versatile yet narrow, expressive yet unimaginative, imprecise, often crude, and always trite.

Holden has many favorite slang expressions which he overuses. In one place, he admits:

> "Boy!" I said. I also say "Boy!" quite a lot. Partly because I have a lousy vocabulary and partly because I act quite young for my age sometimes. (12.)

But if Holden's slang shows the typically "lousy vocabulary" of even the educated American teenager, this failing becomes even more obvious when

---

[9] Heiserman and Miller, *op. cit.*, p. 136.
[10] *Ibid.*

we narrow our view to Holden's choice of adjectives and adverbs. The choice is indeed narrow, with a constant repetition of a few favorite words: *lousy, pretty, crumby, terrific, quite, old, stupid*—all used, as is the habit of teenage vernacular, with little regard to specific meaning. Thus, most of the nouns which are called "stupid" could not in any logical framework be called "ignorant," and, as we have seen, *old* before a proper noun has nothing to do with age.

Another respect in which Holden was correct in accusing himself of having a "lousy vocabulary" is discovered in the ease with which he falls into trite figures of speech. We have already seen that Holden's most common simile is the worn and meaningless "as hell"; but his often-repeated "like a madman" and "like a bastard" are just about as unrelated to a literal meaning and are easily as unimaginative. Even Holden's nonhabitual figures of speech are usually trite: "sharp as a tack"; "hot as a firecracker"; "laughed like a hyena"; "I know old Jane like a book"; "drove off like a bat out of hell"; "I began to feel like a horse's ass"; "blind as a bat"; "I know Central Park like the back of my hand."

Repetitious and trite as Holden's vocabulary may be, it can, nevertheless, become highly effective. For example, when Holden piles one trite adjective upon another, a strong power of invective is often the result:

He was a goddam stupid moron. (42.)
Get your dirty stinking moron knees off my chest. (43.)
You're a dirty stupid sonuvabitch of a moron. (43.)

And his limited vocabulary can also be used for good comic effect. Holden's constant repetition of identical expressions in countless widely different situations is often hilariously funny.

But all of the humor in Holden's vocabulary does not come from its unimaginative quality. Quite the contrary, some of his figures of speech are entirely original; and these are inspired, dramatically effective, and terribly funny. As always, Salinger's Holden is basically typical, with a strong overlay of the individual:

He started handling my exam paper like it was a turd or something. (13.)
He put my goddam paper down then and looked at me like he'd just beaten the hell out of me in ping-pong or something. (14.)
That guy Morrow was about as sensitive as a goddam toilet seat. (52.)
Old Marty was like dragging the Statue of Liberty around the floor. (69.)

Another aspect in which Holden's language is typical is that it shows the general American characteristic of adaptability—apparently strengthened by his teenage lack of restraint. It is very easy for Holden to turn nouns into adjectives, with the simple addition of a *-y*: "perverty," "Christmasy," "vomity-looking," "whory-looking," "hoodlumy-looking," "show-offy," "flitty-looking," "dumpy-looking," "pimpy," "snobby," "fisty." Like all of English, Holden's language shows a versatile combining ability: "They gave Sally this little blue butt-twitcher of a dress to wear." (117) and "That magazine was some little cheerer upper." (176). Perhaps the most interesting aspect of the adaptability of Holden's language is his ability to use nouns as adverbs: "She sings it very Dixieland and whorehouse, and it doesn't sound at all mushy." (105).

As we have seen, Holden shares, in general, the trite repetitive vocabulary which is the typical lot of his age group. But as there are exceptions in his figures of speech, so are there exceptions in his vocabulary itself, in his word stock. An intelligent, well-read ("I'm quite illiterate, but I read a lot"), and educated boy, Holden possesses, and can use when he wants to, many words which are many a cut above Basic English, including "ostracized," "exhibitionist," "unscrupulous," "conversationalist," "psychic," "bourgeois." Often Holden seems to choose his words consciously, in an effort to communicate to his adult reader clearly and properly, as in such terms as "lose my virginity," "relieve himself," "an alcoholic"; for upon occasion, he also uses the more vulgar terms "to give someone the time," "to take a leak," "booze hound." Much of the humor arises, in fact, from Holden's habit of writing on more than one level at the same time. Thus, we have such phrases as "They give guys the ax quite frequently at Pency." and "It has a very good academic rating, Pency." (7). Both sentences show a colloquial idiom with an overlay of consciously selected words.

Such a conscious choice of words seems to indicate that Salinger, in his attempt to create a realistic character in Holden, wanted to make him aware of his speech, as, indeed, a real teenager would be when communicating to the outside world. Another piece of evidence that Holden is conscious of his speech and, more, realizes a difficulty in communication, is found in his habit of direct repetition: "She likes me a lot. I mean she's quite fond of me." (141), and "She can be very snotty sometimes. She can be quite snotty." (150). Sometimes the repetition is exact: "He was a very nervous guy—I mean he was a very nervous guy." (165), and "I sort of missed them. I mean I sort of missed them." (169). Sometimes Holden stops specifically to interpret slang terms, as when he wants to communicate the fact that Allie liked Phoebe: "She killed Allie, too. I mean he liked her, too." (64).

There is still more direct evidence that Holden was conscious of his speech. Many of his comments to the reader are concerned with language. He was aware, for example, of the "phony" quality of many words and phrases, such as "grand," "prince," "traveling incognito," "little girls' room," "licorice stick," and "angels." Holden is also conscious, of course, of the existence of "taboo words." He makes a point of mentioning that the girl from Seattle repeatedly asked him to "watch your language, if you don't

mind" (67), and that his mother told Phoebe not to say "lousy" (160).
When the prostitute says "Like fun you are," Holden comments:

It was a funny thing to say. It sounded like a real kid. You'd think a prostitute
and all would say "Like hell you are" or "Cut the crap" instead of "Like fun
you are." (87.)

In grammar, too, as in vocabulary, Holden possesses a certain self-consciousness. (It is, of course, impossible to imagine a student getting through
today's schools without a self-consciousness with regard to grammar rules.)
Holden is, in fact, not only aware of the existence of "grammatical errors,"
but knows the social taboos that accompany them. He is disturbed by a
schoolmate who is ashamed of his parents' grammar, and he reports that
his former teacher, Mr. Antolini, warned him about picking up "just
enough education to hate people who say, 'It's a secret between he and
I'." (168).

Holden is a typical enough teenager to violate the grammar rules, even
though he knows of their social importance. His most common rule violation is the misuse of *lie* and *lay*, but he also is careless about relative pronouns ("about a traffic cop that falls in love"), the double negative ("I
hardly didn't even know I was doing it"), the perfect tenses ("I'd woke
him up"), extra words ("like as if all you ever did at Pency was play polo
all the time"), pronoun number ("it's pretty disgusting to watch somebody
picking their nose"), and pronoun position ("I and this friend of mine,
Mal Brossard"). More remarkable, however, than the instances of grammar rule violations is Holden's relative "correctness." Holden is always intelligible, and is even "correct" in many usually difficult constructions.
Grammatically speaking, Holden's language seems to point up the fact
that English was the only subject in which he was not failing. It is interesting to note how much more "correct" Holden's speech is than that of
Huck Finn. But then Holden is educated, and since the time of Huck there
had been sixty-seven years of authoritarian schoolmarms working on the
likes of Holden. He has, in fact, been overtaught, so that he uses many
"hyper" forms:

I used to play tennis with he and Mrs. Antolini quite frequently. (163.)
She'd give Allie or I a push. (64.)
I and Allie used to take her to the park with us. (64.)
I think I probably woke he and his wife up. (157.)

Now that we have examined several aspects of Holden's vocabulary and
grammar, it would be well to look at a few examples of how he puts these
elements together into sentences. The structure of Holden's sentences indicates that Salinger thinks of the book more in terms of spoken speech than
written speech. Holden's faulty structure is quite common and typical in

vocal expression; I doubt if a student who is "good in English" would ever create such sentence structure in writing. A student who showed the self-consciousness of Holden would not *write* so many fragments, such after-thoughts (e.g., "It has a very good academic rating, Pency." [7]), or such repetitions (e.g., "Where I lived at Pency, I lived in the Ossenburger Memorial Wing of the new dorms." [18]).

There are other indications that Holden's speech is vocal. In many places Salinger mildly imitates spoken speech. Sentences such as "You could tell old Spencer'd got a big bang out of buying it" (10) and "I'd've killed him" (42) are repeated throughout the book. Yet it is impossible to imagine Holden taking pen in hand and actually writing "Spencer'd" or "I'd've." Sometimes, too, emphasized words, or even parts of words, are italicized, as in "Now *shut up*, Holden. God damn it—I'm *warning* ya." (42). This is often done with good effect, imitating quite perfectly the rhythms of speech, as in the typical:

> I practically sat down on her *lap*, as a matter of fact. Then she *really* started to cry, and the next thing I knew, I was kissing her all over—*any*where—her eyes, her *nose*, her forehead, her eyebrows and all, her *ears*—her whole face except her mouth and all. (73.)

The language of *The Catcher in the Rye* is, as we have seen, an authentic artistic rendering of a type of informal, colloquial, teenage American spoken speech. It is strongly typical and trite, yet often somewhat individual; it is crude and slangy and imprecise, imitative yet occasionally imaginative, and affected toward standardization by the strong efforts of schools. But authentic and interesting as this language may be, it must be remembered that it exists, in *The Catcher in the Rye*, as only one part of an artistic achievement. The language was not written for itself, but as a part of a greater whole. Like the great Twain work with which it is often compared, a study of *The Catcher in the Rye* repays both the linguist and the literary critic; for as one critic has said, "In them, 1884 and 1951 speak to us in the idiom and accent of two youthful travelers who have earned their passports to literary immortality." [11]

Study Questions

1. Make a study of the slang in a few pages of *The Catcher in the Rye*. Look up the terms in Wentworth and Flexner, *Dictionary of American Slang*, determine the meaning, and decide whether the expression is teen-age or general slang.

2. Does Holden Caulfield use the same slang as teen-agers you know? Select a representative passage from the book and substitute terms which would be used by your subgroup.

[11] Charles Kaplan, "Holden and Huck: the Odysseys of Youth," *College English*, XVIII (1956), 80.

3. Select the slang terms from one of Salinger's short stories, and compare them with those Costello discusses. Is slang as frequent and as vulgar as in *The Catcher in the Rye?* What subgroups do the speakers or narrators represent?

Part **IV.** *Literary and Colloquial Aspects Subjects for Brief Papers or Written Reports*

1. Examine Benjamin Franklin's *Poor Richard's Almanac* and write a brief discussion of his use of learned and popular words.

2. Analyze Lincoln's "Gettysburg Address." Which words are popular? Which are learned? Write a short paper on the diction and the effect, with particular attention to popular words used for dignified effect, such as *forefathers* and *brought forth.*

3. Although *Pygmalion* is British, the theme of the social and economic importance of language applies, somewhat less stringently, to the United States. Write a brief paper on the speech of *one* of the characters in *Pygmalion.* Discuss how the character's speech reveals his social class and note expressions that are British rather than American.

4. Discuss the varieties of style which you consciously employ, with examples of how you would orally express the same idea in different situations. You may find it amusing and helpful to indicate how you would be dressed on each occasion.

5. From your own observation or from a glossary of "faulty diction" in a textbook make a list of a dozen or so terms which you find acceptable, according to one of the books on modern American usage—Bryant, or Evans—in colloquial use, and report on the treatment of those expressions in *Webster's Third International.* What examples are given? What context is suggested? Would you find the information adequate as a guide to use of the expression?

6. Study a recorded interview with a famous American author, in *Writers at Work* (New York, The Viking Press, Compass Books, 1959). Write a brief analysis of colloquial aspects of the writer's speech, with special attention to any regional characteristics. Would it be justifiable to regard this mode of expression as "below" the author's literary style?

7. Report on the use of *levels* in reference to language and style in the freshman composition text used in your institution; compare the patterns of classification with Kenyon's, using Kenyon's technique of analyzing and illustrating.

8. Present as a factual report the survey of college slang on your campus suggested in the second question on Roberts's "Slang and Its Relatives." See William White, "Wayne University Slang," *American Speech* (December, 1955), 301–05, for suggestions as to sources and method.

9. Write a brief paper on changes in slang as represented by three generations, yourself and your friends, your parents, and your subteen or early-teen acquaintances. Use both a general dictionary and a slang dictionary for status and meanings.

10. In Robert Penn Warren's *All the King's Men,* compare a passage from Chapter Four from Cass Mastern's journal with a passage comparable in seriousness and emotional quality by Jack Burden, the narrator. In a short paper discuss the chief differences in tone, idiom, diction, and sentence structure which may be ascribed to the difference in historical period.

11. Look up one or several of Frank Sullivan's "cliché expert" pieces: football (1938), politics (1940), war (1940), radio (1941), the atom (1945), campaign oratory (1948), baseball (1949), drama satire (1951), the campaign (1952). Write a "cliché expert" sketch of your own on a different subject, one which you read about and hear about frequently.

12. In a chosen portion of Wentworth and Flexner's *Dictionary of American Slang,* classify and discuss the words and meanings of words which do not appear in a collegiate dictionary. Evaluate the contribution of a slang dictionary to knowledge of spoken and written American English. (Note sources given in Wentworth and Flexner.)

13. Compile a glossary of space-age slang; list your sources and add analytical comments.

14. Write your autobiography in terms of the slang vocabulary associated with each phase of your life and the subgroups from which you acquired it.

15. Report on the cant or jargon of an occupational subgroup with which you are familiar: give a classified list of characteristic terms used, with comments on social and economic status of the users and the general tone of their language. Consult the Preface, Wentworth and Flexner, *Dictionary of American Slang,* for a discussion of cant and jargon, and examples.

16. Compile a glossary of teen-age slang or of the slang of a sport or activity. Comment on the relation of the slang terms to nonslang—different meanings for regular words, clipped forms, and so forth—and the characteristics of the words which occur only as slang. What proportion of the terms are monosyllables? Do your findings support Flexner's observation that monosyllables are prominent in slang?

17. Analyze the slang used in a few pages of *The Catcher in the Rye,* in one of Salinger's short stories, or in some other modern short story. Use Costello's article as a model.

18. Study one of George Ade's *Fables in Slang* or one of Ring Lardner's "You know me, Al" stories and report on differences between past and present slang. Which terms are still used? Which have ceased to be used but have a modern equivalent? Which are obsolete with no substitute? Is there any difference between the life of general slang and of slang which belongs to an activity or sport, such as baseball?

V. SOCIAL OR CLASS ASPECTS

These selections consider various facets of the problem of using language appropriate for different groups in a mobile society. These groups, which can be classified into categories, such as educational, occupational, or social, act as status symbols for those who feel inferior or insecure. By imitating the language of those they admire, the insecure hope to gain assurance, advancement, prestige, and status. In order to preserve certain social or class distinctions, some grammarians and lexicographers have tried to set themselves up as dogmatic guardians of linguistic stability, issuing rules and pronouncements while they mistakenly assume that they can arrest the changes of a living language. Although their prescriptions provide a comfortable crutch for the socially insecure to lean upon, they do not stop the changes or provide a permanent solution to the problem of appropriateness. As most of the writers in this section indicate, the prescriptions are of necessity relative, and any generalizations may be qualified by the four aspects of language considered in this collection of readings.

21. STANDARD ENGLISH
Charles C. Fries

In this passage from *American English Grammar* (1940) Professor Fries defines standard English as the particular language habits which have become socially acceptable in most communities throughout the United States.

In order to grasp the significance of . . . social differences in language practice for the obligation of the schools one must understand clearly what is meant by "standard" English, and that can perhaps best be accomplished by tracing the course by which a particular kind of English became "standard." As one examines the material written in England during the twelfth and thirteenth centuries—a period from one hundred to two hundred years after the Norman Conquest—he finds a situation in which three things are of especial note:

1. Most of the legal documents, the instruments which controlled the carrying on of the political and the business affairs of the English people, were not written in the English language but in French or in Latin. This fact was also true of much of the literature and books of learning familiar to the upper classes.

2. Although some books, especially historical records and religious and moral stories and tracts, were written in English, there was no single type of the English language common to all English writings. The greatest number used what is called the Southern dialect. This particular kind of English had been centered in Winchester, which was the chief city of King Alfred and his successors until the time of the Norman Conquest.

3. There was, therefore, no "standard" English in twelfth and thirteenth century England, for no single type of the English language furnished the medium by which the major affairs of English people were carried on. Instead, English people used for these purposes French, Latin, and at least four distinct varieties of English. The particular kind of English spoken in southern England came nearest to fulfilling the function of a "standard" English because more writings and more significant writings were produced in this type of English than in any other.

In the fourteenth and early fifteenth centuries, however, this situation changed. London had become the political and in some respects the social head of English life in a much more unified England. Many of the major affairs of the realm had to be handled in London. More and more the English language, the English of London, was used in the legal documents of politics and business. Solely because of the fact that more of the important affairs of English life were conducted in this London English rather than in Winchester English, London English became "standard" English. Naturally, then, the growing use of this particular type of English for the important affairs of English life gathered such momentum that even writers to whom other types of English were more natural felt constrained to learn and to use the fashionable London English. Gower, for example, a Kentishman, did not write his native kind of English but practically the same forms, constructions, and spellings as Chaucer, a Londoner born. Naturally, too, this London English gained a social prestige because of the fact that its use connoted or suggested relations with the center of affairs in English life, whereas the inability to use London English suggested that one did not have such social contacts. "Standard" English, therefore, is, historically, a local dialect, which was used to carry on the major affairs of English life and which gained thereby a social prestige.[1]

Many changes occurred in this dialect of English and these changes especially affected the usage of the younger rather than of the older generations in the centers of fashionable social life. Thus the continued use of the older forms rather than the newer changes always suggested a lack of direct contacts with those who were active in the conduct of important matters. In this connotation lay the power of "standard" English to compel the ambitious to conform to its practices.

In America, however, we have had no one recognized center for our political, business, social, and intellectual affairs. More than that, the great distances between various parts of the United States made very difficult frequent actual social contacts in the earlier days. Our coast cities, Boston and New York, maintained direct relations with London long after the earlier settlers had moved west, but the middle western settlements had practically no relations with Boston and New York. This fact can probably explain the differences between our middle-western speech and that of nineteenth century Boston and New York. Because of the fact that New England so long dominated our intellectual life there has been a good deal of feeling in many parts of the United States that the language usages of New England connoted a connection with a higher culture than did the language of the Middle West. Hence the rather widespread attempt to imitate certain New England speech characteristics. On the whole, however, if we ignore the special differences that separate the speech of New England, the South, and the Middle West, we do have in the United States a set of language habits, broadly conceived, in which the major matters of the political, social, economic, educational, religious life of this country are carried on. To these language habits is attached a certain social prestige, for the use of them suggests that one has constant relations with those who are responsible for the important affairs of our communities. It is this set of language habits, derived originally from an older Lon-

[1] "Standard" French, "Standard" Italian, "Standard" Dutch, etc., have similar histories.

don English, but differentiated from it somewhat by its independent development in this country, which is the "standard" English of the United States. Enough has been said to enforce the point that it is "standard" not because it is any more correct or more beautiful or more capable than other varieties of English; it is "standard" solely because it is the particular type of English which is used in the conduct of the important affairs of our people. It is also the type of English used by the *socially acceptable* of most of our communities and insofar as that is true it has become a social or class dialect in the United States.

Study Questions

1. The prestige of Harvard University reflects the past prestige of New England. Does Harvard set the standard in pronunciation to a degree comparable with the influence of Oxford and Cambridge universities on British pronunciation? What historical, geographical, and social facts about the United States have both contributed to uniformity and prevented a too restrictive standard of uniformity?

2. Standard English may be called a class dialect. If a person does not come from an environment where he has learned standard English, where can he acquire it? If he does acquire it thoroughly, is he at any real disadvantage in competition with those born to it?

3. Standard English establishes what is considered correct on the social and economic level where it is required. What may be the penalty for "incorrect" language?

4. If a person does not aspire to the social and economic level which demands standard English, does he personally need to acquire it? How does the flexibility of social classes in the United States result in different generations of one family having different speech habits?

5. Will most high school graduates have an absolute need for standard English? Will all college graduates have an absolute need for standard English if they remain among college-educated people? What are the implications of these facts about language for high school students preparing for college and for college students?

6. Like slovenly dress, slovenly speech is likely to suggest either ignorance of or indifference to what is acceptable. Which type of person can *least afford* to risk being considered ignorant or indifferent: the person content with a low social and economic status, the person established in high social and economic status, the person seeking to establish himself in the status he aspires to?

22. SPEECH COMMUNITIES
Paul Roberts

This chapter from *Understanding English* (1958) considers various speech groups and their effects upon the language patterns of speakers who come into contact with them.

Imagine a village of a thousand people all speaking the same language and never hearing any language other than their own. As the decades pass and generation succeeds generation, it will not be very apparent to the speakers of the language that any considerable language change is going on. Oldsters may occasionally be conscious of and annoyed by the speech forms of youngsters. They will notice new words, new expressions, "bad" pronunciations, but will ordinarily put these down to the irresponsibility of youth, and decide piously that the language of the younger generation will revert to decency when the generation grows up.

It doesn't revert, though. The new expressions and the new pronunciations persist, and presently there is another younger generation with its own new expressions and its own pronunciations. And thus the language changes. If members of the village could speak to one another across five hundred years, they would probably find themselves unable to communicate.

Now suppose that the village divides itself and half· the people move away. They move across the river or over a mountain and form a new village. Suppose the separation is so complete that the people of New Village have no contact with the people of Old Village. The language of both villages will change, drifting away from the language of their common ancestors. But the drift will not be in the same direction. In both villages there will be new expressions and new pronunciations, but not the same ones. In the course of time the language of Old Village and New Village will be mutually unintelligible with the language they both started with. They will also be mutually unintelligible with one another.

An interesting thing—and one for which there is no perfectly clear explanation—is that the rate of change will not ordinarily be the same for both villages. The language of Old Village changes faster than the language of New Village. One might expect that the opposite would be true —that the emigrants, placed in new surroundings and new conditions, would undergo more rapid language changes. But history reports otherwise. American English, for example, despite the violence and agony and confusion to which the demands of a new continent have subjected it, is probably essentially closer to the language of Shakespeare than London English is.

Suppose one thing more. Suppose Old Village is divided sharply into an upper class and a lower class. The sons and daughters of the upper class go to preparatory school and then to the university; the children of the lower class go to work. The upper-class people learn to read and write and develop a flowering literature; the lower-class people remain illiterate. Dialects develop, and the speech of the two classes steadily diverges. One might suppose that most of the change would go on among the illiterate, that the upper-class people, conscious of their heritage, would tend to preserve the forms and pronunciations of their ancestors. Not so. The opposite is true. In speech, the educated tend to be radical and the uneducated conservative. In England one finds Elizabethan forms and sounds not among Oxford and Cambridge graduates but among the people of backward villages.

A village is a fairly simple kind of speech community—a group of people steadily in communication with one another, steadily hearing one another's speech. But the village is by no means the basic unit. Within the simplest village there are many smaller units—groupings based on age, class, occupation. All these groups play intricately on one another and against one another, and a language that seems at first a coherent whole will turn out on inspection to be composed of many differing parts. Some forces tend to make these parts diverge; other forces hold them together. Thus the language continues in tension.

The child's first speech community is ordinarily his family. The child learns whatever kind of language the family speaks—or, more precisely, whatever kind of language it speaks to him. The child's language learning, now and later, is governed by two obvious motives: the desire to communicate and the desire to be admired. He imitates what he hears. More or less successful imitations usually bring action and reward and tend to be repeated. Unsuccessful ones usually don't bring action and reward and tend to be discarded.

But since language is a complicated business it is sometimes the unsuccessful imitations that bring the reward. The child, making a stab at the word *mother* comes out with *muzzer*. The family decides that this is just too cute for anything and beams and repeats *muzzer*, and the child, feeling that he's scored a bull's eye, goes on saying *muzzer* long after he has mastered *other* and *brother*. Baby talk is not so much invented by the child as sponsored by the parent.

Eventually the child moves out of the family and into another speech community—other children of his neighborhood. He goes to kindergarten and immediately encounters speech habits that conflict with those he has learned. If he goes to school and talks about his *muzzer*, it will be borne in on him by his colleagues that the word is not well chosen. Even

mother may not pass muster, and he may discover that he gets better results and is altogether happier if he refers to his female parent as his ma
or even his old lady.

Children coming together in a kindergarten class bring with them language that is different because it is learned in different homes. It is all to
some degree unsuccessfully learned, consisting of not quite perfect imitations of the original. In school all this speech coalesces, differences tend
to be ironed out, and the result differs from the original parental speech
and differs in pretty much the same way.

The pressures on the child to conform to the speech of his age group, his
speech community, are enormous. He may admire his teacher and love
his mother; he may even—and even consciously—wish to speak as they
do. But he *has* to speak like the rest of the class. If he does not, life becomes
intolerable.

The speech changes that go on when the child goes to school are often
most distressing to parents. Your little Bertram, at home, has never heard
anything but the most elegant English. You send him to school, and what
happens? He comes home saying things like "I done real good in school
today, Mom." But Bertram really has no choice in the matter. If Clarence
and Elbert and the rest of the fellows customarily say "I done real good,"
then Bertram might as well go around with three noses as say things
like "I did very nicely."

Individuals differ, of course, and not all children react to the speech
community in the same way. Some tend to imitate and others tend to force
imitation. But all to some degree have their speech modified by forces
over which neither they nor their parents nor their teachers have any real
control.

Individuals differ too in their sensitivity to language. For some, language
is always a rather embarrassing problem. They steadily make boners, saying the right thing in the wrong place or the wrong way. They have a hard
time fitting in. Others tend to change their language slowly, sticking
stoutly to their way of saying things, even though their way differs from
that of the majority. Still others adopt new language habits almost automatically, responding quickly to whatever speech environment they encounter.

Indeed some children of five or six have been observed to speak two
or more different dialects without much awareness that they are doing so.
Most commonly, they will speak in one way at home and in another on the
playground. At home they say, "I did very nicely" and "I haven't any";
these become, at school, "I done real good" and "I ain't got none."

Throughout the school years, or at least through the American secondary
school, the individual's most important speech community is his age group,
his class. Here is where the real power lies. The rule is conformity above
all things, and the group uses its power ruthlessly on those who do not

conform. Language is one of the chief means by which the school group seeks to establish its entity, and in the high school this is done more or less consciously. The obvious feature is high school slang, picked up from the radio, from other schools, sometimes invented, changing with bewildering speed. Nothing is more satisfactory than to speak today's slang; nothing more futile than to use yesterday's.

There can be few tasks more frustrating than that of the secondary school teacher charged with the responsibility of brushing off and polishing up the speech habits of the younger generation. Efforts to make *real* into *really*, *ain't* into *am not*, *I seen him* into *I saw him*, *he don't* into *he doesn't* meet at best with polite indifference, at worst with mischievous counter-attack.

The writer can remember from his own high school days when the class, a crashingly witty bunch, took to pronouncing the word *sure* as *sewer*. "Have you prepared your lesson, Arnold?" Miss Driscoll would ask. "Sewer, Miss Driscoll," Arnold would reply. "I think," said Miss Driscoll, who was pretty quick on her feet too, "that you must mean 'sewerly,' since the construction calls for the adverb not the adjective." We were delighted with the suggestion and went about saying "sewerly" until the very blackboards were nauseated. Miss Driscoll must have wished often that she had left it lay.

When the high school class graduates, the speech community disintegrates as the students fit themselves into new ones. For the first time in the experience of most of the students the speech ways of adult communities begin to exercise real force. For some people the adjustment is a relatively simple one. A boy going to work in a garage may have a good deal of new lingo to pick up, and he may find that the speech that seemed so racy and won such approval in the corridors of Springfield High leaves his more adult associates merely bored. But a normal person will adapt himself without trouble.

For others in other situations settling into new speech communities may be more difficult. The person going into college, into the business world, into scrubbed society may find that he has to think about and work on his speech habits in order not to make a fool of himself too often.

College is a particularly complicated problem. Not only does the freshman confront upperclassmen not particularly disposed to find the speech of Springfield High particularly cute, but the adult world, as represented chiefly by the faculty, becomes increasingly more immediate. The problems of success, of earning a living, of marriage, of attaining a satisfactory adult life loom larger, and they all bring language problems with them. Adaptation is necessary, and the student adapts.

The student adapts, but the adult world adapts too. The thousands of boys and girls coming out of the high schools each spring are affected by the speech of the adult communities into which they move, but they also affect that speech. The new pronunciation habits, developing grammatical features, different vocabulary do by no means all give way before the disapproval of elders. Some of them stay. Elders, sometimes to their dismay, find themselves changing their speech habits under the bombardment of those of their juniors. And then of course the juniors eventually become the elders, and there is no one left to disapprove.

Speech communities are formed by many features besides that of age. Most obvious is geography. Our country was originally settled by people coming from different parts of England. They spoke different dialects to begin with and as a result regional speech differences existed from the start in the different parts of the country. As speakers of other languages came to America and learned English, they left their mark on the speech of the sections in which they settled. With the westward movement, new pioneers streamed out through the mountain passes and down river valleys, taking the different dialects west and modifying them by new mixtures in new environments.

Today we are all more or less conscious of certain dialect differences in our country. We speak of the "southern accent," "the Brooklyn accent," the "New England accent." Until a few years ago it was often said that American English was divided into three dialects: Southern American (south of the Mason-Dixon line); Eastern American (east of the Connecticut River); and Western American. This description suggests certain gross differences all right, but recent research shows that it is a gross oversimplification.

The starting point of American dialects is the original group of colonies. We had a New England settlement, centering in Massachusetts; a Middle Atlantic settlement, centering in Pennsylvania; a southern settlement, centering in Virginia and the Carolinas. These colonies were different in speech to begin with, since the settlers came from different parts of England. Their differences were increased as the colonies lived for a century and a half or so with only thin communication with either Mother England or each other. By the time of the Revolution the dialects were well established. Within each group there were of course subgroups. Richmond speech differed markedly from that of Savannah. But Savannah and Richmond were more like each other than they were like Philadelphia or Boston.

The Western movement began shortly after the Revolution, and dialects followed geography. The New Englanders moved mostly into upper New York State and the Great Lakes region. The Middle Atlantic colonists went down the Shenandoah Valley and eventually into the heart of the Midwest. The southerners opened up Kentucky and Tennessee, later the lower Mississippi Valley, later still Texas and much of the Southwest.

Thus new speech communities were formed, related to the old ones of the seaboard, but each developing new characteristics as lines of settlement crossed.

New complications were added before and after the Revolution by the great waves of immigration of people from countries other than England: Swedes in Delaware, Dutch in New York, Germans and Scots-Irish in Pennsylvania, Irish in New England, Poles and Greeks and Italians and Portuguese. The bringing in of Negro slaves had an important effect on the speech of the South and later on the whole country. The Spanish in California and the Southwest added their mark. In this century movement of peoples goes on: the trek of southern Negroes to northern and western cities, the migration of people from Arkansas, Oklahoma, and Texas to California. All these have shaped and are shaping American speech.

We speak of America as the melting pot, but the speech communities of this continent are very far from having melted into one. Linguists today can trace very clearly the movements of the early settlers in the still living speech of their descendants. They can follow an eighteenth century speech community West, showing how it crossed this pass and followed that river, threw out an offshoot here, left a pocket there, merged with another group, halted, split, moved on once more. If all other historical evidence were destroyed, the history of the country could still be reconstructed from the speech of modern America.

The third great shaper of speech communities is the social class. This has been, and is, more important in England than in America. In England, class differences have often been more prominent than those of age or place. If you were the blacksmith's boy, you might know the son of the local baronet, but you didn't speak his language. You spoke the language of your social group, and he that of his, and over the centuries these social dialects remained widely separated.

England in the twentieth century has been much democratized, but the language differences are far from having disappeared. One can still tell much about a person's family, his school background, his general position in life by the way he speaks. Social lines are hard to cross, and language is perhaps the greatest barrier. You may make a million pounds and own several cars and a place in the country, but your vowels and consonants and nouns and verbs and sentence patterns will still proclaim to the world that you're not a part of the upper crust.

In America, of course, social distinctions have never been so sharp as they are in England. We find it somewhat easier to rise in the world, to move into social environments unknown to our parents. This is possible, partly, because speech differences are slighter; conversely, speech differences are slighter because this is possible. But speech differences do exist. If you've spent all your life driving a cab in Philly and, having inherited a fortune, move to San Francisco's Nob Hill, you will find that your language is different, perhaps embarrassingly so, from that of your new acquaintances.

Language differences on the social plane in America are likely to correlate with education or occupation rather than with birth—simply because education and occupation in America do not depend so much on birth as they do in other countries. A child without family connection can get himself educated at Harvard, Yale, Princeton. In doing so, he acquires the speech habits of the Ivy League and gives up those of his parents.

Exceptions abound. But in general there is a clear difference between the speech habits of the college graduate and those of the high school graduate. The cab driver does not talk like the Standard Oil executive, the college professor like the carnival pitch man, or an Illinois merchant like a sailor shipping out of New Orleans. New York's Madison Avenue and Third Avenue are only a few blocks apart, but they are widely separated in language. And both are different from Broadway.

It should be added that the whole trend of modern life is to reduce rather than to accentuate these differences. In a country where college education becomes increasingly everybody's chance, where executives and refrigerator salesmen and farmers play golf together, where a college professor may drive a cab in the summertime to keep his family alive, it becomes harder and harder to guess a person's education, income, and social status by the way he talks. But it would be absurd to say that language gives no clue at all.

Speech communities, then, are formed by many features: age, geography, education, occupation, social position. Young people speak differently from old people, Kansans differently from Virginians, Yale graduates differently from Dannemora graduates. Now let us pose a delicate question: aren't some of these speech communities better than others? That is, isn't better language heard in some than in others?

Well, yes, of course. One speech community is always better than all the rest. This is the group in which one happens to find oneself. The writer would answer unhesitatingly that the noblest, loveliest, purest English is that heard in the Men's Faculty Club of San Jose State College, San Jose, California. He would admit, of course, that the speech of some of the younger members leaves something to be desired; that certain recent immigrants from Harvard, Michigan, and other foreign parts need to work on the laughable oddities lingering in their speech; and that members of certain departments tend to introduce a lot of queer terms that can only be described as jargon. But in general the English of the Faculty Club is ennobling and sweet.

As a practical matter, good English is whatever English is spoken by the group in which one moves contentedly and at ease. To the bum on Main Street in Los Angeles, good English is the language of other L.A.

bums. Should he wander onto the campus of UCLA, he would find the talk there unpleasant, confusing, and comical. He might agree, if pressed, that the college man speaks "correctly" and he doesn't. But in his heart he knows better. He wouldn't talk like them college jerks if you paid him.

If you admire the language of other speech communities more than you do your own, the reasonable hypothesis is that you are dissatisfied with the community itself. It is not precisely other speech that attracts you but the people who use the speech. Conversely, if some language strikes you as unpleasant or foolish or rough, it is presumably because the speakers themselves seem so.

To many people, the sentence "Where is he at?" sounds bad. It is bad, they would say, in and of itself. The sounds are bad. But this is very hard to prove. If "Where is he at?" is bad because it has bad sound combinations, then presumably "Where is the cat?" or "Where is my hat?" are just as bad, yet no one thinks them so. Well, then, "Where is he at?" is bad because it uses too many words. One gets the same meaning from "Where is he?" so why add the *at?* True. Then "He going with us?" is a better sentence than "Is he going with us?" You don't really need the *is,* so why put it in?

Certainly there are some features of language to which we can apply the terms *good* and *bad, better* and *worse.* Clarity is usually better than obscurity; precision is better than vagueness. But these are not often what we have in mind when we speak of good and bad English. If we like the speech of upper-class Englishmen, the presumption is that we admire upper-class Englishmen—their characters, culture, habits of mind. Their sounds and words simply come to connote the people themselves and become admirable therefore. If we knew the same sounds and words from people who were distasteful to us, we would find the speech ugly.

This is not to say that correctness and incorrectness do not exist in speech. They obviously do, but they are relative to the speech community —or communities—in which one operates. As a practical matter, correct speech is that which sounds normal or natural to one's comrades. Incorrect speech is that which evokes in them discomfort or hostility or disdain.

Study Questions

1. What examples of the language conservatism of the lower class have appeared in previous selections?

2. How do the article on slang by Roberts and Costello's study of *The Catcher in the Rye* supplement Roberts's account of speech communities?

3. From your own experience or observation, can you cite examples of radical changes in speech communities from home to school and from school to college?

4. Do younger generations influence older generations in dress as well as in speech? How would Whistler's mother be dressed today? How significant is the present American emphasis on youthfulness in speech, dress, and conduct?

5. What kinds of place-names—see Mencken—serve as clues to the migration patterns and dialects Roberts discusses? Do names in your own state agree with Roberts's generalizations? Can you find in your own community speech habits that reveal the history of the area?

6. What examples can you find, in your own experience or observation, of individuals whose language reflects their similar education and occupation, but who were born into widely separated social classes?

7. If "good" English is that spoken by a group in which one is at ease, what are the implications for the college graduate who enters, let us say, a profession and whose parents speak substandard English? Need the parents speak as their son does if they are content to remain with their own age and occupation group? If they wish to enter his group, can they be at ease if their speech is different? Is the essential point "good English" or "correctness," or is it, like good manners, a question of an arbitrary standard? Can natural dignity, poise, and good sense enable a person to be at ease even though his speech and manners differ from those of the group?

8. In the United States, is an individual's rise in social and economic status likely to be regarded as creditable or as a fact to be concealed? What examples can you think of in American politics of aristocrats and of self-made men? Does the phrase "from log cabin to White House" suggest approval or condemnation of such a rise from humble origins? How does social mobility, in contrast with fixed social classes, affect both the language used by self-made leaders and the attitudes of the people to the language of their leaders?

23. THE LANGUAGE OF THE CULTIVATED

Austin C. Dobbins

This article, from *College English* for October, 1956, discusses the problem of determining standards of appropriateness in written and spoken expression. Since there are no absolute standards, the student, often to his own confusion, is forced to rely upon the authority of the handbook or dictionary which he is consulting.

In virtually all modern handbooks of composition, students are advised to confine their language choices in college themes to usages which are appropriate to the writing of cultivated people. The use of colloquialisms is to be avoided. Slang—dread thought—is perhaps better rejected entirely. More appropriately, college themes are to be clothed in language which is appropriate to "the highest level of usage and style" which students are capable of writing.

How is the student to follow this frequently expressed advice of his elders? To what authority is he to turn to determine which terms are or are not suitable to the highest level of usage and style which he is capable of writing? Perhaps study of the statements regarding usage in the handbooks will enable the student to achieve the desired standard. Unfortunately, unless he decides to accept the pronouncements of one particular text, the student who follows this suggestion faces difficulties. To Hodges (*Harbrace Handbook*, 1951) *ugly* (ill-tempered) is a colloquialism. To Marckwardt (*Scribner Handbook*, 1948), however, employment of *ugly* in this sense is clearly sanctioned by literary use. To *fix* (to repair), according to McCrimmon (*Writing with a Purpose*, 1950), is a term which is inappropriate in formal style. Warfel (*American College English*, 1949) considers this a usage acceptable in all but the most formal writing. Kierzek (*Macmillan Handbook*, 1954) asserts that *complected* should not be used in any level of writing. Leggett (*Prentice-Hall Handbook*, 1954) suggests instead that *complected* is acceptable as a colloquialism. Foerster (*Writing and Thinking*, 1952) labels "to feature" (to give special prominence to) as colloquial or as business jargon. Gorrell (*Modern English Handbook*, 1953) states rather that while overused the term is becoming established usage. The list might well be extended. Considerable disagreement exists regarding the status of such words as *bunch, claim, contact, date, farther, humans, lend, mad, nice,* and *tough*.

If the dictionary, which "records the [actual] usage of the speakers and writers of our language," is accepted as the authority, the result is frequently even greater confusion. For example, the *American College Dictionary* ("the best dictionary the English language has ever had") terms colloquial such words as *cop, gripe, holdup,* and *pal*. *Webster's New Collegiate Dictionary* ("the supreme authority") labels these words slang.[1] *Webster's,* in turn, maintains that *guy, kids, medico,* and *to neck* (words chosen almost at random) are colloquial. The ACD identifies these words as slang. Since both dictionaries claim to base their labels upon usage, the question inevitably arises as to which dictionary should be accepted as *the* authority.

Admittedly, the words in these lists belong to shifting classifications. In many cases the differences between slang and colloquial usages are more of degree than of kind. But what of such words as *boondoggle, corny, frisk, liquidate, pinhead, bonehead, carpetbagger, pleb, slush fund,* and *snide*? Which of these words ordinarily would be considered appropriate in themes written by cultivated people? According to the editors of the ACD, the first five of these words are slang; the second five are established usage. To the editors of WNCD, the first five of these words represent established usage; the second five are slang. Which authority is the student to follow?

---

[1] The *American College Dictionary* (1953) and *Webster's New Collegiate Dictionary* (1953) are used primarily for convenience in reference. Similar disagreement may be found if the labels in other standard dictionaries are compared.

Since the pronouncements both of handbooks and of dictionaries prove confusing, perhaps the use of "common sense" on the part of the instructor may resolve disagreement into agreement. But this suggestion also raises difficulties. The instructor is asked to comment upon the level of language found in the following "specimens" of college writing. Should the italicized words in these selections be considered appropriate or inappropriate to the writing of cultivated people?

The *highbinders* took care properly to *grease the palms* of the police. They hired *shysters* who didn't give a *tinker's damn* for law or justice. And, although the other Mongoloids soon became *sick* of the obvious connections between *honky-tonk* and law, honest citizens of all races continued to be *turned down* at the city hall so long as bribery remained unchecked. *Yellow* though the crooks were said to be, no crook was found willing to *spill* enough information to keep the town from being known as a *push-over* for criminal elements.

Flophouse habitués, wrinkled and wary, *skewed* eyed delinquents with *smokes* dangling loosely from their lips, old men shaky from *bootleg* and lack of soda—one and all made *snide* remarks as they listened to the ancient *wheezes* of Rev. Sam. *"Bonehead"* was the least of the taunts they used. But Sam was set in his ways. He paid no attention to their *lip*.

What is the instructor to answer? If he objects to the italicized words, he may be asked to show cause and authority for his objection. If he tries to defend the use of words of this nature by suggesting that levels of language vary in accordance with the demands of speaker, subject, and audience (the doctrine of appropriateness), he may be referred to particular authorities who maintain that "careful writers avoid this usage" in cultivated writing. Then, after laboriously consulting the various authorities, if he is conscientious, the instructor will discover that the authorities disagree. The ACD classifies the italicized words in the first selection as slang (the type of language which usually is to be avoided in college compositions). WNCD regards each of these terms as established usage. The ACD considers the italicized words in the second selection as established. WNCD labels these terms as a mixture of dialect and slang.

Certain words are deemed inappropriate in college compositions. How is the student to recognize these terms which are inappropriate to the highest level of usage and style—inappropriate to the writing of cultivated people? Perhaps the answer is to advise students to study only one handbook, consult one dictionary, listen to one instructor. An alternate suggestion, of course, is for our textbooks more accurately to base their labels upon studies of usage.

Study Questions

1. How does *Webster's Third New International Dictionary* provide material for studies of usage?

2. Consult the glossary of faulty expressions in a composition text. Select expressions which have troubled you and look them up in Evans and Evans, *Dictionary of Contemporary American Usage;* or Evans, *Comfortable Words;* or Bryant, *Current American Usage.* Is the textbook in agreement with studies based on usage?

3. How should a student writing for older readers adapt his style to his readers?

4. If a student addresses himself specifically to his own age group, are colloquialisms and slang appropriate?

5. In *Webster's New Collegiate Dictionary, Webster's New World Dictionary,* and the *American College Dictionary,* check the usage labels Dobbins uses in his second paragraph. What labels are now applied to these words?

24. GRAMMAR FOR TODAY
Bergen Evans

Professor Evans's essay, which appeared in the *Atlantic Monthly* in March, 1960, attacks the prescriptive approach to grammar and usage which has dominated language teaching for almost two centuries.

In 1747 Samuel Johnson issued a plan for a new dictionary of the English language. It was supported by the most distinguished printers of the day and was dedicated to the model of all correctness, Philip Dormer Stanhope, Fourth Earl of Chesterfield. Such a book, it was felt, was urgently needed to "fix" the language, to arrest its "corruption" and "decay," a degenerative process which, then as now, was attributed to the influence of "the vulgar" and which, then as now, it was a mark of superiority and elegance to decry. And Mr. Johnson seemed the man to write it. He had an enormous knowledge of Latin, deep piety, and dogmatic convictions. He was also honest and intelligent, but the effect of these lesser qualifications was not to show until later.

Oblig'd by hunger and request of friends, Mr. Johnson was willing to assume the role of linguistic dictator. He was prepared to "fix" the pronunciation of the language, "preserve the purity" of its idiom, brand "impure" words with a "note of infamy," and secure the whole "from being overrun by . . . low terms."

There were, however, a few reservations. Mr. Johnson felt it necessary to warn the oversanguine that "Language is the work of man, a being from whom permanence and stability cannot be derived." English "was not formed from heaven . . . but was produced by necessity and enlarged by accident." It had, indeed, been merely "thrown together by negligence" and was in such a state of confusion that its very syntax could no longer "be taught by general rules, but [only] by special precedents."

In 1755 the *Dictionary* appeared. The noble patron had been given a great deal more immortality than he had bargained for by the vigor of the kick Johnson had applied to his backside as he booted him overboard. And the *Plan* had been replaced by the *Preface*, a sadder but very much wiser document.

Eight years of "sluggishly treading the track of the alphabet" had taught Johnson that the hopes of "fixing" the language and preserving its "purity" were but "the dreams of a poet doomed at last to wake a lexicographer." In "the boundless chaos of living speech," so copious and energetic in its disorder, he had found no guides except "experience and analogy." Irregularities were "inherent in the tongue" and could not be "dismissed or reformed" but must be permitted "to remain untouched." "Uniformity must be sacrificed to custom . . . in compliance with a numberless majority" and "general agreement." One of the pet projects of the age had been the establishment of an academy to regulate and improve style. "I hope," Johnson wrote in the *Preface*, that if "it should be established . . . the spirit of English liberty will hinder or destroy [it.]"

At the outset of the work he had flattered himself, he confessed, that he would reform abuses and put a stop to alterations. But he had soon discovered that "sounds are too volatile and subtle for legal restraints" and that "to enchain syllables and to lash the wind are equally undertakings of pride unwilling to measure its desires by its strength." For "the causes of change in language are as much superior to human resistance as the revolutions of the sky or the intumescence of the tide."

There had been an even more profound discovery: that grammarians and lexicographers "do not form, but register the language; do not teach men how they should think, but relate how they have hitherto expressed their thoughts." And with this statement Johnson ushered in the rational study of linguistics. He had entered on his task a medieval pedant. He emerged from it a modern scientist.

Of course his discoveries were not strikingly original. Horace had observed that use was the sole arbiter and norm of speech and Montaigne had said that he who would fight custom with grammar was a fool. Doubtless thousands of other people had at one time or another perceived and said the same thing. But Johnson introduced a new principle. Finding that he could not lay down rules, he gave actual examples to show meaning and form. He offered as authority illustrative quotations, and in so doing established that language is what usage makes it and that custom, in the long run, is the ultimate and only court of appeal in linguistic matters.

This principle, axiomatic today in grammar and lexicography, seems to exasperate a great many laymen who, apparently, find two hundred and five years too short a period in which to grasp a basic idea. They insist that there are absolute standards of correctness in speech and that these standards may be set forth in a few simple rules. To a man, they believe, of course, that they speak and write "correctly" and they are loud in their insistence that others imitate them.

It is useless to argue with such people because they are not, really, interested in language at all. They are interested solely in demonstrating their own superiority. Point out to them—as has been done hundreds of times—that forms which they regard as "corrupt," "incorrect," and "vulgar" have been used by Shakespeare, Milton, and the Bible and are used daily by 180 million Americans and accepted by the best linguists and lexicographers, and they will coolly say, "Well, if they differ from me, they're wrong."

But if usage is not the final determinant of speech, what is? Do the inhabitants of Italy, for example, speak corrupt Latin or good Italian? Is Spanish superior to French? Would the Breton fisherman speak better if he spoke Parisian French? Can one be more fluent in Outer Mongolian than in Inner Mongolian? One has only to ask such questions in relation to languages other than one's own, languages within which our particular snobberies and struggles for prestige have no stake, to see the absurdity of them.

The language that we do speak, if we are to accept the idea of "corruption" and "decay" in language, is a horribly decayed Anglo-Saxon, grotesquely corrupted by Norman French. Furthermore, since Standard English is a development of the London dialect of the fourteenth century, our speech, by true aristocratic standards, is woefully middle-class, commercial, and vulgar. And American speech is lower middle-class, reeking of counter and till. Where else on earth, for instance, would one find crime condemned because it didn't *pay!*

In more innocent days a great deal of time was spent in wondering what was the "original" language of mankind, the one spoken in Eden, the language of which all modern tongues were merely degenerate remnants. Hector Boethius tells us that James I of Scotland was so interested in this problem that he had two children reared with a deaf and dumb nurse on an island in order to see what language they would "naturally" speak. James thought it would be Hebrew, and in time, to his great satisfaction, it was reported that the children were speaking Hebrew!

Despite this experiment, however, few people today regard English as a corruption of Hebrew. But many seem to think it is a corruption of Latin and labor mightily to make it conform to this illusion. It is they and their confused followers who tell us that we can't say "I am mistaken" because translated into Latin this would mean "I am misunderstood," and we can't say "I have enjoyed myself" unless we are egotistical or worse.

It is largely to this group—most of whom couldn't read a line of Latin at sight if their lives depended on it—that we owe our widespread bewilderment concerning *who* and *whom.* In Latin the accusative or dative form would always be used, regardless of the word's position in the sentence, when the pronoun was the object of a verb or a preposition. But in English, for at least four hundred years, this simply hasn't been so. When the pronoun occurs at the beginning of a question, people who speak natural, fluent, literary English use the nominative, regardless. They say "Who did you give it to?" not "Whom did you give it to?" But the semiliterate, intimidated and bewildered, are mouthing such ghastly utterances as a recent headline in a Chicago newspaper: WHOM'S HE KIDDING?

Another group seems to think that in its pure state English was a Laputan tongue, with logic as its guiding principle. Early members of this sect insisted that *unloose* could only mean "to tie up," and present members have compelled the gasoline industry to label its trucks *Flammable* under the disastrous insistence, apparently, that the old *Inflammable* could only mean "not burnable."

It is to them, in league with the Latinists, that we owe the bogy of the double negative. In all Teutonic languages a doubling of the negative merely emphasizes the negation. But we have been told for a century now that two negatives make a positive, though if they do and it's merely a matter of logic, then three negatives should make a negative again. So that if "It doesn't make no difference" is wrong merely because it includes two negatives, then "It doesn't never make no difference" ought to be right again.

Both of these groups, in their theories at least, ignore our idiom. Yet idiom—those expressions which defy all logic but are the very essence of a tongue—plays a large part in English. We go to school and college, but we go to *the* university. We buy two dozen eggs but a couple *of* dozen. *Good and* can mean *very* ("I am good and mad!") and "a hot cup of coffee" means that the coffee, not the cup, is to be hot. It makes a world of difference to a condemned man whether his reprieve is *upheld* or *held up*.

There are thousands of such expressions in English. They are the "irregularities" which Johnson found "inherent in the tongue" and which his wisdom perceived could not and should not be removed. Indeed, it is in the recognition and use of these idioms that skillful use of English lies.

Many words in the form that is now mandatory were originally just mistakes, and many of these mistakes were forced into the language by eager ignoramuses determined to make it conform to some notion of their own. The *s* was put in *island*, for instance, in sheer pedantic ignorance. The second *r* doesn't belong in *trousers*, nor the *g* in *arraign*, nor the *t* in *deviltry*, nor the *n* in *passenger* and *messenger*. Nor, so far as English is concerned, does that first *c* in *arctic* which so many people twist their mouths so strenuously to pronounce.

And grammar is as "corrupted" as spelling or pronunciation. "You are" is as gross a solecism as "me am." It's recent, too; you won't find it in the Authorized Version of the Bible. *Lesser, nearer*, and *more* are grammatically on a par with *gooder*. *Crowed* is the equivalent of *knowed* or *growed*, and *caught* and *dug* (for *catched* and *digged*) are as "corrupt" as *squoze* for *squeezed* or *snoze* for *sneezed*.

Fortunately for our peace of mind most people are quite content to let English conform to English, and they are supported in their sanity by modern grammarians and linguists.

Scholars agree with Puttenham (1589) that a language is simply speech "fashioned to the common understanding and accepted by consent." They believe that the only "rules" that can be stated for a language are codified observations. They hold, that is, that language is the basis of grammar, not the other way round. They do not believe that any language can become "corrupted" by the linguistic habits of those who speak it. They do not believe that anyone who is a native speaker of a standard language will get into any linguistic trouble unless he is misled by snobbishness or timidity or vanity.

He may, of course, if his native language is English, speak a form of English that marks him as coming from a rural or an unread group. But if he doesn't mind being so marked, there's no reason why he should change. Johnson retained a Staffordshire burr in his speech all his life. And surely no one will deny that Robert Burns's rustic dialect was just as good as a form of speech as, and in his mouth infinitely better as a means of expression than, the "correct" English spoken by ten million of his southern contemporaries.

The trouble is that people are no longer willing to be rustic or provincial. They all want to speak like educated people, though they don't want to go to the trouble of becoming truly educated. They want to believe that a special form of socially acceptable and financially valuable speech can be mastered by following a few simple rules. And there is no lack of little books that offer to supply the rules and promise "correctness" if the rules are adhered to. But, of course, these offers are specious because you don't speak like an educated person unless you are an educated person, and the little books, if taken seriously, will not only leave the lack of education showing but will expose the pitiful yearning and the basic vulgarity as well, in such sentences as "Whom are you talking about?"

As a matter of fact, the educated man uses at least three languages. With his family and his close friends, on the ordinary, unimportant occasions of daily life, he speaks, much of the time, a monosyllabic sort of shorthand. On more important occasions and when dealing with strangers in his official or business relations, he has a more formal speech, more complete, less allusive, politely qualified, wisely reserved. In addition he has some acquaintance with the literary speech of his language. He understands this when he reads it, and often enjoys it, but he hesitates to use it. In times of emotional stress hot fragments of it may come out of him like lava, and in times of feigned emotion, as when giving a commencement address, cold, greasy gobbets of it will ooze forth.

The linguist differs from the amateur grammarian in recognizing all of these variations and gradations in the language. And he differs from the snob in doubting that the speech of any one small group among the language's more than 300 million daily users constitutes a model for all the rest to imitate.

The methods of the modern linguist can be illustrated by the question of the grammatical number of *none*. Is it singular or plural? Should one say "None of them is ready" or "None of them are ready"?

The prescriptive grammarians are emphatic that it should be singular. The Latinists point out that *nemo*, the Latin equivalent, is singular. The logicians triumphantly point out that *none* can't be more than one and hence can't be plural.

The linguist knows that he hears "None of them are ready" every day, from people of all social positions, geographical areas, and degrees of education. He also hears "None is." Furthermore, literature informs him that both forms were used in the past. From Malory (1450) to Milton (1650) he finds that *none* was treated as a singular three times for every once that it was treated as a plural. That is, up to three hundred years ago men usually said *None is*. From Milton to 1917, *none* was used as a plural seven times for every four times it was used as a singular. That is, in the past three hundred years men often said *None is*, but they said *None are* almost twice as often. Since 1917, however, there has been a noticeable increase in the use of the plural, so much so that today *None are* is the preferred form.

The descriptive grammarian, therefore, says that while *None is* may still be used, it is becoming increasingly peculiar. This, of course, will not be as useful to one who wants to be cultured in a hurry as a short, emphatic permission or prohibition. But it has the advantage of describing English as it is spoken and written here and now and not as it ought to be spoken in some Cloud-Cuckoo-Land.

The descriptive grammarian believes that a child should be taught English, but he would like to see the child taught the English actually used by his educated contemporaries, not some pedantic, theoretical English designed chiefly to mark the imagined superiority of the designer.

He believes that a child should be taught the parts of speech, for example. But the child should be told the truth—that these are functions of use, not some quality immutably inherent in this or that word. Anyone, for instance, who tells a child—or anyone else—that *like* is used in English only as a preposition has grossly misinformed him. And anyone who complains that its use as a conjunction is a corruption introduced by Winston cigarettes ought, in all fairness, to explain how Shakespeare, Keats, and the translators of the Authorized Version of the Bible came to be in the employ of the R. J. Reynolds Tobacco Company.

Whether formal grammar can be taught to advantage before the senior year of high school is doubtful; most studies—and many have been made—

indicate that it can't. But when it is taught, it should be the grammar of today's English, not the obsolete grammar of yesterday's prescriptive grammarians. By that grammar, for instance, *please* in the sentence "Please reply" is the verb and *reply* its object. But by modern meaning *reply* is the verb, in the imperative, and *please* is merely a qualifying word meaning "no discourtesy intended," a mollifying or de-imperatival adverb, or whatever you will, but not the verb.

This is a long way from saying "Anything goes," which is the charge that, with all the idiot repetition of a needle stuck in a groove, the uninformed ceaselessly chant against modern grammarians. But to assert that usage is the sole determinant in grammar, pronunciation, and meaning is *not* to say that anything goes. Custom is illogical and unreasonable, but it is also tyrannical. The least deviation from its dictates is usually punished with severity. And because this is so, children should be taught what the current and local customs in English are. They should not be taught that we speak a bastard Latin or a vocalized logic. And they should certainly be disabused of the stultifying illusion that after God had given Moses the Commandments He called him back and pressed on him a copy of Woolley's *Handbook of English Grammar*.

The grammarian does not see it as his function to "raise the standards" set by Franklin, Lincoln, Melville, Mark Twain, and hundreds of millions of other Americans. He is content to record what they said and say.

Insofar as he serves as a teacher, it is his business to point out the limits of the permissible, to indicate the confines within which the writer may exercise his choice, to report that which custom and practice have made acceptable. It is certainly not the business of the grammarian to impose his personal taste as the only norm of good English, to set forth his prejudices as the ideal standard which everyone should copy. That would be fatal. No one person's standards are broad enough for that.

Study Questions

1. Why does *who* at the beginning of a sentence in spoken English seem natural and permissible, regardless of its function in the sentence? If you were writing a letter to a well-educated, older person of some importance, would it be appropriate to write, "Who should I consult for further information?"

2. Look up *inflammable* and *flammable* and the prefix *in*. What does *in-* most frequently mean? By analogy, what is the ordinary person likely to think *inflammable* means? (The change to *flammable* was more likely a safety measure than a concession to purists.)

3. Look up *get* and note its idiomatic uses. Which uses would be suitable in any context? Which would be suitable in conversation?

4. Compare Evans's comments on geographical and social differences in speech with Roberts's discussion of speech communities.

5. If usage is the basis for determining correctness, and the usage of noted

authors is cited, should a *single* occurrence of an expression be regarded as representing the author's usage? When a noted linguist says, "She invited my wife and I," should that sentence be regarded as sanctioning a semiliterate usage, or should the linguist's speech and writing be studied to determine whether he habitually uses a nominative pronoun as object of a verb? Choose one of the expressions in the *Dictionary of Contemporary American Usage* by Evans and Evans and investigate one of the authors they cite as an example. Is the quotation representative or not?

6. Should a student accept majority usage as a basis for his own practice without regard to the fact that, although many people use *like* instead of *as*, many others have an aversion to that usage? If there is a choice between two forms, of which one may be questioned and the other not, which form would it be well to use in writing or in formal speech?

7. College students will seek positions in which they will be subject to the critical observation of older, experienced, well-educated people. Is it the responsibility of the teacher to accept without comment any form that is sanctioned by usage, or should the teacher point out that some expressions may be offensive to people sensitive to language? Is it the student's responsibility to know why one form may be preferred to another and to be able to make an intelligent choice, or should he be content with what most people say?

25. WHAT IS GOOD ENGLISH?

Margaret Nicholson

In the *Atlantic Monthly* for May, 1957, Miss Nicholson considers some of the differences in usage and spelling between the English used by Americans and British and concludes that nationality is not an important factor in determining what is good English.

1

Some thirty years ago a professor of English at the University of California introduced his students to Fowler's *Dictionary of Modern English Usage*. That was in 1926 or 1927. I wish I could remember which, because it would be interesting to know that, without the fanfare of today's publicity, a scholarly reference book published in England could have found immediate enthusiasts in California that first spring of its publication. But I can't remember. Nor can I remember, I am ashamed to say, which of my English professors made the introduction. I do know that he spent the full hour that day reading snatches from it, and that I, for one, was an immediate convert. I stopped in at Sather Gate Book Shop that noon and bought a copy, and from that day on "MEU" has been my delight and mentor.

I never in those days felt that Fowler was particularly British or difficult.

During the three years I taught high-school English MEU was always on the classroom reference shelf and to the best of my memory it was used, even by suburban California teen-agers of the "roaring twenties." I can't remember any complaints about its being un-American.

It wasn't till several years later, after I had abandoned teaching and was working at the Oxford University Press in New York, that I became aware of the battle between American-English and English-English. Oxford was militantly British at the time and the staff was virtuously conscious of representing one of the last outposts of British civilization. We addressed letters to our authors "John Doe Esq."—*Mr.* was allowed only for printers, paper men, and unpaid accounts. Posted above each desk was a list of English spellings to be rigorously adhered to in all correspondence: *analyse* with an *s*, *judgement* with an *e*, *pyjamas* with a *y*—though in what context *pyjamas* would appear in our daily correspondence I can't imagine. It became almost natural for me to speak of my *holiday*, rather than my vacation; *in the circumstances* (not *under*—though I should have remembered Fowler's remarks on that bit of foolishness), of course, I should need new *luggage*. I even remember once saying unblushingly that I should leave *Wednesday fortnight*. If my friends suspected me of snobbism (which they probably in their ignorance called snobbishness) it is hardly surprising. Today it all seems like a foreshadowing of "U. and Non-U." under the guise of "Brit. and Non-Brit.":

Brit.	*Non-Brit.* (or *"chiefly U.S."*)
tin	can
biscuit	cracker
chemist	druggist
packet	package or pack
ill	sick
shop	store
braces	suspenders
I fancy	I think (or worse, *I guess*)
increase (of wages)	rise (in salary) or lamentably, a *raise*
lodger	roomer
sweets	candy

And so on. Fortunately, before very long Oxford New York changed its policy. American spelling became the standard, our mimeographed lists were tossed into the basket, I graduated (a good Americanism) into editorial work, and the war of Brit. and Non-Brit. was forgotten. *Modern English Usage* remained on my desk, an indispensable help in editing both English and American manuscripts. But it was then that I began wondering about the possibility of a slightly simplified Fowler with American variations. Some fifteen years later, to my delight and apprehension, I was invited to undertake the task of preparing one.

Of course there is an English idiom and an American idiom, but in scholarly or serious speech and writing, as opposed to informal talk and fiction, the difference is not as evident as many of us believe. In books that do not contain dialogue, and that have not been deliberately edited for the American reader, our first clue that the writer is British is the spelling; in speeches that seem typically British, it is chiefly the accent that gives this impression; read in the newspaper there is often little that would not be the natural expression of any literate American. I consciously watched for expressions and constructions that one could label peculiarly English or peculiarly American in all my reading during the five years or so that I was working on the "American Fowler" and found many times that I could read chapters in succession without finding any example that could be cited as one or the other without qualification.

The other day I decided to make a random test of my theory in a book I was reading for pleasure (and what a pleasure it is to be able to give one's whole mind to the meaning rather than reserving at least half of it for spotting idiomatic usage and construction!). I found nothing in the first hundred pages, and rather desperately stopped on page 108 when I came to "Here we are back *full circle* to theories long familiar to philosophers." There is nothing in that that an American could not have written, but I suspected that "full circle" so used would come perhaps more natural to an Englishman. But very soon after that I found "A novelist who disregards major public events is either *a footler* or a plain idiot." A footler? If I had not consciously been watching for Briticisms I should have passed this over without noticing, but having stopped I realized I had no reliable idea of what a footler is; I reached for my dictionaries. Both *Webster's Collegiate* and *The American College Dictionary* give *footle*, n., "twaddle, drivel," and label it slang, but whether British or American slang they do not say. *The Concise Oxford Dictionary* gives *footle*, v., "to trifle, play the fool," and n., "twaddle, folly"—also both slang. I am no authority on slang, so I gave up, but my feeling is that as current slang *footler* is chiefly Brit., not U.S. Then I found a term that I felt would justify me in stamping the writer British (if I had not already known he was): "Civilization can lift itself up by its *boot-tags.*" *Boot-straps* is the American for that; no American would write *boot-tags* unless he was deliberately affecting familiarity with British idiom. Our man is English. I wish I had closed the book before I read the last sentence on the same page: "An electoral system *gerrymandered* in the interest of the moneyed class." Gerrymandered? What is our man now?

To be fair, I must admit that as I read on into the more specific chapters of the book I came across many individual words and phrases that would identify it as English rather than American: *motor-cars, tinned food, the greengrocer,* "old maids biking to Holy Communion through the mists of the Autumn morning," "posh tailor-made clothes." (*Webster's Collegiate* doesn't even list *posh; The Concise Oxford* defines it "smart, tip-top," and labels it slang. What about *tip-top?*)

2

And what about the reverse of the picture? What is it that tells the English reader "this book was written by an American"? First, of course, as with us, the spelling. We wantonly omit hyphens when they are needed and insert them when they are unnecessary; we use *z* when *s* is called for and discard the *u* in -*our* endings; we do not realize (or realise) that *worshiped* and *kidnaped*, without doubling the penultimate consonants, are not only wrong but invite flagrant mispronunciation. So let us forget the spelling. Wanting to have something more than a theoretical opinion, I asked some English friends how they identified a nonfiction book as American. "By its illiteracies," one of them retorted immediately. And what are the peculiarly American illiteracies? I insisted. Although it is rather unfair, since this was an informal, off-the-record conversation, I am going to give his list in the order in which it was presented.

Improper use of *will* for *shall*, first person future. This delighted me. It is true that the distinction between *will* and *shall* is less and less observed in America, even by good speakers and writers. Those of us who were brought up on traditional English still observe it instinctively; we are a minority. But is *will* for *shall* in this usage peculiarly American and indisputably an illiteracy? Sir Ernest Gowers, in his *ABC of Plain Words*, published in England for English writers in 1951, does not agree. He points out that "I will go" has always been the plain future for the Celts, that Americans have followed their practice, and that "the English have taken to imitating the Americans." "If we go by practice rather than precept," he continues, "we can no longer say dogmatically that 'I will go' for the plain future is wrong." Fowler would not like this. In his article on *will* (MEU) he says: "Of the English of the English *shall & will* are the shibboleth . . . and endow his speech with a delicate precision that could not be attained without it." Opposite views by two men to the manner born. Americans may choose whichever they will.

In back of for *behind.* "All Americans say it," according to my friends. Well, a great many Americans do. Certainly it slips easily from the tongue of many who should know better. I do not remember having come across it in print, and I cannot believe that a serious writer would be guilty of it. I agree that it is an illiteracy. Of *back of* for *behind* (the *in* is completely otiose) Fowler says gently, "An American, not an English idiom."

The omission of the preposition in such phrases as "I'll see you Tuesday," "He works nights," "I'll write you as soon as I know." These are all standard American usage now; the Englishman, however, would say *on Tuesday, at night,* and *to you.* In recording *write you* when there is no direct object,

The Oxford English Dictionary says, "freq. c.1790–c.1865" and gives several examples.

He aimed to (be) rather than *at (being)*. Whatever the purists may say, this is now standard American usage, although it is no longer condoned in England. OED lists it as obsolete, *Webster's Collegiate* without qualification, and ACD as "U.S.," contrasting it with the English *at* plus the gerund.

Different than instead of *different from*. How long this battle has been going on! It was in full swing in my own schooldays, and quite recently when I was discussing Americanisms with a college professor she exclaimed in horror, "I hope you're not going to allow *different than!*" Allow it? We have it, whether we like it or not. Again I turn for comfort to OED: "The usual construction is now with *from*. . . . The construction with *than* is found in Fuller, Addison, Steele, DeFoe, Richardson, Goldsmith, Miss Burney, Coleridge, Southey, De Quincey, Carlyle, Thackeray, Newman, Trench, and Dasent, among others"—the others, I am afraid, including two thirds of the American public.

So much for peculiarly American illiteracies. We have them, yes. But I was happy that my friend selected the examples he did.

Apart from so-called illiteracies, there are some words that have different meanings on the two sides of the Atlantic. For example, *faculty* is used on the *campuses* (so used only in America) of both English and American colleges, but as applied to the whole body of teachers and perhaps administrative officers (*A faculty meeting was called for Wednesday night*) it is "U.S. only." *Sabbatical* is used in England in its religious sense but not for an academic *sabbatical leave. The Humane Society* in England rescues the drowning and has nothing to do with the prevention of cruelty to animals.

Differences of this kind can be misleading, and it is well not to have too sanguine an acceptance of dictionary definitions. Even in the most recent edition of *The Concise Oxford Dictionary*, which helpfully uses an asterisk to indicate words and meanings "chiefly or originally American," one discovers some surprising things. "*Faucet* (chiefly U.S.), tap for a barrel." "*Filibuster* . . . *obstructionist in legislative assembly." "*Barn-dance* (orig. U.S.), dance in which partners advance side by side & then dance a schottische step." "*Bat*, v. (U.S. & dial.), to wink (*never batted an eyelid = did not sleep a wink*)." "*Beauty Parlour* (orig. U.S.), establishment in which the art or trade of face massage, face lifting, applying cosmetics, &c. is carried on." A *bouncer*, U.S. slang, is a *chucker out. Call down*, U.S. colloq., means *challenge*.

There are of course many words that we—and the British—now use without being conscious of the fact that they are Americanisms: a *blanket* ruling, a blood *donor*, the Red Cross *drive*, to be *through* one's work, to *grill* the prisoner, to meet the *deadline*. Most of these were at one time slang or colloquial, but are now standard, at least in informal use.

Understandably it is in slang and colloquialisms that the differences between British and American are greatest and most apparent. Even in one country there is difference in regional, occupational, and social slang. If slang has color, if it expresses some idea or feeling with an economy not found in standard English, it may pass its own boundaries and even become part of the permanent language. No one thinks now of *mob, bus,* or *cab* as slang. It is my belief that *gangster, hold-up,* and *hoodlum* are also in the language to stay (although it is regrettable that they reflect so unsavory an element of American life). The R.A.F. *gremlins* are as much at home in the United States as they are in England and may live to rival pixies and elves. Americans *grouse* (British slang) about their troubles and the British have little sympathy with *grouches* (U.S. slang).

Fowler says, speak as your neighbor speaks. True, the advice comes from his article on pronunciation, but it is as applicable to the use of English-English and American-English idiom. Personally I am unable to go the whole way and concede that if a large enough number of my neighbors say or write a thing in a given way, that way is right—or at least not until enough time has elapsed to give its blessing to the usage in question. To me *adviser* is so spelled, no matter how many times I see *advisor* in print, even in scholarly books. I prefer *John's going to Boston amazed me to John going to Boston . . .* even though I am assured that the gerund in America is dead. Speak as your neighbor speaks—but today our neighbor is the English-speaking world. If we have an idea to give to our neighbor, whether it is a commercial product or a global (U.S. vogue word) philosophy, we are inefficient if we allow disputed constructions or local peculiarities in our language to distract his attention. English-English and American-English are coming closer together, not growing farther apart. Two world wars, our publications, motion pictures, radio, television, and even the UN are seeing to that.

My feeling is that good English is good English, whatever the nationality of the writer. In every community there are local meanings, terms, and constructions, arising from the circumstances and environment of that particular locality. Some of these should be treasured, some should be eschewed in formal speech and writing. There is no essentially American-English or English-English. There are only not-too-important regional variations.

Study Questions

1. If you have listened to British speakers on radio or television, what are some of the pronunciation differences you have noticed?

2. What facts in recent history and culture account for increasing use of Americanisms in England? Is there a corresponding increase in use of British expressions in America? Why? If not, why not?

3. On the basis of what you know about conversational language and slang, why does the greatest difference between American and British English lie in colloquialism and slang?

26. THE KING'S ENGLISH IN A DEMOCRATIC WORLD

Charlton Laird

This selection, one of the chapters in *The Miracle of Language* (1953), considers the question of usage in its historical perspective. Like Bergen Evans, Professor Laird is interested in the forces which determine the patterns of acceptable usage.

If you mispronounce an American Indian word in an Indian household the adults will probably be polite enough not to laugh, but the children are likely to giggle. Ethnocentrism is so strong in the human animal that most of us assume, until and unless we have the assumption ironed out of us, that our way of doing things is the right way, that strange ways are inevitably wrong ways. A laugh is a powerful tool of social control, perhaps the most powerful, and thus from the earliest days strong forces have promoted standards and control in language.

Language always changes slowly. Even when it changes rapidly in historical perspective, it changes so slowly that the speakers of it are not usually much aware of the change. Thus unconscious controls upon language are sufficiently lax so that language can usually change freely even though it is subject to constant and quite exacting pressure the aim of which is to standardize it and keep it fixed. But as society becomes more complicated, as the users of a language become more numerous and more varied in their spread and occupation, as the necessities for communication become greater, and standardization becomes more and more the pattern of social living, the pressure to impose standards, rigid standards, upon language increases. We are forced to ask ourselves very seriously, what are the relationships of language and life, and how much do the requirements of human welfare at home and abroad require that we police our language? Who is to do the policing, and how?

We have already noted that medieval speakers of English were apparently highly tolerant of variations in language. A Middle English poet mixed up his dialectal forms in any manner that gave him the rhymes and rhythms he wanted, and we have little evidence that anyone thought this practice exceptionable or even unusual. During the Renaissance correctness was much discussed, but apparently not much enforced. During the authoritarian eighteenth century, however, the *ipse dixit* pronouncement, the fiat which assumes that "it's so because he says it's so" reached its height, a height from which it has till now not much declined in some quarters.

A grammarian like Robert Baker, for instance, as the late Professor Sterling Andrus Leonard of the University of Wisconsin has observed, would blandly condemn all sorts of expressions with a positive, "There is no such word," "This is an expression of great barbarity," "This is not English," "That is a deformity in the language." But of course what was a deformity to Baker was not necessarily a deformity to Baker's contemporaries, Lowth, Murray, or Webster. Baker even admits—though he seems unaware that he is making an admission—that the reason one usage is "not English" and another one is unexceptionable "would be perhaps no easy matter to tell." It would have been no easy matter, but the difficulty seems not to have deterred those who set themselves up to do the telling.

Many of these policemen of usage were not close students of the language. If they appealed to linguistic history they were inclined to assume that there was a universal grammatical truth as there was a universal religious truth—indeed, a number of them were divines, and Lowth was a bishop—and that universal grammar was for all practical purposes embodied in Latin grammar. Thus, if they appealed to authority at all, they appealed to Latin. But most of them did not appeal. They asserted. The reviewers of Baker's grammar, even the favorable reviewers who applauded his methods and most of his conclusions, found Baker's composition, as Baker found others' compositions, replete with barbarisms, "vile phrases," and locutions which made "one inelegance necessary by another." Many pronouncements of this sort were drowned in the mutual recriminations of the self-constituted justices of the peace in language, but others became commandments from the linguistic Sinâi, to be copied or miscopied blindly thereafter into handbooks of usage.

The supposed distinction between *shall* and *will* as future auxiliaries provides a pleasant example of eighteenth-century dictatorial procedures and modern echoes in language standards. A mathematician who signed himself Johannis Wallis when he wrote in Latin decided that *shall* and *will* should be distinguished in usage, and asserted that *shall* was properly used to indicate simple futurity in the first person, determination and purpose in the second and third persons; that *will* was used for determination in the first person, and for simple futurity in the second and third. There seems to have been no justification for this dictum among Wallis's contemporaries in seventeenth-century England, nor among his eighteenth-century followers; as Professor Leonard has observed, not even Lowth, who fought for the rule, observed it himself. Nor was there any historical justification. This distinction had never been made between *shall* and *will*, nor has there ever been a time, apparently, when *shall* and *will* were consistently distinguished by Englishmen as signs of different sorts of futurity.

In Anglo-Saxon the words were not used to signal a future; Anglo-Saxon used the simple present, as we do to a degree, to imply future. *Sculan*, from which we get *shall*, meant "ought to," and *willian*, from which we get *will* meant "to desire," "to wish," "to expect." They were not signs of the future, but they became so, very much as *ought to go, have to go, want to go*, and *expect to go* are becoming future forms. They retained their original meanings, in part, but they never became consistently divergent in any way to confirm the arbitrary rule proposed by Wallis. But once the new rule had been announced, nothing could stop it. Joseph Priestley doubted its validity, and said so; his contemporary, Withers, condemned it. But Priestley was a dissenting divine as well as a dissenting grammarian; that he was also a schoolmaster and a chemist did not save him. His voice, along with Withers's, was drowned beneath the authority of Lowth, Murray, and dozens of others. Grammarian after grammarian copied Lowth and Murray; generations of schoolteachers endeavored to enforce the rule and genera-tions of groaning children tried to learn it—or to learn just the opposite, for some handbooks managed to reverse the rule in process of copying it. Until today, ability to follow a dictum concocted by a seventeenth-century teacher whose business was mathematics, has become one of the tests of knowing one's grammar, although on this basis very few have ever known their grammar, or know it now. Most of us who try to be consistent are not. Seemingly we can resist very stubbornly dicta for which we have no native feeling.

Latterly the procedures of a pontiff like the grammarian Baker have found little favor among thinkers about language. We have been inclined to ask why one man more than another has the right to decide what is and what is not "barbaric" or "vile." What makes a vile word vile, or a barbaric construction barbaric? If language grows from the nature of human beings and by the experience of all sorts of people, who is to decide what the lan-guage is to be, except those whose minds and lives make the language? If language has always grown and always changed, why should that which has been "right" necessarily continue to be so? If language always has changed and apparently always will change, why should anybody try to stop it?

These are pertinent considerations, but not the only possible ones. Lan-guage must not only have flexibility to live and grow, it must have currency to be understood. Like money, it is no fit medium for exchange unless it has sufficient currency so that he who gives the coin values it in roughly the same terms as he who receives it. And like money, it must have sufficient stability so that what is given today has approximately the same value to-morrow. Without stability we might never learn to speak, because the lan-guage could be changing faster than we were able to learn it; without currency, even if we learned to speak we could not communicate widely, because our medium of exchange would not be acceptable to enough others to make it usable. We understand each other only because large numbers of people over great areas of the earth have lived in mutual if unconscious agreement that certain words are symbols for certain meanings and not for other meanings; that strictly determined ways of handling these symbols reveal their relationships. We agree that the symbol *table* stands for a flat surface supported from beneath, that it is not a container used to enclose fire for heating purposes. We agree that in the construction *the red table, hot from the red-hot stove,* the table has a permanent color and the stove a temporary one, and that this distinction is apparent in part through the varying positions of *red* and *hot* in the sentence.

Thus there is a fundamental inconsistency in language and in the way in which we make it and use it which forever prevents the establishment and the upholding of any standards from being entirely logical. Language is a living thing. It must survive in men's minds and on their tongues if it survives at all. In so doing, it changes with minds, lives, and the use of vocal apparatus. But at the same time, language can function only if it has stability in time and place. Change is inevitable in language, and yet all change damages language, although it may at the same time revitalize it. We may be able to minimize the effects of this inconsistency, but we cannot remove it.

Thus if students of language were to be guided only by the logic of the situation, they would find themselves neatly spitted on this dilemma, that stability and change are both imperative in a living, serviceable language. How can the difficulty be avoided? Surely not by allowing any man who can print a book to decide questions of standards by his own whim, as some commentators of the eighteenth century tried to do, and many authoritarian people would like to do yet. Surely not by appealing to Latin grammar or to some other supposed universal grammar. As far as we know, there is no universal grammar. There may be universal principles in language, but the laws of grammar, if they can be called laws, are descriptions of what human beings do with language. They are not pronunciamenta concerning what is "right" and what is "wrong." All words and ways of using words are right if the users of the language want them that way; they are wrong if the users of the language do not want them. If they are right now they will be wrong when the users of language want them no longer.

Obviously questions of standards must depend upon usage. In language, whatever is, is right—provided it "is" enough so that enough people want it that way for a long enough time. In short, in his own small way, every man is his own Webster, deciding what language is and what it is not. Even more, every woman is her own Webster. For as we have seen, the great arbiters of language are the women who speak it in the presence of children. There is a theory that men have made all the great innovations in language. Whether or not this hypothesis is sound—and there might well be women who would point out that the theory was propounded by a man—

there is no question as to who preserves the language, through what medium language is handed on to the next generation, by whom some language is allowed to die and other parts saved. Mainly, women do it. What the women pass on to the next generation is "right" and what they do not bother to pass on to their children sooner or later becomes "wrong."

The authoritarians of the eighteenth century, however wrong they were, did not lack for sound counsel. There had been wise men enough from Aristotle to John Locke who seem to have understood the nature of language. Plenty of men from Horace to Priestley had said quite clearly that standards must be based upon usage. And a considerable portion of the grammarians of the eighteenth century themselves, including authoritarians like Lowth and Johnson, paid at least lip service to the importance of usage while condemning "vulgar use, in which the caprice of Custom is apt to get the better of analogy." Even Webster, who asserted that "The business of a grammarian is not to examine whether or not national practice is founded on philosophical principles; but to *ascertain* the national practice," nonetheless found himself relying upon "the principle of analogy" and "the rules of the language itself," and condemning what he called "the well-nigh universal misuses of English." If the usages were "well-nigh universal," and the rightness or the wrongness of a use was to depend upon currency, how could they be "misuses"?

Perhaps one should remind oneself of the nature of the times. Few people in the eighteenth century, presented with the necessity of answering a difficult question, thought of going about to collect evidence, expecting thereafter to extract the answer from the evidence. This is the scientific procedure and it serves us well; it has served us so well and so long that most people can now think of no other way to attack a problem, and they assume that there is no other way. But if the scientific method serves us well, it also blinds us. Surely it must be obvious that we make the most egregious blunders, national and international, public and private, because we do not sit down and think long and seriously about things. We like to work things out, not think them out.

Men of the eighteenth century used, on the whole, the latter method; they liked to think things out. It was the method beloved of Socrates and Plato and of many who came after them. It was the method which seemed to be suited to an orderly world created and run by a Supreme Being in accordance with good, sound logic. Eighteenth-century seekers after the truth liked to use their minds in perceiving the order of the world and in telling the world how to continue to be orderly. Furthermore, it was a habit with them. It was one with respect for God, King, and Country. It was like the British climate and strong, black tea with milk; good or bad, eighteenth-century Britons had grown up with it, and it was a part of their lives, something to be loved and to be done automatically, not to be questioned, surely not long to be deviated from. Thus writers upon language, even when they professed other faiths, reverted mainly in their daily practice to authority in grammar as in theology. An occasional maverick like Priestley, who with some consistency tried to submit questions of standards to the court of usage—whenever he could convene the court—was not very influential. Lowth and Murray, not Priestley, were the accepted grammarians.

As a matter of practical fact, the court of usage is not readily convened. How is one to know what is the national practice concerning the multifarious details of language? How, to use Webster's phrase, is a grammarian "to *ascertain* the national usage"? Webster solved the problem neatly, and apparently to his own satisfaction, by assuming that the practices of Noah Webster and his neighbors in Connecticut were, for all practical purposes, "the national usage." This method had its obvious limitations, but Priestley, who made a more serious effort in England, fared in the end not much better. Even when he could shake himself sufficiently free of the shackles of the time to seek the national usage he had little machinery for discovering it.

And yet, in his century the machinery was being developed, and in the very seat of authoritarianism, in the bulky person of Dr. Samuel Johnson. The good doctor's own discussion of grammar allowed but twelve lines to syntax, which is obviously the heart of English grammatical usage, and his pronouncements come clothed as in the voice of Jove. But Johnson was known mainly as a lexicographer—it was he who, in one of those moments of whimsy and self-deprecation which make the Great Bear a charming fellow, defined a lexicographer as "a writer of dictionaries, a harmless drudge." He was authoritarian to a fault, and yet his work became a foundation for the modern practice of resting standards upon usage.

Johnson spent many of the prime years of his life making a dictionary, employing the best theory that had been worked out by the French and Italian academies, and resting his definitions not upon the usage of his day, but upon the best usage he could discover in the great writers of the British past. The French had made use of the practice, albeit with a different purpose. On the theory that the French language had now become a perfect linguistic instrument, the French Academy endeavored, in the interests of France and civilization, to collect their perfect language and put it in a book so that it should not decay. They thereby attested their ignorance of one of the fundamental principles of language, that a living language always changes and will change however authoritarians try to stop it. But they did advance lexicographical knowledge and practice. Johnson advanced them still further—his friend Garrick jubilated that "he beat sixty Frenchmen, and could beat sixty more," and there was some truth in the boast. Johnson, almost single-handed, created one of the best works of its day in any language, a book which saw the British Empire in and very nearly saw it out. Adapting French techniques, he relied upon usage, even though past conspicuous usage, not as a means of preserving a perfect language, but as the instrument for refining a faulty one.

After Johnson the next step was obvious if onerous. If enough people could be found to read carefully all the important writings in the language, from the earliest documents to today, a whole history of the language could be built upon citations from these writings. The result was the *New English Dictionary on Historical Principles*, the so-called *Oxford English Dictionary*, and accordingly known as the OED or the NED. Begun in 1858, it required three-quarters of a century to prepare and edit, killed off editor after editor, required the ungrudging labor of hundreds of scholars on both sides of the Atlantic, and was finally printed with the aid of the Almighty himself—the printing bill having been guaranteed by the Oxford University Press, relying upon its lucrative privilege to print Bibles in England. Beyond all comparison the *New English Dictionary* records the English language as no other language has ever been recorded, and it has sired a whole sequence of more detailed dictionaries, of which the *Dictionary of American English*, and what might be called its progeny, A *Dictionary of Americanisms*, are now in print; the *Dictionary of Middle English* is announced, and the *Dictionary of Early Modern English* has been in the editing almost a quarter of a century; the *Dictionary of the Older Scottish Tongue* and the *Dictionary of Later Scottish* are in process.

But our concern here is not with wordbooks, except incidentally. Samuel Johnson presumed not only to define words but to endeavor to remove from the language "improprieties and absurdities." In this, Noah Webster, in spite of his theoretical professions, followed him. But the *New English Dictionary* established, apparently for all time, that dictionaries are henceforth to be made by harmless drudges, even more harmless and more faithful drudges than Johnson conceived. The job of lexicographers is now to discover usages, sift them and record them, not mainly to legislate among them. Dictionary editors work on what are called "historical principles," as follows: if a word is recorded in writing it belongs in the dictionary; until it is recorded it will not be entered in the dictionary; when it is entered it will be defined and described in accordance with its usage in printed citations. This procedure, like any other, can occasionally be a bit ridiculous. We thus have the spectacle of a lexicographer refusing to put into a dictionary a word which he knows quite well because he cannot find it used in some piece of published writing. Recently one of our greatest lexicographers, the soundness of whose practice is amply attested by the excellence of his publications, wrote to an American language journal thanking them for publishing a certain article because it contained words which belonged in his dictionary, but which he had been troubled to find published anywhere. And so we have a man greatly learned in the language deliberately disenfranchising himself; though he knew quite well these words existed, and what they mean and how they are used, he could not put them into his dictionary until he could catch somebody using them, even though the user knew less about the words than he did. But even in spite of an occasional absurdity of this sort, the principles and practice of modern British and American lexicographers have given us dictionaries which are justly the envy of the world.

Perhaps we should notice at this point the dilemma of the modern lexicographer endeavoring to deal with grammar. He has troubles to which Johnson was immune. Johnson thought he knew what the grammar of English was, and he said so. The modern lexicographer may think he knows what the grammar of English is, but he will presume to say so only if he can find that there is agreement among those who should know. Johnson thought that making decisions in grammar was part of his business, but the modern lexicographer no more endeavors to decide what are the essentials of English grammar and how our grammatical statement should be formulated than he presumes to decide what are the essentials of chemistry or what is questionable in the quantum theory.

As we have seen, however, grammarians do not agree. The grammatical thinkers of our day are sharply at odds with the accepted grammatical statement. By the tenets of his profession the modern lexicographer should employ the accepted grammatical statement as the basis of his grammatical classifications. But modern lexicographers are learned people, learned especially in language. They do not need me to tell them that adjectives often cannot be distinguished from adverbs and that words like *up, out, off,* and *by* are frequently not prepositions but some part of the verb or complement. But where will they find a grammatical statement sufficiently standardized so that they can use it as the basis of the grammatical treatment in their dictionaries?

There is no such statement. Lexicographers are, on the whole, conscientious men and good. Hence, one can almost hear them, like Launcelot Gobbo, listening to an angel with one ear while listening even harder to a devil with the other, and agreeing with both.

"Record faithfully the conventional statement," warns the angel of traditional grammar.

"Angel, you counsel well," says Launcelot Gobbo Lexicographer.

"But you will be printing nonsense," says the little devil, the modern grammarian.

"Devil, you counsel well," says the lexicographer.

And so in the end the lexicographer runs off with the devil of modern grammar, but he does not feel entitled to run very far. Anyone who wishes to observe this little morality play may do so by examining carefully the desk dictionaries which have recently been put on the market—and there have been excellent ones.

Consider, for instance, the entries under *preposition. Webster's New Collegiate Dictionary* says that a preposition is a word showing any of various abstract relations "used to connect a noun or pronoun, in an adjectival or adverbial sense, with some other word." This definition would seem not to stray far from the conventional statement. Since an adverb is elsewhere defined as a modifier or a qualifier, presumably there is no intent here to suggest that the so-called prepositions can become involved in verbs or complements. (The *New International Dictionary*, however, upon which the *Webster's Collegiate* is based, has an entry *prepositional object* which suggests that a preposition can be "felt to be a loose affix giving transitive force to a verb." This entry was dropped from the *Collegiate*, presumably for reasons of space.)

The *American College Dictionary* goes several steps farther. The definition of *preposition* there reads, "(in some languages) one of the major form-classes or 'parts of speech,' comprising words placed before nouns to indicate their relation to other words or their function in the sentence." Another usage makes clear that a preposition need not be one word, but "any construction of similar function or meaning, as *on top of*." Here are considerable changes. Not only have the editors made clear that they do not much trust the notion of parts of speech by putting these words within quotation marks, they have asserted that a preposition may indicate the noun's "function in the sentence." There is no mention of "adjectival or adverbial." Presumably if the user of the ACD wishes to assume that a noun after a preposition can "function in the sentence" as a complement of the verb he may do so.

Similarly the most recent desk dictionary, and one of the most liberal, *Webster's New World Dictionary of the American Language*, defines a preposition as a "relationship word" or "any construction of similar function (e.g., *in back of*, equivalent to *behind*)" that "connects a noun, pronoun, or noun phrase to another element of the sentence, as to a verb (e.g., he went *to* the store). . . ." Here again, although the words of the definition suggest the conventional statement, they leave the reader free to call *store* the complement of the verb if he wishes.

That is, the editors of all three of these dictionaries are aware of the inadequacy of the conventional statement upon which they must, as yet, mainly rely. Being aware, each lexicographical staff has written a definition which does no violence to the accepted practice, but each insofar as he dares has framed a statement which permits a grammatical interpretation which is relatively liberal. As such an editor recently wrote me—he prefers to remain anonymous—"We like to imagine that we are infinitesimally avant-garde in our treatment of purist notions and especially in our inclusion of thousands of phrasal units constituting 'ungrammatical' idioms." A handsomely chosen phrase that, "infinitesimally avant-garde." It suggests at once the liberality of lexicographers as a group, and the strain they labor under these days in endeavoring to find their way among the uncertainties of grammarians and the differences among grammar books.

The same problem and a similar difficulty arise with questions of usage. Lexicographers now agree that just as words mean what they mean by common consent, so a given spelling, pronunciation, or construction is "right" or "wrong" depending upon its currency. Should we say "all the boys" or "all of the boys"? Must we say "Everybody took his hat" because *body* is singular, or may we say "Everybody took their hats" because *everybody* is popularly felt to be plural? Formerly such questions were decided by thunders out of grammatical Sinais. Now they are determined by mild-voiced drudges, with ears attuned to the mumblings of the multitude.

How can the drudge do this? Admittedly, he has his problems. Written work can be read, if the publisher will supply a sufficient staff of readers, and all good dictionary-makers do some reading, or at least some sampling. But language, including usage, is basically oral, and how can the drudge listen to all the babblings of the world? Partly, he can use scholarly studies of oral speech, and does. Partly, he has had to guess. Just now there is promise that he may soon have great help. A national study is in progress, sponsored by the National Council of the Teachers of English, the Modern Language Association, the American Dialect Society, the Linguistic Society, the Speech Association of America, and perhaps others. Soon there will be hundreds, probably thousands of students of language all over the country, looking and listening for the currency of certain usages, and some day the results of all this industry will be accumulated in a monumental *Dictionary of Current American Usage.*

Students of language are more and more becoming harmless and faithful drudges in search of what George Campbell, in his own declaration of independence in 1776, his too-much-neglected *The Philosophy of Rhetoric,* defined as "national, reputable, and present use."

How far is it desirable to standardize speech? Granted that standardization is desirable, how much can it be standardized?

Of course questions like this cannot be answered with any exactness, but in a general way the first almost answers itself, and the second is being very practically answered for us. Obviously language should be allowed to change without great restriction. It always has changed, and it needs to change if it is to fit our changing lives. Quite as obviously it should not change so fast that it loses its currency and its relative stability. Slang is fun, but we should be worse off if the Constitution of the United States had been written in slang; we should be worse off if a candidate for the presidency could not talk to all the people, confident that his words would be understood. No one can well deny that the language should be allowed to change, but that it should be discouraged from changing too rapidly.

We can perhaps agree then, without necessarily agreeing about the details, that language should have restrictive but not coercive standards. There are two requisites for such standards: we must have some way of determining them, and some way of enforcing them. The second would seem the harder, but it is not. There are dozens of regulatory agencies, organized and disorganized. A very large part of our population is under considerable pressure to be "correct." All sorts of people are under all sorts of pressures not to be caught doing something "wrong." I lately heard a man giving a speech before an educated group. He was discussing the action of a committee, and you could see him hesitate before he used a pronoun. Should he refer to the committee as *it* or *they?* But he dared not hesitate long. He had to say something. He took the plunge with *it.* Then you could see him scrutinizing his audience to discover whether or not they were laughing at him. After all, there were five men on the committee. Were they not plural? People in the audience were not visibly laughing, but they were polite. He went on. He was still discussing the action of the committee, and we could see him trying to frame sentences in which he would not have to say either *it* or *they.* But he could not go on saying, "The committee . . . the committee . . . the committee." When he sat down, probably sooner than he meant to, he was red and sweating.

We are all subject, more or less, to pressures of that sort, and in addition there are planned and organized means of supporting standards. Parents correct their children, teachers rebuke their pupils, employers scrutinize their employees. Publishers have style sheets and copyreaders to enforce them. Broadcasters endeavor to police the pronunciation, diction, and grammar of language they send out upon the air, particularly language for which their employees are responsible. Various agencies will enforce any dictum in language if only they can believe that they have a touchstone by which they can determine what is "right" and what is "wrong." In fact, most regulatory agencies are so zealous to regulate that they embarrass the experts on whose authority they endeavor to act. They want to consult "the dictionary," and to ignore that dictionaries, being the products of human beings, differ. If they then find that two pronunciations, two spellings, two constructions are approved, they wish to know which one is preferred, and they wish to admit only the preferred.

Thus there are regulating agencies aplenty, even though we have no official ones. Do these regulating agencies depend upon sensible advice, sensibly arrived at, founded upon usage? In this we are not doing badly. The best dictionaries have all been edited at great expense, and several publishers of dictionaries maintain more or less permanent staffs of considerable size, composed of highly trained students of language, whose function is to determine current usage by wide reading, by consultation with specialists in geographical areas and technical fields, and by relating apparent shifts in language to the known linguistic practices of our past. Modern dictionaries are planned to take account of changes in language as these can be discovered from sampling of current practice, but to admit no change as accomplished until a new form gains considerable currency, and has maintained this currency for a reasonable period of time. Dictionary-makers endeavor, also, to determine levels of usage by observing who uses the language and how. In general they endeavor to distinguish three levels of speech as follows: (1) formal English, that is, the language of scientific and academic composition, of official documents, of the more dignified platform speech, and the like; (2) informal English, that is, the sort of language which cultured people use in their daily speech, which serves as the medium for most broadcasts, and which appears in written form in popular periodicals; (3) vulgate English, that is, slang, neologisms, barbarisms, and all locutions confined to the use of illiterate persons.

As with dictionaries, so in a lesser degree with handbooks concerned with grammar. Thus far the makers of dictionaries have gone much farther than the makers of grammar books in resting standards upon usage, although even the dictionaries vary in the hospitality which they show to new words. Some are more conservative than others, so that anyone who cares to compare two dictionaries, even two dictionaries which have been recently edited (and not all dictionaries with recent dates are recent dictionaries), can find words which are accepted in one dictionary and frowned upon in the other. But all good dictionaries, even the most conservative, are today supposedly based upon usage. Until recently most handbooks of composition were authoritarian, although no thinker about language for generations has given makers of handbooks a shadow of authority for their authority. But now the tide has apparently turned. Most of the good new books rest standards of grammatical correctness frankly upon usage; the old books are dying out, even though they die a stubborn death.

The study and control of our medium of communication require both scholars with brilliant insight and harmless drudges with a great love of language.

Study Questions

1. Why are stability and change both imperative in language?
2. How do dictionaries serve both to stabilize and to permit change? How do dictionaries slow down the rate of change?
3. How did the *Oxford English Dictionary* establish a standard and method for other dictionaries? Which previous lexicographers had recognized usage as the basis of standards? What usage did Noah Webster consult?
4. Why is slang unsatisfactory for permanent documents? Why is slang essential for drama and fiction? Why are slang expressions in Shakespeare's plays often difficult for modern readers to understand? (See *King Lear*, II, ii, 1–40.)
5. Why do many parents, teachers, and employers want the dictionary to be an authority? Why is such an authority more desired in a society with free movement up the social ladder than in one with fixed social classes?
6. Can individuals do for themselves what the trained staffs who work on dictionaries can do for them? Can individuals make choices on the basis of recorded usage without knowing the writers or the context of the quotations?

Might intensive study of a single contemporary author noted for his correct and easy style—E. B. White or James Thurber, for example—provide a sound basis for sentence structure, grammar, and idiom? E. B. White ends an account of his experience in Hurricane Edna with: "I never did get to hear the wrap-up." Read the article, "The Eye of Edna," *The New Yorker* (September 25, 1954), 34–49, or any similar personal experience article by White to determine whether such colloquialism is typical.

7. In following usage as a standard, a person has to decide whose usage—what writers and what kinds of works—will be most suitable for him to follow. In the professional field you plan to enter, what current writers are most highly regarded? Which of them write especially well? Study them with attention to style and, if possible, read some of their more personal and colloquial writing. The dictionary must cover *all* areas; the individual should make his choices from the areas relevant to his own needs.

8. What criticism would Kenyon make of Laird's use of *levels?* In Kenyon's terms, what *levels* does Laird refer to? What varieties?

9. Comment upon Laird's use of *farther* in the second sentence of the second paragraph from the end.

27. RIGHT VS. WRONG
Robert A. Hall, Jr.

In this selection from *Linguistics and Your Language* (1960) Professor Hall considers the effect of social acceptability upon linguistic behavior.

What is it . . . that makes some forms "incorrect" and others not? This is not a matter of legal or quasi-legal authority. . . . It is not a matter of universal condemnation, nor yet of incomprehensibility; in fact, some "incorrect" forms . . . would be clearer or simpler than the corresponding "correct" forms. It all boils down, really, to a question of acceptability in certain classes of our society, in those classes which are socially dominant and which set the tone for others. Whether a form is accepted or rejected does not depend on its inherent merit nor yet on any official approval given it, but purely on whether its hearers like it or not—on whether they will react favorably or unfavorably towards a person they hear using it. "Correct" can only mean "socially acceptable," and apart from this has no meaning as applied to language.

The social acceptability, and hence "correctness," of any form or word is determined, not by reason or logic or merit, but solely by the hearer's emotional attitude towards it—and emotional attitudes naturally differ from person to person, from group to group, from social class to social class.

Forms and words also change in social acceptability in the course of time: in the early seventeenth century, conservative speakers and purists objected violently to *ye* and *you*, used in speaking to one person, instead of the earlier *thou* and *thee*; and there must have been a time when *cows*, instead of the older plural *kine*, seemed an objectionable innovation.

Nevertheless, the difference in social acceptability between *I ain't* and *I am not*, between *hern* and *hers*, and so forth, is a real fact. If my child is likely to run into trouble later on for saying *I done it* or *hisn*, I will try to keep him from getting into the habit of using those forms which are actually not acceptable socially and which may cause others to react unfavorably towards him. But, if I am sensible about it, I will realize that the reason I want him to avoid these "incorrect" forms is not any inherent badness or evil character that they may have, but a purely practical consideration, that of their social acceptability. His choice of language will be used by others as a purely arbitrary means of classifying him socially among the sheep or the goats. All we need to do in the case of *I ain't*, etc., is to reword the traditional instructions, and say that we avoid using such turns of speech, not because they are "bad" or "wrong" or "ungrammatical," but because they are socially unacceptable. Of course, as soon as people in any given group stop treating, say, *he don't* as socially unacceptable, it automatically becomes "correct."

There is a close parallel between acceptable usage in language and "correct" behavior in other social customs, such as personal garb or table manners. What is it that makes it perfectly good manners to eat some things, such as bread-and-jam, with the fingers, and not others, like meat or vegetables? Certainly not the decree of any official or self-appointed authority; and certainly not any inherent feature or characteristic of what we eat or do not eat with the fingers. Some things that we eat with our fingers are much more messy than others that we would always take up with knife and fork. Here again, it is social acceptability that determines whether we may or may not eat a given item of food with our fingers, or wear a four-in-hand tie with a tuxedo. This acceptability varies from place to place, and from one period of time to another. Thus, in England it is perfectly good manners to pile your peas up on the back of your fork, using your knife as a pusher, and to eat the peas from the back of the fork; but it is very much frowned upon to keep changing the fork from the left hand to the right and back again, as Americans normally do. And the permissibility of, say, table behavior is constantly changing; for instance, I was brought up always to eat bacon with knife and fork or in a sandwich, whereas by now it has become much more widely "correct" to eat it with the fingers.

For cases like those we have been discussing up to now, the situation is clear: we will avoid forms like *I seen him, he don't* because they are used as shibboleths, disregard of which may lead to unfortunate results for us in our living and relations with others. There are many instances, however, where reality and what we are taught do not correspond as to the actual "correctness," the actual acceptability, of what we are told to avoid. Take the case of *it's me*. Grammarians tell us that a rule exists that "the verb *to be* never takes a direct object," and that hence we must always say *it is I* and never *it's me*. The rule itself is found in plenty of grammar books, but that is no guarantee of its accuracy or relevance; in reality, this rule is meaningless as a statement of the facts of English usage. It was taken over by English grammarians from Latin grammar, where it is an accurate statement of the facts of Latin usage: in Latin, you said *sum egō* "[it] am I," never *sum mē* "[it] am me." The facts of actual acceptable usage in English are quite different: we normally say, and have said for hundreds of years, *it's me, it's us*, and so forth.

This is not merely an unsupported assertion on my part; statistical studies have been made which show *it's me* to be by far the most frequent and normal usage in current English, as compared with *it is I*. Professor Charles C. Fries made a detailed study of many such points that are often the objects of dispute and condemnation, in his *American English Grammar*, by analyzing thousands of letters which had been written to the War Department by people of all levels of education and social standing. He found very clear documentary proof that many forms and many constructions that are often condemned are actually in perfectly good standing in the usage of educated persons, and hence by definition acceptable or "correct." He found, for instance, that it is normal to say *it's me, these kind of things, none of the children are here, everybody should take off their hat*, in standard English, and that there is no real difference in such respects between standard and vulgar speech. The story is told of a certain very puristic lady —let's call her Miss Fidditch—who was teaching her class very strictly to avoid *it's me*:

MISS FIDDITCH: You must always say *it is I*. The inflexible rule of grammar is that the verb *to be* never takes a direct object.

(A few minutes later:)

PRINCIPAL (outside the door, knocking): Who's there?
MISS FIDDITCH: It's me—Miss Fidditch.

Miss Fidditch was right when she said *it's me*, naturally and normally, in a give-and-take conversational situation and without reflecting; she was wrong when she tried to force on her class an artificial, unrealistic rule that applied to no one's, not even her own, usage in actual fact. And we all know the old story about the grammarian who said "Never use a preposition to end a sentence with."

We are often told that such-and-such a form or combination of forms is "in accordance with the rules of logic," which make other competing forms or combinations "illogical" and hence inadmissible. Such a rule as *everyone* or *everybody* is singular and hence a word referring to it must be in the singular" is an instance of this, or the rule that "a double negative makes a positive" and that hence we mustn't say *I didn't see nobody* except when we really did see somebody. It is perfectly true that, in strictly ordered systems like mathematics or symbolic logic, a violation of the rules of discourse will introduce confusion and make a statement into its opposite or into something else from what was intended. The purists' error here lies in identifying language and logic, and expecting normal linguistic usage to be strictly logical. As a matter of fact, no language ever was strictly logical, nor can we make it so by preaching at its speakers. To begin with, we should have to define what "logical" meant—and we would find that each different language would, from the outset, give its speakers different ideas as to what "logic" is. To us, for instance, it seems logical, and, in fact, inescapable to say *one book*, but *two books, three books, five books*, using the form *books* when we refer to more than one of them, and thus distinguishing between "one" and "more than one" or (to use the traditional grammatical terms) singular and plural. To someone brought up speaking Hungarian, that difference seems useful in general—a Hungarian will say *könyv* for "book" and *könyvek* for "books," with *-ek* indicating the plural for him just as *-s* does for us—but when he has a numeral to tell him how many books there are, he uses, not the plural, but the singular form of the word for "book." The Hungarian says *egy könyv* "one book," *két könyv* "two book," and likewise *három könyv* "three book," *öt könyv* "five book" and so forth. To him it seems silly, needless and illogical to say "five *books*" where the indication of plurality is already given by the number, so that "five book" will do just as well. Which is more logical, English or Hungarian, in this respect? One could argue both ways, and perhaps the Hungarian way of saying "two book, three book" might prove to be more strictly logical. It all depends on what you are brought up to say.

The same thing holds for such points as the "double negative," which many persons condemn violently—*I didn't see nobody* instead of *I didn't see anybody*. They tell us that "logically" a double negative makes a positive, and that therefore *I didn't see nobody* "really" means *I did see somebody*. Here again, our traditional grammar rule is based on Latin, as it is in so many other instances—as if the rules of Latin could be applied to English. In Latin, those who spoke it about the time of Caesar, Cicero and Augustus normally took a double negative to mean a positive. So for them, *nōn nihil* "not nothing" meant "something," and *nōn vīdī nēminem* "I didn't see nobody" could only have meant "I saw somebody." That was right, logical and natural *for them*, because that was the way they used Latin. But later, in the course of the centuries, those who spoke Latin and the Romance languages which developed out of Latin, got in the habit of using a double negative with *negative* meaning. In Spanish, for instance, it is downright incorrect (because nobody will accept it) to say such a thing as *vi a nadie* in the meaning of "I saw nobody." You *must* say *no vi a nadie*, literally "I didn't see nobody," with the two negatives *no* "not" and *nadie* "nobody," whenever *nadie* "nobody" follows the verb; otherwise what you say is meaningless. It may be "illogical," and it may be "incorrect" from the point of view of Latin grammar; but in Spanish, French, and Italian, for instance, the requirement of a double negative is so absolute that no one would be able to get away with condemning it on the grounds of logic. The reason that the point can be raised at all in modern English is that we have a divided usage: in actual current speech, when there is no emphasis, a double negative and a single negative both have a negative meaning, and everybody will understand what we mean whether we say *I didn't see nobody* or *I saw nobody* or *I didn't see anybody*. But when we are putting emphasis on the verb or the pronoun, then *I DIDN'T see NObody* does have positive meaning, and would be normal as an answer, say, in contradiction to *You saw nobody*. The drift of our language is inevitably toward the use of the double negative; this is as normal and natural as anything else in English, and as logical in English as it is in Spanish and French.

Now with regard to this second group of "wrong" usages, the situation is essentially different from that of *ain't* and *hisn*. Such forms as *ain't* are both socially unacceptable and condemned by purists; whereas *it's me* and *those kind of things*, although grammarians may condemn them, are nevertheless in normal, everyday use by socially accepted people and hence are socially acceptable and by definition "correct." And when it comes to such pronunciations as KEW-pon, ad-ver-TISE-ment, AD-ult, the purists' condemnations are absolutely fanciful, without any rhyme or reason whatsoever. Both KEW-pon and KOO-pon, both ad-ver-TISE-ment and ad-VER-tise-ment, both AD-ult and ad-ULT are normal, regular, and acceptable variants; to call either member of these pairs "correct" and the other "incorrect" is quite arbitrary. Language is not an either-or proposition, in which no variation, no deviation from a strictly maintained party line is permissible; in many instances, such as those of *coupon* and *advertisement*, more than one alternative exists and both are equally acceptable or "correct."

Aside from these two types of "incorrectness" we have just discussed, there are other kinds of usage that are condemned, and (although this is not always realized) on somewhat different grounds. The largest group of forms of this sort are those which are under a social taboo of one kind or another. In our society, we tend to shy away from casual public discussion of certain topics, particularly two: sexual reproduction and elimination of bodily waste; and we carry over our repugnance to terms which imply casual discussion of these subjects. This is of course a real repugnance with the classes of people who set the dominant tone of what is and what isn't acceptable in our society, and it establishes a taboo which absolutely *must* be observed on pain of very severe social sanctions: if you use the so-called "four-letter" or taboo words in mixed company in any except the lowest classes of society, you will immediately be subjected to extreme disapproval, condemnation and ostracism. But there are two things to be noticed about these taboos of decency, real as they are: 1) they are partial, and 2) they are relative, in that they are peculiar to our West European society.

On the first point, that these taboos are partial, note that I can use the terms *sexual reproduction* and *elimination of bodily waste*, as I did in the preceding paragraph, without fear of reproach or condemnation, although I would never wish or dare to use, in conversing, lecturing, or writing this book, the equivalent taboo words—words which most readers probably know as well as I do. It offends our sense of "decency" to discuss those subjects casually or to imply casual discussion of them; but it is acceptable to use more formal, learned terms that imply serious discussion on a scientific level. In the meanwhile, of course, the "four-letter" words go on in the normal, everyday usage of folk who are untroubled by social taboos, and are the only terms they know for the activities and body parts connected with sex and elimination. Many of us have doubtless heard the anecdote of the doctor who kept asking a constipated patient if he had *defecated*, and, always receiving the answer "No," kept prescribing more and more laxatives until he finally (and with considerable reluctance) used the taboo word, when he found out that his patient's intestines had nearly been ruined by the excessive purgation. The patient simply didn't know the fancy word *defecate*, and kept giving the answer "No," whereas he would have known and understood the "four-letter" word from the beginning. Which was more sensible—for the doctor to observe the taboo and ruin the patient's intestines, or to use the "four-letter" word at the start and get the result he was aiming at?

Such taboos, also, although certainly very real, are relative. Not all societies have the same taboos. Most societies do not have our feeling that sex and elimination are indecent; on the other hand, another society may taboo the mention of one's relatives, or of dead people's names, or of certain game animals. With the Cree Indians, it is taboo to speak one's sister's name; the Cree will say that he "respects her too much," and he would feel as much repugnance towards mentioning her name as we would towards using a "four-letter" word. In some societies, especially in the islands of the Pacific, such taboos on one class of words or another have become very elaborate. We can imagine, for instance, a person from a society which tabooed the mention of one's relatives' names, as being highly shocked at such a comedy as *Charley's Aunt*, with its irreverent treatment of family relationships, whereas at the same time he might, without violating any of his society's taboos, sing his baby daughter a lullaby in which her sexual parts and their function were prominently mentioned. It would be extremely naive on our part to condemn such a person for not knowing the difference between decency and indecency: standards of decency, like other standards, are relative, not absolute, and no society can claim that its ideas of decency are right and all others wrong. So it is with our taboo words; they are condemned, it is true, and we would do extremely well to avoid using them in "decent" society; but the reason for avoiding them is, not that such words are inherently evil, but simply that they run counter to particular taboos of the dominant classes of our society.

Closely similar to the taboo on words that refer to sex and elimination is that on words that have a serious religious meaning, when they are used in any other connection: *Jesus, God, Christ, damn, hell* used as "swear-words." Here again, I can use any of these words in serious discussion: *Jesus Christ died to save us from damnation,* etc. But used frivolously, as in *Christ, am I tired!* or *Ouch! Damn it to hell!*, these words shock a great many of us. They used to shock still more people; in the 1880's, when Clarence Day, Sr., was in the habit of saying *damn!* in the middle of the pastor's sermon and elsewhere, it was a serious breach of etiquette—and part of our amusement over his behavior in that respect comes from the difference in attitude between that day and this. Objectively speaking, *damn it!* is simply a succession of sounds that we use when we are angry, and even *damn you!* implies no desire on our part that the person or persons spoken to should literally roast in hell-fire for eternity, but simply that we're more or less irritated at them. The "badness" of swear-words of this kind comes from the fact that some people—people who are dominant in our society—are displeased by them and will act unfavorably towards people who use them. . . .

And even with rules that do state normal, current usage accurately—have they any authority beyond that of simple statements of fact? We have already seen that there is no legal sanction, not even any semi-legal academic backing, for any claim to "authority" in language and its use. Suppose that usage should change, and that what we now say universally (such as *he goes, she sings*) should go out of fashion and be replaced by some other usage which we now wouldn't accept (like *he go, she sing*). Would the old be "right" and the new be "wrong"? By no means; if people's habits and usage change, then there is no "authority," no law that can keep them from doing so, and the new is just as good as the old. Not necessarily better, of course: neither better nor worse, but just different. Some of us are inclined to think that because a habit, a custom, or a thing is old, it must necessarily be better than something new. This was the prevailing attitude all through ancient times and the Middle Ages, and has lasted even up to now in some matters like those of language; it is the only reason some grammarians have for preferring one usage to another.

Another norm that is often set up for deciding disputed points is the usage of great writers: do we find *it ain't, he don't* or split infinitives in great writers, men who must have had great knowledge of their own language in order to write their great books? First of all, though, we must ask *which* great writers—those of the present, or those of the past? Our choice is difficult here; if we go too far back, the literary language is obviously archaic, and nobody nowadays, not even the most conservative grammarian, would recommend every feature of Milton's or Dr. Johnson's prose for our modern usage. If we come too close to the present, it is hard to tell just who is a really great writer and who is not; and, even if we have our great writers picked out, we find that very often they use freely the very forms we want to condemn, especially the more "realistic" writers like Steinbeck and Farrell. Then let's restrict our choice of great writers to, say, the late nineteenth and early twentieth century, so that they will fit what we want to prescribe. Even so, we find that their actual usage was considerably freer than we want to think. Hence the defensive accusations we often hear dogmatic purists make, that "even the greatest writers" make this, that or the other "mistake."

Furthermore, just how much bearing does great literature and its language have on normal everyday usage? That great literature gives us examples of the *artistic* use of language, we can easily grant; and that studying the way a Thomas Hardy or a Henry James has manipulated his language will be of use to us if we want to write literature—likewise granted. But such men as Hardy or James (to say nothing of authors like Carlyle or Meredith) are not typical, they are exceptional, in their language as in their content; and the very fact that they are exceptional disqualifies them as examples for everyday, normal, non-literary usage. Wouldn't it be nice if we all tried to talk like great literature in our daily contacts? It would be almost like trying to handle everyday affairs in the style of grand opera.

The entire attempt to set up absolute standards, rigid norms, for regulating people's language is destined to failure from the outset, because, as we have seen in this chapter: 1) there is no authority that has either the right or the ability to govern people's usage; and 2) such an authority, even when it has been set officially (as were the French and Spanish Academies), can never find valid standards by which to govern usage. Logic, Latin grammar, the usage of literature, appeals to authority as such—none have any applicability. In our country, especially, attempts to prescribe rules, to set up a normative grammar, have been very widespread, and have battened on our insecurities, on our fears for our social standing in the face of linguistic shibboleths. But all such attempts have been, and will continue to be, failures.

Is there any definition at all that we can give for "good" language? Only, I think, something like this: "good" language is language which gets the desired effect with the least friction and difficulty for its user. That means, of course, that "good" language is going to vary with the situation it is used in. In elegant or puristically inclined society, "good" usage will include *it isn't he, he doesn't,* and also *this kind of people, it is I,* since those forms will get the best results in favor and compliance with what we desire. In normal everyday situations with normal everyday people, *it isn't him, he don't, these kind of people, it's me* will be good usage, since ordinary people speak that way normally; and we won't be too worried about saying *damn!* unless our hearers have specific objections. With people who customarily say *it ain't him, he don't, we seen them, hisn,* those forms will be good usage, provided they serve to get results most effectively.

One type of confusion which often crops up at this point, and which we should be on our guard against, is that between language and style. We are often inclined to think that "correctness" is the same thing as good style, particularly in writing. Actually, the two are not the same, though the situation is parallel for both. "Good" style is simply that style of speaking or writing which is most effective under any given set of circumstances. When we speak of "good style," what we usually mean is clarity, absence of ambiguity, orderly structure, and the like—and these are, indeed, important in most situations. But they are not the same thing as type of language, and "good style" is possible in any dialect. Aesthetic considerations— whether a given way of expressing ourselves is pleasing or not to our listeners or readers—of course enter into the picture, too, with regard to "good" style. But all matters of aesthetics depend so much on individual preference, and differ so much not only from one language to another but from one speaker to another, that no one can presume to set up objective standards for them, nor legislate or make authoritative pronouncements on what is or is not pleasing to the ear or to the eye. . . .

In short: the entire structure of our notions about "correctness" and "right" vs. "wrong" in language is not only inaccurate, erroneous and useless; it is definitely harmful, and we would do well to outgrow it. When purists tell us that we are using "bad" or "incorrect" or "ungrammatical" language, they are simply telling us that what we say would not be acceptable in the upper social levels; sometimes they are right as to the facts of the case, and sometimes they are just talking through their hats. What our purists give us in the way of rules and laws to observe has no authority, no validity aside from their own preference, and is often based on specious pseudo-logic or on the structure of a distantly related language, Latin, which has no relevance to English. If an "error" or "mistake" is frequent, if almost everybody makes it, if it is found in even the greatest writers, then it is no error: as the great Byzantine emperor and law-codifier Justinian put it, *commūnis error facit iūs*—a mistake that everybody makes is no longer a mistake. We need to look at our language realistically, not feeling "inferior" about it and taking nobody's word as to its being "right" or "wrong." Often enough, we may find we need to change our usage, simply because social and financial success depends on some norm, and our speech is one of the things that will be used as a norm. In a situation like this, it is advisable to make the adjustment; but let's do so on the basis of the actual social acceptability of our speech, not because of the fanciful prescriptions of some normative grammarian or other pseudo-authority.

Study Questions

1. Which forms should be corrected in a child's speech? Which ones should not? What must a parent or teacher know about language in order to make the necessary distinctions?

2. "It's me" is acceptable because the expression occurs chiefly in conversational situations where unnatural "correctness" is inappropriate. One of the rare exceptions is seen in the Biblical "Lo, it is I, be not afraid." In the context, one of the utmost dignity and solemnity, "Look, it's me, don't be scared" would be as unsuitable as "It is I" would be in the usual context. Can you think of other expressions which suitably deviate from formal patterns because the context is almost invariably informal?

3. In the "test scenes" in Act III of Shaw's *Pygmalion,* what social taboos does Eliza Doolittle violate? Would the violations be equally shocking to Americans? How does the reaction of Clara show how fashions in speech develop?

4. In dialogue in modern realistic fiction, can the reader assume that what characters say will be acceptable in other contexts? What must the reader know about time, place, and social class, and about the author's own qualifications as a recorder of speech in reaching any conclusions as to whether the dialogue can be regarded as representing standard usage? How would a small-town group react to the sophisticated speech of New York or Hollywood society?

5. Can one have a "good style" in writing and speaking without understanding basic sentence patterns and without a good vocabulary within the limits of the subject?

6. William Faulkner in *The Town,* at the end of Chapter 16, shows Ratliff trying to overcome his substandard speech habits and young Charles Mallison, his superior in class and education, protesting because of the vigor of Ratliff's substandard forms. Analyze the passage to determine just what the substandard forms are and how they may be explained. Is Ratliff's natural expression "good style" for him, a traveling sewing-machine salesman? Would his substandard forms be "good style" for Charles or for his uncle, Gavin Stevens, members of the upper class?

28. THE GENTEEL TRADITION

Albert H. Marckwardt

This section from *American English* (1958) deals with the factors which affect the connotations of words in American English.

Another manifestation of the same tendency ["to make the ordinary seem somewhat grander than it actually was"] is to be observed in connection with our terms for educational institutions and various types of training schools. In fact, there is if anything a double impulse here. The first is to be found in the tendency to dignify academic institutions of all kinds with a name that is a degree above, or at best somewhat more impressive than, that which they would merit in England. . . . A telling illustration of how this tendency operates is furnished by the state of Michigan where, in the decade of the 1930's, all but one of the normal schools in the state officially became Colleges of Education and in the 'fifties dropped the modifying phrase. This change was officially justified by the establishment in each of them of a liberal arts curriculum leading to the bachelor's degree, but the fact remains that *college* clearly seemed to the educational authorities a more desirable and respectable term than *school*. That *university* underwent a similar extension for much the same reason is evident from the exultant statement of a misguided patriot of the 1870's quoted by Schlesinger and Fox: "There are two universities in England, four in France, ten in Prussia, and thirty-seven in Ohio." Even *high school*, the American use of which dates from 1824, is seldom used for a secondary school in England, and in Europe it regularly denotes an institution of college or university rank. Here, however, American usage may have had its roots in Scotland.

The secondary tendency is to apply to trade schools and other establishments devoted to the training of artisans the same labels which have in the past been reserved for academic institutions. Again evidence is scanty, but *business college* as a term for a stenographic and secretarial training venture, is to be found as early as 1865. The dictionaries are strangely silent on *barber college*, but it was current in parts of the United States early in the twentieth century. Its sister institutions, the schools and colleges of cosmetology, devoted to initiating the beginner into the mysteries of the permanent wave, probably do not go back beyond the 1920's.

Occupational terminology in America has undergone a series of changes quite similar to those which have already been observed in connection with the educational institutions: old terms have been extended in application; new ones have been created. The words *doctor* and *professor* are obvious instances of extensions in application. Both of these are carefully restricted in their use in England, where surgeons are *Mr.* even if they do hold the M.D. degree, and professorships are naturally much less numerous than in the United States. In America, dentists, osteopaths, chiropractors, optometrists, chiropodists, and veterinarians are all doctors, and in addition the tremendous extension of the doctorate in American graduate schools, and the lavish manner in which American colleges and universities distribute honorary degrees add to the number of doctors on other levels as well. Even so, this does not take into account such jocular applications, either in full form or the clipped *Doc,* which, as the *Dictionary of Americanisms* indicates, was extended to logging camp cooks late in the nineteenth century.

Professor has developed in much the same direction; in fact, it may have begun earlier and gone farther. We find an enterprising bookseller styling himself a Professor of Book Auctioneering as early as 1774, and virtually every attempt at a glossary of Americanisms during the nineteenth century mentions the extension of the title to such groups as dancing teachers, magicians, and phrenologists. Certainly in most small towns the title was regularly applied not only to superintendents of school and principals but even to male grade-school teachers as well. The inevitable result of this wholesale doctoring and professoring is, of course, an avoidance of the titles by those who are normally entitled to them, an outcome suggested by the mock-serious society organized at the University of Virginia "for the encouragement of the use of *mister* to all men, professional or otherwise."

Academic usage in the north of the United States as contrasted with the south also offers a striking illustration of the operation of what might be called scarcity values. In the colleges and universities of the North there are many holders of the doctorate who have not yet attained professorial rank in a teaching faculty. Consequently, one who is both a professor and a doctor is customarily addressed as *professor.* In the South, on the other hand, until quite recently many college faculty members of professorial rank did not possess a doctor's degree. In this part of the country one who has both the rank and the degree is normally addressed as *doctor.*

In a sense the extension of the use of both *professor* and *doctor* is closely related to the American passion for honorifics, but a further discussion of these must be postponed until we take a hasty glance at the creation of other so-called professional titles and occupational terms. *Mortician,* frequently thought of in this connection, appears to have been created about 1895 on the convenient analogy of *physician,* and the same process of derivation has given us *beautician, loctician,* and six or eight others, all somewhat bizarre. It is possible that *mortician* may owe its creation quite as much to the age-old and constant search for euphemisms for terms connected with death and burial as to the desire for professional status. There is, after all, a somewhat gruesome pun in the word *undertaker*, and though it has served the English from 1698 on, they do at times soften the effect by substituting *funeral furnisher*.

Realtor, another oft-cited instance of the American creation of pseudo-professional terms, could be excused by the generously inclined on the ground that it permitted a single word to replace the somewhat cumbersome *real-estate agent*, but there is probably more truth than fiction in the sentiment expressed by Sinclair Lewis's Babbitt to the effect that, "We ought to insist that folks call us 'realtors' and not 'real-estate men.' Sounds more like a reg'lar profession." Though the Lewis citation comes from the early 'twenties, the term itself dates from 1915.

American regard for technology is shown by the overwhelming popularity of the word *engineer*, used in strange and numerous combinations. Our early use of the term in connection with railroading was a portent of things to come; the English in general content themselves with the somewhat more humdrum sounding *engine driver*. But since that time we have employed the word in an astounding number of combinations, running to well over 2000. H. L. Mencken reported that the Extermination Engineers, namely the rat and roach eradicators, have had a national association for some thirty years. Such further terms as *patent engineer, recreation engineer, erosion engineer,* and *casement window engineer* illustrate the variety of uses to which the term has been put.

The proposal of a Janitor's Institute, held at Mt. Pleasant, Michigan, in 1939, to the effect that janitors henceforth be called *engineer-custodians*, reveals as well the temporary nature of the satisfaction to be derived from verbal glorification, for historically *janitor* represents quite the same state of mind that gave rise to *realtor* and *mortician*. Derived somewhat artificially from the mythological character Janus, it was first used for a doorkeeper or porter, and its application to the sweeper of floors and builder of fires has been confined primarily to the United States; in England *caretaker* is the common term. As is evident from the action of the institute, even twenty years ago the word had become sufficiently tarnished that *engineer, custodian,* or both, sounded more attractive. One of the amusing sequels of the shift in terminology from *janitor* to *custodian* in one American university was that the title of the head of a research library had, in turn, to be changed from *Custodian* to *Director*, since there was some danger of confusing him with the janitor of the place.

Nor was the tendency to glorify the commonplace limited to the professional and work-a-day world. The American household bears some marks of this, even today. For example, the Lynds in their study *Middletown in Transition* find occasion to quote this very revealing excerpt from a current newspaper:

> The time will easily be remembered when masculine and juvenile members of a household received glaring looks punctuated by lifted eyebrows when

they forgot in the presence of guests and referred to the evening meal as "supper." But time has changed that. Smart folks are having buffet suppers, . . .

Disregarding for the moment the recently regained prestige of a certain type of supper, we may conclude that in the 'twenties and 'thirties it was considered proper, particularly by women, to refer to the evening meal as *dinner* and presumably to the midday meal as *luncheon,* and that this terminology had quite recently replaced *dinner* as the term for the noon meal and *supper* for the evening meal.

This shift is a slightly delayed reflection of the changed eating habits of many American families which developed from the increased urbanization and industrialization of American life, and has, of course, some justification in fact. For the farming and small-town families at the beginning of the present century, the heaviest meal of the day was served at noon, and the evening repast was considerably lighter. Thus for that time, *dinner* and *supper* were accurate descriptions. The present tendency toward lighter meals at noon, frequently consumed away from the home by the male members of the family and by the children, has resulted in the heavier meal being served at home in the evening, with a resultant change in terminology and a prestige-loss for *supper.*

In this connection it is interesting to observe that *supper* not only continued in common use in America some sixty or seventy years longer than in England, but that this was a matter for comment by at least two mid-nineteenth century British travelers. In 1859, Gosse in a series of letters from Alabama wrote, "The meal which we are accustomed to call 'tea' is by Americans, universally, I believe, called 'supper,' and it is the final meal, there being but three in the day." Five years later we find C. Geithe reporting, "I chatted . . . till tea, or as they called it, supper."

As American domestic architecture has changed, so too have the names given to the various rooms. The principal phenomenon over the past century has been the disappearance of a "best room," rarely occupied on weekdays, and used only to entertain guests and for holidays or festive occasions. In American usage this was the *parlor.* This in itself was a shift from British English, for there the term *parlor* was applied to a rather small intimate chamber, whereas the more pretentious one was called the *drawing room,* a term which never caught on with the Americans. In the United States, as long as the parlor was an institution, the room which was ordinarily used by the family circle was the *sitting room,* but as the parlor disappeared, the sitting room became the *living room,* and the former term came to be felt as somewhat rustic and old-fashioned.

It may be noted that only in America was the term *cuspidor*—an importation from Portuguese through Dutch—adopted for what was at one time a not uncommon accessory in the home, to say nothing of clubrooms and legislative halls. This somewhat delicate word was also introduced in England as early as 1781 but never gained any real currency.

Finally, the tendencies toward verbal elegance and sentimentality appear to have combined to produce a more extensive use of *home* in America than in England. At the close of the last century, George Warrington Steevens commented, "As to the home, the American talks about it a great deal. He never builds himself a house; he builds himself a home." Consequently, contractors for domestic dwellings are *home builders*, the householder is a *homeowner*, vacuum sweepers, dishwashing machines, ironers, and the other manifold mechanical appurtenances of the American household are *home appliances*. School instruction in cooking and sewing has become *homemaking*, and when exalted to a more learned level, *home economics*. Even the housewife became a *homemaker* by formal resolution of the Long Island Federation of Women's Clubs, as Mencken has pointed out. Moreover, the institutions of refuge for the needy and those of detention for troublesome juveniles are quite regularly *homes*, to say nothing of the *funeral home*, which now customarily serves as the setting for final rites.

Travelers to America, almost from its very beginning as an independent country, have taken great delight in pointing out what seemed to them a fundamental inconsistency between the theory of equality upon which the government of the country is based and the fondness of the American people for titles of honor. Although Crevecoeur, reflecting on his pre-Revolutionary experience, stoutly insisted that lawyer, merchant, and farmer were the fairest titles our country at that time afforded, observers from the 1840's on have a quite different story to tell. As late as 1896, George Warrington Steevens inquired somewhat petulantly in describing the American, "Why does he cling all his life to the title of some rank or office he held twenty years ago?" Two answers to the question were offered some years before Steevens phrased it, and without question there is some truth in each. In 1849 the Scotsman Alexander Mackay defended the Americans on the ground that, "the fondness for titles which they display is but a manifestation of the fondness for distinction natural to the human mind." A somewhat different opinion was voiced a decade later by Thomas Colley Grattan, who concluded, "Were a well-established national self-reliance felt among the leading men in the United States, there would be none of the melancholy parodies of 'High Life,' none of the yearnings after aristocratical distinctions which are now so flagrant."

When American honorifics are examined in a dispassioned light, it must be said that they are still a far cry from Teutonic usage, for example. They are notable chiefly for some extension of such bogus military titles as *Colonel*, the retention of legislative and judicial titles, as noted by Steevens, beyond the period of service, and the somewhat comic extension of the word *Honorable* itself. Judged by either general European or Latin American standards in these matters, the English-speaking American becomes almost a shrinking violet. It is only in the light of English practice that our use of honorifics seems somewhat overweighted, and even the English have their silly periods, as anyone who witnessed the furor over the proper application and meaning of *Esquire* which raged in the autumn of 1953 can well testify.

In this connection it is well to remember that the United States came into being as the result of a political rather than a social revolution. The latter frequently does result in a highly conscious effort to do away with artificial titular distinctions; witness the adoption of *Citizen* in the French Revolution and that of *Comrade* in post-revolutionary Russia. This did not occur in the United States, for there was no nobility to displace, no class of governing officials to turn out of office. If anything, some offices and distinctions had to be created, and even the title to be given to the chief executive of the country was for a time a moot question.

In consequence of H. L. Mencken's picturesque and entertaining assault upon *Honorable*, little remains to be said except to point out the problem posed by the vastness of the country and the complexities of its governmental machinery. To begin with, we have the President and the members of his cabinet and the justices of the Supreme Court. No one would be inclined to doubt that any one of these merits the term. But if the executive and judicial branches of our government are thus entitled to the distinction, and so far we have imaginarily conferred it upon no more than thirty individuals, our very concept of the equality of all three branches of our government demands that all members of the Senate and the House of Representatives receive it as well. Thus at a single stroke we have added some 550 *Honorables*. Going back to the executive and judicial branches, we must now ask whether we stop with Supreme Court justices and cabinet secretaries. What about appellate and district judges, to say nothing of undersecretaries and assistant secretaries? There is the whole diplomatic corps in addition, and officials in special governmental agencies not represented in the cabinet.

Leaving the national government and pursuing the same problem on the state level, we must now multiply by forty-eight the possibly 2000 *Honorables* we have already conferred. Nor can we stop here, for surely a metropolitan mayor has a position equal in dignity and responsibility to the governor of one of our smaller states. Ultimately we arrive at the township justice and the village fire marshal. Moreover, many of these offices are no longer than a biennium in duration, and once a man has acquired the title he is not likely to relinquish it. The wonder is that anyone at all escapes the term, or perhaps that we have not attempted to create distinctions within it, that is to say, degrees and classifications of honorability.

A further sector of the American vocabulary which scarcely has a counterpart in British life comprises the wide variety of names given to fraternal orders. The last two decades of the nineteenth century gave rise to an almost unbelievable number of these, very nearly 500, in fact. Schlesinger and Fox, in commenting upon this gaudy variety, among which are included such choice items as the American Order of Druids, the Prudent Patricians of Pompeii, and the Concatenated Order of Hoo-Hoo, make the very sound observation that "the nomenclature of fraternalism will someday offer interesting material for the student of suppressed desires and wishful thinking." Although they do not develop the point, there can be little question that the motivating force behind these is of a class with what we have just observed.

Euphemism, verbal prudery or the avoidance of the unpleasant word, is another somewhat indirect product of the frontier which, from a semantic and lexical point of view at least, is often closely allied to verbal glorification. In fact, it is often difficult to decide whether the motive behind such a substitution as that of *casket* for *coffin* was primarily that of suggesting something more elegant or that of avoiding a term connected with death and burial. Much of the verbal prudery, however, for which we became notorious in the nineteenth century, may be traced to two factors: the position of woman in American society and the predominantly middle-class character of American culture.

The second of these points is so obvious as not to require extensive elaboration. Within the history of modern societies it has always been the middle class which has manifested a greater and more anxious concern for the proprieties than either the lower class, which has tended toward indifference, or the upper, which has been protected by a thick coat of self-assurance. Among the proprieties thus affected, that of language has usually assumed a prominent position. It was the English middle class, or at least the upper sector of it, which created the demand that led to the excessive schoolmastering of the language in eighteenth-century England. That the Puritan settlers of New England—also predominantly middle class—were intensely concerned with linguistic propriety is indicated by the amount of colonial legislation directed against profanity. Noah Webster interested himself in expurgating the Bible, and considered this one of his important works. There is ample evidence in a dozen sociological studies that most Americans today are prone to think of themselves as belonging to the middle class. Consequently, there is every reason to expect from American English a typical middle-class delicacy, expressed in a multitude of linguistic taboos. The record, as we shall see, in no way dispels our expectations.

This verbal delicacy received a strong reinforcement from the position which women enjoyed in our frontier society. In his *Society and Thought in Early America*, Harvey Wish points out that:

. . . their relative scarcity and economic opportunities made them more difficult to please in courtship. While the South enjoyed a latter-day chivalry with roots deep in feudal times, the North, too, had its ritual of courtesies due to women. Everywhere seduction and breach of promise suits were apt to be prejudiced in the woman's favor. Here one addressed a mixed audience as "Ladies and Gentlemen" instead of the traditional "Gentlemen and Ladies." Women travelled alone without losing caste, and their daughters dispensed with chaperones (even if they belonged to the well-to-do class). While the Industrial Revolution was emancipating western European women as well as their American sisters, the American woman was definitely ahead in status.

Because of this scarcity value, American women seem to have been in a position to foster an extreme sensitivity in linguistic matters. Calhoun in his study of the American family cites one letter written a few years before 1850 which asserts, "Women can alter the dialect, change the manners, dictate the dress and habits of life, and control the morals of every community." Captain Frederick Marryatt's comments on this point have furnished what is often considered the classic example of verbal delicacy. He tells first of how he offended an American woman by saying *legs* instead of limbs and then goes on to the account of the girls' seminary where the piano "limbs" were "dressed in modest little trousers with frills at the bottom of them." That the veracity of the latter story has been questioned is of little importance; it is true in spirit to the segment of American life it purported to reflect. Nor was this cult of super-refinement one of short duration only. The Lynds in their study of Middletown cite a commencement essay at the local high school as late as 1891 bearing the title, "Woman is Most Perfect When Most Womanly."

The first and most prominent linguistic effect of female dominance and middle-class morality was an extreme reticence on matters directly or even remotely connected with sex. Again the Lynds' *Middletown in Transition* furnishes corroborative evidence from a society studied less than two decades ago:

> Sex is one of the things Middletown has long been taught to fear. Its institutions—with the important exception of the movies and some of the periodicals it reads, both imported from the outside culture—operate to keep the subject out of sight and out of mind as much as possible.

In language, of course, questionable subjects are kept out of sight and mind, ostensibly if not actually, by developing new and less shocking terms to replace those which have taken on taboo characteristics. All languages do this to some extent. It is the degree to which these euphemistic tendencies have operated in American English that is of particular interest.

One outlet for verbal delicacy of this nature was the creation of a host of more or less thinly disguised terms for houses of prostitution. *Assignation house* is cited by the *Dictionary of Americanisms* for 1854; *house of assignation* preceded this by twenty years. *Sporting house,* which in England meant first merely a house frequented by sportsmen and later a gambling house, was finally applied to a brothel in America in 1894 in a book which bore the somewhat disconcerting title, *If Christ Came to Chicago.* None of the dictionaries, however, seem to record the related use of *sport* for a prostitute, which was current about the same time. *Crib* also reflects the same transition from a gaming house to one of prostitution, though somewhat earlier, and such terms as *cat house, fancy house, cow bag,* and *call house* were all in use at one time or another; and on a somewhat more dignified level, *disorderly house* and *house of ill fame.* Cadet as a euphemism for procurer seems to have flourished from the first to the third decades of the twentieth century. There was also an equal reticence with respect to naming specific venereal diseases, but this has been generally overcome within the past twenty years.

Another object which has particularly invited euphemistic terminology is what the English call a *water closet* and the Americans a *toilet.* Commenting on the use of *toilet,* the *Oxford English Dictionary* says, "In the U.S. especially a dressing room furnished with bathing facilities; in a restricted sense, a bathroom, a lavatory," but it is difficult to fix the time when the precise application to the water closet itself occurred. The first citation which may be so interpreted with reasonable certainty bears the date 1909, though it must have had this meaning considerably earlier. *Rest room* (1909) and *comfort station* (1904) were also concocted during the first decade of the century, and Mencken credits *powder room* to the speakeasies of the Prohibition era. The American use of *washroom* in the same sense goes back to 1853.

It is to be expected that during a period of extreme verbal delicacy there will be many taboos for various parts of the body, particularly those which have any connection with sex or with the excretive functions. Mid-nineteenth-century America was no exception. This topic, however, has been so fully treated by Mencken and by Pyles that it will be necessary only to point out one or two matters which seem to have been overlooked.

For example, despite Captain Marryatt's oft-quoted stories of the woman who was offended at the mention of *limb,* it should not be forgotten that this word acquired the meaning of "leg" not in America but in England as early as 1400. *Oxford English Dictionary* citations show that it was in constant use in England from the beginning of the fifteenth century until 1837. Marryatt's account of his American experience bears the date 1839, and from that time until 1924 all the citations are American. What we have here then is the continuation of a British euphemism rather than an American invention.

The taboo against *leg* was extended to fowl prepared for the table, as is frequently pointed out, but *drumstick,* one of the euphemisms which appeared on the scene as a substitute, is clearly of British origin, and on the basis of dictionary evidence, at least, was as much used in Britain as in the United States. The extension of *joint* from its British use in connection with such meats as beef, mutton, and venison, to roast fowl seems clearly to have originated in America, and so too the further distinction between a first joint and a second. An English traveler in America in 1845 reported himself as being "requested by a lady, at a public dinner table, to furnish her with the first and second joint." The presumed indecency of the word *leg*, coupled with an almost equally strong taboo against *breast*, gave rise to another pair of American euphemisms used in this connection. Thomas C. Grattan, in his *Civilized America* (1859) explained that, "some . . . would scarcely hesitate, though almost all call it the 'white meat,' in contradistinction to the 'dark meat' as all ladies and gentlemen designate the legs of poultry." *White meat* as a term had previously existed in England, but was limited in its meaning to milk, cheese, and other dairy products, literally white food.

Undergarments for both men and women likewise offered a fertile field for mid-nineteenth-century ingenuity. *Unmentionables*, which refers at times to trousers and at others to drawers, is cited as early as 1839; *subtrousers* as late as 1890. Between these dates a wide variety of terms appeared, though it should be noted that *inexpressibles*, sometimes classed with American euphemisms of this type, is actually British in origin and seems to have been used in England throughout the greater part of the century.

Death, dying, and burial constitute another area of the lexicon in which most languages develop a large number of euphemisms. America was no exception, and Professor Louise Pound has dealt with this subject most exhaustively. Of the American terms which developed in this way, I have already mentioned one of the best known and most widely used today: *casket*, which serves as a delicate substitute for *coffin*. It seems to have entered the language by way of the compound *burial casket*, which along with *burial case* was coined in the 'fifties and 'sixties of the last century. It must have caught on very rapidly, for by 1870 a British news correspondent in New York was able to make the flat statement, "In America a coffin is called a casket." That the term did not immediately win universal favor is shown by Nathaniel Hawthorne's comment in *Our Old Home* (1863): "'Caskets!'—a vile modern phrase which compels a person . . . to shrink . . . from the idea of being buried at all." The perfumed practices of the modern mortician have, of course, resulted in a host of evasive expressions, against which Evelyn Waugh trained the shafts of his wit in the novel *The Loved One*.

The Puritan prohibition of profanity has already been mentioned, and although the number of violations of their laws clearly indicates that this was more often honored in the breach than in the observance, yet the fact that the laws should have existed at all, as well as the length of time they remained on the books, offers satisfactory evidence of an active taboo against profanity in the Puritan conscience. As a consequence of this, it would seem, American English has developed a whole lexicon of near-swearing, including *darn, drat, doggone, blasted, Sam Hill, gee whittaker, gee whiz*, and their progeny of sixty or seventy others, most of them still bearing more or less phonetic resemblance to the particular morsel for which they have been substituted.

Darn offers a fairly satisfactory example of the way one of these terms developed. We need not concern ourselves here with the debate which went on some years ago over whether *derne,* the Middle English word for "secret," was its real progenitor, or whether it emanated from an aphetic form of *eternal,* with the *er* pronounced as in British *clerk (clark).* The facts are simply that we do have *darnation* used as an adjective as early as 1798, and a quarter of a century later as an interjection. The earliest examples indicate use by, or with reference to, coastal New Englanders. If we assume that by this time post-vocalic *r* was either weakened or had disappeared entirely, and that the coastal New England *a* before *r* was a low central vowel with something of the quality of present-day Bostonian *park* [pa:k], the close resemblance of this to the ordinary pronunciation of *damnation* is clear enough. They are virtually the same except for the medial *m. Darn* appears by itself a decade or so later. A contemporary but very shrewd and accurate analysis of the whole situation was given in 1832 by J. T. Buckingham, writing in the *New England Magazine:* "We have 'Gaul darn you' for 'G— d— you' . . . and other like creations of the union of wrath and principle."

Nor is it merely the nineteenth century and the standards of propriety peculiar to it which give the impetus to usages designed to soften the harsh facts of life. We have at hand at least one twentieth-century phenomenon which has fostered a similar development—present-day American educational practices. The extension of elementary and secondary education to virtually all of the youth population, coupled with the determination on the part of educational psychologists to avoid injury to budding juvenile or adolescent personalities, no matter how academically inept, has resulted on the one hand in almost a total abandonment of the practice of failing a student, thus causing him to repeat a grade or unit of work, and on the other, in the creation of a host of special courses designed for those who are clearly unfitted for even the watered-down academic regimen of the present era. Consequently the practice of advancing the academic failures has become known as *social promotion* in some quarters, and high-school curricula now include courses which bear such strange labels as *Social English* and *Social Mathematics.* Moreover, the "exceptional" child may mean one of less than normal intelligence.

It is important to recognize that taboos and the resulting euphemisms have always operated in language. We have had them in English from the time that some Anglo-Saxon monk with an over-keen sense of propriety, coupled with a distinctly worldly knowledge of what went on in harbor resorts, coined the term *port-civene* (port woman) to translate "harlot" in the parable of the Prodigal Son, up to the present era when one of our recent governmental administrations was careful to characterize a slight economic depression as a *recession*. The interesting aspect of the mid-nineteenth-century development of euphemisms in America lies in the peculiar combination of cultural circumstances which brought it about, the lavish scale upon which it operated, and the extremes which it often attained.

Every movement has its counter-force, and the genteel tradition of the past was no exception. Nineteenth-century America was not without those individuals who not only accepted their lack of culture and refinement as an established fact but who gloried in it, and indeed flaunted it. The "I don't know anything about art but I know what I like" cliché—and the attitude it portrays—is a patent instance of this resistance to culture with a capital *C*. There is a good deal of this, for example, in Mark Twain, some of it undoubtedly sincere and some clearly with tongue in cheek. The extreme of such an attitude has at times been called the "mucker pose," one which certain politicians and others dependent upon large-scale popular support have at times found it profitable to adopt. Linguistically the mucker pose is frequently manifested by the conscious employment of features of sub-standard English. A case in point was the thoroughly cultured millionaire candidate for the presidential nomination recently, who rarely made a speech or television appearance without using *ain't* at least once. Currently this is scarcely a potent factor on the linguistic scene, but it is present to some extent, and its existence cannot be overlooked.

Study Questions

1. In each subject classification, see how many euphemisms you can add to those that Marckwardt lists.

2. Have you observed the "mucker pose"—the deliberate use of substandard English as a rejection of propriety and a kind of anti-intellectualism? What is the difference in effect between this kind of speech and the occasional facetious use of local varieties of substandard English among close friends?

3. Which do you think is more dominant in current American euphemisms, the influence of women or the influence of advertising? *Coffin* became *casket*, and one kind of *casket* is called an *eternity bed*. Can you supply other examples in which products are made more attractive by terms which disguise the harsh facts? What are some of the trade names by which unmentionables are made mentionable? BVD was one of the first.

29. SOME SOCIAL DIFFERENCES IN PRONUNCIATION
Raven I. McDavid, Jr.

In this article, which first appeared in *Language Learning* for 1952–53, Professor McDavid discusses some of the implications which pronunciation has upon the social status of speakers in various regions of the United States.

When we compare varieties of American English, we generally assume that differences in grammar reflect social differences, and that differences in vocabulary or pronunciation reflect regional differences. Yet we must often modify this useful practical rule. The word *bastard* occurs everywhere, but everywhere it seems to be a cruder term than *illegitimate child*. In all regions where *jacket* and *vest* are synonymous, *jacket* is apparently more rustic and old-fashioned. Conversely, Atwood's monograph [1] shows that the differences in status between the preterites *dove* and *dived, woke up* and *waked up, sweat* and *sweated,* are more regional than social. Moreover, though /klɪm, kləm, klom, klæm, klam, klum/ all have less prestige as preterites than *climbed,* at least three of these forms occur in definite regional patterns: /klɪm/ in the North and South, /kləm/ in the Midland, /klom/ in eastern Virginia.[2] Even /ɛt/ as the preterite of *eat*—a social shibboleth to many speakers—turns out to be the socially elegant form in Charleston, South Carolina, where the use of /ɛt/ (and of *ain't* in informal speech) sets off those who belong to the best Charlestonian society from those who would like to belong but don't.

We should therefore not be surprised if some pronunciations carry connotations of social prestige or lack of it. We can discuss a few of these pro-

[1] E. B. Atwood, *The Verb Forms of the Eastern United States* (Ann Arbor: University of Michigan Press, 1952).

[2] The regional designations are those found in H. Kurath, *A Word Geography of the Eastern United States* (Ann Arbor: University of Michigan Press, 1949), and in articles by Kurath, E. B. Atwood, Raven McDavid, and A. L. Davis. Linguistically the North includes New England, the Hudson Valley (including New York City) and derivative settlements in upstate New York, Pennsylvania, and further west. The Inland North is the northern area exclusive of the Hudson Valley and eastern New England. The Midland includes most of New Jersey and Pennsylvania, with derivative settlements to the west and south. The North Midland includes most of New Jersey and Pennsylvania, plus northern West Virginia. The South Midland includes the Shenandoah Valley, southern West Virginia, southwest Virginia, and the mountain and upper Piedmont areas of the Carolinas and Georgia. The South includes the older plantation areas of eastern Virginia and the coastal plain and lower Piedmont of the Carolinas and Georgia. The boundaries between these sections are much less sharp west of the Appalachians than along the Atlantic Seaboard.

nunciations by examining the evidence collected for the Linguistic Atlas of the United States and Canada. This evidence has been collected in the field by trained investigators using a finely graded phonetic alphabet and a questionnaire of selected items dealing with everyday experience. The persons interviewed are strongly rooted natives of their communities, typical of various age or social groups. Usually there is one person, as unsophisticated as possible, from the oldest generation, and another either younger or more sophisticated or both. Besides, there are enough cultured informants to indicate the local or regional standards. For the Atlantic seaboard states alone, the field workers for the Atlas interviewed over 150 cultured informants—a greater number of cultured informants than even the largest standard dictionary has utilized for the entire United States.

Besides the relative status of informants in their own communities (indicated by the field worker after he has completed the interviews), one must evaluate communities, or groups of communities, against the whole body of American English. Previous work in linguistic geography, especially Kurath's *Word Geography of the Eastern United States*, enables us to judge pronunciations by the type of dialect areas in which they occur.

Focal areas are those areas whose economic, social, or cultural prestige has led to the spread of their linguistic forms into other areas. Examples are eastern New England (Boston), eastern Pennsylvania (Philadelphia), the Hudson Valley (New York City), the Virginia Piedmont (Richmond), and the South Carolina Low-Country (Charleston). Pronunciations characteristic of focal areas are likely to have prestige, especially when used by the younger and more sophisticated speakers.

Relic areas, on the other hand, are those whose geographical or cultural isolation, and relative lack of prestige, has caused the retention of older forms or prevented the spread of forms characteristic of these areas. Examples are northeastern New England, the eastern shore of Chesapeake Bay, and eastern North Carolina. Pronunciations characteristic of relic areas are likely to lack prestige, especially if they are chiefly used by the older and less sophisticated speakers.

A third problem we must consider is the attitude of speakers towards particular pronunciations—whether we call them "secondary responses" with Bloomfield or "metalinguistic details" with Trager. Here, incidental comments of the informants are of great value. For instance, the American *vase* /ves/ is a /vaz/ in Southern British Received Pronunciation. We might expect /vaz/ to have prestige in the United States, especially in those areas of New England and the Old South where British customs are admired and British speech forms are often adopted into local cultured speech. However, not only is /vaz/ rare as a spontaneous pronunciation, but the frequent comments of informants that "if it costs over $2.98 it's a /vaz/" suggest that many people who say /vaz/ are judged as parvenus who have acquired the pronunciation during a recent exposure to culture and who wish to use it to impress their neighbors. Judgments that pronunciations are characteristic of less privileged social groups—Negroes, unsuccessful farmers, recent immigrants—indicate for such pronunciations a lack of prestige in the community, regardless of their status elsewhere or their occurrence in the informant's unguarded conversation.

Finally, some informants may deliberately stick to pronunciations they know are considered old-fashioned, unprivileged, or simply peculiar. New Yorkers generally consider it substandard to pronounce a curl of hair and a coil of rope the same way, yet I know at least one prosperous and well-educated New Yorker of colonial stock who does not distinguish such pairs. The most sophisticated informant interviewed in Charleston proclaimed that she personally said /tə'mætəz/, though she knew other people said /tə'metəz/ or /tə'matəz/—"because Grandmother H—— always said /tə'mætəz/, and what Grandmother H—— said is good enough for me." One cultured informant near Galt, Ontario, consistently says /bul, pul/ for *bull, pull*, instead of /bʊl, pʊl/ because these pronunciations have come down in his Scotch-Canadian family. Such examples of "rugged individualism," family pride, or personal stubbornness do not give us patterns of prestige, but they warn us to go slow in condemning what we do not say ourselves.

As Kurath has often pointed out, there are three types of differences in pronunciation:

(1) Differences in the pronunciation of the individual phonemes.

(2) Differences in the occurrence of the individual phonemes.

(3) Differences in the system of phonemes.[3]

Differences in the pronunciation of the individual phonemes are hardest to detect and evaluate. Some of these pronunciations are fairly striking, and do denote social status:

1. The ingliding diphthongal pronunciation of *date* and *boat*, as [deət] and [boət] is generally confined to the Charleston area.

2. The fronted [ʉ] in *two, boot* is very common in the Midland and the South.

3. The monophthongal or near monophthongal variety of /ai/ occurring finally and before voiced consonants in *high, hide*. This type of pronunciation is chiefly found in Southern and South Midland dialects. Though sometimes ridiculed by speakers from other regions, it is rarely considered an unprivileged form in the areas where it occurs—and then only if the speaker does not differentiate *high* from *hah*, *blind* from *blond*, *hide* from *hod* or *hard*.

4. The fronted beginning of /au/ ([æʊ, ɛʊ]) in such words as *cow* is

[3] The particular type of analysis one favors will often determine the category to which he assigns these differences. The analysis here used is basically that of *The Pronuncia-*

found in northern New England and the New England settlement area, and in the South and South Midland. In the North they are generally considered old-fashioned or rustic, and are disappearing. They are very common in the Richmond area and seem to be spreading nearly everywhere in the South except in South Carolina.

5. The centralized beginning of /ai, au/ ([əɪ, əʊ]) in *rite, ride, lout, loud*. Sometimes this occurs only when the diphthong is followed by a voiceless consonant, sometimes in all positions. In the inland North the centralized beginning may occur regardless of the consonant following the diphthong, but in this region the centralized beginning is often considered somewhat old-fashioned and rustic, though it is used by many cultured informants. The centralized beginning when the diphthong is followed by a voiceless consonant, but not otherwise, is characteristic of the speech of three well-defined areas: Canada (especially Ontario), the Virginia Piedmont, and the Atlantic Tidewater area from Georgetown, South Carolina, to St. Augustine, Florida. In view of the social prestige of the Richmond and Charleston areas, the pronunciations of *light* and *lout* as [ləɪt, ləʊt] probably have privileged status.

6. An ingliding vowel with a rather high beginning sometimes occurs for /æ/ in such words as *calf, bad* [æ͡ə, ɛə] or for /ɔ/ in *law* [ɔ͡ə, o͡ə]. These pronunciations are most common in such cities as New York, Philadelphia, and Baltimore. They are especially common in families with a cen-

---

tion of the Eastern United States as adapted to the system of transcription generally used in *Language Learning*. Phonetic symbols are enclosed in brackets; phonemic symbols in slanting lines. Phonemic equivalents are as follows:

Vowels:
/i/   as in *beet*
/ɪ/   as in *bit*
/e/   as in *bait*
/ɛ/   as in *bet*
/æ/   as in *bat*
/a/   as in *hot, father*
/ɔ/   as in *bought*
/o/   as in *boat*
/ô/   the New England "short *o*" as in *coat, road, home*
/ʊ/   as in *put*
/u/   as in *boot*

Diphthongs:
/ai/   as in *write*
/au/   as in *rout*
/ɔi/   as in *oil*
/æi/   as in the common Southern and South Midland *bag, half*
/ɔu/   as in the common Southern and South Midland *law, hog*. This diphthong also occurs in New Hampshire.
/iu/   as in the common New England *beautiful, music*. This diphthong also occurs along the south Atlantic coast.
/ˈ/   primary stress
/ˌ/   secondary stress

tral or eastern European background, and the more extreme varieties are often considered substandard.[4]

There are relatively few differences in the system of phonemes that all students would agree upon.

1. For some speakers the "New England short *o*," /ŏ/, occurs alongside /o/ in such words as *coat, road, home, whole*. It probably is found everywhere in the New England settlement area since it has been recorded as far west as Montana. On the other hand, even in New England it is losing ground, since it is found chiefly in smaller and relatively isolated communities and in the speech of the older and less sophisticated informants.

2. A falling diphthong /iu/ occurs alongside /yu/ (or /u/) in such words as *puke, beautiful, music, tube, due, new, suit, sumach, grew, blew*. It is found chiefly in the New England settlement area, but also occurs along Chesapeake Bay and the Carolina and Georgia coast. It is slightly old-fashioned, especially in the North (it occurs most frequently in *puke*, which does not have a "schoolroom pronunciation"); yet it still occurs in cultured speech.

3. In the Pittsburgh area the vowel /a/ occurs only before /-r/, with both *cot* and *caught, collar* and *caller* having /ɔ/. This feature also seems to occur frequently in western Canada and in the Minneapolis area. If anything, it seems to be spreading among younger and better educated speakers.

Differences in the occurrence of individual phonemes are most common and easiest to evaluate. They may be grouped according to several social types, though we must remember that these groupings are only tentative ones.

1. Some differences are purely regional:

In such words as *whip, wharf,* and *whoa*, some speakers have /hw-/, others /w-/.[5]

For *humor*, the pronunciation /hyumər/ occurs sporadically and chiefly in the Northern area, though elsewhere there are indications it is being sponsored by the schools as a spelling pronunciation. /yumər/ is far more common, at all levels of usage. For other words of this group, however (though the evidence is less adequate), the forms with /yu-/ seem to be less widespread and somewhat lacking in prestige.

For *without*, the middle consonant may be either /θ/ or /ð/ at any social level. In the North and eastern North Carolina /ð/ is overwhelmingly predominant; in Canada, the Midland area, eastern Virginia, South Carolina, and Georgia /θ/ is very frequent.

[4] These differences in the pronunciation of the individual phonemes are sometimes analyzed as phonemic or systematic differences. See George L. Trager and Henry Lee Smith, Jr., *An Outline of English Structure* (Norman, Oklahoma: Battenburg Press, 1951).

[5] Raven I. McDavid, Jr., and Virginia Glenn McDavid, "h before semi vowels in Eastern United States." *Language*, Vol. 28, 1952, pp. 41–62.

Ewe is /yo/ in most of the country where people have knowledge of sheep. Since this pronunciation is never heard from those who have not lived where sheep were raised, it may be considered an occupational pronunciation among sheep herders.

Bleat, the cry of a calf, is prevailingly /blæt/ in the North and /blet/ in the South, being replaced by *bawl* in the Midland; /blit/ is almost exclusively a city pronunciation.

Because is frequently pronounced /bɪ'kəz/ in the North and in South Carolina, but rarely in other regions. Where this pronunciation occurs it is used by speakers of all degrees of sophistication.

The unstressed vowel of *without* is always /ɪ/ in the North and the South, but usually /ə/ in the Midland.

Beside the usual /ču-/, Massa*chu*setts is often /ju-/ in New England, but /tyu-/ or /tu-/ in the South and South Midland.

Instead of /wɔnt/ (or the common Southern /wɔʊnt/) *want* is very often /want/ in Massachusetts and Vermont, /wənt/ in New Jersey and Western Pennsylvania. Both of these pronunciations occur sporadically in western areas settled ultimately from New England.

Words such as *orange, Florida, borrow,* and *tomorrow* may have either /a/ or /ɔ/ before /-r-/. In the Atlantic seaboard states /ɔ/ is most likely to occur in these words in northern New England, western Pennsylvania, and the Charleston area. For such words as *Florida* and *oranges,* /ɔ/ is practically universal in the North Central States and westward, but in these same areas /a/ or /ɔ/ may occur in *borrow* and *tomorrow.*

For *bulge, bulk,* and *budget,* both /ʊ/ and /ə/ occur: /ə/ in the North and North Midland, /ʊ/ in the South Midland, eastern Virginia, and the Piedmont of the Carolinas and Georgia, /ə/ again along the southern coast south of Chesapeake Bay.

For *won't,* /wont/ occurs everywhere. In addition there are four forms with regional distribution: (1) /wənt/ in the North, outside of the Hudson Valley; (2) /wɔnt/ in North Carolina; (3) /wunt, wʊnt/ in Canada, New York City, the Hudson Valley, Chesapeake Bay, eastern North Carolina, and the Charleston area. All of these forms occur in cultured speech.

For many of the words derived from Middle English /o:/—and some borrowings that have fallen into the pattern—both /u/ and /ʊ/ occur, without social distinction but with sharply differing regional patterns. This is true of *coop, cooper, hoop, goobers, room, broom, root, cooter, food, hoof, roof, spooks,* and probably others. For instance, I—a native of upper South Carolina—normally have /u/ in *root, cooter, food, roof, spooks,* and *goober,* /ʊ/ in *coop, cooper, hoop,* and either /u/ or /ʊ/ in *room, broom, hoof.*

For such words as *tube, dew, new,* we find /iu/ in the North and occasionally along the southern coast, although it is somewhat old-fashioned in both areas. In the South and South Midland, /yu/ is predominant. It occurs as a prestige form in some communities in the North and North Midland. In northeastern New England, the Hudson Valley, and the North Midland, /u/ is almost universal and is spreading in other parts of the North.

Such pairs as *horse* and *hoarse, morning* and *mourning, border* and *boarder* are usually distinguished in the North, the South, and the South Midland, but not in the North Midland. In many parts of the Inland North and in Canada the distinction is disappearing.

2. A few pronunciations seem to lack prestige everywhere. *Italian* as /ˌai ˈtælyən/ is generally looked down upon; /dif/ (instead of /dɛf/) for *deaf* and /ˈwaundɪd/ (instead of /ˈwundɪd/) for *wounded* are generally considered old-fashioned.

3. Other pronunciations lack prestige, but occur in limited regions.

Along Chesapeake Bay, *fog* and *hog* occasionally have /o/.

Rinse is rarely /rmč, rɛnč/ in the North, but these pronunciations are common in the Midland and the South. They are slightly old-fashioned, but not uncommon in cultured speech. The hyper-form /rmz/ is less common, limited to the same areas, and chiefly found in the speech of the half educated.

Coop occurs with /-b/ on Delaware Bay and along the southern coast south of Chesapeake Bay. This pronunciation is not common in cities, is slightly old-fashioned, but is used by many cultured speakers.

In parts of the South Midland and the South (but not in the Virginia Piedmont) *took, roof,* and *hoof* frequently have /ə/ in uneducated speech.

In much of the South and South Midland, the less educated speakers have /ə/ in *put,* to rime with *cut.*

For *loam* and *gums,* the pronunciations with /u,ʊ/ are confined to the New England settlement area, with /ʊ/ more common in Maine and New Hampshire than elsewhere. Although generally lacking in prestige, /gʊmz/ and /lʊm/ sometimes occur in cultured speech in Maine and New Hampshire. In other areas cultured speakers occasionally say /gumz/ and /lum/.

Two pronunciations of *can't*—/kent/ and /kæmt/—occur chiefly in parts of the South and South Midland. Although both pronunciations seem to have spread from the Virginia Piedmont, /kent/ seems to be the older and /kæmt/ the more recent form. Consequently, although both forms occur in the speech of all types of informants, /kent/ is often considered just a little more old-fashioned.

4. Several pronunciations may lack prestige in one region but be acceptable in another:

In the South and South Midland the pronunciation of *creek* as /krɪk/ is usually considered very quaint and lacking in prestige, since it is largely confined to the uneducated Negroes of the Carolina and Georgia coast. Even in the South, however, /krɪk/ may occur in the speech of cultured Charlestonians. In the North both /krik/ and /krɪk/ occur, with some pressure from the public schools to enforce /krik/ as a spelling pronunciation. However, /krɪk/ is very common in northern cultured speech. In the North Midland, especially in Pennsylvania, /krɪk/ is practically universal.

In the Atlantic seaboard states, *farm* and *form* are rarely homonymous, and where this homonymy occurs, as occasionally in South Carolina and Georgia, it is only in uneducated speech, and consequently frowned upon. In parts of Louisiana and Texas, however, this homonymy is normal among all classes of speakers.

Soot is most frequently pronounced as /sʊt/, except in Pennsylvania. In many parts of the country /sət/ is looked upon as old-fashioned, rustic, or uneducated. In the South, however, it is the pronunciation used by a majority of cultured speakers.

Many scholars, even C. C. Fries,[6] have labeled the pronunciation of *catch* with /ɛ/ as lacking in prestige. However, /kɛč/ is overwhelmingly the normal pronunciation, for the nation as a whole and for all regions except southern New England, the Hudson Valley, Pennsylvania, and the city of Charleston, where /kæč/ is the majority usage. In the areas where /kæč/ is the usual pronunciation, it is naturally preferred by educated speakers. In Virginia, and to some extent in North Carolina, /kæč/ is a prestige pronunciation, used by a majority of the cultured informants but by few others. In other parts of the country, however, a majority of the cultured informants say /kɛč/.

5. For some words, one pronunciation may have prestige in one region and another pronunciation have prestige somewhere else.

For *raspberries*, the "broad *a*" pronunciation with /a/ seems to have some prestige in eastern New England, and to a lesser extent in New York City and eastern Virginia. In other parts of the country, however,—particularly in the Inland North—the pronunciation with /æ/ is socially preferred, and the /a/ pronunciation considered old-fashioned or rustic.

For such words as *hog* and *fog*, pronunciations with /a,ɔ,ɔʊ/ have been recorded from speakers on all social levels. The /a/ pronunciations seem to have social prestige in Boston, New York City, Philadelphia, Charleston, Richmond (but not in smaller communities in the Virginia Piedmont), western North Carolina, northwestern South Carolina, and northern Georgia. In other southern communities the cultured informants have /ɔ,ɔʊ/. It is probable that /ɔʊ/ is an older prestige pronunciation that has spread from the Virginia Piedmont, with /a/ replacing it in cultured Richmond speech and in the cultured speech of other metropolitan centers.

Almost everyone knows that the two pronunciations of *greasy* sharply divide the eastern United States, with /-s-/ more common in the North and North Midland but /-z-/ usual in the South and South Midland. In some areas where both pronunciations occur, they are associated with dif-

6 Charles C. Fries, *American English Grammar* (New York and London: Appleton-Century-Crofts, 1940), p. 10.

RAVEN I. MC DAVID, JR.   249

ferent social levels or social contexts. Trager has frequently pointed out
that among his boyhood playmates in Newark the /-z-/ pronunciation was
confined to such derogatory phrases as a *greasy grind*. In South Carolina
and Georgia the /-s-/ pronunciation is regular among the Gullah Negroes
but almost never occurs in the speech of whites.

6. Occasionally a pronunciation may have social prestige in one area but
elsewhere be only one of several acceptable pronunciations. For instance,
office with /a/ has social prestige in eastern Pennsylvania and eastern
Virginia; in other areas /a/ or /ɔ/ or /ɔʊ/ may occur without any implication of social distinction.

7. Some pronunciations have prestige in the limited areas in which they
occur.

The pronunciation of *can't* with /a/ is the socially preferred form in
eastern New England, and to a lesser extent in New York City, Philadelphia, and eastern Virginia. Elsewhere it is extremely rare.

The pronunciation of *soot* as /sut/ is largely confined to the northern
areas. Wherever it occurs, it is likely to be found in the speech of the
moderately or better educated.

The lack of constriction of post-vocalic /-r/ (the so-called "loss of /r/")
in *burn, barn, beard* occurs mostly in eastern New England, New York
City and the South Atlantic States. In the areas where it occurs, it is most
likely to appear in the speech of the younger and better educated informants. In some communities in the South Atlantic States the rustic and uneducated white speakers preserve the constriction of /-r/, while Negroes
and the more sophisticated whites lack constriction. In such communities
visitors from the Inland North or the North Central States, where the constriction of /-r/ occurs in the speech of all classes, are likely to be at a
social disadvantage. Conversely, in some Inland Northern communities,
the only residents who lack constriction of /-r/ are the Negroes who have
come from the South in the last generation. In these communities, Southern
students have had difficulty securing rooms. In telephone conversations,
landladies may identify the lack of consideration of /-r/ as a Negro characteristic and announce that no rooms are available.

8. A few pronunciations are always somewhat prestigious since they
occur most frequently in cities and in the speech of the younger and
better educated informants. However, if the group of informants using
such a pronunciation is very small, the prestige of the pronunciation may
be lost since the pronunciation will be interpreted as a mark of conscious
snobbery.

The pronunciation of *soot* as /sut/ always has social prestige, not only
in Pennsylvania where /sut/ is the usual pronunciation but in the North
where /sut/ is a common pronunciation among educated speakers and in
the South where /sət/ is the usual pronunciation among speakers of all
classes.

The pronunciation of *vase* as /vez/ (less frequently /vaz/), and of *nephew* as /'nɛvyə,-yu/ (much less commonly /'nɛvi/) are largely confined to cultured informants—chiefly in Southern Ontario, Boston, New York City, Philadelphia, Richmond and Charleston, where British speech forms are likely to have prestige. Inland informants who say /vez/ or /'nɛvyə/ usually have strong family or cultural ties to one of those centers.

The pronunciation of *sumach* with /siu/ instead of the more common /su-/ is also largely confined to the larger coastal cities and to a relatively few inland cultured informants.

Such words as *suit, blew, threw* are normally pronounced with /u/. Although the pronunciations with /yu/ have social prestige in England they are extremely rare in this country, occurring almost exclusively in the North. Most Americans consider them unnatural and affected.

9. Sometimes the pronunciation of a word may involve a number of intricately related cultural, historical, and political facts. One of the most complex of these is *Negro*, where the pronunciations involve not only the status and the attitudes of those who use them, but the reactions of those the pronunciations designate. The historical pronunciation /'nɪgər/ is by far the most common, and in many communities it is the normal pronunciation used by speakers of both races. However, since it is used by many people as a term of contempt, it is actively resented by Negro spokesmen —regardless of the intent behind it. The spelling pronunciation /'nigro/ is comparatively new, but it has been actively sponsored as a polite pronunciation and is so used by most cultured speakers of the North and North Midland. However, /'nigro/ is very rare south of the Mason-Dixon line, partly because it is recognized as a Northern pronunciation of a word about which most Southerners have strong prejudices, partly because it violates the normal Southern tendency to have /ə/ in unstressed syllables. The pronunciation /'nɪgro/ is also a common polite form in the North and North Midland, but relatively uncommon in the South. The normal polite form in the South (and occasionally in other sections) is /'nɪgrə/. Most cultured informants in the South do not use /'nɪgər/, which they feel is both derogatory to the Negro and characteristic of poor white speech. The difference in status and implication of /'nɪgrə/ and /'nɪgər/ is very sharply maintained in the South, though frequently outsiders do not understand the distinction and wonder why the Southerner does not say /'nigro/, which to the Southerner seems unnatural.

Even such a limited approach to the problem of social differences in pronunciation indicates that it is very complex and that the person who attempts to label the status of a pronunciation must have information about such social forces as trading areas, educational practices, and community structure. Nor will it be a simple matter for teachers to apply the knowledge gained from studies such as this. Yet one may suggest certain procedures.

Those who teach English in the public schools should be fully aware of the socially preferred pronunciations in the communities in which they are teaching. They should not waste time and energy attempting to force exotic pronunciations upon their students, regardless of how desirable or elegant such pronunciations seem. They should also be aware that other types of pronunciation may be acceptable in other communities. Such awareness will not only make it easier for teachers to deal with the student who has moved to the community from another region, it will also make it easier for them to teach in communities outside their own dialect area.

Teachers of English to foreign students must also recognize this problem. In universities with a cosmopolitan student body, the instructors and drill-masters may speak any one of several varieties of American English. Even if it is possible to choose instructors and drillmasters from one dialect area, or require them to use something like a uniform dialect in their classes, as soon as the foreign student goes into his regular classes he will hear other types of pronunciation from the professors and his fellow students. The problem would be less difficult at smaller colleges where the faculty and the student body are predominantly from one region. Even here, however, the students will occasionally encounter other varieties of English. The longer they are in the United States and the broader their contacts—by travel, movies, radio, or television—the more frequently they will hear other pronunciations than those they have learned. How much attention the teacher should pay to variant pronunciations is a matter of practical pedagogy, depending on circumstances—it is much more important for the student to master one American pronunciation of *can't* than to learn a little about several pronunciations—but certainly the advanced students should know that speakers may differ markedly in the details of their pronunciation, and yet all speak socially acceptable American English.

Study Questions

1. Supply examples from your own observation of as many as possible of McDavid's kinds of differences in pronunciation.

2. What local pronunciations are you aware of in your own community? Proper names of places, such as street names, are likely to acquire local pronunciations. In some areas, for example, *Lafayette* is pronounced *La-fay'-ette.*

3. Using the words McDavid gives as examples, observe the pronunciation by members of a group who come from as many different parts of the country as possible. Residents of a dormitory are likely to provide good subjects for such an investigation.

4. Compare McDavid's observations with Whitehall's "survey of the four principal varieties of American speech," *Webster's New World Dictionary,* 1.16, and his table of primary phonemes of North Central American English, pp. xvii-xviii.

30. TODAY'S COLLEGIATE ENGLISH

J. N. Hook

The results of Professor Hook's survey of the grammar and usage patterns of college students originally appeared in *Word Study* for February, April, and May, 1951.

Recently, about 120 juniors, seniors, and graduate students who were enrolled in my classes in modern English grammar spent part of their time in eavesdropping. They were assigned the problem of discovering and describing some of the characteristics of present-day collegiate English, as reflected in the conversation of University of Illinois students. It was not an error-hunt in which they engaged; rather, it was an attempt to observe and record whatever facets of usage caught their attention and interest. Those who wished to narrow the problem to a particular phase, such as agreement of verbs or case of pronouns, were permitted to do so.

My purpose in giving the assignment was to make my students more deeply aware of the fact that our language is living and changing. Their findings, even though not startling, seem to me to be sufficiently interesting to merit a better fate than a wastebasket affords. Hence this article.

Although no exact numerical count was required, it appears that on the average each of the 120 students made notes on the conversation of 25 or more persons. At a conservative estimate, then, the colloquial English of 2,500 or more persons was represented in the survey. Some of the researchers supplemented their eavesdropping with simple questionnaires.

In this paper I shall present the findings in the students' own words. My task has been to select and group the most representative findings. Let me emphasize *most representative*. Unless several students made approximately the same observation, it has not been included here. Thus each quotation is to be interpreted as standing for several others that said virtually the same thing.

Case of pronouns after *to be*

"All but two of the thirty-eight girls in my house say *This is she* when answering the phone. Of these thirty-six, however, only fourteen say *That is I* when indicating themselves in a group picture."

"Almost all the boys say *It's me*. However, when I questioned fifty-eight of them, forty-nine said that they believe *It is I* to be the 'correct' form."

"In one semester of listening, I have heard six people say *It is I*."

"One student says she uses *It is me* in familiar conversation but reserves *It is I* for people she is trying to impress."

"I noted the answers of twenty girls who knocked on my bedroom door and replied to the question *Who is it?* Twelve of the girls gave their names, six said *Me*, and two said *It's me*. Not one of the twenty said *It is I*."

"Betty, who says *That was me*, contrarily says *If it were I*."

"This was a dirty trick, but I also questioned twenty professors over the phone. Ten I asked whether they normally say *It is I* or *It is me*. Five of them said that they use *It is me* but are aware that it is 'incorrect.' The other ten I told first that I was doing some research for a class in grammar. All of these ten asserted that they always say *It is I*."

"In twenty-seven instances in which a personal pronoun was needed after a form of *be*, the nominative was used six times."

"In long distance calls, *This is he* is used more frequently than *This is him*, but the reverse is true of local calls."

"The girls in my house, when meeting strangers or when talking to a new young man on the telephone, say *This is she, It was I, It is he*, etc. Otherwise, they use the objective form."

"Nine students said that they use the nominative on formal occasions and the objective on informal ones."

"English majors use the nominative case more frequently in this construction than do other students."

"Faculty members who come to South Reserve all seem to use the nominative form, graduate students use both about equally, and undergraduates generally use the objective."

"More upperclassmen than freshmen say *It is she*."

"The nominative case of the pronoun after *to be* is apparently being discarded on this campus. Does this mean that when the present college group is absorbed into the business and political world, the use of the objective case in this situation will be generally accepted?"

Case of pronouns in other constructions

"Playing 'dumb,' I made the rounds and asked twenty-five seniors, juniors, sophomores, and freshmen whether I should use the nominative or objective forms in *Between you and* (*I, me*); *Are you going with Dick and* (*I, me*)?; and *Let us be candid, you and* (*I, me*). Twenty of the twenty-five said that to be 'correct,' I should use *I* in each expression, although several of them said that they would use *me* informally."

"There was an unconsciously inconsistent use of the nominative and objective following *than: She's a better swimmer than he is. Why, she's even better than me!*"

"Girls tend to say *She is prettier than I.* Men say *He's stronger than me.*"

"The few persons (usually freshmen) who say *Him and I left* tend also to say *He talked to her and I* and *She sent him and I.*"

"Such sentences as *Jerry and myself will do it* are common, but *himself, herself,* and *themselves* are seldom used alone as subjects."

"No one attempted to use *whom* in ordinary conversation. Occasionally I heard students use *whom* in speaking to a medical doctor or to a member of the faculty."

"Usually when the preposition immediately precedes the pronoun, *whom* is used. I did, however, hear *He was secretary of state under who?*"

"At the beginning of a sentence, students tend to use *who;* in the middle, they sometimes pause to decide whether *who* or *whom* is preferable."

"I asked sixteen people how they would write and say *Give the package to (whoever, whomever) opens the door.* All sixteen said that they would write *whomever* but say *whoever.* Ah, correctness, thy name is error!"

"To most of us, *I don't know who you mean* seems to be the same construction as *I don't know who he is.* . . . Because the distinction between *who* and *whom* is often a fine one, *whom* seems to be losing prestige at the U. of I."

"I asked twenty students what baffles them most in English usage. Fifteen said '*Who* and *whom.*'"

Number in pronouns and verbs

"Undergraduates have *everybody* doing *their* own work and *each girl* taking *their own seats.* The same students say *One of these poems are by Browning.*"

"I asked sixteen students which pronoun they would use in this sentence: *He is one of those people who always think (he, they) cannot be wrong.* Ten of them chose *he.* In the sentence *I have one of those flowers which the florist said will not shed (its, their) leaves,* fifteen of the sixteen chose *its.*"

"There is less use of *he don't* by upperclassmen than by freshmen."

"*There's* plus a plural is much more frequent than *There are* plus a plural. One often hears *There's five classes opened, There's six of us girls,* etc."

"Vegetables are often referred to with a singular verb: *Is there any more potatoes?*"

"Sometimes a speaker is inconsistent: e.g., *there aren't any more seconds, is there?*"

"With indefinite pronouns and with plural nouns between subject and predicate, the number of the verb is rather often confused: e.g., *Neither were going our way. Each have done their work* (spoken by a professor). *Oh, Sally, one of the fish are dead* (spoken by an honor student)."

Shall and Will

"In an effort to gain information regarding *shall* and *will* I conducted a survey among the fifty men in the house where I live. I had them fill in blanks: 'Restricting yourself to a simple future meaning, fill in the blank spaces below with *shall* or *will*. I ...... go. You ...... go. He ...... go. We ...... go. You ...... go. They ...... go.' Only two of the fifty used *shall* in first person singular and plural, and *will* in second and third person singular and plural."

"The following example is the prize of my otherwise repetitious collection: Boy—*What time shall we go to Bidwell's?* Girl—*We shall go at four o'clock. We will both be ready, and Betty and her date shall be there.*"

"I found that *shall* is being replaced by *will* except in questions with the meaning of *ought. Will* is used predominantly in all expressions of future time, except when supplanted by *going to* or a present tense form."

"The conscious 'correct' use of *shall* and *will* to show determination or promise is almost non-existent on this campus."

"Contractions such as *I'll, he'll, she'll,* etc. can and do stand for both *shall* and *will,* and no one, including the speaker, knows which."

"No one of the twenty students used *shall* at any time except in questions."

"Although I seldom heard *shall* used, five of fifteen students told me that they normally use *shall* with the first person."

"*Shall* is regarded with awe by most of my friends."

"The present progressive (*are going*) seems to be used chiefly to denote the very near future, but *will* refers principally to the more distant future."

"Ordinarily they say *I won't go,* but to express strong determination they say *I will not go.*"

"Puristic grammarians may be responsible for the changes occurring in statements of future time. By insisting upon subtle and useless distinctions between *shall* and *will*, they have driven people to the substitution of *going to.*"

"There is something almost pathetic about this haughty old aristocrat *Shall*, an air of decadent grandeur—another of those inevitable tragedies that must accompany the growth and development of language."

Miscellaneous verb forms

"Once in a while a student, usually a freshman, says *have drove* or *blowed*. Now and then students *have went* to a show."

"Occasionally I hear *hadn't ought.*"

"*Lay* and *lie*, *sit* and *set*, *rise* and *raise* are often confused, even by upper-classmen."

"Principal parts of *lie* seem to be *lay*, *laid*, and either *laid* or *lain*. One girl who uses *lay, laid, lain* was corrected by someone for saying *Do you mind if I lay on your bed?* Twenty minutes later she retorted with *You don't mind if I lie my head on your pillow, do you?* . . . Some use the present tense of *lie* correctly and take a chance of hitting the right form when they use the past or perfect tenses."

"The few *ain't*-boys whom I heard are majoring in engineering or physical education."

"*I have to* and *I have got to* are used more often than *I must.*"

"Infrequently, auxiliaries are omitted, as in *I been to that show. Of* is sometimes substituted for the auxiliary *have*, although perhaps the students are saying *'ve.*"

"Perhaps they mean *used to be*, but it sounds as if they are saying *use to be.*"

"The adverb *never* is often used almost as an auxiliary verb along with a past tense form: *I never ate breakfast this morning. I never got the assignment.*"

"I am sorry to have to report that I have not yet heard anyone on the campus split an infinitive."

"In the house in which I live there is a surprising lack of interest in splitting the infinitive, effectively or otherwise."

"Five students, when questioned, told me that it is incorrect to split an infinitive. Two were aware that the split is now accepted. Thirteen did not know what I was talking about, but suspected vaguely that splitting an infinitive is akin to pursuing your mother-in-law with a hatchet."

"One of my friends will distort a sentence to avoid splitting an infinitive: *John found himself hopelessly to be involved with the others.*"

"Occasionally I hear a sentence like this: *Her behavior prompted us to seriously question her sanity.*"

Double negatives

"All in all, I heard comparatively few examples of the double negative."

"Double negatives smash against my ear four or five times a day."

"My own sister said *I can't do nothing right.*"

"Professor —— confided to us, *It isn't nothing compared to his 'Prelude.'* "

"A fellow LAS student of whom I asked a light answered *I don't have none.* The reply was given in an offhand manner which suggested that such a trivial question did not deserve being answered grammatically."

"When *but* has negative force, *not* is often used to strengthen it: *There aren't but five men left.*"

"With *hardly*, the second negative appears most often as a contraction; *can't hardly* is frequent, but *cannot hardly* is infrequent."

"There is a tendency to say *haven't hardly* but not *haven't scarcely.*"

Prepositions

"The once *verboten* terminal preposition now flourishes."

"In two years as a student librarian, I have never yet heard a student say *the book for which I asked.*"

"The terminal preposition is certainly defensible in such expressions as *something worth looking at* or *How can that be accounted for?*"

"I asked fifty students whether a sentence such as *What did he send for?* would be acceptable in both formal and informal language. Thirteen said that the terminal preposition should be avoided in formal writing, and four said that it should never be used."

"The most common use of prepositions at the ends of sentences is in questions: *What are you laughing at? What are you worrying about? What are you majoring in?*"

"*Which side are you on?* is more emphatic than *On which side are you?* I can't imagine an Illinois fan screaming that at a basketball referee."

"Instead of saying *It is for that purpose,* nearly everyone says *"That's what it's for."*"

"I heard the preposition used to end a sentence eighty-seven times. I was able to question twenty-six of the persons who had used it thus. All twenty-six were unaware that I had overheard their conversations. The questions and answers were as follows:
Is it a grammatical error to end a sentence with a preposition?
Yes—21. No—5.
Would you do so in a formal paper or speech? Yes—0. No—26.
Would you do so in a familiar conversation? Yes—23. No—3."

"A current colloquialism or slang expression (I don't know which), used especially by students from Chicago, is *May I go with?*"

"The final preposition without an expressed object is sometimes heard: *Eat this to go with. It fits between.*"

"Double final prepositions, or an adverb plus a preposition, are heard occasionally: e.g., *What did it turn out into? What time is he on at? What have you got that jacket on for? They didn't know what I was going to grow up into. They've got something to hold their heads up about. Who shall I stand opposite of?*"

"I noticed two glaring errors in prepositional usage—redundant prepositions, as in *Where are you going to?* and duplication, in such sentences as *With whom are you going to the party with?* and *That is the goal for which I have been working for.*"

"Unnecessary prepositions are often used: *divide up, eat up, outside of, off of, up over, in under, check up on, where are you at?*"

"But it was a professor who said *an idea of which Coleridge was fond of.*"

"Errors in pronoun case sometimes result from using the terminal preposition: e.g., *Who are you going with? Who did you speak to?* Few use the wrong case of the pronoun when the preposition comes just before it."

"Almost everyone says *Wait on me*, not *Wait for me.*"

"*Try and* is used more often than *try to.*"

"Occasionally a preposition is omitted: *I can give you a couple extra days.*"

Adjectives vs. adverbs

"Referring to health, nine students who answered my questionnaire said *I feel well*, six *I feel good*. When I questioned the nine, four said they thought they were using *well* as an adjective, five as an adverb. Nine said *I feel bad*, six *I feel badly*. Nine said *She looks good in her new dress*, six *She looks well*. Fourteen said *She writes well*, one *She writes good* (explaining that it means she is a good writer). Fourteen said *The apple tastes bad,* one *The apple tastes badly.*"

"Adjectives and adverbs are often confused: *wounded bad, awful show, sure sing loud, beat Indiana easy, feel badly.* But the same persons often use the 'right' forms."

"I occasionally hear the word *muchly.*"

"*Real* is consistently used as an adverb."

"There is extensive use of *sure* for *surely.*"

"*Due to* and *because of* are used almost interchangeably."

Often-used expressions

"*I'm sure* may mean assurance, consent, comment, or denial. The tone in which *Hmmm* is spoken shows its meaning. *Kinda* and *sorta* are the campus-wide substitutes for *rather.*"

"*Terrific* may mean spectacular, beautiful, difficult, pretty, interesting, breathtaking, enormous, frightening, detestable, dull, or adorable."

"In conversations, I have never heard *I understand,* but always *I see.*"

"Yes, *cute* is still used widely."

"One of the most overworked words in the collegian's vocabulary is *very.* In a twenty-five minute conversation, one coed used *very* eighteen times. Girls use *very* more often than men do. *Very much* is also overused."

"*So* is an almost campus-wide intensifier, not only in such expressions as *so clever,* but also in sentences such as *I will so go with you.*"

"*Sharp* means attractive, neat, well, witty, or intelligent. It may be used in almost any expression of approval."

"Some G.I. terms still survive, especially *chow, G.I., sack, gob, fly-boy,* and *tank-jockey.*"

"*Like* is used much more than *as if* in such sentences as *It looks like it will rain.* An especially interesting use of *like* is in *I feel like an apple,* meaning *I want an apple.*"

"*Get* contributes to the expression of these meanings and probably more: obtain, baffle, have sudden insight, annoy, be obliged to, possess, cause to be in any position or condition (*He got me drunk*), cause to move or be removed (*Get your dates out of here*), induce, establish communication with, fetch, buy, and arrive at a state or position (*I can't get comfortable*). Besides, it is used in various expressions that I find hard to classify: *get by, get so down, get to go, got to get at it.* Were the word to fall into disuse, there would be a considerable gap in the collegiate vocabulary."

"Some of the items are understood only in a small clique or in a particular school within the university."

"College students would shudder if they heard anyone use numerous current slang expressions in close proximity. The parodies of campus slanguage are not at all accurate."

"The primary shortcoming is the unhappy paucity of expressive words in the average college student's vocabulary. For example, I overheard this in a cafeteria line: *Oh, her! I think she's awful, just awful! Her tests are so hard, and the way she marks! But I have Mr. X for geography, and he's swell, nice and easy, and such a doll!*"

Miscellaneous

"Most of the sentences are nonperiodic."

"It seems that the tendency is to use the superlative when two things are compared."

"Words are often omitted, especially *you* and *I* as subjects."

"Students speak as wordlessly as possible."

"If any one characteristic is used to describe the language of college students, it might well be the use of short cuts, particularly sentence fragments, omitted words, contractions, and shortened forms such as *psych, journ, chem, abpsych, bak-t, buzz-law,* and *stix* (statistics)."

"Most of students' English seems to be based upon the books they read and the language they hear spoken, but seldom upon grammatical reasoning."

Levels of Usage

"We reserve formal English for a very few situations involving oral language, and for themes, term papers, and examinations."

"It seems to me that the student has three levels of speaking: informal (with close friends), intermediate (with people he knows slightly), and formal (with people who are older or to be especially respected). Similarly, he (or she) has play-clothes, streetwear, and formal attire. . . . The formal language is least spontaneous; the speaker mentally phrases each sentence before speaking it."

"The college student is quick to adapt his level of speech to that of the person with whom he converses."

"One may ask a close friend, *Going to the game?* He may inquire of an acquaintance, *Are you going to the game?* But in a formal conversation he would probably say, *Are you planning to attend the football game this afternoon?*"

"When grammatical constructions are awkward or illogical or difficult to learn, one of these things apparently happens: the 'correct' form gradually evolves into a more easy and natural form; people continue to use the difficult form but are ordinarily hampered or slowed up somewhat in their speech; or a second form appears and is used in colloquial situations as an alternative to the 'correct' one."

From the reports of these 120 students I draw six earth-shaking conclusions:

1. Most of the 2,500 persons who unconsciously took part in the study are aware that formal and informal English are not always identical. Intentionally or unintentionally they attempt to adapt their language to the audience and the occasion.

2. Information like that contained in *Current English Usage* is trickling but slowly into the collegiate consciousness, perhaps because too few professors are aware of the linguistic research of the past twenty years.

3. In an attempt to be "correct" when using formal English, some persons use constructions not now regarded as acceptable in either formal or informal speech and writing.

4. Some persons are inconsistent in their use of a particular construction; they may employ different forms when there is no reason for variation, or they may prescribe one usage and follow another.

5. Upperclassmen, by and large, violate fewer of the current taboos of usage than do freshmen.

6. Professors who are inclined to criticize students' usage should cast only small pebbles.

Study Questions

1. For each of Hook's problems in usage, consult a composition textbook and one of the recent books on American usage, such as Evans's or Bryant's. What do you discover concerning the relation between standards of "correctness" and recorded usage?

2. For any one of the problems, take a poll of class members to determine (a) which form the person uses spontaneously, (b) which form the person considers correct, (c) the basis of the person's choice.

3. Write a paragraph using forms from Hook's list which the book on usage designates as acceptable *without* qualification. Ask an English teacher, an English major, and a freshman to "correct" the paragraph. Are there any notable discrepancies in the "corrections"? Are any of the "corrections" unacceptable according to the authority on usage?

Part **V.**   *Social or Class Aspects*
Subjects for Brief Papers or Written Reports

1. Prepare, from your own experience, a comparative analysis of two distinctly different speech communities, for example, a small private school and a large university, and discuss how you adapted to them.

2. Using the biography or autobiography of a self-made man who has risen from one social level to another, with or without formal education, prepare a brief account of his attitude toward language and the relation of language skill to his success. *George,* by Emlyn Williams, is a recent example of such an autobiography. Abraham Lincoln is an obvious subject.

3. In *The Rise of Silas Lapham* William Dean Howells contrasts the speech patterns of the Laphams and the Coreys as a means of showing their social differences. Analyze and classify the types of speech contrasts. Comment also upon Howells's use of contrasts in clothing to show the difference in social status between the upper class and the *nouveaux riches.*

4. Examine other readings in this text which exemplify some of the trends and problems Roberts discusses, and report on similarities and differences between his approach and that of other writers.

5. Collect your own examples of one of the faulty expressions in the glossary of a composition text. Consult at least three authorities on usage, including *Webster's Third International,* and report in the form used by Bryant, *Current American Usage:* summary, data, other evidence. You may use selections in this text as sources of examples.

6. Look up *who, whom* in Bryant, *Current American Usage.* Conduct your own investigation of spoken and formal written English in your speech community and report on examples of colloquial, formal, and hypercorrect usage of *who* and *whom,* using Bryant's form.

7. If a copy of Johnson's *Dictionary* is available, a facsimile of it, or even a quotation of a full entry, compare an entry with the entry for the same term in *Webster's Third New International Dictionary.* Report on the differences in information presented and technical aspects of the presentation.

8. Examine a recent edition of Woolley's *Handbook of English Grammar* in light of the selections you have read in this text and explain in your report why Bergen Evans singles it out for ridicule (p. 200).

9. Examine a copy of William Strunk's *The Elements of Style,* with E. B. White's introduction and concluding essay on style. Analyze one or several other examples of White's writing. Report on White's style as following or deviating from Strunk's precepts. What are the merits of Strunk's approach? What are the limitations?

10. Listen to several television or radio programs with British announcers and report on the chief differences from American speech that you observe in pronunciation and usage, arriving at a general conclusion as to typical differences.

11. Take one letter of the alphabet and compare the treatment of usage prob-

lems in Nicholson's *A Dictionary of American-English Usage* and Fowler's *Dictionary of Modern English Usage*. Report on changes and additions in Nicholson· which reflect distinctive aspects of American English.

12. In the *Oxford English Dictionary*, *Webster's Second International Dictionary*, and Wentworth and Flexner, *Dictionary of American Slang*, look up *brawl*, *loon*, and *cuckoo*. In what senses did Shakespeare use each term? Report briefly on the relation between the Shakespearean and the modern slang meanings.

13. Write an analytical report on an article by an eminent current writer in your chosen field: consider variety of style, diction, and usage, particularly usage that represents such problems as *who* and *whom*, *like* and *as*.

14. Study the dialogue in a contemporary American short story and, in a short paper, show how levels of usage and colloquialisms reflect time, place, and social class and how the dialogue differs from the nondialogue passages.

15. In Faulkner's *The Town*, study the speech of Gavin Stevens, Ratliff, and the various Snopeses and write a paper on the social levels represented and on colloquial standard and colloquial substandard deviations from formal usage.

16. Examine in Fries's *American English Grammar* the discussion of the usage examples cited by Hall, "Right vs. Wrong." Write an analytical report on how Fries's treatment exemplifies the approach of the scientific linguist.

17. Discuss Professor Higgins in Shaw's *Pygmalion* as representing self-confident freedom in speech and manners. What is Higgins's social status? His professional status?

18. Choose a nonfiction selection in *The New Yorker* written in the first person, with some dialogue, and analyze it as standard colloquial, with special attention to usage problems which have been called to your attention.

19. Read Raven I. McDavid's article in *American Speech*, May, 1950, and sum up his findings on *don't* and *ain't*.

20. Look up *ain't* in *Webster's Second* and *Third International*, in Evans and Evans, *A Dictionary of Contemporary American Usage*, and Bryant, *Current American Usage*. Report on the present status of *ain't*. Is it ever permissible in speech? If so, with what meaning and in what circumstances? In what parts of the country is it most acceptable? Least acceptable? How is it used in fiction and drama?

21. Analyze the colloquial quality and informality in the dialogue in a short story by Irving, Poe, or Hawthorne.

22. Compare passages of dialogue from Henry James's *The American* (1877) and *The Ambassadors* (1903) and analyze the colloquial quality and informality of each.

23. Compare the colloquial quality of the dialogue in a story by Washington Irving with that in a story by a modern writer, such as John O'Hara, John Cheever, Irwin Shaw. Make the same comparison with another pair of writers, one from the nineteenth century and one contemporary, who deal with the same part of the country.

24. Write a paper on the euphemisms used in social situations, in advertising, or in a profession.

25. Report briefly on the controversy over the application and meaning of *Esquire*.

26. Investigate and summarize H. L. Mencken's "assault upon *Honorable.*"

27. Write a short report on local pronunciations of proper names which differ from standard pronunciations.

28. For each of Hook's problems in usage, compare a composition textbook with Bryant, *Current American Usage*. Classify your findings and report on "correctness" as related to recorded usage.

29. Report on the results of a poll of class members on a specified problem. (See question 2, p. 261.)

30. Report on the paragraph "test" results. (See question 3, p. 261.)

SUGGESTIONS FOR LONGER PAPERS

A number of subjects suggested for short papers may be extended in scope for long papers. The subjects given below, however, generally cover material from more than one part. Roman numerals indicate parts most relevant to the topic. Part I is not specifically indicated because the general principles it covers should be referred to whenever pertinent to any subject.

1. From an issue of *American Speech* that is at least five years old, select ten or fifteen new words and look them up in the most recent dictionary available. Compare the *American Speech* and the dictionary entries and arrive at some conclusion as to what kinds of words achieve a place in the language and what kind of evolution they may go through. (II)

2. Compare selected sections of different editions of the same dictionary to show changes in vocabulary and meanings of words and to identify the language processes represented. (II)

3. Study the dialogue in a pair of comparable British and American plays or short stories to determine differences in British and American vocabulary and idiom, with special attention to cultural levels. (IV)

4. Compare a few selections in this text as representing current usage, applying Evans and Evans, *A Dictionary of Contemporary American Usage*. (V)

5. Study the place-names in a limited area of your own state to ascertain how they illustrate principles of naming and characteristics of American English and how they reflect social and historical background. (II and III)

6. Examine the discussions of colloquial English and slang in this text to determine whether the confusion between cultural levels and functional varieties is evident. If it is, analyze the selections involved, following Kenyon's method. Or make a similar study of half a dozen composition texts for college courses. (IV)

7. From the materials in this text select passages which represent formal style, informal style, and colloquial style. By comparative analysis determine the characteristic features of each. Make intensive use of dictionary usage classifications for vocabulary and idiom. (IV)

8. Study definitions of *colloquial* in both collegiate and unabridged dictionaries. Study the vocabulary and idiom of at least two selections in this text for the use of colloquial language, selecting one which seems relatively formal and one which seems relatively informal. Note that *Webster's Third New International Dictionary* does not use *colloq.* (IV)

9. Study the regional variations in the dialogue in a play, a short story, or a novel in which locality is important and discuss how they represent special aspects of American English. (III)

10. Analyze the slang vocabulary of a special group, such as Beatniks, to show language processes and principles at work. (IV)

11. From Kurath, *A Word Geography of the Eastern United States*, make a list of common regional variants and test a number of individuals on terms and pronunciations used to determine what factors have influenced usage. (III)

12. Study the vocabulary and idiom of a specific group—such as a group in a dormitory—that represents varied backgrounds, and report on the effects of family, class, and region on speech habits. (III and V)

13. Make a collection of slang used by members of a family including different ages and distinct subgroups to determine sources of slang vocabulary, the "lifetime" of slang, and the effect of the age group on frequency and kind of slang used. (IV)

14. Classify and analyze current slang among college students to demonstrate which of the psychological motives for the use of slang seem to be most prevalent and what emotional and intellectual attittudes are revealed. (IV)

15. From sources in Part III of the text, identify the speech area in which you live and, with the additional aid of dictionaries, write a short documented account of the characteristics of the speech in your region, providing examples from your own observation. (III)

16. "Words are more easily transferred than regional types of pronunciation." Test the truth of this statement by comparing the speech of students from distinctly different regions, noting vocabulary and pronunciation. (III and V)

17. "Within a small area a number of interesting variants for the same thing can often be found in the half-hidden recesses of popular speech." Test this by observing variants for names of common objects in everyday life. Clerking in a store is likely to offer opportunities for observation. (III)

18. Following the techniques described by McDavid, pp. 112–13, but, if necessary, limiting yourself to vocabulary and idiom, collect data on your home community, including descendants of foreign-language groups. Classify your results and compare them with the generalizations in this text on pertinent points. (III and V)

19. If you have lived in different areas, write a paper on the chief differences in pronunciation, vocabulary, and idiom which you have observed, classifying and analyzing the speech habits of both areas according to regional dialects. (III)

20. "Words of course spread with people, following routes of migration." Test this by observing routes of migration indicated by place-names from another section of the country and investigating vocabulary and idiom in a community known to be settled by a group from another area, such as New England groups in the Middle West. (II and III)

21. If you know someone who retains vocabulary and speech habits acquired in another dialect area or derived from a foreign-language background, assemble and classify deviations from local speech and apply principles of word migration and dialect variations to see if the deviations can be fully explained by such principles. (III and V)

22. "Literacy always blunts the edge of dialects." If you know a group or community with marked difference in "book-learning" between generations, see what evidence you can find to prove or disprove the quoted statement. Consider vocabulary, grammar, idiom, and pronunciation. (III and V)

23. If you have traveled widely in the United States, especially by auto, classify dialect differences you have observed and see if you can explain why they have resisted "leveling." (III and V)

24. If you live in a large city and have opportunity to make comparisons, test the truth of McDavid's statement about differences between urban and rural

vocabulary, p. 115. In what ways is the commercial influence of the city apparent in the surrounding area? (III and V)

25. Read all of the available reviews of *Webster's Second International* and *Webster's Third New International* dictionaries and write a paper on prevailing attitudes therein revealed toward dictionaries and language. Refer specifically, for comparison or contrast, to principles of language represented in I and II in this text. (I and II)

26. Study the language "coined" for fictional purposes in a work of science fiction, and write a paper on the language processes apparent in the neologisms. Aldous Huxley's *Brave New World* would be a suitable subject, embracing both British and American settings in the future. (II and IV)

27. Certain religious groups, such as the Quakers or the Amish or the Mennonites, have preserved distinctive speech patterns, which in some groups retain foreign elements. From personal observation or from study of a work of fiction, such as Jessamyn West's *The Friendly Persuasion*, write an analysis of vocabulary, grammar, and idiom of such a group. (III and IV)

28. Mr. Micawber, in Dickens's *David Copperfield*, is probably the literary character most noted for use of literary rather than colloquial language. The dialogue in *David Copperfield* ranges from Micawber's pompous formality through the nonstandard speech of Mr. Peggotty and Ham. Analyze the distinctive characteristics of these varieties of style in dialogue: Micawber's formal speech, standard colloquial, and nonstandard colloquial. What conclusions do you arrive at concerning the degree of informality in standard colloquial in nineteenth-century England in comparison with twentieth-century America? (IV and V)

29. In Faulkner's "The Bear" a wide range of colloquial style is represented. Study the dialogue of all the characters, classify it from most formal standard through illiterate substandard, and discuss the social and regional characteristics most notable in each variety. Note particularly individual social motivation or ambition as reflected in speech and comparable personal dress and behavior. (III, IV, and V)

30. Select a practical number of topics, such as double negatives, from among those dealt with by both Bryant, *Current American Usage*, and Evans and Evans, *A Dictionary of Contemporary American Usage*, and compare the technique and content in the parallel entries. Where sources for quotations are given, look them up and examine the contexts. Arrive at a conclusion as to the soundness of the methods and sources used by Bryant and Evans and Evans in comparison with the treatment of the same points in a recent edition of a standard composition text. (IV)

31. Select a category of television or radio dramatic programs, such as domestic comedy or Westerns, and make a study of the levels of usage and varieties of style and their social implications. Use as a model for method and technique Theodore Williams's "Soap Opera Grammar," *American Speech* (May, 1957), 151–54. (IV and V)

32. Make a study of the special vocabulary, slang, and idiom of a regional occupational group, such as Southern cotton-growers, or Middle Western dairy-farmers, and prepare an analytical report of your findings. Arrive at a conclusion concerning the general principles illustrated by this speech group. Except for the lack of such a conclusion, a model may be found in Audrey Duckert's "The

Lexical Cherry Orchard," *American Speech* (February, 1959), 65–67. (III, IV, and V)

33. Trace the history of a single common word, such as *dame* or *blue* or *head*, from its origin through its current standard and slang uses and determine the factors affecting denotation and connotation. Use at least the *Oxford English Dictionary*; Mathews, *Dictionary of Americanisms on Historical Principles*; *Webster's Third New International Dictionary*; and Wentworth and Flexner, *Dictionary of American Slang*. (II, III, IV, and V)

34. Make an analytical study of a fairly recent bound volume of *American Speech, The English Journal*, or *College English* to determine what aspects of language study are represented, what the prevailing approaches are, and what qualifications the writers possess in their subjects. Discuss and evaluate your findings about the periodical for the student who is seeking to attain understanding of language and acceptable language habits. (I, II, III, IV, and V)

NOTES ON THE AUTHORS

ALLEN, HAROLD B.

Harold B. Allen, Professor of English at the University of Minnesota and Director of the *Linguistic Atlas of the Upper Middle West*, was recently President of the National Council of Teachers of English and is the editor of *Readings in Linguistics*, a collection of essays covering the whole field of linguistic studies.

BAUGH, ALBERT C.

Albert C. Baugh, Professor of English at the University of Pennsylvania, is the author of *A History of the English Language*.

COSTELLO, DONALD P.

Donald P. Costello is Assistant Professor of English at the University of Notre Dame.

DOBBINS, AUSTIN C.

Austin C. Dobbins is chairman of the Department of English at Howard College.

EVANS, BERGEN

Bergen Evans, Professor of English at Northwestern University, opposes the prescriptive, authoritarian approaches to grammar and usage, as his recent books, *A Dictionary of Contemporary American Usage* (with Cornelia Evans) and *Comfortable Words*, and his nationally televised program, *The Last Word*, clearly reveal.

FRANCIS, W. NELSON

W. Nelson Francis, Professor of Linguistics at Brown University, has written one of the revolutionary grammars, *The Structure of American English*, which has been widely adopted as a textbook for courses in modern American English.

FRIES, CHARLES C.

Charles C. Fries, Professor Emeritus of English at the University of Michigan, is one of the American pioneers in the scientific study of language. His *American English Grammar* and *The Structure of English* are two landmarks of American linguistic scholarship that have won the respect of other students in the field.

GREENOUGH, JAMES B.

James B. Greenough (1833–1901) was Professor of Latin at Harvard University and a specialist in Latin grammar and vocabulary.

HALL, ROBERT A., JR.

Robert A. Hall, Jr., Professor of Linguistics at Cornell University, has made scholarly studies in Romance philology and in pidgin and creole languages. His publications include *Linguistics and Your Language* (a revised edition of *Leave Your Language Alone!*), *An Analytical Grammar of the Hungarian Language, Spoken and Written French,* and *Italian for Modern Living.*

HILL, ARCHIBALD A.

Archibald A. Hill, Professor of English at the University of Texas, has studied linguistic problems in Latin and English and is the author of *Introduction to Linguistic Structures.*

HOOK, J. N.

J. N. Hook, Professor of English at the University of Illinois and formerly Executive Secretary of the National Council of Teachers of English, is interested in the problems of teaching English grammar and usage to high school and college students.

KENYON, JOHN S.

John S. Kenyon was Professor of English at Hiram College, and his research in scientific linguistics resulted in *American Pronunciation* and in *A Pronouncing Dictionary of American English* (with Thomas Knott).

KITTREDGE, GEORGE LYMAN

George Lyman Kittredge (1860–1941) was Professor of English at Harvard University. His wide-ranging interests included Chaucer, Shakespeare, and the development of the English language.

KURATH, HANS

Hans Kurath, Professor of English at the University of Michigan, is editor of the *Middle English Dictionary* and author of *A Word Geography of the Eastern United States.*

LAIRD, CHARLTON

Charlton Laird, Professor of English at the University of Nevada, is the author of *The Miracle of Language* and coeditor of *English as Language* (with Robert M. Gorrell).

MARCKWARDT, ALBERT H.

Albert H. Marckwardt, Professor of English at Princeton University, is co-author of *Facts About Current English Usage* (with Fred G. Walcott) and author of *Introduction to the English Language* and *American English*.

MC DAVID, RAVEN I., JR.

Raven I. McDavid, Jr., Professor of English at the University of Chicago, has been a fieldworker for the *Linguistic Atlas* and is coauthor of *The Pronunciation of the Eastern United States* (with Hans Kurath).

MENCKEN, HENRY L.

Henry Louis Mencken (1880–1956), a journalist and magazine editor by profession, was a self-trained philologist whose collections of material relating to all aspects of American English were published in *The American Language* (1st ed., 1919; 4th ed., 1936) and in *Supplements to the American Language* (1946, 1948).

NICHOLSON, MARGARET

Margaret Nicholson, Head of the Contract and Copyright Department of The Macmillan Company, edited *A Dictionary of American-English Usage*, an adaptation of H. W. Fowler's *Dictionary of Modern English Usage*.

ROBERTS, PAUL

Paul Roberts, Professor of English at San José State College, has applied the methods of descriptive linguistics to the problems of English composition, grammar, syntax, and usage in *Understanding Grammar* (1954), *Patterns of English* (1956), *Understanding English* (1958), and *English Sentences* (1962).

SLEDD, JAMES

James Sledd, Professor of English at Northwestern University, wrote *A Short Introduction to English Grammar* (1959), in which he applies scientific linguistic principles to modern English grammar.

BIBLIOGRAPHY

Allen, Harold B., ed. *Readings in Applied English Linguistics.* New York: Appleton-Century-Crofts, Inc., 1958.

Baugh, Albert C. *A History of the English Language,* 2d ed. New York: Appleton-Century-Crofts, Inc., 1957.

Bloomfield, Leonard. *Language.* New York: Holt, Rinehart and Winston, Inc., 1933.

Bradley, Henry. *Making of English.* New York: The Macmillan Company, 1904.

Bronstein, Arthur J. *The Pronunciation of American English.* New York: Appleton-Century-Crofts, Inc., 1960.

Brook, G. L. *History of the English Language*. New York: Oxford University Press, 1958.

Bryant, Margaret M. *Current American Usage*. New York: Funk and Wagnalls Co., Inc., 1962.

———. *Modern English and Its Heritage*. New York: The Macmillan Company, 1948.

Carroll, John B. *The Study of Language*. Cambridge: Harvard University Press, 1953.

Evans, Bergen. *Comfortable Words*. New York: Random House, Inc., 1962.

———, and Cornelia Evans. *A Dictionary of Contemporary American Usage*. New York: Random House, Inc., 1957.

Francis, W. Nelson. *The Structure of American English*. New York: The Ronald Press, 1958.

Fries, Charles Carpenter. *American English Grammar*. New York: Appleton-Century-Crofts, Inc., 1940.

———. *The Structure of English*. New York: Harcourt, Brace & World, Inc., 1952.

Gleason, H. A., Jr. *An Introduction to Descriptive Linguistics*, 2d ed. New York: Holt, Rinehart and Winston, Inc., 1961.

Greenough, James B., and George Lyman Kittredge. *Words and Their Ways in English Speech*. New York: The Macmillan Company, 1901.

Hall, Robert A., Jr. *Linguistics and Your Language*. New York: Doubleday and Company, Inc., 1960.

Hill, Archibald A. *Introduction to Linguistics*. New York: Harcourt, Brace & World, Inc., 1958.

Hockett, Charles F. *A Course in Modern Linguistics*. New York: The Macmillan Company, 1958.

Hughes, John P. *The Science of Language*. New York: Random House, Inc., 1962.

Ives, Sumner. *A New Handbook for Writers*. New York: Alfred A. Knopf, Inc., 1960.

Jespersen, Otto. *Language, Its Nature, Development and Origin*. New York: The Macmillan Company, 1922.

Kenyon, John S. *American Pronunciation*, 10th ed. Ann Arbor: George Wahr Publishing Company, 1961.

Kurath, Hans. *A Word Geography of the Eastern United States*. Ann Arbor: University of Michigan Press, 1949.

———, and Raven I. McDavid, Jr. *The Pronunciation of English in the Atlantic States*. Ann Arbor: University of Michigan Press, 1961.

Laird, Charlton. *The Miracle of Language*. New York: Harcourt, Brace & World, Inc., 1953.

Lloyd, Donald J., and Harry R. Warfel. *American English in Its Cultural Setting*. New York: Alfred A. Knopf, Inc., 1956.

Marckwardt, Albert H. *American English*. New York: Oxford University Press, 1958.

———, and Fred Walcott. *Facts About Current English Usage*, English Monograph No. 7, National Council of Teachers of English. New York: Appleton-Century-Crofts, Inc., 1938.

Mencken, H. L. *The American Language.* New York: Alfred A. Knopf, Inc., 1937.
———. *The American Language, Supplement One.* New York: Alfred A. Knopf, Inc., 1946.
———. *The American Language, Supplement Two.* New York: Alfred A. Knopf, Inc., 1948.
Myers, Edward D. *Foundations of English.* New York: The Macmillan Company, 1940.
Newsome, Verna L. *Structural Grammar in the Classroom.* Milwaukee: Wisconsin Council of Teachers of English, 1962.
Nicholson, Margaret. *A Dictionary of American-English Usage.* New York: Oxford University Press, 1957.
Partridge, Eric, and John W. Clark. *British and American English Since 1900.* New York: Philosophical Library, 1951.
Pyles, Thomas. *Words and Ways of American English.* New York: Random House, Inc., 1952.
Roberts, Paul. *English Sentences.* New York: Harcourt, Brace & World, Inc., 1962.
———. *Patterns of English.* New York: Harcourt, Brace & World, Inc., 1956.
———. *Understanding English.* New York: Harper & Brothers, 1958.
———. *Understanding Grammar.* New York: Harper & Brothers, 1954.
Robertson, Stuart, and Frederic G. Cassidy. *The Development of Modern English,* 2d ed. Englewood Cliffs: Prentice-Hall, Inc., 1954.
Sapir, Edward. *Language.* New York: Harcourt, Brace & World, Inc., 1921.
Sledd, James A. *A Short Introduction to English Grammar.* Chicago: Scott, Foresman and Company, 1959.
Stewart, George R. *Names on the Land.* Boston: Houghton Mifflin Company, 1958.
———, and Wilma R. Ebbitt. *Dictionaries and That Dictionary.* Chicago: Scott, Foresman and Company, 1962.
Sturtevant, Edgar H. *An Introduction to Linguistic Science.* New Haven: Yale University Press, 1947.
Thomas, Charles K. *Phonetics of American English.* New York: The Ronald Press, 1958.
Trager, George L. "Language." *The Encyclopaedia Britannica,* Vol. 13. Chicago: Encyclopaedia Britannica, Inc., 1960.
———, and Henry Lee Smith. *An Outline of English Structure,* Studies in Linguistics, Occasional Paper No. 3. Washington, D.C.: American Council of Learned Societies, 1957.
Warfel, Harry R. *Language: A Science of Human Behavior.* Cleveland: Howard Allen, Inc., 1962.
Wentworth, Harold, and Stuart Berg Flexner, comps. *Dictionary of American Slang.* New York: Thomas Y. Crowell Company, 1960.
Whatmough, Joshua. *Language, A Modern Synthesis.* New York: St Martin's Press, 1956.
Whitehall, Harold. "The English Language." In *Webster's New World Dictionary.* Cleveland: The World Publishing Company, 1959, pp. xv-xxxiv.
Whitehall, Harold. *Structural Essentials.* New York: Harcourt, Brace & World, Inc., 1956.

A
B
C
D
E
F
G
H
I